QUEERING REHOBOTH BEACH

THE
PINK PONY
A
COCKTAIL LOUNGE

QUEERING REHOBOTH BEACH

BEYOND THE BOARDWALK

JAMES T. SEARS

TEMPLE UNIVERSITY PRESS *Philadelphia* • *Rome* • *Tokyo*

TEMPLE UNIVERSITY PRESS
Philadelphia, Pennsylvania 19122
tupress.temple.edu

Design by Kate Nichols

Frontispiece: Pink Pony exterior. (Courtesy of Delaware State Archives.)

Library of Congress Cataloging-in-Publication Data

Names: Sears, James T. (James Thomas), 1951– author.
Title: Queering Rehoboth Beach : beyond the boardwalk / James T. Sears.
Other titles: Beyond the boardwalk
Description: Philadelphia : Temple University Press, 2024. | Summary: "This
    volume explores the story of how a conservative southern Delaware beach
    town was transformed into a major East Coast summer queer resort"—
    Provided by publisher.
Identifiers: LCCN 2023044359 (print) | LCCN 2023044360 (ebook) | ISBN
    9781439923801 (paperback) | ISBN 9781439923818 (pdf)
Subjects: LCSH: CAMP Rehoboth (Organization)—History. | Sexual minority
    community—Delaware—Rehoboth Beach—History. | Seaside
    resorts—Delaware—Rehoboth Beach—History. | Rehoboth Beach
    (Del.)—History. | Rehoboth Beach (Del.)—Social conditions.
Classification: LCC F174.R44 S43 2024 (print) | LCC F174.R44 (ebook) |
    DDC 975.1/700866—dc23/eng/20231214
LC record available at https://lccn.loc.gov/2023044359
LC ebook record available at https://lccn.loc.gov/2023044360

Printed in the United States of America

9 8 7 6 5 4 3 2 1

FOR LUIS

CONTENTS

ACKNOWLEDGMENTS

W ithout the assistance of those whom I interviewed, this book would not have been possible. CAMP endorsed this oral history project and granted me access to the organization's documents and board members. Additionally, much appreciation goes to Nancy Alexander, director of the Rehoboth Beach Historical Society and Museum, and the staff at CAMP Rehoboth, the Delaware Technical College Library, the Delaware State Archives, and the Rehoboth Beach Public Library. Finally, acknowledging that the "first draft of history" is penned by reporters, I am indebted to the *Whale*, *Washington Blade*, *Cape Gazette*, *PGN*, and Wilmington's *Morning News* and *Evening News*, among others.

I thank the anonymous reviewers at Temple University Press as well as its board for their comments and suggestions. My editor, Shaun Vigil, provided critical structural recommendations in earlier drafts and substantive comments throughout the process. His availability, diligence, insight, and criticism were invaluable.

Special thanks to J. Dan Marshall—my writing partner and friend of more than forty years—for his indulgent readings and critical suggestions. Several readers also provided helpful conversations and critical suggestions on the penultimate draft: David DeWitt, Paul Shaker, and two anonymous lesbian reviewers. Special assistance was also provided for research on the Paradise Inn by innkeeper Tom Kelch.

Most importantly, my thanks to those who shared their experiences and insights through what was, at times, a demanding interview process. This book could not have been written without the telling of their stories.

NOTES ON LANGUAGE USE

Various nouns are used with reference to non-heterosexual identities as well as identities related to gender, disability, social class, and race/ethnicity. Generally, I have followed guidelines from the American Psychological Association for bias-free language. Its *Publication Manual* (7th ed.) underscores: "Language changes over time, and it is important to use the terms that individuals and/or communities use to describe themselves, their experiences, and their practices."[1]

When appropriate, such terms as *homosexual* and *homophile* have been used with reference to the period through the 1960s or as a pre-Stonewall attitude. *Gay and lesbian* or *gay men* and *lesbian women* are used when distinctions of gender are relevant, while *gay* is used more generically, reflecting a change in political identities beginning with Stonewall. Different acronyms, such as LGBT or LGBTQ+, are employed when representing a more complex thinking about sexuality/gender that began in the 1980s. *Queer* in its various forms is used in several ways: to reflect an extreme homophobic mindset; to embrace the very word wielded by homophobes; to bracket heteronormativity; and to capture the fluidity of sexualities/genders.

In discussing people who are transgender and gender-non-conforming (e.g., non-binary, agender, gender queer), participants' chosen proper names, pronouns, and terms are used.

Woman or *women* is used throughout the book, with *girl* reserved for reference to a female child. Exceptions are when quoted directly from a participant or when used within a historical context, such as feminist perspectives where *womyn* is employed.

Individuals with physical disabilities are identified by using "person-first" language rather than by the disabling condition (e.g., people with substance-use disorders rather than substance abusers, or people with AIDS rather than AIDS victims) and by respecting the person's preference or that of the community (e.g., people who are deaf versus Deaf people).

When conveying socioeconomic status, I have tried to avoid overly broad or pejorative words and phrases. However, when relevant and quoted directly from a participant, such terms as *redneck, greaser, good old boy, jet-setter,* and *sugar daddy* are used. Similarly, such phrases as *War Between the States* are occasionally used to fit the individual's perspective and historical era.

Regarding race and ethnicity, capitalization is used when a word is used as either a noun or an adjective, such as Blacks or a White person. *African American* and *Anglo* are occasionally employed, as is *Person(s) of Color*. In contrast, *Negro, Afro American,* or *colored people* are exclusively used when quoting from a dated vantage point. For people of Hispanic descent, *Latino/Latina* or *Latinx* is used, depending upon the participant's preference. Hyphenated identities, such as *Asian-American*, are not used. However, when it is important to convey a participant's racial mindset, pejorative nouns, such as *Orientals*, are used within a quotation.

This work includes descriptive words that many readers may find problematic. These include *queers, fags* or *faggots*, and *bitch*. Apart from the first term (for reasons explained earlier), these derisive nouns are used very judiciously and only when the homophobic or sexist context is critical to convey. Nevertheless, there is a substantive distinction between the occasional use of *fag* or *faggot* and publication of the N-word, which a queer victim uttered during a Boardwalk assault. Certainly one is that although I am a gay man, I am also Caucasian. Further, these two gay epithets (as well as the word *queer*) have been appropriated and reappropriated in recent decades by sexual minorities, including me. However, given the four-hundred-plus-year history of systemic racism in this country, the racial epithet is understandably objectionable on multiple levels. Thus, the singular use of the N-word in this book has been elided.

CAST OF NARRATORS

Fezuk, Carol. *Letters* manager who cofounded the competing gay paper, *RBG*

Hodge, Wayne. Longtime manager of Renegade and principal assistant to Thompson

Lawson, Jr., Gene. Businessman turned lawyer who co-owned The Strand

*Pusey, Bertha and Ray. Nemeses of The Strand and Baltimore Avenue gay scenes

Stiff, Libby. Cofounder of Women's Fest and past president of RBHA

Sudler, Hassan. Fiction writer who serialized "Summerville" in *RBG*, which he later edited

York, Libby. Cofounder of the Back Porch and later a well-known jazz singer

OTHERS

Ackerman, Jack. Part of the "quiet generation" of Rehoboth's homosexuals of the 1960s and 1970s

*Aumiller, Richard. University of Delaware theater instructor fired in 1976 for being a "gay activist"

Carpenter, Kathy. Local school male athlete turned drag performer and then trans activist

Courville, Bill. With his partner, Jerome, owned the RB Guest House from 1987 to 2013

Decker, Michael. Successful musician who, at age twenty-one, was immersed in the 1970s scene

*Fisher, Ted. Family owned a nearby appliance store, married York, and co-owned Back Porch

*Godwin, Randall. Owner, with his wife, Betty Jean, of Nomad Village

Gossett, Patrick. Former Planning Commission member and second openly gay commissioner

Greenberg, Michelle. Niece of gay man who owned a guesthouse that became Paradise Inn

Jacobs, Fay. Lesbian author, veteran *Letters* writer, and former director of RB Main Street

Janssen, "Babo." Lambda Rising manager and first openly lesbian commissioner candidate

Jerome, Bob. With his partner, Bill, owned the RB Guest House from 1987 to 2013

Kanter, Sharon. Baltimore educator who operated Open Secrets and DJ'd at the Nomad

*****Koerber, Herbert.** Operated Paradise Inn with his lover, Mami

Mosiej, Annette. Local artist and sign maker

Moss, Natalie. Longtime staff member for CAMP, overseeing its legal filings and bookkeeping

Park, Forrest. Leader of the drag volleyball group along with Curt Leciejewski, Brent Minor, and Mark Kimble

*****Short, Jimmy.** Nomad bartender, a former teacher, and the last person convicted of sodomy in Delaware

Slavin, Jeffrey. Maryland mayor, original Strand investor who had a group house for twenty years

Spain, Dolph. With his partner, Lloyd, a former DC-area educator and longtime RB resident

Stevenson, Neil. Grew up in RB from the 1950s onward with his police officer father

Thompson, Robert. B&B owner

*****Vane, James Robert.** First Delaware lobbyist for gay rights from the late 1960s into the early 1970s

Welch, Jim. Early gay and AIDS activist, CAMP cofounder, and Dominguez's partner

Williams, Frank. Graphic artist who coedited *RBG* with Carol Fezuk

Yochim, Chris. DuPont chemist and an "A-list" gay man during the 1980s

*Deceased or inaccessible for interview with author

ABBREVIATIONS

ARG: Rehoboth Beach Alliance for Responsible Government

Blade: *Gay Blade/Washington Blade*

CAMP: CAMP Rehoboth

Cape: *Cape Gazette*

CNJ: *Central New Jersey Home News*

Coast: *Coast Press*

Daily Commercial: *Wilmington Daily Commercial*

Daily Republican: *Wilmington Daily Republican*

Evening Journal: *Wilmington Evening News Journal*

Homeowners Association: Rehoboth Beach Homeowners Association

Letters: *Letters from CAMP Rehoboth*

Meeting Association: Rehoboth Beach Camp Meeting Association

Morning News: *Wilmington Morning News*

PGN: *Philadelphia Gay News*

RBG: *Rehoboth Beach Gayzette*

RBHS: Rehoboth Beach Historical Society

RBHA: Rehoboth Beach Homeowners Association

Sears Papers: Sears Papers, Duke University, Rubenstein Rare Book and Manuscript Library

State Journal: *Delaware State Journal*

Sunday News Journal: *Wilmington Sunday News Journal*

UnderGround: *Rehoboth UnderGround*

Whale: *Whale*

PREFACE

Oral sources tell us not just what people did, but what they
wanted to do, what they believed they were doing and what they
now think they did.
                        —**Alessandro Portelli,**
                    The Death of Luigi Trastulli and Other Stories

While shared memories are rarely uniform, uncontroversial, or
uncontested, the fact that certain individuals, events, places,
and legacies are shared through this network of memory helps to
craft us as a collective, as an "us."
                    —**Matthew Houdek** and **Kendall Phillips,**
                            Public Memory

s an undergraduate history student during the early 1970s, one of my
first assigned readings was Cambridge historian E. H. Carr's *What Is
History?*[1] However, as my historical studies progressed, more positiv-
ist-oriented scholars, such as Geoffrey Elton, dominated my professors'
reading lists. Working on my senior thesis about political transformation
in a New England town at the onset of the nineteenth century, I dispassion-
ately mined newspapers, letters, and related documents. Triangulating
these subjective sources would reveal historical truth—or so I was trained.
Portelli's idea that subjects' motives and intentions *animate* historical
events or Houdek and Phillips's assertion that shared memories *create* historical realities were not my scholarly lodestars. In the process, however, I
determined that being a historical scribe was not my calling. I departed to
pursue graduate study in political theory and political psychology at the
University of Wisconsin, where discordant interpretations and interdisci-
plinary analyses were valued.

When I entered the ranks of the professoriate, I began conducting oral
histories. During the mid-1980s, there was an urgency to document queer

lived experiences precariously built upon heteronarrative lives and heteronormative lies. There, too, were few resources for LGBT youth and an absence of nonfictional accounts about the everyday lives of Southern queers—
either in the present or in the past. Twenty years later, the social and
political landscape had changed, largely through grassroots efforts of people
confronting the enormities of prejudice and pain, death and deception, suicide and silence. My works—ranging from a biographical history of the early gay movement to queer activism in the American South—were prefaced
on the naïve belief that social progress was as inevitable as it was slow.

What is history? Carr defines it as a continuous "process of interaction
between the historian and his facts, an unending dialogue between the
present and the past." Based on his series of lectures, he argues that history
making is not science; it is created, not discovered. Carr challenges the his-
toricism of Leopold von Ranke and others who established the *empirical*
study of history in the nineteenth-century German university curriculum—largely copied in U.S. colleges. They viewed history as fact-based and
event-driven, objective and linear. Yet making history, as Carr and such
others as Benedetto Croce and Carl Becker practiced, is not a science; it is a
craft. What is critical is not the methodological tools but the acumen of the
one who wields them.

What constitutes a fact? Why are some "facts" more important than
others? For instance, why has the *New York Times* 1619 Project set the origin of the United States with the arrival of the first slaves, whereas Hillsdale College's 1776 K–12 curriculum begins with the nation's founding? The
former curriculum sets its core narrative within the Black experience and
the impact of enslavement upon the national psyche. In contrast, selected
historical documents chronicle the "complete" history of the Christian republic. Acknowledging that the school's curriculum is devoid of "highly
charged subjects like racism and sexuality," Hillsdale president Larry Arnn
has argued that these difficult subjects "should be broached, not by teachers, but by the child's own parents."

Historical "facts," however, do not exist *a priori* to the writing of history, just as sources—even primary documents—cannot speak for themselves. History is neither value-free nor fact-dependent. It is a product of
shared, albeit often contested, meaning-making within a specific sociopo-
litical context. Of course, disguising opinions as truths is as disingenuous
as it is dangerous, especially during this era, when MAGA falsehoods mas-
querade as facts.

"While we may all agree at the event-level that something happened," writes historian Alun Munslow in his 1997 review of *What Is History?*, "its significance (its meaning as we narrate it) is provided by the historian." Historians do not just impartially sift fact from fancy; they weigh the importance of each to the story they choose to tell. Too often, they have employed the pen of the master to scribe a narrative of god and guns, American exceptionalism and Christian benevolence, consumer capitalism and rugged individualism. This American story is what I read in my Scott-Foresman history books and later heard satirized in Bob Dylan's "With God on Our Side" and Pete Seeger's "What Did You Learn in School Today?" Yet, as historian Howard Zinn writes, history also "has a special ability to reveal the ludicrousness of those beliefs which glue us all to the social frame of our fathers."

Unlike many countries, the United States does not have a formal curriculum for its ninety-nine thousand schools. However, textbooks' hegemony in the American classroom, the textbook industry's market sensitivities, and classic textbook politicians and their media ecosystem have resulted in a *de facto* national curriculum, which has been challenged by the Right as well as the Left. A Christian nationalist educational and political backlash has exposed the long simmering cauldron of misogyny, racism, sexual phobias, and biological binaries. In contrast, a countervailing narrative of America, reading history from the "bottom up," accompanied late-twentieth-century progressive social movements (e.g., *Bury My Heart at Wounded Knee*) and alternative history textbooks, such as Howard Zinn's *A People's History of the United States* and Ronald Takaki's *A Larger Memory: A History of Our Diversity, with Voices*.

Now that *Roe v. Wade* has been overturned, Red State legislatures have all but eliminated a woman's right to choose. As I write this Preface, a Trump-appointed federal judge in Texas—wielding the Comstock Act of 1873 that banned the mailing of anything "designed, adapted, or intended for producing abortion, or for any indecent or immoral use"—has effectively prohibited FDA-approved abortion medication. Earlier in his legal career, Judge Matthew J. Kacsmaryk lamented the destruction of the "four pillars" of marriage: statutory no-fault divorce, freedom for "fornication and adultery," legalization of contraception and abortion, and acceptance of same-sex marriage and gender fluidity. Meanwhile, drag performance has been banned in Tennessee, revisiting an earlier era when those wearing fewer than three pieces of gender-conforming clothing were jailed. It also became the eighth state to bar trans-affirming educational policies and medical procedures for youth. In Florida, K–12 educators are prohibited from discussing gender or sexuality. Further, PEN America reported that school districts in twenty-six states have banned more than 1,500 books, mostly focused on "race and racism in American history, LGBTQ+ identities, and sexual education in schools."

Given this polarization and demonization, few have entered into conversations with the Other. Leery of entering the apocalyptical cultural wars, the willingness to engage in *Conversations for an Enlarging Public Square* within a "fabric of public reason" appears slim. Yet this precise strategy was adopted by a handful of community members in Rehoboth Beach. Thus, a history of a southern Delaware beach town morphing into a major East Coast queer vacation spot and of the transformation of conservative townsfolk attitudes is especially timely. *Queering Rehoboth Beach* is a narrative history from a handful of individuals—and those opposing them—who successfully gained equality and access to the levers of power within a century-old town that was a beachhead for Methodism. It also chronicles missed opportunities, aborted projects, and blind prejudice.

One lesson I hope that readers take from *Queering Rehoboth Beach* is that we are subjects—not objects—of history; we can become agents of history, not merely consumers. This tale is centered during the AIDS pandemic, the advent of the Moral Majority, and the transubstantiation of Twentieth-Century Fox into Fox Broadcasting and, later, the Fox News Channel. During the 1980s and 1990s, a handful of misfit queers erected bridges across the heterosexual divide as they fought for dignity and equality. In the process, a community and many of its residents were transformed.

Traditionally trained historians and readers of conventional queer histories may shudder at the primacy I afford to individual narrators as they engaged in the "Battle for Rehoboth" and interacted with others. From their perspective, a tight and orderly timeline, documenting relevant factual events and principal actors, is the historian's *modus operandi*. Personal stories of protagonists and antagonists are, at best, "tangential" filler. Yet how can we understand people's adult behaviors without understanding the formative events that contoured their psychologies of action and being? Spiraling, intersectional narrative histories in overlapping timelines are the human experience. Making history, like reading history, is existentially messy, epistemologically agnostic. Historians Ethan Kleinberg, Joan Wallach Scott, and Gary Wilder write:

If we think of the historian as akin to the interpreter of dreams, we see that those who look to make literal sense of the dream by presenting it in a chronological, realist, and self-evident manner, are recognized and rewarded. But those whose inquiries lead to the obscure navel of the dream, the place where narratives and interpretation stop making conventional sense, are ignored or dismissed. The danger of a guild so highly disciplined is that the organization of meaning only allows for a narrow band of interpretation that is always aligned with what has come before, with what already "makes sense" (i.e., common sense). Structures of temporality, politics, or even identity that do not conform with convention are ruled out or never seen at all.

This is one meaning of *Queering Rehoboth Beach: Beyond the Boardwalk*.

The Italian historian and philosopher Croce emphasized that *"ogni vera storia è storia contemporanea"* (all genuine history is contemporary history). It is refracted from the presence of memories. History is subjective in its remembering, researching, writing, and reading. Therefore, its principal subjects' psycho-historical experiences are critical to understanding and interpreting their actions in pivotal events. In the words of Pulitzer Prize–winning historian David McCullough: "The pull, the attraction of history, is in our human nature. What makes us tick? Why do we do what we do?"

James Sears
Rehoboth Beach, 2023

PROLOGUE

A "FAMILY" RESTAURANT

Room for Us All?

On an indistinct Friday night, my husband, Luis, and I decide to dine out. We have only been residing in Rehoboth Beach for a few months, having moved from DC in the summer of 2019. Our impression of this small ocean resort town is quite positive. CAMP Rehoboth's goal of gay and lesbian inclusivity—set three decades earlier, after locals had proudly displayed "Keep Rehoboth a Family Town" bumper stickers—seemed a reality. Rehoboth, managed by an open lesbian hired from Provincetown, is overseen by an elected Board of Commissioners that has included gays since 2002. Gay flags hang in shop windows. The number of overflowing gay bars nearly equals that of welcoming houses of worship. Same-gender couples walk along the mile-long Boardwalk and hand-in-hand down gentrified Baltimore Avenue. Lining "The Avenue" are gay-owned boutiques and upscale restaurants, and, at its heart, housed in a quaint turn-of-the-century cottage next to a modernist gay community center, is CAMP. On this longtime community organization's porch are copies of its publication, *Letters from CAMP Rehoboth*, freely available in newspaper stands throughout the town. Its very acronym—**C**reate **A M**ore **P**ositive Rehoboth—is a message of progress and inclusiveness.

As we sit at our table, I stroke my husband's cheek—more than once. I feel at home. As in Washington, homophobia, if not racism, seems to have ebbed in most neighborhoods.

But, as I would soon learn, we are in *southern* Delaware. The pace is slower; the speech is often lumbering; Trump flags fly proudly along county roads. Its southern roots are never far from the surface, sitting just a few miles north of the infamous Mason-Dixon Line.

Our waitress welcomes us. Luis begins speaking Spanish. However, it is evident that her "Spanglish" is not up to the task. But he adroitly orders our wine and entrées. I show her my Locals Season card. "No problem," she volunteers. "You have a 10 percent discount."

As we sip our chardonnay, we hear raucous laughter drifting from an adjoining table of Anglos—three pairs of women and men. They, too, seem to be enjoying drinks after a long week's work.

We finish dinner, and the check arrives. I notice that the discount has not been applied. The new waiter tells me that it does not apply to "specials." I explain that at the time we ordered, our waitress had informed us that we would receive that discount. He agrees to speak with the manager, who soon presents himself to apologize for her mistake.

Meanwhile, a crew-cutted fellow at the neighboring table speaks above the din of a noisy restaurant: "You're just cheap!" His table of friends fancy his cross-table wisecrack.

I'm astonished by the unprovoked comment and even more so at its reception. Am I "cheap" for simply asking for what I had been promised?

I explain, "I'm retired, so this *is* important." Before things escalate, I dangle the bromide: "Let's just agree to disagree."

He casts a few dismissive scowls in our direction as his table enjoys hard-to-hear jokes, seemingly at our expense.

As we wait for a new check, I wonder whether such an outburst is normal in this town. Even in the Deep South of South Carolina—where I was an openly gay professor, activist, and author—this ungentlemanly behavior would never have been acceptable.

I gaze at these three couples. Ensconced within our queer space, we are really living in their heterosexual world [see my Note on Language for the usage of this and related epithets]. Homosexual couples like Luis, a Latino Green Card holder, and I, his older White husband, are, at best, marginal in Trump's world.

After paying the corrected check, we depart. At the threshold of the restaurant's double doors, my Scottish temper surfaces. Turning to our neighboring diners, I show them a defiant middle finger in muted tribute to all those queers of color, mixed-race couples, and limp-wrist homosexuals who have been trashed and bashed across the generations.

Exiting the restaurant, I zip up my jacket and gaze through the plate-glass window to the other side. The women's stares meet my gaze; no longer unseen, my middle finger is acknowledged with their own.

Meanwhile, the crew-cutted man has arisen from the table and is dashing toward the front doors. He brushes me aside. Confronting Luis, he spits a string of indistinguishable epithets.

I retreat into the restaurant and ask the hostess to phone the police to report this ongoing assault. Out of nowhere, a second man from that table plants himself in front of me: "We're state police."

"I don't care who the fuck you are, he's assaulting us." Tersely, he replies, "Watch your language. No one touched you. There is no assault. This is a *family* restaurant. Go back home."

Luis reenters the restaurant: *"Vámonos!"* (Let's go!)

My husband is from Nicaragua. Its government has jailed or murdered many of its citizens during years of Sandinista rule. There, as I have experienced firsthand, police officers have godlike authority. They can enter your house without a warrant, toss you in jail with a fictitious accusation, plant drugs on your property for its quick seizure. Aside from avoiding any interaction with La Policia Nacional, the safest alternatives are to meekly comply or to pay them off. Assault, corruption, bribery, obstruction of justice, and autocratic rule are the norm.

Before the Trump regime, I really had never fathomed that this could also be America's dystopian future. Although Luis is here legally, I realize that the most prudent course of action is a quiet retreat. As we depart onto the rain-soaked sidewalk of Rehoboth Avenue, I query: Does this beach town's portrait of inclusivity match reality?

Safely at home but unable to sleep, I go to my desk. Before dawn, I have written up our encounter. Surely, the story would be of interest to the readers of *Letters from CAMP Rehoboth*.

I email my draft the next day to David Mariner, who has recently immigrated from DC with the daunting task of replacing the late Steve Elkins as CAMP's executive director. The Georgia-born Elkins, a former Carter White House aide, cofounded this gay community service organization in 1991. Following his death in 2018, the mayor and his six commissioners named a walkway in Steve's honor.

A few days later, I stop by the CAMP office. David, whom I have met a month earlier, is sitting uncomfortably at his cluttered desk in a neatly organized office overlooking The Avenue. He welcomes the unscheduled intrusion, if not my inquiry about the article I've submitted. I hand him a revised copy.

Scanning my account of the dinner encounter, David questions whether these officers' actions indeed represented homophobia.

"The reader can't be sure *this* was their motivation, right?"

"Well, I wrote it so it could be read from a variety of privileged perspectives."

I have in mind the privilege of unawareness—the privilege of *not seeing*. Skin color, gender, nationality, social class, sexuality, and other social markers, positioning us in our everyday interactions, mask the benefits derived from those positions and even allow the marginalized to disregard or even defend them. But the intersection of these privileged positions, constituting our lived experiences, seems too much to explain at that moment.

"What do you mean?"

In the spirit of CAMP, I offer a reconciling response.

"Perhaps they weren't homophobic but simply reacted to my emasculating middle finger, or my husband's poor English, or my public reproach of the waitress."

This is precisely how the wily brave new world of Trumpian bigotry manifests itself. There is no smoking gun—only ambiguity, misdirection, and gaslighting.

He dodges: "Perhaps it would be better placed in another local publication, like the *Cape Gazette*."

"CAMP is about creating a more positive community. Let your readers decide; let them discuss it. Surely that is worthwhile."

He dawdles: "Besides, *Letters from CAMP* doesn't publish again until early spring."

"This story is timeless; it's universal. It's a confrontation among folks living in different worlds and the difficulty of naming it . . . nailing it down for what it is."

He defers: "Maybe it's something better taken up quietly with the state police commander." His voice trails off, seemingly tiring of our exchange.

"Well, I guess that's it?"

He parleys my question with a question: "You already emailed me a copy of this article, right?"

Before I can answer, he tears it up, explaining: "I already got too much paper on my desk."

QUEERING REHOBOTH BEACH

PART I

INTRODUCTION

BEYOND THE BOARDWALK

We are fortunate to live in a community that long ago
determined that it, too, would be a place where there is room for
all. Our town celebrates the diversity of God's creation.

—**Steve Elkins**, *The Way I See It*

T his is a story of a southern beach town, which, like so many others of
the not-too-distant past, concealed a secretive queer world of lesbians,
gay men, bisexuals, and trans folks evolving across multiple generations. The story of Rehoboth is much more complex and nuanced than in-
dicated by airbrushed newspaper and magazine articles published over the
years. *Queering Rehoboth Beach* begins with the establishment of Rehoboth
as a Methodist Church meeting camp in the late nineteenth century, attracting not only Methodist moralists but secular capitalists. Their struggle
to maintain Rehoboth's "special character" has cascaded through the generations and rests at the root of the conflict between the townsfolk and
queers during the 1980s and 1990s, in what the *Washington Post Magazine*
would headline as "The Battle for Rehoboth."*

HISTORIC HETEROSEXUAL REHOBOTH

Queering the contemporary history of Rehoboth Beach requires an understanding of heterosexual terrain contoured by southern geography and
Methodist theology.[1] Like many southern stories I have chronicled, Re-

---

* My use of *queer* along with other terms to describe persons attracted to the same
or both genders or various gender identities is explained in "Notes on Language Use"
at the beginning of this book.

hoboth's history was sculpted by conservative White Christian men of privilege—the old guard. These elders' antipathy toward progressivism, pluralism, and populism was evident from the town's late-nineteenth-century origin as a church camp blessed by the state. This rigidity was most apparent in the adoption of "Discipline"—a set of strict rules within the governing covenant for the Rehoboth Beach Camp Meeting Association. These rules were grouped into six categories: immoral conduct, neglect of the means of grace, impudent conduct, dissension, disagreement in business/nonpayment of debts, and insolvency. In everyday life, these rules limited one's dress (wearing gold or expensive apparel), mandated church attendance, and prohibited worldly indulgences (e.g., dancing, playing cards, going to the theater, consuming alcohol and tobacco). These disciplinary provisions, however, were not principally about saving souls; they "ha[d] but one object in reality and that [wa]s the growth and increase of the Church." J. B. Quigg, the leading Methodist minister on the Delaware peninsula and cofounder of the association, further stated coldly, "The reformation of the erring and the expulsion of the unworthy are only incidents of this progress."

In the farm soil that became Rehoboth, Methodist evangelists sowed seeds of fellowship and unity by works of mercy and piety. Some grew amid thorns of discord, others were trodden on the path of avarice, and a few fell between rocks of intemperance. These were early tensions between commercialism and evangelism, between the Great Awakening in revivalism and the Great Convulsion in real estate, and between believers of the sacred and practitioners of the profane. These divisions, streaming through the town's 150-year history, were laid bare during the "Battle for Rehoboth."

Most historical accounts and anecdotes of Rehoboth's founding fail to detail Rev. Quiggs's efforts, preferring to highlight the younger Rev. Robert W. Todd's vision of a camp by the sea that inspired Christian souls of means to establish the association in 1873. The internecine warfare between Elder Quigg and the Confederate sympathizer, capitalist, and Democrat James Bright—also a fellow Rehoboth founder and Methodist—is seldom mentioned, but the story is chronicled in Chapter 1. Further, the struggles between Methodists who fully embraced the "Discipline" and those who tempered it with drink and dance or tempted it with usury and luxury are typically glossed over with a few humorous passages or anecdotes.

This Methodist project, unlike other camp meeting sites in Delaware, extended well beyond ocean evangelism. Lots were sold, tents pitched, and cottages erected. A train station was built, telegraph lines raised, and a newspaper published. Boardinghouses welcomed excursionists from Baltimore, Philadelphia, Washington, and throughout Delaware. Yet within fifteen years of its founding, the association had disbanded, and camp meetings ceased. In the newly chartered Henlopen City (soon renamed Rehoboth Beach), just a couple of financially blessed churches remained. In the wake of acrimony and recrimination about this "failed project," the righteous held tightly to Mark 8:36: "For what shall it profit a man. . . ."

This archetypal 1870s and 1880s conflict between an emerging secularized business class, seemingly fueled by hordes of Visigoth interlopers and Bacchanal vacationers, versus religious conservatives and gentry property owners, supported by sullied politicians, is strikingly parallel to the "Battle for Rehoboth" a century later. For this reason, the opening chapter for *Queering Rehoboth Beach* is the story of Rehoboth's early years, with its focus on the conflict between Quigg and Bright.

REHOBOTH'S CONTEMPORARY SAINTS AND SINNERS

Today, Rehoboth residents, although distant in time from their Methodist forbearers, are as homogenous as the town's boundaries are narrow.[2] Within a square mile of land are fewer than 1,500 souls, 98 percent White, a median age of sixty-five, and $100k+ household income. A short walk north, past the mile-and-a-quarter wooden-plank boardwalk and just over the town line, is Deauville Beach. To its northwest is the even smaller village of Henlopen Acres. Col. Wilbur Corkran, an architect and engineer, established this private community in 1930, exclusively for a "quiet-loving, cultured people." Like many American communities formed during this era, racial covenant restricted ownership to people of "the Caucasian Race." Although such covenants were judged unenforceable by the U.S. Supreme Court in 1948 and made illegal twenty years later, it was not stricken until 1982. Today, only four of its 102 residents are non-White. Farther north lies Cape Henlopen, a state park whose public land was established centuries ago by William Penn, and old Fort Miles. Wedged between the park and Henlopen Acres is North Shores community and North Beach, an area formerly known as Whiskey Beach. At the southern end of the Boardwalk, near Queen Street, is Poodle Beach, where gays have sunbathed since the early 1980s, when they tired of hauling coolers and volleyball nets past the Carpenter's compound. Farther south lies a two-block sliver of land separating Rehoboth Bay from Atlantic waters, mile-long Dewey Beach. Here, generations have been drinking, dancing, and gaming, first at the nineteenth-century Douglass House, then the Depression-era Harry Shaud's Bottle & Cork, then the rock-n-roll-era Starboard and, later, the Rusty Rudder.

Water protects Rehoboth's eastern and western borders. The Atlantic's surf and breeze attract beachgoers, but its storms have ravaged the Boardwalk and swept out to sea businesses and homes as well as bathhouses and pavilions. In 1903, the newly built Horn Pier, jutting 150 feet into the ocean, was destroyed, as was much of the hundred-foot-wide Surf Avenue adjacent to the beach. The Great Storm of 1913 completely washed that street off the map and destroyed the Boardwalk, pier, and a rebuilt Horn's Pavilion. But "nothing compared" to the Ash Wednesday Nor'easter of 1962. As one veteran of both storms recounted, "That [1913] storm was just a good blow compared to this one." Its gale force winds with forty-foot waves not only wrecked the Boardwalk and battered its hotels but flooded businesses far up Rehoboth Avenue.

Across the decades, it has been no less quiet on Rehoboth's western front. The Lewes-Rehoboth Canal, completed in 1916, sliced through "the Grove," the original camp meeting site, to connect the Chesapeake and Rehoboth Bays. With the canal serving as a water thoroughfare, canneries processed tomatoes, lima and string beans, and peas. The canal, too, separated the town's residents from an unincorporated spit of land occupied by Blacks; Whites separately christened it "West Rehoboth." Born on the west side of the canal in 1937, Ada Burton stresses that "it was just called Rehoboth" among her family and neighbors. "But to the officials at City Hall, it was an important distinction," observes novelist Alexs Pate. These citizens "d[id] not vote, were not counted, and had virtually no social services." Like his novel's title, a reminder of Jim Crow segregation, it is best characterized as "West of Rehoboth."

Generations of African Americans had settled in this area and surrounding countryside since the emancipation of Blacks following the Civil War. In 1884, Elijah Burton donated an acre of his farm, which became Mt. Pleasant United Methodist Church in 1899, located on Church Street. However, following WWII, Charles Mills, a Quaker who had managed the Stokely cannery since 1929, parceled out some of his farmland to Black workers who had difficulty finding lodging. Such streets as Duffy, Burton, and Harmon were named after them. They built modest homes, grew staple food crops, and raised livestock on the eighty-nine lots that sold for $1,100 to $2,700 (in 2022 dollars). Known as "one of the county's more powerful figures," the progressive-minded Mills lived on Maryland Street and served as president of the Rehoboth School Board, was a town and county commissioner, and was a mayoral candidate. Mills called the separate unincorporated development "West Rehoboth," a term that local Whites welcomed. According to him, their viewpoint was "Blacks are good and useful, but shouldn't be mixed in residentially."

Throughout the Jim Crow era, men and women who lived West of Rehoboth—together with seasonal workers of color—served and cooked at Rehoboth's restaurants, labored in the fields and nearby canneries, kept houses and laundered clothes, mowed lawns and shucked crabs, and transported residents by hacks, carriages, and taxis. Those without family in the area could board at John Allen's eleven-room Pink Elephant (so called because of its pinkish-brown shingles), the nearby cabins, or at his adjacent Wayside Inn, which had a dance hall with a beer garden. Scattered among the shacks and trailers, which lacked sewer connections, were hog pens and garden plots, churches and cemeteries, jazz and "jook joints." Those few Whites who visited simply hankered a plate of Miss Lillian's fried chicken, bought liquor as underage drinkers at the Bloody Bucket, played pool and craps at Walter Harmon's Do Drop, scored drugs at "the corner" near dead-end Hebron Road—or busted one of these illegal operations.

Glen Thompson, who would figure prominently in the "Battle for Rehoboth," frequented the Bloody Bucket when he was underage, visiting from DC in the 1950s. "When this area was totally segregated, White people didn't want Black people in their bars," Thompson explains. So, "they would set up in their house or garage a little business where they sold liquor. The state knew about it, did nothing." Thompson remembers walking West of Rehoboth and onto a wooded path where there "was sort of like a shack or an oversized garage" with a jukebox. At the Bloody Bucket, the old Black man "didn't care" about the color of his customers' skin or their age, as long as "he was going to get his money."

Thompson's future nemesis, Joyce Felton, also sojourned West of Rehoboth, frequenting the 007 Club during the early 1980s. She describes it as "a community unto itself." Across the canal in Rehoboth, "there was not a whole lot of Black presence in the day-to-day except in the service industry. There were kind of lines in the sand." When the canal could no longer impede pent-up real estate demand, many properties fell under the bulldozer's blade driven by speculators, clearing the land for craft beer brewers, luxury homebuyers, and franchise businesses.

Billed as "the Nation's Summer Capital," Rehoboth Beach has long been a town for Washington's elite seeking solace in sun and surf. Politicians and their families have summered over the decades. Richard Nixon brought his family in the late 1950s, and years later "the girls" rented a house. Lynda Byrd Johnson, with then-boyfriend Chuck Robb, enjoyed partying at Whiskey Beach and then moving her retinue to the swank Henlopen Hotel. It is now the "summer White House" for the Biden family. On some summer mornings during the 1970s, walkers could spot Judge John Sirica walking the boards, while syndicated columnist Jack Anderson, disliking the Boardwalk crowds, hunkered down for summer weekends with some of his nine children. There, too, were former ambassadors, owners of professional sports teams, and Fortune 500 executives.

The disgraced have also walked along Rehoboth's tree-lined streets. Outed former Maryland congressman Robert Bauman strolled arm-in-arm through town with two effeminate-looking men. Former Rehoboth lifeguard Michael "Sean" Scanlon laundered his illegal lobbying monies with Jack Abramoff at their fake American International Center on Baltimore Avenue. In short, Rehoboth, as longtime newspaper man Dan Terrell writes, is a town of saints and sinners. At times, it has been difficult to distinguish between them.

QUEERING HISTORICAL NARRATIVE AND MEMORY

Queering Rehoboth Beach is set within these historical and geopolitical markers.[3] It is a narrative history rich in memories, with deep emotional undercurrents. It is also a queered history. What was assumed to be heterosexualized space—on the beaches, within houses of worship, at artist gatherings, in restaurants and businesses, along the Boardwalk—is revisited. It also looks beyond a Boardwalk familiar to seasonal visitors to glimpse at the Other. In *Queering Rehoboth Beach*, the simple narrative familiar to leisurely readers of the magazine *Letters from CAMP Rehoboth*—that homosexuals triumphantly transformed a once-sleepy homophobic town by rehabbing historic homes, opening upscale businesses, and networking into civic life to create an inclusive community—is queried.

The temporal spine of this newly queered story moves linearly from the origins of the Back Porch Café, opened in 1975, to Renegade, closed in 2003. Yet it begins where it ends: with the 2018 death of Steve Elkins, who was the consensus builder bridging the chasm among the town's late-twentieth-century factions. In queering these decades, I also explore earlier generations of Rehoboth's saints and sinners, progressives and stand-patters, miscreants and misfits—beginning with its late-nineteenth-century founders, who engaged in some of these factional battles.

Also absent from this narrative history is a sole storyteller. As its author, I have assembled an ensemble of women and men who collectively queered the history of Rehoboth Beach. Bear in mind that this choral narrative is not always harmonious and, at times, is downright discordant.

Stories we tell our families, friends, neighbors, and even ourselves are refractions of lived experiences. Some memories are privileged; others are purged. Some, we freely tell but may misremember; others, we selectively recall or distort; and a few comport with "objective" reality. We weave each story from a set of important yet imperfect threads embroidering precariously remembered pasts. A challenge of writing a community history is to quilt disparate members' stories together without dismembering their narrative dissonance. A narrative history—quilted from inchoate stories—requires envisioning the unseen, decoding the tacit, and bracketing the accepted. It also requires recognizing the symbiosis between knower and known.

Scholars from a variety of disciplines "have carefully sifted through historical memory in an effort to recapture the lost voices of LGBTQ individuals and open spaces for different ways of remembering." Cultural studies professors Matthew Houdek and Kendall Phillips, in their discussion about public memory, continue, "While shared memories are rarely uniform, uncontroversial, or uncontested, the fact that certain individuals, events, places, and legacies are shared through this network of memory helps to craft us as a collective, as an 'us.'" In short, memories are as much a collective process as an individual one. That is, the meanings we associate with our remembered experiences are, in part, an artifact of our collective psychology. Consequently, those who "know" Rehoboth, even "gay Rehoboth," should prepare for remembering those people, places, and events of their imagined communities.

Alfred Young, a pioneer in writing social history, observes in his biographical tour de force of an American revolutionary, *The Shoemaker and the Tea Party*, "My subject was not only his experiences . . . but the *way* he remembered them." Young chooses to "unravel his memory from his experiences, and then intertwine them anew." Quoting the editor of the *Journal of American History*, he writes that "memory, private and individual, as much as collective and cultural, is constructed." Young adds that "this construction is not made in isolation but in conversations with others that occur in the context of community." This queering of history acknowledges that objectivity is not possible. Realities are shaped and reshaped by interactions with others as well as with our past and present selves. A challenge for any historian is affording space for individuals to present their memories (historical fairness) while contextualizing those presentations (historical accountability).

Chapter 2 introduces most of the principal characters in *Queering Rehoboth Beach*. However, given the lengthy timeline, the cast of characters is long; a brief bio of each is included along with references and notes at the beginning of this book. Among those who are living, several dozen agreed to interviews, lasting from one to ten hours. These are available at the Rehoboth Beach Historical Society and at Duke University's Rubenstein Library Special Collections. For those who are deceased, portraits were developed based on interviews with others who knew them. I also gained insight from personal correspondence as well as secondary historical documents. Triangulation of these storied memories occurred through historical and legal documents, newspaper, journal and magazine articles, and books and interviews with others.

This project began after I reflected on the restaurant incident and as I wrestled with seemingly incongruous mental images of Rehoboth: an ostensibly queer-friendly resort where prejudice endures; an organization (CAMP) committed to making Rehoboth "room for us all," yet its director unwilling to publish an account challenging that narrative. In the process of seeking to understand the queer history of Rehoboth, I was startled to find just a few anecdotal stories published in *Letters*. So, my journey began.

The story of CAMP is an integral part of the town's queer history; it is not synonymous. Jeffrey Slavin, a longtime supporter of the organization, observes, "There's a lot of people who are part of Rehoboth gay history who have no connection to CAMP Rehoboth," ranging from Annette Mosiej to Jack Ackerman. Few are aware of CAMP's other founders, most notably Jim Bahr, who prospered with Victor Pisapia in Australia. Many are unaware of homosexuals' contributions throughout Delaware's contemporary history—from James Robert Vane to Ivo Dominguez Jr.—or how age-old conflicts, cascading through Rehoboth's generations, influenced struggles for queer visibility and equality during the late twentieth century. Those who have read airbrushed local histories, therefore, may find this book unsettling.

In his quasi-fictional mid-century travelogue of America, John Steinbeck admits:

I've always admired those reporters who can descend on an area, talk to key people, ask key questions, take samplings of opinions, and then set down an orderly report very like a road map. I envy this technique and at the same time do not trust it as a mirror of reality. I feel that there are too many realities. What I set down here is true until someone else passes that way and rearranges the world in his own style.

Acknowledging that realities are constructed, as are our shifting remembrances of them, I welcome other readings beyond the Boardwalk.

As an academic carpetbagger, I realize that *Queering Rehoboth Beach* has shortcomings. One is that I simply have never been a resident (only residing west of the canal for three years) or a native Delawarean. The state, of course, no longer considers this lack of residency a liability for a political appointment, but historical analysis may be an exception.

At the end of the day, *Queering Rehoboth Beach* means queering the normalcy of everyday Rehoboth life, querying taken-for-granted beliefs and assumptions, and, in the process, queering pejorative and outdated understandings of those who chose to live beyond them.

1

FOUNDING PRINCIPLES

And he removed from thence, and digged another well; and for
that they strove not; and he called the name of it Rehoboth; and
he said, for now the Lord has made room for us all.

—**Genesis 26:22**

e are familiar with the statement "Those who cannot remember the past are condemned to repeat it," from the late Harvard philosopher George Santayana.[1] One of his many accomplished students was Pulitzer Prize–winning historian and cultural critic Van Wyck Brooks. Brooks's 1915 classic *America's Coming of Age*—dedicated to his lifelong friend, poet John Hall Wheelock—is an insightful and brilliant, albeit uneven, critique of the American schism between idealism and pragmatism. Like "highbrow" and "lowbrow" art (terms he coined), Brooks argues that there is "no community, no genial middle ground"; there is no public space to engage one another, as each holds the other in "mutual contempt." Nevertheless, to progress—as a community, as a person—one has to engage. Everyday "catchpenny realities" must be attuned to grand visions. To begin this process, Brooks advises "go[ing] back to the beginning of things." While Brooks's analyses begin with the origins of Puritanism, I begin with Rehoboth's genesis set within a biblical brotherly conflict among Methodists. Far from being tangential, this story threads conflicting perspectives, such as a commercially oriented versus family-based town and one based on secularism or sectarianism, that would undergird the Battle of Rehoboth a century later.

Immediately after the so-called War of Northern Aggression, "open southern sympathy and efforts to aid the southern cause" were common sentiments on the so-called Delmarva Peninsula, especially in lower Delaware, where most of the state's two thousand slaves had labored. In 1868, the Methodist Congress of Philadelphia debated whether to create a separate district for the peninsula, given the "strong sectional feeling owing to the war." Its most ardent advocate was forty-two-year-old Rev. John Bolton Quigg. A self-educated Philadelphia man, he received his first ministerial appointment in 1850 at a small church near Dover, Delaware. Quigg "demonstrated his great powers of oratory," as he fervently argued that this area "demand[ed] a set of men especially consecrated to God's works." The result was the new peninsula district: the Wilmington Conference. Five years later, this conference organized the Rehoboth Beach Camp Meeting Association, from which the town of Rehoboth Beach would eventually be chartered—and from which its early crucible would be a legacy for future generations.

VISIONARIES AND INVESTORS

Among the many ministers attending the 1868 annual meeting was Rev. Robert W. Todd. Five years Quigg's junior, Todd also led a church in the Dover area, having earned a theology degree from Dickson College. Both men were uncompromising advocates for Methodist discipline and shared a love for books and oratory. But unlike his elder, Todd had been raised in rural Eastern Maryland. His nearby hometown, Denton, was known for its southern sympathizers. Priding himself as a Union man, he described "devoted friends of the 'lost cause' [who] were not only inconsolable, but also angry and vindictive."

Four years later, in 1872, Quigg became presiding elder of the Wilmington District. Todd was now ministering at the well-regarded St. Paul's Methodist Episcopal Church, an imposing structure at 9th and West Streets. In late summer—exhausted from preaching duties at various camp meetings, leading a newly formed temperance union, and losing his wife, Margaretta—Todd sought rejuvenation of body and soul at the Ocean Grove Meeting Camp along the Jersey Shore.

Upon returning to his Wilmington parsonage, the forty-one-year-old regaled his Methodist congregation with his vision of a camp meeting place on the Atlantic. A man steeped in theology and with a fondness for history, he appropriated the Old Testament text from the prophet Isaiah, "The sea (יָם) hath spoken (אָמַר)," in a Sunday sermon. This message captivated the interests of some of his influential and affluent congregants, who often merged John Wesley's regeneration of the human spirit with Adam Smith's invisible hand of capitalism. Among early visionary investors were William

Bright, a member of Wilmington's city council; Washington Hastings, a founder and trustee at St. Paul's who operated the Seidel & Hastings iron rolling mill; and sheet iron manufacturer Joshua J. McCullough.

In October, ministers and businessmen from Wilmington, Lewes, and Baltimore (including Todd and Quigg) traveled to Rehoboth Bay. They agreed that its location was perfect. The following month, contracts for two large parcels of land were drawn up, and, two weeks before Christmas, Methodists of means met in the St. Paul's lecture room. During this all-day gathering, they vowed "to maintain a seaside resort where everything inconsistent with Christian morality . . . shall be excluded and prohibited." They formed the Rehoboth Beach Camp Meeting Association with a thirty-member board of directors to oversee its operation and the mortgage purchase of several hundred acres. Stock was authorized, not to exceed three hundred shares, with no more than two shares held by a man of "good morals" who complied "with the regulations of the Association."

At the beginning of the new year, the state assembly approved the charter for the association. It authorized the sale of stock and whose holders could vote and assume office. In March 1873, the town's grid was laid out in a way that favored ocean breezes, with such street names as Baptist, Christian, Presbyterian, Quaker, Episcopal, and Methodist. Lots were numbered and divided into 50×100-foot parcels, with a lottery set for April 22 to determine their order of selection.

Ten days later, at five o'clock in the morning, 120 stockholders and a roughly equal number of other hopeful lot buyers departed Wilmington's P. W. & B. Depot for Rehoboth. Lots had already doubled from their original $50 price. Prominent men—judges and politicians, ministers and merchants—peered out windows as the train rumbled through the Delaware countryside. "A succession of well-fenced, well-tilled farms, prolific gardens and peach orchards," observed James P. Matthews, who had drawn the first option for lot selection. "Evidences of thrift and industry."

At the end of the line, passengers disembarked at the quaint Swedish immigrant town of Lewes and boarded carriages "drawn by fat and sleek looking horses." Some with lesser means chose "rattle-traps" for the remaining seven miles. On that sunny mid-morning, they passed fields "clothed in Spring's freshest green" and smelled "the delicate pink of the numerous peach trees in full bloom." About a half mile from the beach, they arrived at a huge oak grove "with trees so large that they look as if they had thrown their giant shadows over a hundred generations."

After a catered lunch at the old Martin farmhouse, prospective property owners gathered with their notes, proxies, and receipts. Association
officers, led by its president, Reverend Todd, stood tall in an old wagon
overlooking the crowd. Among others overseeing this process were association officers William Bright, who had arranged the farm sale to the association; Presiding Elder John Quigg; and Wilmington building contractor
William H. Foulk.

After the 204th stockholder's name had been called, non-stockholders
seeking lots were free to choose. Slightly before 8:00 P.M., the contented
and malcontented boarded the Wilmington-bound train at Lewes. Unsold
lots were later advertised for upward of $150, with the association offering
a 20 percent ministerial discount.

SALVATION AND SPECULATION

Board member Foulk stayed on to oversee the construction crew.[2] With lumber from nearby Millsboro, workers erected the preacher's lodge and several
cottages, costing each new owner $1,500 or more. The first set of eight-foot
oak Boardwalk planks were laid upon virgin ocean sands. By June 1873, a
34×105-foot beachfront hotel was enclosed with a first floor that included a
large dining room, men's and ladies' parlors, and a reading room. The association let concessions for the three-story, thirty-eight-room Surf House
along the hundred-foot-wide beach boulevard of Surf Avenue.

Deeming these accommodations insufficient for the July camp meeting, Todd penned an open letter to Wilmington entrepreneurs: "Thousands
of people will be here who will have no tents and must be provided with
food and shelter. There is a fine chance for business." Some of the faithful,
though, expressed concerns about such commercialism and opening Rehoboth to the secular-minded. "Tell us, pray," asked one Methodist Delawarean, "what is to make this a Christian sea-side resort and whether any
of the unconverted will be allowed to resort thither?"

During this first season, people came from Baltimore, Washington, and
Philadelphia as well as Delaware, arriving by train or steamer to Lewes and
then overland in one of Morris & Arnold's hacks. Some only stayed a few
hours, while others pitched canvas tents or boarded at one of the plank
tents in the Grove. Those who could afford $10 to $12 a week stayed at Surf
House, three blocks north of Rehoboth Avenue. Bright enjoyed an upper
room at the overflowing Surf House, where the less fortunate slept on

floors with mattresses. With a capitalist eye, he spotted "the need for two more large boarding houses." Bishop Levi Scott and his son arrived a few days early to pitch their tent. Wealthy entrepreneurs, such as James E. Hooper, Baltimore's leading cotton manufacturer, and Wilmington's John Morton Poole, a producer of rolling mill equipment, were already settling into their new cottages.

Immediately after breaking camp, Reverend Quigg was elected the new president of the association's board. Reverend Todd became the camp superintendent. His son, Jacob, also a minister, was appointed to the Finance Committee, along with Bright and Hastings. Other committees, including Order, were tasked with enforcing the rules of the association based on the strict Discipline of Methodism. The Rehoboth Beach Camp Meeting Association approved rigid bylaws in accordance with church precepts. Prohibited were the playing of cards and tenpins, dancing, and theatergoing, along with any Sabbath Day toil, including shaving. Naturally, the selling or consuming of alcohol was banned. This prohibition extended a mile *beyond* the association's boundaries. Surf House stayed open until early September, reopening the following June and establishing Rehoboth's traditional three-month season.

So successful were the first two summers that some believed that they would "soon have the camp of *the* country." Share values, too, had increased twofold, with the association selling forty-four additional lots. Sales from private owners fetched a minimum of $186, with some selling at six times their original price. A few Baltimore believers in salvation and speculators of property earnestly considered building a cooperative rather than separate cottages exclusively for those of their city. All agreed that more hotels and boardinghouses were needed.

DISSENT AND GROWTH

As early as 1875, there were challenges to the strict interpretation of Methodist Discipline and informal discussion about separating the camp meeting from the association.[3] At the third annual summer meeting, some even claimed "that the camp, under the auspices of the Association, was of no benefit but rather a detriment to the latter." Dover entrepreneur Col. William C. Fountain recognized a business opportunity and opened the Douglass House in 1877. This sixty-room hotel was one mile and seven feet south of the camp's property line, in Rehoboth City (what is now Dewey Beach).

Here, hotel revelers indulged in some of if not all the deadly sins, including whiskey drinking, card playing, shuffleboarding, and dancing.

Growth continued within Rehoboth's circumscribed boundaries during the late 1870s. One-room wooden cottages replaced sailcloth tents. The wood-clad Scott Chapel, on what is now Baltimore Avenue, complemented the open-air tabernacle in the Grove. The *Rehoboth Beacon*, a folio newspaper, was published under ministers Jacob Todd's and J. B. Quigg's watchful eyes. Additional boardinghouses were approved for construction, a pavilion erected, and the Boardwalk extended to five thousand feet. Surf House was expanded to include a covered portico whose roof reached above the second story and extended along the three sides facing the ocean. By 1877, nearly seven hundred lots had been sold, ten of which were purchased by investors to build a second hotel along the beach. The next year, the partnership between the Rehoboth Beach Camp Meeting Association and the secular Rehoboth City Association, a privately held commercial real estate firm, resulted in the railroad's extension from Lewes to the Grove at Rehoboth.

The new Junction & Breakwater railway line, through such investors as Bright and McCullough, brought more pilgrims, profiteers, and pagans. Daily "excursionists" could now enjoy a "few hours at this famous summer resort" or stay at one of the several hotels or boardinghouses. Many of these visitors stayed or dined at Bright House, which had opened in 1876. The eighty-room four-story hotel designed by Bright was set on the seashore and fronted by "an elegant piazza" and one hundred bathhouses. Mrs. J. B. Grubb, whose family also operated a Wilmington hotel, served hundreds of meals daily and could lodge two hundred guests. It was generally agreed that Bright provided "princely entertainment" and that his private hotel was the "most popular place of resort."

BRIGHT AND HIS NEMESES

Bright, now in his second term as association president, was a shrewd Wilmington businessman.[4] Like Quigg, he was a native Pennsylvanian and self-made. After moving to Delaware, he started building houses. In 1852, at age thirty-eight, he purchased a Wilmington grocery store and then parleyed his success into real estate ventures, eventually becoming the city's largest property owner.

As a Democrat, Bright did not support Abraham Lincoln, but he was troubled by the rapidly escalating secessionist crisis. Following the Battle of Gettysburg, fought by Delawareans on both sides of the conflict, he was arrested and held without bail or trial at Fort Delaware. The fort, located on Pea Patch Island near Delaware City, warehoused nearly thirteen thousand Confederate soldiers and sympathizers. A few escaped via the southern Underground Railroad. Many more, like Bright, with their health broken, were released after swearing allegiance to the Union. Later, it was revealed that Bright's arrest had been instigated by those seeking control of his properties.

Following the war, Bright was elected to city council in the Republican-controlled city of Wilmington and became its president in 1867. He then helped the association acquire the original two tracts of farmland and later bought the notes from the farm owners. These were held against the association's land, earning him a solid 6 percent interest. Further, as the note holder, he did not pay periodic assessments levied on other lot owners, some of whom, without stock, lacked any say in the governing of the association.[5] For many years, Bright continued serving as an officer of the association as well as a director of two banks and the president of Delaware State Fire and Marine Insurance.[6] He was known as a generous benefactor to individuals and causes.

As commerce expanded, Rehoboth excursionists increased, and cottages multiplied, the hegemony of Methodism weakened. In 1876, the association, under Bright's leadership, had changed its bylaws to allow non-Methodists to comprise fully a third of its directors. There was also an informal proposal to permit tenpin alleys and billiard tables on the grounds. Not everyone was happy with the growing influence of the secularists, the influx of the unconverted, and the seemingly spiritless path embraced by some directors of the Camp Meeting Association.

Among those ministers preaching at the camp's Sunday school convention of 1878 were New Castle's Rev. A. H. Bristol. He expressed shock upon his arrival at this "den of dancing, card playing, and whiskey drinking." Another preacher, J. B. Mann, damned such dancing as "the lowest and most vulgar amusements by which the Devil takes young people from Christ." Reverend J. H. Caldwell, who chaired this convention, reported hearing "that the directors were manipulated by influencers which winked at these things."

Association president Bright opened the 1878 mid-July stockholders meeting at the preacher's tent, declaring that "the future and full success of Rehoboth is assured." Following routine business, Reverend Caldwell levied his charges of dancing and card-playing against Bright House, now under the proprietorship of Walter Burton, a former state legislator, and

Dr. Thompson of Lewes. Reverend Quigg moved "to expel from these grounds anyone guilty of the violation of the rules." Those in opposition pointed out that the hotel was privately owned and expressed doubt about the capability of the Committee on Order to enforce it. Board member Hastings, a prominent Wilmington mercantilist and a leader of the city's Republican Party, moved unsuccessfully to exempt the hotel. The resolution passed, with Bright abstaining. However, those supporting it found no "teeth of the order," as no one was "disturbed" at Bright House, whose guests "[we]re very strong in their determination to amuse themselves as they please[d]." Dancing to music from a string band continued nightly in the main hall. Euchre and other card games persisted in the parlors. Nightly roller skating was popular on the Boardwalk after supper. A special excursion train from Milford even brought fifty couples to a complementary dance at Bright House.

QUIGG'S CRUSADE

"Politics seems to have encamped at Rehoboth," declared a Wilmington newspaper, reporting that some had launched "a crusade against dancing and the 'wicked Bright House.'"[7] Meanwhile, politicians, ranging from an assistant to President William McKinley and his entourage to state officials and county judges, camped out at Bright House or the Douglass Hotel rather than cloister themselves at the "more quiet and repose" association-owned Surf House.

In July 1878, a special board meeting was held in Wilmington. Unlike those attending the larger stockholder meeting, most board members had direct financial interest in Rehoboth beyond their lots or cottages. After two hours of heated discussion, the Committee on Order was denied permission to enforce the association's rules. Quigg, who headed that committee, acquiesced to "the authority of the board." However, "as a private stockholder," he reserved the right "to take any action."

Immediately, Quigg filed for injunctive relief against the association and the Bright Hotel, claiming that "dancing being permitted there has long been a subject of grievance." In an all-day session at the Court of Chancery in Dover, the case of *Quigg v. Bright et al.* was heard before a packed courtroom. In defending Bright *and* the association, Jacob "Jake" Moore, Delaware's portly former attorney general, stipulated that dancing did occur, but that it was beyond the enforcement role of the court. In his four-hour presentment, Moore acknowledged that the association's charter granted it police power through its Committee on Order, but he stressed that its board chose not to wield it. Thus, he asked if an injunction was issued, what would stop others from seeking a similar legal remedy against Methodist proscriptions, such as "wearing costly apparel . . . or use of tobacco?" He further argued that Quigg lacked standing as a stockholder because he had not first demanded monetary redress from the board.

"Amusements," Quigg's attorney firmly reminded the court, "were against the morality of the M. E. Church." Further, he claimed that Bright's veiled "attempt had been made to divert it [the association] from the object of its originators and of its charter." All other remedies had been exhausted by Quigg, he contended; therefore, the court was his last recourse.

In his ruling, the judge agreed that amusements occurring at Bright House were indeed contrary to Methodist Discipline and that their proscription was incorporated into the deed held by Bright. Further, he ruled that the association, under its police power, could rightfully enter any Rehoboth property to enforce its rules, request their immediate end, and even eject violators from the camp's boundaries. Nevertheless, any such action was the sole province of the association controlled by the mercantilists, not the courts. Ironically, five generations later, another association controlled by influential families would engage in legal contests against commercial interests.

SEEKING SOLOMON

One Christian observer pontificated that board members "will have either to exorcise the devil or the devil will exorcise them."[8] The former, though, was doubtful, given the influence of such directors as McCullough, Hooper, Hastings, Poole, and, of course, Bright. It also was common knowledge that many of the "sons and daughters of the Methodist preachers and leaders in the church were the most persistent participators in the dance." Most notably, the rebellious fifteen-year-old Ely Quigg had a propensity for "the dance and dexterously shuffling the cards."[9]

These legal proceedings and court ruling affected the Methodist Church on the peninsula and the Rehoboth Camp Meeting Association. Throughout the fall and winter, the "question of the day was, 'Is or Is It Not Practicable to Enforce the Discipline of the Methodist Church?'" Reporters were barred from the meeting of the Wilmington Methodist Preachers' Association as ministers quarreled. There were more accusations that "camp meetings were run as a money-making scheme" and complaints of whiskey drinking, card playing, and cigar smoking occurring not only at Rehoboth but at the crown jewel campsite of Ocean Grove. Despite Reverend Quigg's vigorous efforts to end such undesirable practices, he summarily rejected those clergy who wanted to terminate Methodist camp meetings. "We *are* a camp meeting church," he bellowed, and we "must go out and try and reach those who never go inside of a church!" The group, exasperated by the wearisome deliberation, directed Quigg to prepare a paper on the question, which was widely published in newspapers throughout the state. In it, he argued that the purpose of church discipline was to bring those violators "to repentance and a reformation of life" with "excommunication [as] the last resort."

Throughout autumn and into early winter, ministers debated the meaning of church discipline and its enforceability. Meanwhile, the association's board, after accepting the resignation of Rev. Jacob Todd, formed a committee to consider whether to separate the camp meeting from the association. Both groups, each with their peculiarities, vainly sought a Solomonesque balance between the interests of resort businessmen and excursionists, who yearned to be "free from some things that the Church could not consistently countenance," with those of Methodist preachers and pilgrims, who were committed to church discipline.

In early January 1879, stockholders of the Camp Meeting Association gathered at St. Paul's in Wilmington to separate "the sheep from the goats." The committee proposed to strip the words *Camp Meeting* from its charter to become simply the Rehoboth Beach Association. Moreover, it recommended deleting *Discipline* appearing before *Methodist*. The charter would read: "Everything not consistent with Christian morality as taught by the [*omitted:* Discipline of the] Methodist Episcopal Church shall be excluded and prohibited." Thus, committee chairman Hastings explained, the resort would not "*appear* to be conducted under the auspices of a Camp Meeting Association or the M. E. Church." While horned goats had the amended charter forwarded to the state assembly, Christ's lambs received teeth to enforce its regulations through its Committee on Order. Yet neither was harmony realized or hostility abated.

TWO SLATES: SINNERS AND SAINTS

At the beginning of the season in June, Rehoboth hotels and boardinghouses were already overflowing with excursionists, and many tents and cottages had been rented for the entire season. Anticipating crowds, Bright House expanded its kitchen, and Surf House was freshly staged. Most anticipated, the annual meeting of stockholders promised to "be the warmest and liveliest that has taken place since that corporation has been in existence."[10]

Despite a sunny outlook for a record-breaking 1879 season, storm clouds hovered on the horizon in the "coming struggle between the Rehoboth Beach Association and the worldly minded." However, Quigg's supporters were splintered between unrelenting crusaders demanding certain and rigid enforcement of the discipline vis-à-vis those, with "heavy financial interests at stake," supporting a dance ban *only* on the Sabbath and questioning "the evil influence" of croquet and tenpins.

On a mid-July late afternoon, stockholders met at the Grove to choose a third of its board. There were two slates: "Bright's Ticket," which promised to keep the "land sharks" at bay, and "Quigg's Ticket," which was "rather restricted in their ideas of liberality." Unlike previous summers, there was an unsettling quietness, with sparse debate before voting. Elderly Bishop Scott was a witness to the startling "rebuke." Bright's "sinner" slate, including prominent industrialists Hooper and Poole, defeated Quigg's so-called saint slate, mostly composed of ministers, by a margin of nearly four-to-one. Stockholders now aligned themselves with an even more progressive board that outnumbered the anti-dancing faction by three-to-one.

REBUKE AND RETRIBUTION

Divine retribution was swift. In the predawn hours of August 22, 1879, "lurid flames were flashing athwart the sky." A "colored servant," sleeping near the laundry in Surf House, was "awakened by the crackling and snapping of the flames." He rushed through the three-story building, shouting "Fire!" In less than a half hour, its wooden frame structure was little more than a "smoldering mass of ruins," with few contents salvageable. Among the sixty or so terrified guests fleeing the "fire and blinding volumes of smoke" were families of board members and the party of President Rutherford Hayes's private secretary. Without the efforts of servants, "many lives might have been lost." The *Daily Gazette* singled out the efforts of the laundry servant, whose "hands and face were burned painfully"; other newspapers omitted his heroism entirely.

Word of the fire quickly reached Wilmington by telegram, with more details provided by those returning home that day. A crowd of investors soon gathered at Fourth and Market to discuss their options. Association president H. F. Pickels, who hurried from his nearby stove dealership, becalmed investors. The fire would "lose some money but Rehoboth, as a watering place, w[ould] not feel the disaster at all. It may prove a blessing in disguise." Surf House was never rebuilt. Lots were placed in the hands of sales agent Bright, who purchased an additional hundred feet on Surf Avenue to expand his hotel.

Between the demise of Surf House and the elevation of a more tolerant board, it was not surprising that the 1880 season brought noticeably fewer camp attendees. Many tents were reportedly unoccupied; the two remaining hotels—Bright and Douglass—were filled with excursionists. Before "many young dancers commence[d] their tripping 'o nights to quick music in the Bright House," the "staid Methodists" were alone, "singing psalms in the Grove." Observers promised that Rehoboth would "rank among the best watering places on the Atlantic Coast" and "become the Atlantic City of Delaware."

Nevertheless, the steadfast disciplinarian, fifty-four-year-old Quigg, was in summer attendance. In his second stint as presiding elder of the Methodist Conference, he had assiduously prepared for the July stockholders' meeting. The "grand old man" stood erect in the gothic Scott Chapel. The tone of his oratory and his presiding stature clearly signaled that he would not forsake Reverend Todd's vision of a seaside Methodist retreat. He made what surely in his mind was a modest motion: that a ninety-nine-year lease of the campgrounds be awarded to the Methodist Episcopal Church "to be used according to the *original* design." Having heard little opposition to his resolution, Quigg was "very much surprised" when it was "summarily" rejected. "Rehoboth is admitted to being a failure," asserted the stockholder majority that argued "goodness under such high pressure w[ould], if continued, so handicap the city's future that all anticipations of success must be put aside." It was "another step," the *Wilmington Morning News* observed, "where the world scored a point against the Godly."

On the evening of the secularists' victory, the "new order of things" in Rehoboth was celebrated by a grand ball at Bright House. A Wilmington symphony played "the most worldly music" as uninhibited guests danced throughout the night. The "mutterings . . . among the extreme moralists" could not be heard above the orchestra, which was promptly engaged for the entire season, with dances scheduled *every* night. "However much the goody-goody people may grumble," ventured Wilmington's *Daily Morning News*, "it is not likely the new board of directors will take the least notice."

In early 1881, the board met to further amend the association's charter, subject to approval of the stockholders and the state assembly. It unanimously voted to delete *all* references to the Methodist Episcopal Church, alter the requirement that twenty of its thirty board members be church members, reduce the number of directors to fifteen, and give *all* lot-holders a voice in governance. Although the sale of liquor was forbidden, these recommendations, concluded the *Delaware State Journal*, "make Rehoboth Beach another place entirely." The adopted changes, effectively "secularizing the resort," eliminated the political issue of taxing lot-holders without representation. The association was no longer in the camp meeting business; its business was business. A century later, leaders of another hegemonic homeowners' association would be adversaries to progressive businesspeople, antipathetic to its queer citizenry, and disturbed by hordes of excursionists.

QUEER GENERATIONAL APERÇUS

And who shall declare his generation?

—**Acts 8:33**

During the first decades of the twentieth century, strong female friendships, if not sapphic relationships, were not uncommon, yet they were seldom visible within a male-dominated world.[1] In Rehoboth Beach, women joined women to better the town through their Village Improvement Association and to share canvases at summer exhibitions of an emerging art colony, which later gave rise to the Rehoboth Art League. One such woman was Anna Burton S. Hazzard. One of the first women to receive a Delaware real estate broker's license, she would later become the president of both organizations. "Miss Annie" never married.

Other resolute women entered heterosexual marriages as avenues into the corridors of power. In 1872, five-year-old Mary Wilson first visited the Rehoboth area with her family, headed by her father, a decorated Union Army cavalry officer, Maj. Gen. James Harrison Wilson. Following private schooling and travels abroad, at age nineteen, she married Wilmington textile mogul Henry B. Thompson; the couple became "leaders of Wilmington society." At Wilmington and Rehoboth social functions, Mary Thompson was—to borrow from Felix Dahn's classic study of the sixth-century clash between the Eastern Roman Empire and the Gothic tribes—"the ostiarius [who] looked prudently through a secret aperture in the wall" before allowing admittance. She founded Rehoboth's July Holiday Ball, a fundraiser for Beebe Hospital held each season at the Fireman's Hall on Rehoboth Avenue, and was single-handedly responsible for initiating the town's mosquito-eradication efforts.

In 1916, Mrs. Henry B. Thompson wrote a family friend, President Woodrow Wilson, cautioning him of the perils of the suffragist movement. A woman seeking entry into the world of men, she warned, was "dangerous, treacherous & revengeful—therefore the sooner her political activity is curbed the better." As Delaware's steely-headed anti-suffrage leader, she condemned the modern, freewheeling woman.

In the spring of 1920, Delaware was the battleground state for adopting the Nineteenth Amendment. As chair of the Association Opposed to Woman Suffrage, Mary, "brilliant in her use of charm, cajolery . . . and dramatic speechifying," was "instrumental" in the general assembly's overwhelming vote against it. Historian Richard Carter also observes, paradoxically, that "had she lived in a slightly later age, she could easily have won election to high political office."

Cherishing Mary's Rehoboth childhood memories of "forests of pines" and a "white beach," the Thompsons built their cottage—*Mon Plaisir*—with its "enormous porches on all sides," which captured "perfume in the air" from towering pines. Completed in 1927, it was designed by their Princeton-educated son, James. He also designed other Rehoboth homes as well as the town's bandstand and public lavatory. During his twenties and thirties, this handsome, gregarious blue-eyed heir to wealth and privilege was known as a "carefree young bachelor, always ready for a dance, a theater party, a hunt, always rumored about to marry this or that young heiress but never quite doing so." After serving in WWI as an army intelligence officer, James formed the Thai Silk Company and constructed his landmark house in Bangkok. Known for his fondness of antiquities, ballet, and cockatoos—and rough trade—he famously vanished from Malaysia's Cameron Highlands in 1967.

Easygoing James Thompson was a good friend to du Pont heiress Louisa d'Andelot Carpenter, whose family had supported suffrage. As adolescents, they and social acquaintances visited Rehoboth during the 1920s. Escorted by Mary, they often stayed at Judge David Marvel's ten-bedroom cottage. Louisa, the daughter of R. R. M. Carpenter, was attending Miss Porter's School in Connecticut, where she became the closest of friends with Sophia McLane of Baltimore. A frequent ribbon winner at various East Coast horse shows, the blond-haired Louisa, with her piercing blue eyes, "set a fashion . . . when she appeared in tuxedo coat, wing collar, and bow tie." Another paper's society section described the style as "mannish."

During Wilmington's 1925 debutante season, Louisa was presented to society in December at the Hotel DuPont Gold Ballroom. Receiving more than six hundred guests at the foyer leading to the great doors of the ballroom, she sparkled in silver slippers and stockings, with a matching gown of "white crepe threaded with silver over a silver slip trimmed with a flounce of silver lace." Louisa stood in front of an "iridescent fountain banked with poinsettias," complemented by the fragrance of dozens of bouquets sent in her honor. The *Morning News* judged it "one of the brilliant occasions of the season." In 1929, her parents announced Louisa's engagement to Princeton-educated John K. Jenney, an executive with the DuPont Company. After a quiet marriage ceremony and honeymoon, Louisa soon moved to New York City. Living apart from her husband, she was often spotted with her women friends at Harlem's lesbian haunt, the Clam House. The couple divorced in 1935.

Beginning in the 1930s, the butch bohemian Louisa entertained guests at the family's private Rehoboth Beach compound, often accompanied by her on-again, off-again lover Libby Holman. She had met the jazz singer and Broadway actress at a New York horse show through Clifton Webb, who was appearing with Holman in a Broadway revue, *The Little Show*. The impetuous Holman was also in a sham marriage. In July 1932, her husband, twenty-one-year-old tobacco heir Zachary Reynolds, was murdered after one of the couple's boisterous nights of arguments and drinking. Louisa—dressed in a man's jacket and slacks—discretely paid Holman's $25,000 bail and stealthily moved her to Rehoboth, far away from tabloid reporters. Along with other celebrities, such as Noël Coward, Tennessee Williams and occasional lovers, Tallulah Bankhead, her sister Eugenia, and Greta Garbo, they frolicked and picnicked on the beach just steps from Rehoboth. Behind the gates, however, she and her flamboyant friends enjoyed hedonistic Sunday night parties. An aviatrix, skilled equestrian, and first female Master of the Hounds, Louisa was also a mother of two adopted children and a philanthropist. No one in Rehoboth dared utter the L-word, although some suspected. A local historian, elder Evelyn Thoroughgood, remarked, "In Louisa's time, we vaguely knew that she was gay, but nobody talked about it. You just didn't."

Sexual silence was also the norm during World War II. Just north of Rehoboth, Fort Miles housed 2,500 soldiers tasked with keeping the sea routes free from Nazi U-boats. Five-story concrete towers along the beach housed sentinels triangulating readings to target the enemy with 2,700-pound shells shot from sixteen-inch barreled guns. There, too, men

Louisa Carpenter on July 17, 1941. (Courtesy of Delaware State Archives.)

on horseback patrolled the mostly desolate beach from Cape Henlopen to the Virginia tidewater. Hidden amid sand dunes and salt grass were lonely GIs, some of whom found momentary sexual solace with a comrade-in-arms. Men (and women) bivouacked at the Rehoboth Civil Air Patrol anti-submarine Base 2 at the old Rehoboth airport. Octogenarian Glen Thompson recalls, as a teenager, meeting older men who relayed such experiences: "Rehoboth was an R & R area where the soldiers would come in who had mental or physical problems or they did their relaxing." The gay scene "was kept under wraps because if you exposed yourself to the wrong people, you could be in real trouble. Where they used to congregate—the gay guys— was right where Poodle Beach is now. They wanted to be outside of the city, and it was really dark back in that area."

Maryland-born Ross Alexander was an ambulance driver in Europe and India during the war. In 1954, he opened Joss, a "connotation of good luck and happiness associated . . . with all good things," explained Alexander. A seasonal Rehoboth shop, it showcased Christmas ornaments, candles, and even paper clothes used as cutouts at the annual ball of the Rehoboth Art League. Joss was Rehoboth's first acknowledged gay-owned business. When Alexander relocated his business to Baltimore Avenue in the mid-1970s, it "set the standard for renovating that commercial block"; it was the first business to receive the local chamber of commerce's business of the year award. By the time Alexander retired in 2001, with his longtime part-ner, Fran Hueber, a paleobotanist at the Smithsonian, once-quiescent Bal-timore Avenue had long morphed into the gay commercial street, known to some simply as The Avenue.

Meanwhile, during the Cold War, Fort Miles was transformed into a se-cret intelligence installation, as McCarthy-era witch hunts claimed the pro-fessional lives of many homosexuals in the military and government. One of those worried was a thirty-something Pentagon naval assistant, Bob Gray, who was living a "double life." When President Dwight Eisenhower named him his appointments secretary, Gray was "absolutely terrified they [the FBI] would find something." After Eisenhower's presidency, Gray joined the PR firm Hill & Knowlton as director of its DC office.

Not surprisingly, Rehoboth became a furtive beach destination. The ap-peal lay in its short distance: just a few hours' drive over the newly con-structed Chesapeake Bay Bridge, yet far from prying eyes. A Pentagon-based senior military officer explained years later, "People didn't go down there in an aura of fear, but they certainly went in an aura of absolute caution."

From the 1950s and into the 1960s, closeted locals and DC government folks cruised secluded beach dunes or attended weekend afternoon cocktail parties with pitchers of manhattans or martinis. The most exclusive were near Silver Lake, at the summer home of Gray, who was becoming DC's most sought-after lobbyist. "His travels on the social circuit were so exten-sive," detailed the *Washington Post*, that the gentleman who "smiled like a diamond" would wear out "two tuxes annually."

Others hooked up at the Pink Pony, a Boardwalk bar owned by WWII vet-eran Ted Nowakowski Sr. that welcomed gays who mixed amiably with

Pink Pony interior. (Courtesy of Delaware State Archives.)

straights, especially during Saturday's happy hour. There, behind the thick smoked-glass windows framed with latticework, homosexuals freely drank, dined, listened to cabaret, and occasionally danced. Evelyn Dick Thorough-good, whose grandfather, Allee Dick, was the second mayor of Rehoboth, had graduated from Rehoboth High School in 1938. She recalls her "first encoun-ter with gay social life" in the 1950s. Stopping by one night to see her hus-band, George, who occasionally bartended and whom everyone called Bugs, "was the first time I had ever seen this wild, exhibitionist style of dancing."

The Great Nor'easter of March 1962 washed away the original Pink Pony along with much of the Boardwalk. Gays sought other watering holes. One such bar was on First Street, just off Rehoboth Avenue. At first, the owner charged homosexuals double for drinks, but later hired a spotter to identify and eject them. Thirty-three-year-old Jimmy Short was one of those devi-ates. A former Coast Guard officer and high school history teacher, Short had just completed fifteen months at the New Castle County Workhouse— the last man jailed under Delaware's sodomy statute. He met up with a bi-sexual couple, Randall and Betty Godwin, at nearby Bethany Beach. They owned Nomad Village, a dozen A-frame cottages along with a liquor store and bar. Short convinced them to queer one side of their fledgling bar.

Secluded beaches immediately beyond the town's northern and southern boundaries also harbored homosexuals. Caressed by ocean breezes thick with the smell of Hawaiian Tropic, they played volleyball and Frisbee, enjoyed backgammon and cards, and drank sea breezes and colas as Johnny Mathis and Lesley Gore crooned on transistor radios. Away from the curious and outside local jurisdiction, their invisibility was shattered in the summer of 1964 when a Rehoboth man publicly exposed "widespread" homosexuality on its beaches. Harry Bonk, a former All-American who played halfback under the legendary Bear Bryant, told his fellow state highway commissioners, "They congregate like bees in a swarm." A Rehoboth tavern owner backed up Bonk's statement: "They come in groups of six or eight like a bus unloading." It's "an invasion."

The Stonewall riots marked the emergence of queer underground newspapers, campus student unions, and community liberation groups. Even so, Rehoboth, like most towns in the Diamond State, appeared unchanged during the 1970s. Gay sunbathers continued to stroll across "Carpenter's Beach," although there were no longer special holiday tables of food freely available to passersby, as sixty-eight-year-old Louisa Carpenter's twin-engine jet, en route from her Florida horse farm, had stalled and crashed in a field near Easton, Maryland. This stretch of beach area was now roped off from the dunes to the tidemark; epithets or eggs were sometimes tossed at queer "trespassers."

A growing number of gay men were quietly buying and renovating summer homes, retiring to the beach, and starting businesses. Ed Conroy and Roy Anderson had been visiting Rehoboth since the 1950s. Before the Chesapeake Bridge was constructed, Conroy remembers the DC-based couple's time-consuming crossing of the bay in a ferry with their two dogs. Anderson recalls strolling the Boardwalk on summer nights: "You dressed. There were no shorts!"

For a brief time during the early 1960s, they had operated a seasonal shop, the Unicorn Gallery. In 1972, the DC educators and art couple bought a second home behind the old Henlopen Hotel near the beach, known as the Gables for its unique architectural style. Four years later, on Fourth of July weekend, they opened an upscale gift shop. However, first they approached shop owner Ross Alexander to ensure that there would be no problems. "Do you mind if a shop opens up next to you?" Anderson recalls asking. "He said, 'Not if we don't sell the same things.'" Unlike Joss, the Wooden Indian featured upscale Americana, such as pottery, decoys, blankets, and quilts, along with Herald and Waterford china and miniatures that the couple bought on their annual trip to London's West End aboard the *Queen Mary*.

That same 1976 holiday weekend, twenty-something Michael Decker, a gifted musician who often toured with top rock groups, was listening to a popular local radio station. "Rock the Boat," a disco hit by the Hues Corporation, played in the background. The announcer beckoned, "Cruise Down to the Boathouse." Decker recounts, "Any gay person hearing that music— if you weren't listening to the speaking—would be attracted." Homosexuals heeded this siren call and headed to Dewey Beach. The line of mustached men in denim, lusting to join disco dancers at three bars for a $3 cover, stretched two blocks, stopping just short of Rehoboth's southern border, like the Douglass Hotel a century earlier.

Lesbians who enjoyed sunning themselves at North Beach also frequented Nomad Village or the Boathouse. Libby Stiff remembers "drinking screwdrivers with a splash of sloe gin. We called them Sloe Screws." A longtime Delawarean (her family had settled in nearby Milford during the seventeenth century), she and her family had visited Rehoboth in the summers during the 1950s, staying at one of the inexpensive guesthouses. In 1974, she met her life partner, Bea, the first clinical nurse specialist in the state. They raised a family in Wilmington and also owned a small house near Rehoboth at Indian River Bay. On Saturday nights, the couple sometimes visited the Boathouse. "The Nomad seemed as if it was in the boonies," Stiff recalls, but the Boathouse was "a legitimate bar. It was the first step toward liberation. We could actually go there and kiss and hold hands and dance together. It was rustic, but nice."

Most lesbians, though, preferred private gatherings. Those with a bit of money could enjoy dinner or afternoon high tea at the newly opened Back Porch Café. Its closeted co-owner, Victor Pisapia, whose Italian grandparents had immigrated to the country and whose godparents had opened a restaurant in Dover, prepared such meals as fresh trout with mignonette sauce or jerk chicken—unseen on Rehoboth's drone menus of fried foods and pizza. A few, too, sojourned to the salon hosted by the magisterial Anyda Marchant and her partner, soft-spoken Muriel Crawford. The couple, together since 1948, had cofounded Naiad Press in 1973, which published Marchant's pseudonymous lesbian novel, *The Latecomer*. On Saturday evenings, they imbibed Dewars on the rocks and served up cocktails mixed with lively conversations about literature, politics, and art, with an occasional flutist playing in the background.

On Memorial Day weekend in 1980, DC bar impresario Glen Thompson opened Renegade Disco & Lounge, West of Rehoboth. It was the first openly owned gay bar in Delaware. Unlike the dilapidated Boathouse, where cattails pressed against windows and bay waters sometimes seeped between wooden dance planks, his club provided a "first-quality" dance floor and sound system for a "multitude of sweaty bodies." The next summer, the *Washington Blade* proclaimed, "Crowds of younger, more 'blatant' Gays have discovered Rehoboth." Renegade became "a conspicuous symbol of 'the Gay presence.'"

The news story also featured the Blue Moon, which had opened on Baltimore Avenue, a block west from Joss and the Wooden Indian. The gay child of Pisapia's gastronomical gem—the Back Porch Café—and Felton's Manhattan avant-garde eateries, this glitzy restaurant served nouvelle cuisine with New York panache. Felton, a bon vivant bisexual and Brooklyn native, had been a Students for a Democratic Society (SDS) organizer in South Carolina. After being kicked out of that state, she opened a vegetarian restaurant, the Black Cat Café, in a former North Carolina Baptist Church. "It was a motley crew of mostly women," she says. "We had a lesbian separatist dishwasher who didn't want to wash dishes if a man had eaten off them." Living in a commune, Felton created a restaurant, much like the Blue Moon, that became "a hub and safe place for gay men and lesbian women."

Such brazen visibility of lesbians and gay men did not sit well with Rehoboth's old guard, the town commissioners, or high-toned members of the Homeowners Association, whose political endorsement usually guaranteed election. During the summer of 1981, Commissioner John Hughes's political ads, paid for by the association, promised "the continuation of Rehoboth as a family resort." The thirty-nine-year-old mayoral candidate espoused traditional values, warning, "Keep your eyes open when this family resort is advertised in other areas as a gay paradise!"

By the mid-1980s, the number of expressly gay-owned upscale restaurants, B&Bs, and shops had grown to more than a baker's dozen. More followed, particularly along Baltimore Avenue, transforming it into "The Avenue." Rehoboth, as headlined in the state's leading newspaper, had joined the Atlantic Coast "summer circuit" of "vacation spots among gays: Provincetown, Key West, and Fire Island." Frustrated, Mayor Hughes, then seeking his third term, unabashedly told the *Washington Blade* that the town was "still not ready for the sight of two gays walking down the street with their hands in each other's hip pockets."

The advent of a "gay cancer" only heightened fear among Reagan-era Rehoboth citizens. Bumper stickers, funded by the Homeowners Association, proclaimed, "Keep Rehoboth a Family Town." Some local youth formed a wannabe heterosexual militia, the Anti-Gay Vigilante Organization (AGVO). These young men brandished gay-phobic T-shirts and wielded ball bats, stoking fears among some within the nascent queer community. Not surprisingly, incidents of harassment and assaults on gay men and women escalated. Graffiti scrawled outside known gay establishments, bottles tossed toward departing Renegade and Blue Moon customers, and epithets hurled at suspected queer beachgoers became far too common. Near the decade's end, the opening of a downtown gay dance club, The Strand, sparked wholesale rebellion among townsfolk, whose pitchforked elected officials sought to legislate it, if not homosexuals themselves, out of existence. The cover of the *Washington Post Magazine*—a stern-looking lifeguard gazing over sunbathers—declared "The Battle for Rehoboth."

Throughout the 1990s, war waged. There were raids and arrests at gay bars, hastily drawn up ordinances targeting gay-owned businesses, and selective enforcement of laws for customers strolling along The Avenue. Violent assaults by local youth were only slightly less unusual than harassment of queers from youthful cohorts of beach guards or summer police officers. These actions were met with resistance: boycotts of homophobic merchants, street celebrations of gay pride, outlandishly costumed men attending weekend themed parties, gay and lesbian candidates running for elected office, and local gay publications.

The founding of CAMP Rehoboth in 1991 by an odd assortment of gay men was the most significant, however. As this decade progressed, this nonprofit preached an inclusive—**C**reate **A M**ore **P**ositive—middle way. It provided sensitivity training to police recruits, sponsored community-wide AIDS fundraisers, reached out to ministers and merchants, and published the biweekly *Letters*. It also condemned explicit ads, erotic businesses, and overt displays of sexuality. At the decade's end, another story appeared in the *Washington Post Magazine*, but this cover depicted two gay men holding hands, with the title "Rehoboth Beach and Its Gay Constituency, Coming to Terms."

As each summer season further advanced the town toward the twenty-first century, the fault line between the gay and straight communities narrowed. The influence of Rehoboth's generation of homophobes and liberationists diminished, while that of CAMP's grew. Physical assaults on the Boardwalk and arrests for cruising became rarer. "Even the straight boys are serving bottles of beer in the gay bars instead of throwing them," quipped one Rehoboth man.

Diversity and division within the queer community were also more apparent. In 1999, transgender folks began organizing in lower Delaware. A year earlier, Kurt Charles Brown, a star athlete on the local high school wrestling team, had returned from Florida and soon transitioned as Kathy "Carpenter" Brown. That same year, Carol Fezuk, a former *Letters* manager, launched an alternative gay newspaper with the help of illustrator Frank Williams and, later, Black writer and activist Hassan Sudler. The *Rehoboth Beach Gayzette* focused more on social life and devoted more coverage to transgender and racial topics.

In 2002, Mark Aguirre became the first openly gay man (and Latino) to win an election in Delaware. Two years later, Patrick Gossett garnered the most votes cast in that municipal election, joining Aguirre on the seven-member board of commissioners. Meanwhile, the "gay community," along with Gossett and Aguirre, was increasingly split, aligning with various heterosexual factions on issues ranging from building ordinances to affordable housing. Steve Elkins, CAMP Rehoboth's longtime executive director, observes, "Whether a candidate is gay or straight no longer seems to be the issue." The next year, he was honored as Rehoboth's Citizen of the Year.

Following the death of Elkins in 2018, eulogies were additional testaments to the transformation of a town once so divided along a gay-straight axis. "As the area began to expand, change, and grow, unfortunately so did the division," recounts Kathy McGuiness, a former town commissioner. Elkins's "efforts . . . move[d] us forward." Nevertheless, Elkins's passing, as detailed in the next chapter, raises disquieting questions about the future of CAMP after three decades of White male leadership. Within fractured LGBTQ+ millennial space and the graying of the Rehoboth Beach queer "community," some argued that it would soon meet the same fate as mega dance clubs, affordable summer rentals, and Sloe Screws.

PART II

STEVE ELKINS WAY

All you can take with you is that which you've given away.
—*It's a Wonderful Life*,
motto next to portrait of George Bailey's father

A century after the formation of the Camp Meeting Association, a new association wielded "a power base without parallel in the city's history."[1] From 1971, when the Rehoboth Beach Homeowners Association was founded, through the end of that decade, association-backed candidates won eighteen out of twenty-four local contests. It sought to preserve the town's "unique character" as a "family resort." In the summer of 1981, it endorsed a slate of candidates, including John Hughes. As a town commissioner, he had voted to rid Rehoboth of Shaw Park, located where the old Grove camp meetings had been held. A longtime summer trailer camp on land donated to the town for that purpose, it was the last affordable residential refuge for visiting working-class families.

The same summer, Steve Elkins and his partner, Murray Archibald, shared their first summer rental with other gay men. They enjoyed summer weekends, playing afternoon volleyball at Poodle Beach, hosting happy hours along with games of croquet, dining out at the recently opened Blue Moon, and dancing into the wee hours at Renegade. Meanwhile, Hughes canvassed door to door in his mayoral campaign, organized behind the scenes by retired Rear Adm. Francis Fabrizio, who had cofounded the Homeowners Association. Hughes publicly fretted about the "obvious infusion of gays" and pledged, "Rehoboth will continue with its present image as 'family oriented.'" Although Elkins and Archibald were "vaguely aware" of the political campaign, their focus was summering on the beach with friends. Years later, they would be agents of change, dramatically changing Rehoboth's understanding of "family."

Elkins died of lymphoma in March 2018. Like George Bailey in Frank Capra's film *It's a Wonderful Life*, Stephen Wade Elkins, in the view of many townsfolk, was "the richest man in town." The town's flag was set at half-staff. Women and men from the inner corridors of Dover's statehouse to the barrier spit of Fenwick Island's lighthouse praised his legacy of community building and love for others. "He shattered stereotypes and opened hearts with his example, his humor, his attention to detail, and his sheer will," read his obituary.

At the time of Elkins's death at age sixty-seven, Rehoboth Beach boasted a maturing queer community. *Letters from CAMP Rehoboth*, the biweekly seasonal 128-page publication, included original essays and poetry, syndicated articles, letters, and photographs along with dozens of advertisers targeting its mainly affluent readers. Each year, CAMP Rehoboth produced several well-established seasonal fundraisers, most notably SunDance; sponsored programs ranging from CampSafe to the women's coffee talk and the men's discussion group; and hosted such festivals as Women's Fest and Follies. Some of these programs, such as HIV prevention, were based on external funding. Others, such as Women's Fest, were group initiatives brought under the CAMP umbrella, and a few, like SunDance, predated CAMP. There, too, were forums for candidates to local elective office and programs on health and fitness. The atrium at CAMP's twenty-first-century $1.7-million community center, later named in the honor of Archibald and Elkins, housed many such events. "These last thirty years, we were so engrossed in CAMP Rehoboth," reflects Archibald. "When you are working with that kind of passion and intensity, suddenly decades are gone, and you wonder, 'What happened?'"

A generation earlier, the town, its officials, and the Homeowners Association had been far less supportive. That was an era when "a few wearisome individuals" tried "to push gays and lesbians out of Rehoboth or at least back into the closet." To "save the present and seal the future," Jim Bahr, CAMP's first executive director, wrote in *Letters*, "We need to build coalitions." The strategy toward fulfilling this future was not "to imitate Provincetown" but to "promote Rehoboth Beach as a resort welcoming all people, all kinds of families." The inclusivity envisioned in this 1991 mission statement would come from promoting "cooperation and understanding among all people." In this quest, Elkins was the ardent, able, and articulate ambassador of the gay community.

But that future was far from certain during the 1990s. It was a decade of HIV/AIDS, Jesse Helms and Matthew Shepard, the Defense of Marriage Act, and Don't Ask, Don't Tell. When CAMP was launched, the town's small size matched the small-mindedness of its leaders. Contrived ordinances targeting the emerging queer community regulated parking, music, and restaurants. Roving bands of juveniles made routine attacks. There, too, was the random ill-advised arrest for midnight biking on the Boardwalk, for inciting a summer afternoon "riot" on the beach, for talking too loudly when leaving a gay-owned restaurant, or for gathering frogs at a park. Arrests were orchestrated of bartenders by underage undercover cops, of lesbian gift shop owners for selling backroom erotica, and of gay dance club managers for noise violations.

DC ENCOUNTERS

Elkins and Archibald were southern boys with deep family roots in Georgia and Alabama, respectively. Archibald, the son of generations of Methodist ministers on both sides of his family, is an artist. His mother "taught us to exercise our creativity." John, his youngest brother, recollects, "Murray was David Bowie, and I was Bama. He was knee-high suede boots (it was the seventies), and I was cleats. He was out, and he was gay." Archibald agrees with this characterization: "I certainly had a crush on every boyfriend I had growing up." He adds, "I had no name for it." Unlike many boys growing up gay in the South, Archibald "didn't have a whole lot of anguish. . . . I was in that strange age when Stonewall had just happened, so it was like bursting out. I felt I was right where I was supposed to be!"

The liberalness of Archibald's parents made coming out at age sixteen relatively easy: "My family was close, and I was not very good at having secrets." Besides, "they said they pretty much knew." Similarly, his brother John, who was nine years younger, was as accepting as his other siblings. Years later, John remembers everyone embracing Elkins when the couple made their first Christmas visit to the family's Alabama parsonage: "He was Brooks Brothers and business," but he "sang in the church pew like Dad and talked sports (as best he could)."

An Eagle Scout growing up queer in the 1960s South, Elkins remembers when "bars were still raided, and gay and lesbian people carried to jail."

Like Archibald, he was involved in church life, and, as an adult, he returned home every Christmas to attend Liberty Baptist Church with his mother, Lucille. Yet he remained deeply closeted. The son of a successful import businessman, Elkins was president of his class and, as his only sister, Judy, describes, could be a "bossy showman."

After graduating from the University of Georgia with a major in journalism, Elkins took a job as an insurance adjustor in Atlanta. Three years later, finding work increasingly boring, the disenchanted twenty-five-year-old quit "to think about what to do." The following Monday, he entered Jimmy Carter's campaign headquarters "to get a bumper sticker. I walked out with a job!" From March through November, his responsibilities increased as Carter's long-shot 1976 presidential campaign rolled up primary victories and the candidate arrived at the Democratic National Convention as the presumptive nominee. Following the November victory, he moved to Washington for the transition. He stayed on at the White House as an administrative assistant to Hugh Carter Jr., who was special assistant for administration. Elkins would often say, in his characteristic self-deprecating humor, "My big claim to fame was that I had control over who got what parking spot."

That same year, Archibald graduated from Birmingham Southern College. He was "completely obsessed with theater" as an actor and production designer. "There weren't really any local gay organizations those days," he says. "It was all about disco."

As Archibald began working with a theater group performing in Alabama schools, Elkins settled into Washington. The gay communities in DC during the mid-1970s and early 1980s were not unlike those in Atlanta. The capital was still pretty much a southern town or, as John Kennedy once quipped, a city of "northern charm and southern efficiency." The visible gay scene was just expanding from the gritty out-of-sight Warehouse District in southeast Washington to the city's mostly White northwest. In 1975, the city's first official Gay Pride Day had brought more than a thousand people to 20th Street NW, between R and S Streets. Sponsored by the recently opened Lambda Rising Bookstore, it was promoted by the five-year-old newspaper the *Gay Blade*.

When Elkins arrived in late 1976, one of the first gay bars to open near Dupont Circle was the Fraternity House. Attracting a "cruisy, all-male crowd[, with] lots of mustaches, jeans, and plain flannel shirts," it featured two upstairs dining rooms and a back bar with dancing boys aloft. Decades earlier, it had been the Stables, with a small bar downstairs. The real activity, though, was in the private upstairs rooms, where, according to owner Glen Thompson, "The Kennedys were known to go there. Marilyn Monroe. . . ."

Thompson and Elkins were quite different. A mutual dislike dated back to a dustup at the Fraternity House. Thompson allowed Elkins to use an upstairs room for meetings of the Gertrude Stein Democrat Club. "He was such a shit," Thompson disparages. "He came to me one day, screaming because I turned the music up *after* happy hour was over. He said it was 'disturbing' his meeting."

Both, however, valued knowing the community and networking with the more powerful to accomplish their goals. Thompson says, "Steve learned that from being involved in politics; he knew how. He won everybody over. He won the city over. He won the mayor over. He knew how to do it!" But Elkins didn't win him over: "I didn't believe that he was sincere. I still don't."

Elkins was not "out" at work, although he enjoyed the district's gay surroundings. Washington's gender-segregated bar scene, as in many cities, was also segmented according to proclivity and race. At the corner of 9th Street and New York Avenue was the Eagle, offering Thursday night happy hour for anyone wearing a red handkerchief. For those seeking military hookups, there was the long-standing Carroll Tavern. For dancing, there was country and western at the Barn, located just eight blocks from the White House, and the decades-old Hideaway, downstairs from the Barn, with just a jukebox. For those desirous of mega sound systems and packed dance floors, the ClubHouse on Upshur, famous for its "acid punch," catered to a mostly Black membership. Meanwhile, Whites frequented Pier Nine and Lost & Found, which were picketed, boycotted, or fined for discriminatory carding policies. Among show clubs, most notable were Rascals, at Dupont Circle; nearby La Zambra, on 14th; and a long-standing Black club, the Brass Rail. After-hours destinations included Delta Elite, located in DC's African American Northeast section.

One September day in 1978, Elkins received a call from White House security to clear two friends, William and Vicki, who had a large painting bound for the Old Executive Office Building. He recollected Vicki requesting to "clear in Murray Archibald," who had just arrived in DC. Archibald planned a brief visit with William before spending the rest of his vacation in New York City "to see someone I had met a few months earlier." Elkins continued the story: "I'll never forget it. I said, 'Sure. Is he okay?' And she said, 'Oh, yeah, he's real nice. You'll like him.' Thirty minutes later, it was history." Archibald never made it to Manhattan.

Murray Archibald (*left*) and Steve Elkins (*right*), 1979.
(Courtesy of Murray Archibald.)

After small talk, another painting had to be brought from their store. "Will you clear us back in?" Vicki asked. "I'll clear you and Bill back in, but Murray's going to stay here. I'm going to give him a tour of the White House."

Elkins, dressed in an elegant three-piece linen suit punctuated with a stylish tie, escorted Archibald, wearing "torn jeans and sandals," into the Oval Office. "We both knew instantly," Archibald recalls. "It was just a spark the very moment we met." He traded his days in New York for evenings with Elkins in DC to enjoy nights of dining and dancing.

When he returned to Birmingham a week later, Archibald announced the relationship to his parents, who "were just happy that I had found someone." He gave notice to the theater group and packed his bags for DC. They would remain side by side until Elkins's death. "It was just one of those things that just felt like fate," Archibald declares. "Something settled in my soul when we were together."

A few months later, Archibald accompanied Elkins to Steve's new bank job in Missouri. However, soon after the 1980 New Year, they returned to DC. Elkins was often on the road, traveling with Robert Strauss, who headed Carter's reelection presidential campaign. Archibald worked for a graphic design firm housed in a gentrifying block on Corcoran Street. After the ill-fated presidential campaign, Elkins joined the newly formed McMahon and Associates, a DC consulting and research firm that lobbied on progressive policy-related issues. Joe McMahon, who had served on the staff of Massachusetts Sen. Edward Brooke, met Elkins during his White House years. McMahon "organized our very first summer beach house" in Rehoboth.

"I'd never been here at all!" Archibald exclaims. "Steve had come while he was at the White House before I met him."

"Just for a weekend," Elkins interjects.

POLITICIZING REHOBOTH QUEERS

For the summer of 1981, Elkins and Archibald took a share in a house on Norfolk Street, just behind the Christian Science Church.[2] Elkins reminisces, "Those were the days when you'd come home from sitting on the beach all day, and you'd get out those starched Oxford cloth shirts and roll up the sleeves and your starched shorts, and you'd go out and play croquet."

There were three gay watering holes—outside Rehoboth's town boundaries. The oldest, Nomad Village, was also the farthest away and the least appealing, given the absence of a desirable dance floor, the small crowd, and the desolate journey past Indian Inlet Bridge. Although Elkins and Archibald made the "good drive" to Nomad every now and then, they favored dancing at the Boathouse and Renegade.

Opened in the summer of 1976, the Boathouse stole much of Nomad's business. Partially sitting above the waters of Rehoboth Bay, it had been a beer garden and dance hall during the 1930s and, in the early 1970s, a fried-fish restaurant serviced by tuxedoed Black waiters and music played by the Sammy Ferro Trio.

June and Sid Sennabaum, a Wilmington-based Jewish couple, operated the Boathouse. Sid, an affable businessman in his mid-fifties, had opened Delaware Dental Lab in northern Delaware after WWII. His only brush with the law was his arrest in 1974 for practicing dentistry without a license. It seems, in his characteristic altruism, he had fabricated and donated false teeth to lower Delaware's toothless poor.

June was friends with many gay men. Her hairdresser, Francis Murphy Jr., ran Universal Wigs in Wilmington and had opened that city's first gay dance bar, the Gas Lamp, in 1971. Entry into this Shipley Street dance club was gained through an upstairs red door after ringing a buzzer. Weekends after midnight, a hundred or more patrons could be found around the rectangular bar or dancing. One weekend, "Frannie," a professed heterosexual, experienced an entrepreneurial epiphany on the road from Rehoboth. He "saw a lot of really well-educated guys, who seemed to have money, but no place to go." He sought others who believed in his vision to share the risk. The liberal-minded Sennabaums found Murphy's proposal exciting, given Sid's love for the water and boats and June's fondness for gay men and money. One longtime patron recollects:

> The Boathouse was for many a homosexual an almost magical place. Not before nor since have I gotten the same feeling when walking into a gay bar. Many friendships were forged there. More than once, customers grabbed a push broom and helped sweep out the receding tide waters from the brick floor so we could dance.

Elkins and Archibald liked the Boathouse, although "we'd go to Renegade at night," says Archibald. Located just off the highway before entering Rehoboth, it was opened by Thompson in May 1980. For years, it had been the Chicken Pot before momentarily morphing into the Disco Drive In, a restaurant and bar with live music, go-kart racing, and camper rentals on its seven acres. "Rehoboth was very attractive because of Renegade," recalls eighty-eight-year-old Dolph Spain. He and his partner of fifty-seven years, Lloyd, sold their remote Chesapeake Bay summer house because of this emerging gay scene and the beach. "Once Renegade opened, we never went back to the Boathouse . . . [where] you'd be standing at the bar drinking your beer—and then standing in water!"

During his first Rehoboth summer, Archibald remembers seeing the same gender segregation as in DC, but without any sense of fellowship. "There was not a community that was drawing them [lesbians and gay men] all together. Well, except at Renegade, when people would be dancing. There would be men and women, but they didn't interact." Lesbian Sharon Kanter agrees: "There were issues with the women and the men at Renegade."

Kanter grew up as modern Orthodox, marrying "a nice Jewish boy" in 1972. She had been teaching for several years in her native Baltimore before joining a group of "strong, really cool women" softball players: "Unbeknownst to me, most of them were gay." After one game, she was invited to join them. "I went to the bar and realized this is where I need[ed] to be." Kanter experienced a moment of sexual clarity: "Oh my God! I feel at one with myself!"

In 1980, Kanter divorced and took a holiday to "very rural" Rehoboth with one of her teammates. "Very few people lived here full-time," she says.

"So, you may see people just in the summer and not see them again until the following summer." Away from the responsibilities of school and students, "it was fun times." She reminisces, "Renegade was my choice of having a great time dancing."

As years passed, relations between Rehoboth lesbians and gay men would improve, as would Renegade's welcoming of women. However, Kanter remembers the 1980s as "a turbulent time here between the men and the women. That was not just in Rehoboth, that was in Baltimore, too. I remember the gay men in Baltimore not wanting to be with the women."

The idea of building coalitions, let alone inclusive queer communities, during this decade seemed like a pipe dream. Following the assassination of Harvey Milk, the rescission of same-sex protections in many cities, and the formation of the Moral Majority, Stonewall activism appeared to be a chimera. Despite heady feelings from the 1979 March on Washington and the adoption of a nondiscrimination plank at the 1980 Democratic National Convention, small-town queers remained sexually closeted. Aside from an occasional, often distant, bar or cruising spot, there were few queer signs in America's heartlands. Those migrating to cities often entered gendered and racial enclaves of separatism. While gay liberation politics ("Gay is good") was generally a guiding tenet, pre-AIDS organizing consisted of multiple movements of disconnected people embracing discrete identities and engaging in shifting coalitions. For example, in North Carolina during the 1970s, lesbians were publishing *Sinister Wisdom* and rural men were publishing *RFD*; there was music produced by Ladyslipper Records and faerie gatherings at Running Water; and there were campus student organizations, and Metropolitan Community Church (MCC) chapters, Triangle Area Gay Scientists, and dance clubs and bars. It was not until 1981, however, that various groups gathered in Charlotte and Durham to celebrate the state's first gay and lesbian pride events. That same year, the *New York Times* published a page A20 article about a "rare cancer" found in several dozen homosexual men (brief articles in a Centers for Disease Control and Prevention weekly report and the *New York Native* had been published two months earlier). Eventually, the so-called gay cancer would become front-page news. As the decade progressed, coalitions of gay men and lesbians, heterosexuals and homosexuals, People of Color and Anglos developed. Although separatism persisted within many queer territories, a sense of community also emerged. Building queer coalitions was always difficult, but it was nearly impossible in small towns and rural America. However, the emerging national visibility of gender and sexual minorities via mass media, along with the "gay plague," seeped into the country's smallest crannies. By the decade's end, queer organizations appeared in small and mid-sized towns like Rehoboth, Delaware, and Wilmington, North Carolina, which would eventually rival homosexual bars as community hubs.

Although none of the bars frequented by Kanter and others were within Rehoboth's jurisdiction, there were growing concerns among the town's citizenry about the rising visibility of homosexuals, the queering of heterosexual spaces, the expansion of gay-owned businesses, and what soon would be identified as HIV/AIDS. Archibald recollects that this "was the first time gay life really exploded onto the streets of Rehoboth." In August 1981, citizens went to the polls to elect a successor to popular three-term mayor Miriam Howard. On the ballot were two commissioners, conservative John Hughes and moderate Eleanor Lynam.

The boyish-looking, six-foot-six Hughes was a "cross between a tanned lifeguard and a prep school basketball player." A native of Maryland, he had summered in Rehoboth since 1941. After graduating from Georgetown University, he returned to his wife's hometown in the 1960s. In 1974, he bought $600 worth of his father's property to run successfully for resident city commissioner. Working full-time as the operations manager for the state's beach preservation project, Hughes won a council seat with the weighty endorsement of the Homeowners Association. Now a three-term commissioner, the ever-youthful, always aspiring politico championed family values, promised law and order, and pledged planned growth. Among his ten campaign pledges, the "most important of all" was the "continuation of Rehoboth as a family resort"—harking back to his Rockwell-esque town memories and unbridled disdain for queers.

Thompson, who knew Hughes personally, underscores, "If you weren't totally kissing ass with the association, you had no chance" being elected. Hughes was "an ambitious person. He knew if he was going to get somewhere, he had to go along." The Homeowners Association "had money. It controlled the town."

Hughes and the association made homosexuality an issue for the first time in Rehoboth politics. He staunchly declared, "We call ourselves a family resort, but silently watch the vast population of homosexuals flourish within our midst; a population which I feel is antithetical to the term 'family resort.'"

His opponent owned an apartment building, served as a commissioner, and had been a Rehoboth resident for eight years. Lynam campaigned for balancing homeowner and business interests, modernizing city government, "maintaining respect for our laws," and not granting certain citizens "special privileges." Asked about the "great influx of 'swinging' singles and homosexuals," she reassured homophobic worriers, "It is becoming a more accepted way of life and they seem very responsible, fixing up old homes, opening nice shops, and being very thoughtful and considerate." To some, Lynam was a homosexual apologist, if not a fellow traveler; Hughes, whose campaign theme was "A Strong Man at the Helm," cast himself as an unapologetic homophobe.

Despite his antigay rhetoric, Hughes equivocated on specific actions he might take as mayor, promising "not [to] allow harassment of anyone, including homosexuals." At times, he even voiced a laissez-faire attitude: "Asking me to do something about homosexuals is like asking me to do something about seagulls." Some, like Thompson, gave him the benefit of the doubt, distinguishing between public posture and personal prejudice: "How much he really thought that is up for grabs." Yet Thompson acknowledges that Hughes "did think that, at the time, but he was open-minded."

A week or so before the August election, *Whale* news editor Trish Hogenmiller contacted Thompson. Hoping to set up a newsworthy cage match between Hughes and homosexuals, she asked, "Would you be willing to host a gathering of lesbians and gays at Renegade with candidate Hughes?" Thompson, a staunch conservative who prided himself on shielding his political opinions, agreed to offer the space, but not to participate. Hughes "was scared to death, [but] he wanted to meet some people," he remembers. The informal gathering was held in the middle of Renegade's main room, where "anybody who wanted to talk to him could." Several gay businesspeople and property owners stopped in to listen and chat. There, Hughes displayed "a number of misconceptions about gays and still does," Thompson told the *Washington Blade* afterward. However, he predicted that gays "may even be better off" under a Hughes administration.

Lynam lost by a two-to-one margin. Thompson's prediction also succumbed to reality. During Hughes's three two-year terms as mayor, his positions on homosexuality in general and gay-owned businesses in particular were seldom nuanced and never neutral—a stance that allowed him to run unopposed in the next election. In 1985, faced with an opponent, Hughes doubled down on his antigay bombasts, generating nationwide headlines.

During the 1980s, "people didn't want the town to change—and it was changing," says Thompson. He continues, "None of those people during that period liked that. That's not what they wanted in *their* town."

When the polls closed, Archibald and Elkins, along with other out-of-state friends, were enjoying the final weekends of their Rehoboth summer. Aside from the bars, no gay organizations or publications were active anywhere in Delaware, except for a small student group at the University of Delaware. Unlike in DC or Baltimore, Rehoboth offered no illusion of a queer community. Apart from the shifting sands of Poodle Beach, there was no gayborhood where queer-owned businesses flourished, no fields of lesbians playing softball while humming a Cris Williamson tune, no shared cultural or political history, no gay pride marchers or even a gay pride picnic. Although many homosexuals vacationed in Rehoboth, few envisioned its future as a vibrant queer community, let alone a beach resort on the party circuit with Provincetown, Fire Island, and Key West.

"In those first years of coming to the beach, we weren't thinking about building a community. It was summertime!" Archibald declares. While they were "aware" of Hughes's political antics, "the times were different," he says, although "you were *always* aware of being gay when it spilled out from behind and became public."

Ten years later, however, that would be the goal of CAMP Rehoboth: Come out from beyond the Boardwalk, organize a fledgling community, and build bridges across the abyss of prejudice to the heterosexual community. Elkins played an outsize role in this mission, as shown by the words and actions of a once-recalcitrant Hughes. In 2007, still active in local affairs, he rebuffed a Wilmington reporter: "I don't know who's gay and who isn't—and I don't give a damn." He and his wife attended some CAMP events, but he was mostly seen bicycling around town or driving his beloved beat-up Jeep on the beach.

The gradual transformation of Hughes's attitude and those of others in the political old guard in Rehoboth can be attributed in part to the country's parallel evolution, but also to the efforts of Elkins and Archibald. During CAMP's three decades under this couple's leadership, finding their way was transformed into finding our way—what many long-standing CAMP members fondly refer to as the "Steve-Murray Way." Board member Chris Beagle explains, "[They] taught us the meaning of community, how to be inclusive and work productively, and the importance of making our voices heard."

BEACH PLUMS AND FAIRIES

> The permanent temptation of life is to confuse dreams with
> reality. The permanent defeat of life comes when dreams are
> surrendered to reality.
>
> —**James Michener,** *The Drifters*

The day after Christmas in 1974, Victor Pisapia and Libby York strolled along the deserted beach of Rehoboth. It was cold, though sunny. The conversation warmed their souls. Libby, turning thirty, "wanted to make a statement. We were thinking of doing a juice bar somewhere." However, as they walked and talked, it was evident that Victor "was on the fence."[1]

"We stopped," Victor remembers. "She looked at me. 'I really want to do this. But the biggest thing is, I want to do it with *you*.' That was the first time anybody ever said anything like that to me. I immediately said, 'Yes.'"

This personal decision would have political ramifications far into the town's future, marking the beginning of the contemporary queering of Rehoboth Beach. It was a Michener-like instance where pursuing a personal dream would help transform Rehoboth's culinary—and political—reality.

VICTOR'S STORY

Two decades earlier, Pisapia would routinely visit his godparents, who owned a Rehoboth summer cottage on Newcastle Avenue. Like most children, he enjoyed playing on the beach and swimming in the ocean, wandering the Playland arcade, and exploring the Boardwalk.

After the war, his godfather opened a restaurant in Dover. Pisapia's family, including several uncles and aunts, followed from their north Jersey "Italian enclave." He lived down the hill from his godparents' grand home. Loretta, his godmother, prepared southern Italian meals at the popular restaurant from recipes her mother had taught her. "When you grow up in a small state like Delaware . . . it's like being in a fraternity." Pisapia adds, "All these people come into Rehoboth, but it's the people who lived there and the families who are there who created all of that. My family was part of that culture."

From his earliest memories, Pisapia's senses were flooded with this rich culinary heritage where "mothers would have been cooking over many, many centuries and passing it down to their daughters." Family life rotated around his mother, Giussepina, who was not only an excellent cook, like her mother, but very religious. Pisapia was gregarious and funny, and his classmates often visited, devouring after-school treats. He says, "What I realized, as I grew up, is that food has a lot of power."

Dover during this era was "a one-horse town," and there wasn't much of an Italian neighborhood. The students at Holy Cross, though, "knew each other really well." In 1960, the curious curly-headed twelve-year-old had an "epiphany." Pisapia was "starting to think something [wa]s really wrong. I used to read a lot of *National Geographic*. All I could do was to visualize the photos on the front pages and dream about places like these." Entering high school in 1962 and sporting a crewcut, Pisapia was popular, especially with the girls. Yet "there would be moments when I would be at the gym and look at boys. There would be that little bit of emotion; I had no idea what that was."

During the late 1960s, "everything was changing." His University of Delaware dormitory was full of basketball players and hippies who "smoked more pot than anybody I knew." He became "one of those hippie kids . . . just exploring life." Pisapia's senior year of college "was the moment that I *finally* knew something was different about me." He was "looking for answers, trying to figure out who I was." He dated infrequently: "Lots of girls wanted to go out with me. But when it would get down to the nitty-gritty, I didn't feel anything."

Pisapia went to the counseling center: "I tried to get it out . . . that I was really attracted to men. They just looked at me. I can still see the looks on their faces: blank stares." One guidance counselor provided the address of a Wilmington queer bar. One night, in desperation, Pisapia drove to King Street. After sitting in his car for an hour and staring at the bar's sign displaying two boxers, he entered the Golden Greeks. Known affectionately as Stella's after the former sex worker who owned it, inside "was real seedy. At the long bar were a lot of sixty-five- and seventy-year-old queens with lots of gold chains." Few noticed Pisapia, as most eyes followed a jock-strapped youth, silhouetted against bright strobe lights, dancing for dollars. "I just said, 'No, this isn't who I am.' I left and went back into the closet."

Bars like Stella's existed in many medium and large towns, mostly operated by the Mafia or other nefarious owners who paid off police and other city officials. In northern Delaware, closeted homosexuals mostly journeyed to nearby Philadelphia, which offered greater options and presumed anonymity. Although underground bar guides existed, new patrons often arrived through word-of-mouth.

Ironically, as Pisapia sought access to the "gay community," the infamous Stonewall Inn riots had just occurred in Greenwich Village. But shouts of "Out of the Closets, into the Streets" had yet to be heard in Delaware: "There was no such thing as 'gay' back then. I mean *nobody* talked about being gay. They talked about being 'sissies.' They talked about being 'pansies.' They talked about being 'fairies.' And they talked about it as a 'disease.'"

After graduating in 1970, Pisapia began his job search. With no experience and a desire to remain in Wilmington, he received countless rejection letters. In desperation, he applied to Wilmington High School, whose reputation as a "rough school" preceded it. The youngish principal saw something in Pisapia's application and invited him to replace the school's most charismatic social studies teacher. Once the premier all-White school in the city, it became majority-Black due to busing and White flight. Students "were not your normal kids," dutifully addressing him as "Mr. Pisapia." They brought knives to school, fights were common, and rival gangs roamed the halls. There was also a nursery for teen mothers. Pisapia recalls, "This was as far from Holy Cross as possible. But what I loved about the kids was that they were so honest. They just told you what they felt." He grew his hair into "the biggest Afro you ever saw. . . . I wore lots of bell-bottoms, clogs, and paisley ties." Most students found him "hip and groovy" and began addressing him as "Mr. P."

Before the school year began, he lugged the assigned textbooks to the Victorian home he shared with college friends. In frustration, he shouted, "God! This is so boring. It's all taught from a White man's perspective. I have all Black kids!" Pisapia contacted a Boston free school. Reviewing its materials, he developed a curriculum that incorporated group projects, cartoons and drawings, and field trips. He says, "The principal would always call me in the office afterward and just scream his bloody guts at me. I would just say, 'Well, nobody told me I had to have parent permission slips!'" At the end of a stressful school year, "My best friend from college picked me up. We got into the VW bus, lit up a big fat joint, put on Pink Floyd, and took off." This was the beginning of Pisapia's journey "seeing the world."

In the fall of 1972, Pisapia asked students whether they wanted to travel to Italy during spring break. Partnering with another school, he chaperoned twenty-five adolescents, who saved money by working part-time jobs for the two-week excursion. He came back with a different perspective, concluding that social studies teachers should not teach "unless they are well-traveled and have experiences." He walked into the principal's office, which was more than familiar, to submit his resignation. The principal said, "Well, you can't resign. You're getting tenure this year." The novice teacher asked, "What's that?" He rolled his eyes: "Victor, tenure means that you can never lose your job." Frustrated, Pisapia exclaimed, "I don't want my job. I'm telling you I want to *leave* my job, so I can go travel the world, so I can become a better teacher someday."

After his final school year, he convinced two college friends, Keith and Gayle, to quit their jobs too. Beginning in August 1973, the threesome traveled throughout Europe. Pisapia was "taken with the European Café" and the regions' culinary richness. They ate baguettes with slathers of rich butter in France, devoured paellas along with amazing tapas, picked mussels on the cliffs in Spain, and munched on pommes frites with mayonnaise in Belgium. They lived in a castle with a French family in a village known for its fine tapestries. There, Pisapia learned to cook cassoulets. He swigged pints of Heineken in Amsterdam's dark paneled bruin cafés with Afghan rugs draping tables and voyeuristically strolled along De Walden. He bunked for several weeks with a German family whose breakfasts of salami, ham, and cheeses were food "no American would eat."

En route, the trio shared a dog-eared copy of *The Drifters*, which "was pretty much telling our story as we were doing it." This best-selling 1971 novel by former teacher James Michener follows six young Americans traveling through Mediterranean countries. Pisapia recalls, "We were just drifting. We were going from city to city and country to country, eating the food and meeting new people." And, like other packs of youthful explorers, what Pisapia experienced "was a sense of freedom that I never had in America."

He arrived in New York City with 25 cents in his pocket. After Pisapia visited family in Dover, his father dropped him off at Dewey Beach. Before crashing on a friend's floor each night, he bused tables at the Dinner Bell Inn, where he met York. At Rehoboth's best restaurant, guests dined at tables laden with the fragrance of fresh flowers and Miss Edna's famous yeast rolls. Lauded for its chicken salad with oysters and crab imperial, the inn was operated by Rehoboth's indomitable grande dame, Ruth Cowgill Emmert, who began serving meals on four card tables at her Philadelphia Street home during the Depression. The year before Pisapia joined her hundred-plus staff, she was named Delaware Restauranteur of the Year. Within a few years, his Rehoboth restaurants would exceed even her reputation.

LIBBY'S STORY

York had worked summers at the Dinner Bell since 1972.[2] Emmert was a mentor to her and Pisapia: "She was just real smart, independent, not hung up. I don't think she worried too much about what people thought of her." Never afraid to do any job that required her detailed attention, Emmert motivated her employees "to work way harder than we ever thought we could work!" York also remembers Emmert's stories of "Old Rehoboth" and some of "its classy, intelligent, educated older population."

His first week at work, Pisapia bumped into the veteran waitress at the inn's milk counter. Like him, York had taught school, had backpacked in Europe, enjoyed a sense of humor, and itched for adventure. "We hit it off right away," she recalls.

Near the end of the 1974 tourist season, "Libby and I put our heads together. We decided this town was boring as bat shit, and we needed to do something! That was the beginnings of the Back Porch." York credits Emmert as a "very big role model for us; how we do this, how to treat people, and her standards of excellence." At that time, though, Pisapia was unwilling to commit. He told York, "First, I have to live in Boulder." She understood, as patience was a family trait, like music.

The York household in Chicago, overflowing with books, was filled with music. Her parents loved to play the piano and sing. She recalls:

> I heard a lot of Sinatra around the house. My dad wrote a nightlife column for the Northwestern paper, the *Purple Parrot*. . . . They were both smart and had interesting friends like Emmett Dedman, who was the editor of the *Chicago Sun-Times*. They had great parties. I got a sense of a wider world.

During the 1940s and 1950s, her family circled around the radio and listened to WMAQ's late-night broadcasts from Chicago's famous Chez Paree.

For an hour or so, she enjoyed the big band sounds of Cee Davidson or Lou Breese and torch song or jazz singers, such as Libby Holman, Billie Holiday, Dinah Washington, and Ella Fitzgerald: "I always grew up with the feeling that this music was valuable and important."

In 1962, York matriculated to American University. Arriving on a muggy Washington August morning, she remembers "a couple of guys on campus just watching the coeds and checking out the 'talent.' I stopped to ask where my dorm was. That guy was Ted Fisher." She wrote to her parents about meeting a handsome athletic boy driving a bright red Jaguar.

Fisher was a free thinker. "He wasn't big on sororities and fraternities. It was the beatnik era." York details, "He had a group of friends called the Elements." In this era of hootenannies, she and her college roommate joined them to play guitars and sing. They also hung out at the neighborhood Zebra Room, with its shark head glaring down at black-and-white-striped booths. This long-standing beer and pizza joint was operated by Hal Lake, a look-alike liberal version of Archie Bunker, known affectionately as "Prince Hal of the Lake."

She says, "We were in a generation that was straddling two different ways of thinking." Like her mother, York was an activist: "My generation was on the forefront of women who didn't feel they had to get married and have kids. We would have our own careers, our own bank accounts, our own lifestyles." She majored in political science but was also elected homecoming queen.

Libby visited Rehoboth during her first year of school with her new boyfriend. Fisher's parents owned a house on Hickman Street and an appliance store in nearby Milford. "I fell in love with Rehoboth immediately," she says. "It was so beautiful. Just far enough south that there were magnolia trees and some of the more southern vegetation, but also the pines and the gorgeous beaches." The town was "quite conservative" and exuded "a community feeling." It was a community that this couple and Pisapia would soon broaden.

REHOBOTH IN BLACK AND WHITE

Neil Stevenson was about age ten when York first visited.[3] He vividly remembers his boyhood Rehoboth. During the summers, he'd wade into Silver Lake and scoop up golf balls. He first would play the far end of the town's nine-hole golf course with his putter and nine iron stashed in the nearby woods. Then, on his way to the beach, the golf balls would be bar-tered for ice cream. Sometimes, Stevenson visited the Robert E. Lee restaurant (where the long-standing Robin Hood operates today), owned by a "larger-than-life figure," Jake Moore, an ex-Marine who militaristically "ran the lunch counter with booze down the side."

The winters in Stevenson's Rehoboth memories included townies skating on the lake and singing around bonfires. At Christmastime, there was a "community party." He looks back on when the Derricksons showed cartoons borrowed from their movie house and the Lions Club came out to the lake: "Everybody got a little stocking with an orange. You could see Santa Claus! It was completely desegregated. I think that was a wonderful rarity in those days." As if anticipating retrospective criticism, he adds, "We weren't this terrible racist community."

From a different perspective, York says that Rehoboth "was pretty racially segregated." Yet she recalls that "the Dinner Bell was the first time I felt like I had African American friends." It had an interracial softball league with Black players "who worked in the kitchen and some of the [White] seasonal waiters. . . . It was segregated even in who worked the floor and who worked the kitchen."

Nevertheless, some local Blacks remember local history differently. Well before the time of Stevenson and York, during the 1930s, the Rehoboth Fire Department staged "Minstrel Frolics," while a generation earlier, southern "cakewalks" were common entertainment as Henlopen, Baltimore, or Douglass hotel waiters performed the plantation-based dance while guests watched in amusement—unaware that its origin was meant "to satirize the competing culture of supposedly 'superior' whites." Rehoboth had no "sundown" ordinance, but there was just one Black-operated boardinghouse rented from a local White man. Walter Harmon, whose uncle lived West of Rehoboth, noted that before WWII, Black people were not allowed entry into any theater. This rule changed, as the town's three movie houses—Charles Horn Jr.'s Blue Hen, the Center, and the Avenue— opened their balconies to People of Color, sometimes separated by a curtain to allow Whites access. However, this change did not happen until "rich people, coming from Washington DC, Philadelphia, and all around [who] had their help. And the help didn't have any place to go until they got real hard on Horn."

Despite groundbreaking Supreme Court rulings, segregation was integral to American life. In Delaware, Jim Crow legislation, enacted in 1875, was not replaced for nearly a century. Ada Burton was a teenager living west of the canal during the 1950s. She bitterly speaks about family and neighbors who were good enough to work at Rehoboth's restaurants "but could not be served there." The first day that Burton reported to work at the home of a Rehoboth lady, she went to the front door: "[The homeowner] said, 'Now when you come tomorrow, you come to the back door.' I said, 'Okay.' When I had lunch, I had to go down in her basement to eat. . . . She never saw me anymore."

For those cleaning or cooking at White residences, waiting tables or preparing meals at White-only restaurants, or caretaking for White children, Thursday was their day off. Many went to the Boardwalk—more precisely, a narrow strip of beach between two jetties near the Bellhaven Hotel, known locally as the "Crow's Nest." Born in the Rehoboth area in 1925, Henrietta Pierson remembers, "We'd just sit there. Some of them could go in swimming, but they had to stay in that one spot." Ninety-year-old Harmon, whose family has lived in Delaware for centuries, emphasizes, "We knew where we belonged. And that's where we stayed." He and his wife, Edna, schooled their twins: "Keep your hands off people and don't look at *any* White women!" These residents attribute the "Crow's Nest" name to Jim Crow.

Novelist Alexs Pate, who summered there during the 1950s and 1960s, richly describes Rehoboth during this era of de facto segregation:

> Jim Crow was an enigmatic, unseen, but important resident of Rehoboth. He could formulate any disguise, feel comfortable in any surrounding. He could be the manager of the bowling alley, the desk clerk at the Henlopen Hotel. . . . He could be a woman. And she could have muscles in her lips which made them as stiff as a half-opened drawbridge when she slammed the cash register closed in the face of a black person. That was the thing. A perfectly nice person could turn sour, become a blotched red-face swelling when merely presented with the necessity of being civil to someone black.

In addition to the town's three theaters, there was Bill Larsen's Rehoboth Lanes. Along with bowling, it offered pool tables and arcade games, which stayed open until midnight. It had a huge upstairs skating rink, where Stevenson and his friends went every weekend, if there was money from the sale of golf balls. On summer Monday nights during the late 1950s and early 1960s, it hosted a "rock 'n' roll" dance with a local band.

For young adults, though—much like Rehoboth youth a century earlier—the partying place was the adjacent unincorporated hamlet of

Dewey Beach. York and Fisher gravitated to the Bottle & Cork, where they danced to nationally touring bands. They also sojourned to Whiskey Beach—a sobriquet given for its rum-running destination during Prohibition. Throngs of young people hung out at Whiskey during this era. Fisher windsurfed near its jetties. "It was a scene," York remembers. On summer weekends, hordes of body-painted youth, dressed in skimpy bikinis or loud jams, guzzled beer, listened to the occasional band, and danced the "jerk" and the "boogaloo."

The gadfly of Rehoboth, Dave DeRiemer, remembers, "People resented us having live bands and dancing in broad daylight, even though it was all just good clean fun." After local officials banned live music from Memorial Day to Labor Day, DeRiemer, in cahoots with Bottle & Cork owner Jim Lavelle, devised a floating dock where bands performed offshore, beyond the jurisdiction of authorities.

Whiskey Beach was also a place for sporadic semi-gang warfare. For instance, in 1964, nearly a hundred "fist-swinging, pipe-wielding" teen hooligans rumbled in the predawn hours. According to state police, this melee started with a confrontation between Wilmington "rival gangs," the "Yards" and the "Stantons." Cable from nearby fences, car tools, and sickles were also used; five youth were hospitalized. In DeRiemer's version, as explained to a reporter, the Stanton boys actually "hit the beach in search of a DC boy who had dated a Stanton girl"; they were "not a gang," just a "group of boys."

In a series of newspaper articles reporting this "gang riot," state police also warned readers that north and south of Rehoboth, "homosexuality [wa]s rampant." Pledging all available resources "to wipe out both sexual deviation and teen-age gangs," the police superintendent promised, "We will haul them out by the bus load." He warned, "Now is the time to assert authority."

Stevenson, who worked for DeRiemer as a carpenter after graduating from high school, found him to be "a friendly guy, open-minded, full of ideas, and fun. My impression was a lot of the authority of society didn't care for that in an adult." As the 1960s progressed, "there were a lot of undercurrents of resentment towards authority." York agrees: "It was just an era of 'them and us.'" She and Fisher started going over to DC from Rehoboth for antiwar marches. She says, "One of our friends, who was a lifeguard with Ted in Rehoboth, was killed on one of those canal boats not more than a month after he got into Vietnam. It was so tragic."

Michael Decker, a gay man who is a year older than Neil Stevenson, was too young for the war. However, he characterizes Whiskey Beach—which would later become one of the queer beaches—as "a no-man's-land" with random brawls, "a sort of *West Side Story*." Lacking much money, his family stayed at Joseph's Cottages, just past the canal and across from Shaw Trailer Park.

Decker also remembers "a little paseo on the Boardwalk" with his parents one early evening. That was his "first awareness of anything gay." As they strolled by the Pink Pony, he recalls, "I heard a guitar sound." He put his nose against the tinted window. "I said, 'Oh, look! There's a guitar player. Let's go in!' I remember my parents laughing; 'Oh, I think you're a little young for that.'" York and Fisher also "walked the boards" and wandered into the Pink Pony, located at the end of Olive Street. "There was this kind of feeling that something different is going on here," she remembers, noting that at the time, "the whole gay scene was separate." Later, as a teen, Decker went to the Blue Hen Theater. It had just a few rows of balcony seats, "with guys carryin' on sexually."

There certainly were sexualized spaces for gay liaisons in Rehoboth and its outskirts, including the public men's room near the corner of First Street and Rehoboth Avenue. Stevenson, who is heterosexual, vividly describes descending the concrete stairs lined with dingy brick walls and entering through the metal door. There was "a long urinal. Being exposed to gay men for the first time . . . not being intimidated or bothered about it, [but] understanding that [wa]s not supposed to happen here."

Like most youth of that era, Stevenson learned that "you stayed away from queers." He was taught the opposite by his parents. In the early 1960s, two "out-of-towners" built a house across the street from the Stevensons. He describes Henry and Jimmy "as married as anyone else would have been. Jimmy used to come over and have lunch with my mother all the time. They'd watch soap operas together just like any two gals."

In 1964, Wilmington's *Morning News* alerted readers that "deviates [we]re buying property" in Rehoboth and "cluster[ing] in too large numbers" on beaches. This mostly Washingtonian "cult," the newspaper warned, "might shatter the image of Rehoboth as a family resort." As Stevenson points out, it was popular back then "to 'go roll some queers.'"

His father, Albert Wesley Stevenson, grew up in a Depression-era Delaware family of "gleaners." Neil explains, "They would go into fields and gather food after harvest." Later, his dad drove an intercity bus with a route ending in Rehoboth. He stayed overnight at the Marvel Hotel, part of which would eventually become the Back Porch Café. He met Neil's mother,

married, and, through his network of friends, joined the town's small police force.

At his request, his father went undercover to thwart those rolling the
queers. Neil recalls:

> I remember my dad dressed up in old khakis and a shirt. I said,
> "Where are you going?" He said, "I'm going to work." He had a gun
> in his pocket and blackjack in his back pants' pocket. In the vernac-
> ular, he "was dressed like an old queer." He milled around and hung
> around—caught a lot of other crimes also.

In 1967, Neil, now a long-haired teenager, witnessed Rehoboth transform into "a very hip place" with more an "undercurrent of resentment towards authority. There were a lot of hanger-a-rounders. We called them 'the
blanket people.' They showed up at the beach with a blanket." It was the
Summer of Love, and although "we weren't Haight-Asbury, there were people who would fit right in there." York and Fisher were two such people.

SOMETHING ELSE SHOP AND THE ZEN DEN

After finishing college, York and a roommate rented a basement apartment
from Carl Stern, who wrote for the *Washington Post*.[4] Given York's interest
in politics and the family's home in Chicago, he arranged for her to work at
the 1968 Democratic National Convention as a film runner for United Press
International. She says, "All hell was breaking loose. Abbie Hoffman and
the whole protest movement was in full swing."

That autumn, in a far different scene, she married Fisher in a chapel
near American University. Following the reception at the Mayflower Hotel
and a European honeymoon, they moved to Delaware. She taught middle
school in Milford, while he managed the family store. Small-town life was
jarring for this self-described Chicago hippie. Soon, York joined another
teacher to organize demonstrations. Along with protests of the Vietnam
War, the civil rights movement was also militarizing, rocked by the assassination of Martin Luther King Jr. and subsequent urban rioting. "It was
kind of a crazy time," York reflects.

In the summer of 1969, they opened the Something Else Shop on the
first block of Rehoboth Avenue. Showcased near the front were "gift cards,
candles, and posters with corny peace and love quotes." They also sold Mr.

Natural comic books, drawn by West Coast artist Robert Crumb, and Zap Comix. Toward the rear of their tiny store were pipes, rolling papers, beads, black-light posters, lava lamps, and other paraphernalia.

Understandably, the shop attracted quite a few inquisitive visitors. Stevenson remembers that the "dark and cool" space "was always one of the most mysterious places in the world to me. You looked in there, but you wanted to keep walking." One summer evening, as he was standing near the storefront, he encountered Fisher. They sat on a nearby bench and talked for several hours, which "helped change my life," says Stevenson. The two shared a common passion for surfing and were equally suspicious of authority. He admits, "I really didn't know him, but when an older person who's very hip *really* is talking to a younger person, *listening*—that does not always happen."

As summer shop owners, they never experienced problems with local authorities, although they were mindful of the fate of the Zen Den several years earlier. Attempting to combat teen drinking and drag racing, Mayor Joel Stamper had endorsed a nonalcoholic teen nightclub, privately operated by DeRiemer. The twenty-six-year-old, whose father was chief counsel for DuPont's labor law division, had come to Rehoboth in the summer of 1962. He rented a cottage near the corner of 4th Street and Rehoboth Avenue. Wandering youth listened as his friends strummed guitars. The number of kids mushroomed. DeRiemer began playing records and sporadically hosting a band. With Mayor Stamper's blessing, he launched the "beatnicky" Zen Den Club that July. Nearly 1,500 $1 summer memberships sold, including to the mayor's daughter. As the club's nightly presence became noticeable, complaints about noise and concerns about possible "overflow in the busy intersection" arose. There was also gossip about gambling and immoral acts occurring. When DeRiemer sought to purchase the property, sixty residents signed a petition against it.

The following year, DeRiemer bought a building at the corner of 1st Street and Wilmington Avenue to house his club, just a block from the beach and right off Rehoboth Avenue. Employing similar tactics as the town elders would a quarter of century later against a queer dance club, the commissioners and mayor refused to issue a business license. Further, they enacted a noise ordinance with hefty fines. Stevenson, who was at the cusp of adolescence, recalls "an air of mystery about it. I knew that it was something that the community wanted to suppress."

The city summarily shuttered the Zen Den when it opened in June. This move was countered with a restraining order obtained by DeRiemer, who charged that other dancing and entertainment businesses continued "without harassment from the town," including Larsen's Rehoboth Lanes. Petitions for and against the club circulated. Several hundred youth marched to the Boardwalk and protested on the beach. Mayor Stamper claimed that the club was "chasing away tourists," but the court ordered that the Zen Den could remain open, pending trial.

In August 1963, twenty state police ransacked the teen club and arrested DeRiemer for "maintaining and exhibiting a pool table with minors present," but they found no evidence of gambling, alcohol, or drugs. In fact, the *miniature* pool tables—unlike those of standard size at Larsen's bowling alley—were directly in front of the large street window. "I am trying to avoid the smoky pool hall atmosphere and they seized on this good intention," DeRiemer told a reporter.

As 1964 dawned, DeRiemer listed the building for sale with a local gay Realtor, Peck Pleasanton. Meanwhile, the priggish city commissioner, Mrs. Carl Zoller, announced that the town would launch its own teen club. "It will *not* be a Zen Den," she promised. She could not say when it would open, since officials were "pre-occupied" with constructing a new city hall. It would be twenty years before another teen dance club opened.

"The kids can give up their social plans for the needs of the city," quipped DeRiemer, who swore to reopen the club if his building was not sold. With the injunction in force, he renamed it the Sea Horse. City officials accepted his business license application, although they set down "stringent rules of operation." It never reopened after that summer of 1964. "He was ahead of his time," lauds Jan Konesey. It "seemed that everywhere he turned, the city was against it." Ironically, years later, as town commissioner, Konesey would propose ordinances to shut down a gay-owned dance club, The Strand, located at Larsen's former bowling alley.

BACK PORCH BEGINNINGS

Following their head-shop venture, York and Fisher returned to Milford.[5] She waitressed in Rehoboth during summers, where she eventually met Pisapia. After their winter beach walk and his return from Colorado, they "got together to brainstorm. . . . What was [their business] going to look like?" Pisapia continues, "We ate a lot of tofu and brown rice back then. So, we wanted it to be a café and to have a healthy focus." It was to be called the Beach Plum Café. They still had to find a location and persuade Fisher to join.

"We wanted a magic environment, not just another shop on the main drag of town," says Pisapia. Wearing her waitress blazer, York met the owner of the old Marvel Hotel to discuss renting a part of it. The conservative businessman was surprised to see a young woman negotiate his lease. Retrospectively, she comments, "If it was a male starting a business, they would just say he was 'decisive' or 'driven.'" After wrapping up business, he issued York a compliment: "You're tough!" Pisapia gave her the moniker "Libby the Lip."

Fisher was leery about the location. "You had to go down the alleyway; so you had to actually discover us," Pisapia explains. "Ted was very much about being directly on Rehoboth Avenue." His greater concern was that none of the three partners knew much about operating a restaurant. Pisapia argued that, although they had "very little restaurant experience, we ha[d] this burning desire." They "had to kind of drag him in," York admits. She put up her $5,000 inheritance, and Fisher chipped in another $2,000, assuming responsibility for handling finances and renovations. "We were the creatives," Pisapia vaunts.

Given an enclosed back porch with a bare backyard, their original name couldn't work. "Once we had this space, it kind of evolved," York says. The Back Porch Café, in its lumbering structure with "not a right angle in the place," would serve "healthy and beautiful fresh Delaware fruits and vegetables and fresh fish and salads." This farm-to-table concept was popularized in the mid-1970s by Alice Waters at Chez Panisse. Unaware of what was going on the West Coast, "it must have been in the air," supposes York.

Fisher and his "cronies" scraped for materials to build chairs and tables. The Porch, which seated fifteen to twenty diners, was truly a "recycled restaurant." With a worn copy of *Cooking for Crowds*; advice from his mother, who prepared the restaurant's cheesecakes; and mental notes from European cafés he had visited, Pisapia crafted an innovative menu. Aid and advice, solicited and unsolicited, also arose from the community. Rick Sumlin, the chef at the Dinner Bell, who had begun working for Emmert at age twelve, provided insight about how to order enough food. Local grocer Butch McQuay sped deliveries. Michael Quinser, a local youth who worked at the Porch, had a "very debonair" boyfriend who owned a well-known Pennsylvania restaurant. "He showed us how to do French service at the table," credits York. The first walk-in refrigerator, nicknamed Big Bertha, was donated by the Crab Pot owners, who, like Emmert, were Old Rehoboth Quakers. Then, there was Papa John. A Rehoboth eccentric, he operated french fry and burger spots along the Boardwalk. Libby remembers him "snooping around" before their opening. "Where's your deep fryer?" he

Back Porch staff, ca. 1974. (Courtesy of Libby York.)

quizzed. "Papa John, we're not gonna have any deep-fried food." He snort-ed, "Well, you'll never make it!"

As the big day approached, "I remember being very scared. We were so young, and it was such a big project," Pisapia discloses. York remembers "opening the doors, wondering if anyone would show up." They did. On opening night, sixty dinners were served. One reason for the Porch's imme-diate success was the response from Old Rehoboth. "It was truly a Delaware town," Pisapia pronounces. "The du Ponts basically ran the show. Then, you had your big families in Rehoboth," which, he adds, "had its core group who pretty much ran everything." However, "they were well-traveled," and "when they saw something new like this, they brought all of their friends."

Everything was made from scratch: the breads, the yogurt, the muesli. Pisapia traipsed through local strawberry fields and sojourned to Indian River Inlet for ocean fish, seeking out the freshest local foods: "I would do things like mustard chicken, beef bourguignon, fresh trout with mignon-ette sauce." It was his "dream restaurant menu," although he cooked in a "shoebox." York's creativity and musicality created other fresh Rehoboth traditions: exhibiting local artwork, hosting live entertainment, providing al fresco dining—and welcoming lesbians and gay men. "We didn't care," one of the first employees says. "Most of our staff was gay anyway, so there was never any judgment."

Rehoboth "was crying out for something new, but nobody was willing to take the chance," Pisapia observes. When the Porch closed in September, the partners had not only recouped their $7,000 investment; Fisher presented each with a check for $10,000. The threesome were much more than business partners, and Fisher and York were more than simply husband and wife.

CONCHS AND HIGH TEA

"People kept telling us coming into the Back Porch through this little alley 'reminds us of Key West.' We had never been to Key West," says York, "but it seemed like a good idea."[6] The trio rented a trailer at Big Coppitt Key. She enjoyed the beaches and the isolation of the so-called Conch Republic. Fisher loved wintering in a place where he could bike and surf every day. Pisapia, who "had no idea where it was or what it was," knew that despite being in the closet, this would be "my journey into Gaydom."

Although they knew that Pisapia was gay, they respected his decision about when he would "come out to us." Meanwhile, York "met all these wonderful gay friends. We'd go to the Monster, a great discotheque, and dance and dance." For twenty-seven-year-old Pisapia, his first season "was reconnaissance." He "watched. I was trying to absorb a part of gay culture that I just never saw before." He encountered a "joyous" gay community where "everybody knew each other," one that Pisapia had never experienced in Delaware: "They all went to sunset every day." In contrast, "Rehoboth was just straight and boring." Key West was "something out of a Tennessee Williams play."

As they recuperated from their first summer at the Porch, the trio agreed that they were working too hard for too little money. "We decided to try to go for our liquor license," reports York. When they returned, a retired Emmert traveled with them to the Alcoholic Beverage Control Commission (ABCC) hearing. She voiced support for the application and attested to their good character. Once approved, Fisher went to work creating a bar, which he decoupaged with pictures covered with layers of varnish. The small garage on the side of the restaurant now became the Raw Bar, which was managed by Pisapia's old college dorm-mate and fellow European backpacker, Keith Fitzgerald. The Porch began offering fine wines. "We were the first one really to have that kind of ambience, wine list, and sophisticated dining options," York proudly says. The Raw Bar also became a gathering spot. Decker recalls, "It was not a gay bar, but it was certainly a mixed crowd."

"We need to be using this!" York unwrapped the silver tea service received as a wedding gift to launch another innovation: afternoon high tea. For this service, the staff wore 1950s hats, which Mayor Miriam Howard donated. Rehoboth's first and only woman mayor, Howard was "this gorgeous, beautiful older woman," according to York, who loved the Porch and "would bring all of her girlfriends to Sunday afternoon's high tea."

After the Porch's more successful second season, Pisapia returned to Key West. He found a separate place to live, came out, and fell in love: "It was probably the most exciting time in my entire life!" His first boyfriend was "a blond Adonis." He quickly learned, however, the half-life of a 1970s gay relationship: "I had no idea that I was just another notch on his belt buckle." On the road back to Rehoboth the following spring, Pisapia and York "literally cried all the way to Miami."

During the next few years, the Porch grew in size and popularity. Fisher built a side deck and then an upstairs deck. They went from serving sixty to 250 dinners nightly. The menu expanded from three to eight mains with a half dozen appetizers and many more desserts. "The food just got better; I got better. I became more sophisticated," Pisapia explains.

By 1978, word was out. The first gay media coverage about Rehoboth appeared in the *Washington Blade*. Noting that "P Street Beach [wa]s not enough" during a steamy DC summer, the reporter described Rehoboth as "less of a gay resort than a resort that attracts gays." The Back Porch "lends a transplanted Georgetown atmosphere to gourmet cooking" while "300–400 gays converge on Carpenter's Beach."

A few weeks later, on the homophobic heels of Anita Bryant, a two-part, front-page expose was published in the *Whale*. Rehoboth reporter Trish Hogenmiller detailed the "hedonistic lifestyle" and "clout financially" of gay men who, "to some, [we]re 'queers,' 'fruits,' 'pansies,' or 'faggots.'" Residences were "resplendent with antiques and fine art, straight from the pages of *House Beautiful* and a closet of clothes from *Gentleman's Quarterly*." Gays, "as frequent visitors and property owners, ha[d] made their mark, co-existing with the family resort image (which some are afraid they will ruin)."

The reception to this local coverage about a queer presence was mixed. One shop owner admitted, "If it wasn't for the gays I did business with, I wouldn't do business." A clothier grumbled about homosexuals searching for pants with small waists: "I had to make a decision whether or not to cater to them and decided against it." Citing "straights who come to gawk at us as if we were freaks," Boathouse owner Sid Sennabaum reported that his "so-called friends look the other way when I'm around." A *Whale* letter writer wailed: "It took me most of a day just to get down to reading it because I was sickened to see your fine newspaper wasting space on such a subject."

Equally troubling to city leaders during that summer of 1978 was a *Washingtonian* story, "Greetings from Rehoboth." Depicting the "singles scene of the shore's biggest adult playground," the magazine included photographs of a topless bikini-bottomed brunette dancing in the sand and a silhouetted female embracing the surf with the suggestion of an absent bathing suit. The issue quickly sold out from Rehoboth's newsstands; townsfolk penned angry letters to the publisher. "The swinging activities so lasciviously alluded to," wrote Commissioner John Hughes, "take place outside the city limits where they are safe from our body of laws, carefully nurtured over the years." He warned visiting Washingtonians that they "[we]re entering a family resort, where property owners run the show—dull as it may be."

RENEGADE ENTREPRENEUR

The first time I came to Rehoboth, 35 years ago, Renegade was
the place to dance.

—**Murray Archibald,** *Memorial Day Weekend*

"No board unburned" was the *Philadelphia Inquirer*'s description of an
early morning fire at "Delaware coast's most popular gay nightspot."[1] On Fourth of July eve in 1980, Renegade Restaurant & Bar,
located just west of Rehoboth's canal, burned to the ground. Although
some claimed that the arsonists were "rednecks," Glen Thompson was more
circumspect: "If it had been a bunch of rednecks sitting in a bar getting
drunk, they wouldn't have waited outside for everyone to leave and then
gone in and carefully set the fires." But "the season is over," Thompson told
the reporter. "Next year we'll be back better than ever."

Thompson had just returned to his Virginia home from Provincetown.
In the middle of the night, "I kept getting these phone calls. After four or
five calls, I finally got up." After being informed of the fire, he hastily drove
to Rehoboth, arriving at the smoldering scene near dawn. Before arriving,
Thompson "had discussed it briefly with Dolly," who owned the destroyed
building. "I made a very good deal because she wanted nothing to do with it."

Since its opening in May, the old wooden structure had been welcoming
up to nine hundred people on a weekend night and for Sunday-afternoon
tea dances; the Boathouse was attracting more patrons on weekdays. Both
bars advertised side by side in the *Washington Blade*.

Two weeks before the arson, eight cars had been vandalized in Renegade's parking lot. Some local gays expressed concern about the "uptick" of

gay harassment, citing homophobic epithets marked on the Boathouse and a paint-scrawled warning: "You're Next!" The burly fifty-year-old Rehoboth police chief, Harry Maichle Jr., was nonchalant: "We had one or two attacked. A car stopped, called them 'faggots,' somebody jumped out and hit one." Thompson characterizes the chief as "old school." With a quarter century of policing experience, Maichle had entered the police academy in the mid-1950s, eventually rising to the rank of captain. In 1976, he had been hired to lead Rehoboth's seventeen-officer force.

Despite Maichle's indifference, Thompson assessed that these concerns were valid. The arson "made the rednecks feel real brave. They would go down to the bars" in Dewey Beach to drink and prattle. "Then, they would get into their cars and come up." The incidents didn't last that long. The approach he took was typical Thompson: "I found out who they were." Then, "I got that straightened out" by going to the businessman who was the parent of one of the leaders. Thompson bought "stuff from him. He saw how reliable I was, and we got over it."

This, too, was the era of the so-called Anti-Gay Vigilante Organization (AGVO). Sharon Kanter, a Baltimore teacher vacationing for the summer, remembers that the group "scared the crap out of us. They looked like Aryan Nation types." As Thompson explains, it "was not quite an organization; it was very loose." Yet "as long as T-shirts exist," observed one gay man, "the strong potential exists for that name to be a valid entity." Although state police confirmed that "roving bands of straights [we]re routinely beating gays," no one had filed a complaint.

After the blaze, the Boathouse owners hosted a fundraiser to help former Renegade employees. Thompson was dubious: "June and Sid Sennabaum could give a shit less about the gay community. They were counting the money in the register!" Meanwhile, some of his former employees were hired by Frederick Baker, who owned Studio 1 Restaurant & Lounge, a straight dance club a mile up the highway from Renegade. Litz Cox, its new manager, placed a marquee nearby that read, "The former manager and staff of Renegade welcome you." Thompson was incensed and threatened a lawsuit. The sign was removed.

Opening a month after Renegade, Studio 1 had failed to attract a heterosexual crowd. Baker leased the space from Richard Derrickson, who owned Rehoboth's huge Midway complex, including his movie theaters. Studio 1 featured washed-up rock 'n' roll bands like the Boxtops and other live performances, such as the King Clone's Rock 'n' Roll Heaven Revue. As a businessperson, Derrickson—part of an Old Rehoboth family—rented to homosexuals like Baker. His political posture, however, hardly squared with his capitalist spirit. As a town commissioner, he decried the very condition to which he contributed: "I don't think anybody in the city really likes the fact we have a lot of gays." Employing a southern-like aphorism, he apprised a reporter that Rehoboth "citizens do not mistreat" homosexuals.

Baker placed an ad in Philadelphia's *Gay News*: "The Hottest Nightclub in Delaware is Now Gay Studio 1." But, as Thompson would later point out, "the only way that place would have ever survived as a gay bar would have been if it had been the only place." It was torched in the early-morning hours of August 6. Identified as the last person to leave each club, Cox acknowledged that he was a "prime suspect for both fires," but he claimed to have passed the investigator's lie detector test.

There were other suspects as well as rumors of a "gay war," which authorities rejected but many gays believed—and some old-timers still do. Neil Stevenson echoes, "When Renegade burned down, the question I asked myself was 'Who did that?' There was always this netherworld." One newspaper reported that "a funeral wreath of black roses" had been delivered to Studio 1 just prior to the fire. Whispering locals "saw it as possible retribution"; none allowed their names to be used.

GLEN'S STORY

Renegade "fell into my hands," Thompson says. John Hill, "from one of the old families" in Rehoboth, had stopped by one of Thompson's DC bars, informing him about a bar called the Islander: "I knew where he was talking about." The five-thousand-square-foot mostly plywood structure, lacking heat and air conditioning, was a seasonal spot incarnated over the years as Wild Gills, Disco Drive In, Chicken Pot, and Islander. None had been profitable. Its current owner apparently "was in trouble" because her "playboy" son was not focused on managing the bar. Thompson continues, "She didn't want to go into another season." This opportunity piqued his interest.

"Dolly and I got along very well. We were both old school. She was the kind of person who only took a handshake," he recalls. According to Thompson, after the fire, she agreed to sign the insurance money over to him; in turn, he agreed to rebuild and then repay her over a short time span. Donald Pong, his business partner whose name was on the lease, "didn't want to deal with it."[2] Thompson became the sole owner of the building and the bar.

Things went less smoothly with the state of Delaware. "There had been no *openly* owned gay bar in the state before me," Thompson brags. Gay bars had been owned by heterosexuals or corporations controlled by them. Certainly, the Boathouse, licensed under the Sennabaums, and the Nomad, licensed by the ostensibly straight Randall and Betty Jean Godwin, fit that pattern. The Alcoholic Beverage Control Commission (ABCC) "didn't know who I was. They didn't know until *after* they issued the license." Learning of the bar's clientele and the operators' sexual identities after the notoriety from the fire, the commissioners "were not happy." They looked "for a way to take back the license."

The ABCC soon discovered, as Thompson acknowledges decades later, that one local resident voicing support at the commission's initial licensing hearing was his DC accountant. He "got his driver's license real quick just for me from my [Delaware] address." Thompson states, "You make friends with people who can help you." A veteran of DC bars and politics, he learned of the commissioners' effort to pull his license from an inside source. Thompson enlisted a young attorney from a respected Lewes family whom he had known from the DC police force. His lawyer told the ABCC, "Do you know who you are dealing with? Do you know how much power he has? Do you want the whole gay city of Washington at your doorstep?" After that meeting, Thompson emphasizes, "They backed off!"

Thompson had first visited Rehoboth at the age of four with an uncle.[3] In 1944, they began lodging in Lewes on summer weekends. His uncles had taken a bit of pity on the youngster, given their sister's difficult circumstances. The seventh son of eight siblings, he was a voracious reader. He says, "We were, I wouldn't call poor White trash, but we were poor White. We lived in a four-room basement with no electricity and no plumbing" on Maryland's western border with Washington. Later, the Thompson family moved to an Upper Marlboro farm, where his father's business shrewdness is etched in memory: "It was river-bottom land. He sold the sand first. Then, he sold the gravel. Then, he sold off all the trees and then the land."

On his mother's side, Thompson's family dates back at least six Washington generations, coming from seventeenth-century coastal Virginia. Later, the family moved to the Eastern Shore and then on to Washington, "taking advantage" of a new capital in a new country. "We were the scoundrels of the group," he wisecracks. His grandfather's oldest and youngest brothers were also gay. The oldest, Washington Thompson Jr., "piloted a ship that went out of a wharf in southwest Washington, went down the Potomac, and into Chesapeake Bay. I knew he was gay, not because he told me, but from what I was able to read and figure out." The younger grand-uncle "was a little woman. He was so funny. Uncle Harry had this high-pitched voice." He continues, "His role was to take care of the children from his siblings. That was a role a lot of gay people took a hundred years ago."

The couple living next to his family during his childhood "were 'cousins.' Everybody knew who they were, and it was accepted. No one questioned it." Thompson "always knew" that he was different in the same way: "In the eleventh grade, I started rebelling. I couldn't handle it anymore. It was too much. I knew exactly what I was. And I knew exactly who the ones in school were." All the same, he wouldn't associate with them because he "didn't like the way they acted"—sissies.

Thompson was also self-conscious about his social standing at Frederick Sasscer High School. Although he served in leadership roles at school, "in order to be in the 'A' group, your parents had to be somebody of importance." So, the adolescent hung around a half dozen boys with a lower social standing. During the mid-1950s, "we'd wander around, each trying to be more masculine than the other." One afternoon, the more streetwise lad of their gang suggested traipsing to a queer bar on 9th Street NW. The teens knocked on the door of the Carroll Tavern, a rough-trade dive full of sailors and soldiers, mostly seeking easy money, a free weekend at a homosexual's home, or both. Thompson vividly remembers a woman answering the door:

> Gay bars kept the doors locked, with somebody standing at the door. Then, they'd unlock the door. Well, she opened the door. She looked at us. I'm surprised she let us in. She said, "I want you to know that we're all the same here, but you're welcome."

That was his first gay bar experience. He would later return to 9th Street alone.

At the onset of his senior year, Thompson contracted multiple illnesses that left him hospitalized for months. That "changed my life completely. I would have taken an entirely different path had that not happened." Although he had a college scholarship, "I was still in no condition." Eventually, he enrolled at the University of Maryland, but halfway through the second semester, he knew "this ain't for me," concluding, "I prefer the real world."

Believing that he "wouldn't live very long," Thompson spent much of his twenties traveling the world: "I was *always* able to figure out how to make a living." He stayed a year in Hong Kong, studying Chinese art and porcelain. Although mainland China was closed to foreign exporters, "I found that you could make a lot of money" if one was knowledgeable and "knew *how* to go and *where* to go." Near the Portas de Cerco, Macau's old border gate with the mainland, he bought collectible possessions from peddlers. Similarly, in London, he became versed in antiques. He scoured the British countryside in a van, astutely buying choice heirlooms and exporting them to U.S.-based dealers. From these travels, he grasped that "the rest of the world doesn't think the way we think." He learned "to assume that every single person you meet is a liar and a thief. Because that's what the world is." In short, the impresario realist "learned how to play their games."

During the 1960s, Thompson periodically returned to "the city where I've always been drawn back." Washington "was just a little southern town," he stresses. "You're talking about a period where gay men still married, and everything was kept quiet." There, too, were divisions within the homosexual community. "You had your Capitol Hill gays, Georgetown gays, Dupont Circle gays, and suburban gays. They were all different breeds of people, and they didn't mix that well," yet "I could fit into any of the groups." For instance, Thompson went to Sunday brunches, hosted by the "prissy" Hill clique dressed "in their little designer outfits." He emphasizes, "Even though I was just the little poor White trash boy with no education, I had a good personality, and I could be quite clever."

When in DC, he sometimes ventured onto the Eastern Shore, whose rich Maryland soil produced wealthy families. It was "famous for its little blue-blood gay underground community." Thompson visited Louisa d'Andelot Carpenter's thousand-acre Springfield Farm on the Chester River. At the iron gates, bronze statues of her prize-winning horses stood guard: "It was sort of like what you see in the movies." The Federal-style home had a terrace walled by bricks, relics from nearby colonial Chestertown. It overlooked stables, boarding some of the country's finest thoroughbreds owned by Louisa and her special friend, Eugenia Bankhead, Tallulah's less famous sister. On one visit, among those present were Eugenia and another of Carpenter's former lovers, Libby Holman. Thompson also remembers this "bunch of women all dressed as men," with the exception of "crazy lady Holman."

The Eastern Shore gay men "were fairly quick-witted themselves. None of them did anything, but they knew a lot." Thompson continues, "They would act very proper when they would come out to the bars. They would *never* travel alone." On visits to Baltimore and Washington gay bars, they whispered to desirables "how lovely it was on the Eastern Shore in their eighteenth-century homes and to please come. And they would."

Thompson also mingled with Carpenter and her entourage in Rehoboth. Aside from the Carpenter's family compound, sandwiched on secluded property between the Atlantic Ocean and Silver Lake, there was a rambling home at Henlopen Acres. She had purchased the property, near the corner of Pine Reach Road and Dodds Lane, in early 1966. He recalls, "The first time I went there, I was so fascinated that they had valet parking." In addition to her women friends, "there were artists who I didn't know and some local celebrities from upstate" along with the blue-blood boys. There also were genuine celebrities, ranging from Noël Coward to Efrem Zimbalist Jr. Thompson attended only the afternoon parties, where de rigueur was beach couture; formally attired servants served hors d'oeuvres from silver trays.

In the late 1960s, Thompson permanently returned to the United States, "where I got legitimate for a while." Still, he was coy about his sexuality:

> I came along at a time where we were looked down upon. However, when I worked at A-M [Addressograph-Multigraph], I never ever once hid what I was—and never once displayed it. They all knew what I was, and they all accepted me because I was better than any of them. . . . You had to be better in order to be equal.

BACK TO THE PORCH

Although Thompson was furious regarding Baker's encroachment on his gay-bar turf, he was more focused on getting Renegade rebuilt.[4] By his calculations, he had fifty-six days to reopen for the lucrative 1980 Labor Day weekend. From those who remained "loyal," he formed a work crew and rented out two houses. "I gave them rent, and I gave them food, but paid nobody." Working around the clock, they swiftly cleared all the debris, with "nothing left but five thousand square feet of cement." When the county building inspector arrived for his initial review, two assistants accompanied him. Thompson observed him directing the pair to "measure the sides." They calculated "the exact size of that platform. I couldn't figure out quite why."

Occasionally, Thompson would stop by the Back Porch Café. Sometimes, Mayor Miriam Howard was there, wearing one of her colorful signature hats. The sixty-eight-year-old retired federal employee championed restricting group housing rentals, mandating decibel measurements to reduce noise, and preserving Rehoboth as a "family resort."[5] Like Howard, Thompson was a Republican, awaiting Governor Ronald Reagan's "Morning in America." On one visit, his eyes wandered toward the legs of a nearby waitress. He was appalled to see them unshaven. This was the first time Thompson recalls encountering Joyce Felton.

Felton had arrived at the Porch that summer via Victor Pisapia, who had spent the first months of 1980 in New York City. Tiring of Key West, where he already "knew about celebrity personality, the drug scene, the sex scene," he wanted "to step it up again and go someplace where there were intellectuals, career-minded people, and where I could learn more." Just a few days after arriving, he attended a Greenwich Village house party.

In a classically cramped walk-up, Pisapia met Felton. She remembers overhearing a sun-tanned man in jeans and a jean jacket chatting about his restaurant. Felton welcomed him into her cocktail conversation. Like Pisapia, she was a restauranteur, managing four restaurants at Macy's famed flagship store on 34th Street. In contrast to the mild-mannered Pisapia, she was, like her mother, "a ball-busting warrior." Felton had earned a City University of New York degree in English; had opened a queer-friendly, vegetarian restaurant in Charlotte; had married and divorced; and was now working on the corporate side of restaurant management.

The two became "buds" immediately. "He was lovely," Felton reminisces. He talked to her about Rehoboth and his restaurant, inviting her to visit. "We became really close friends quickly," confirms Pisapia. Felton schooled Pisapia on how to jump the subways and introduced him to the gay scene. He recalls, "Joyce knew about every gay man in New York City. They all loved her because she was pretty much a party girl." He remembers "dancing our brains out" at Studio 54 and at the Lime Light, where "you had to prepare for days in advance: Go to the gym; sleep until two o'clock in the afternoon; get all of your drugs in line; outfits had to be talked about."

That spring, after visiting Rehoboth, Felton quit her Macy's job and returned to this "under-realized, mid-Atlantic, southern beach town" to work at this "cool, hippie restaurant serving really good food." Candidly, Pisapia "didn't think she would actually want to stay in Rehoboth." Nevertheless, "I think the whole idea of a small town . . . and the fact that I was there gave her something new she could do." He quickly realized, though, that "a lot of people were not quite sure about Joyce because she did bring a different element into the town."

When the Porch had closed for the prior 1979 season, the three owners weren't getting along. Pisapia was frustrated with the year-to-year lease on the property. Libby York, with a passion for jazz, had tired of the restaurant grind—and her husband. For Ted Fisher, though, the café had become his life. At that juncture, thirty-year-old Pisapia "was thinking as a business-person, not as a chef. I wanted to *own* something." York, reflecting on the breakup of her business and marriage, recalls the split-up as "a gradual process."

Perhaps the first jolt to the couple's once-solid relationship had occurred several years earlier in Key West, where Pisapia met the store manager of Fast Buck Freddies. She wore "big bandanas around the head, cigarette hanging out from the mouth, big hoop earrings coming down, and huge Guatemalan caftans." They started cooking together and hosting dinner parties. He asked her to join the Porch's 1976 summer kitchen staff, saying, "She brought an entourage of gay boys from Key West. *Finally*, Rehoboth was getting a little bit more interesting!" Eventually, she proposed that the trio partner with her to open a restaurant. They agreed to back the restaurant as silent partners. Pisapia later admitted that it was "a very bad business decision."

In 1977, the Rose Tattoo, named after a Tennessee Williams play, opened on Duvall Street, near the Monster, Delmonico's, and La Te Da in Key West. Pisapia considers it "probably the most beautiful restaurant we ever did." It attracted the gay glitterati—Tennessee Williams, Truman Capote, Calvin Klein—the accompanying paparazzi, and more ordinary diners seeking a Hollywood-like experience.

After two years of helping out without any voice in its actual management and confronted with the constant partying of its owner and staff, the Porch partners were embittered. "It changed Key West for us. Suddenly, it was no longer a place we could just relax," says Pisapia. "That's when I started making a transition to leave that town." York gracefully declares it "a good learning experience" that "didn't end well."

And yet it was at the Rose Tattoo where York had a rendezvous with fate. Jazz musician Franklin Micare was on the balcony. "We got to talking that I was a singer, 'Well, come sit in with me at the Pier House.' It went well." Micare then offered, "'If you're ever in New York, come sit in with me at my gig in the Village.' Well, that's all I had to hear!" Several weeks later, someone announced the availability of a sublet on a West Village apartment. The opportunity was tantalizing: "I was seeing my new future!" York did not return for the Porch's 1980 season, choosing to perform "the Great American Songbook, our classical American music, a great jazz repertoire."

Key West's climate had been stormy for the threesome throughout the winter of 1979. York remembers "lengthy discussions about how we [would] work out the deal for the sale of my shares." Her husband was "just a very understanding guy," despite the fact that "our marriage was breaking up." Her shares were paid over the next five years, becoming "my music scholarship."

As they entered Rehoboth's 1980 season, the relationship between Pisapia and Fisher soured further. Pisapia, who continued to push for relocating the Porch to Baltimore Avenue, remembers Fisher responding, "No one is going to go over to Baltimore Avenue!" Despite its being "a hard summer," Pisapia's kitchen team "was quite tight" and included talented young chefs who would become well known.[6] The business was "running like a little machine," as his team served upward of two hundred dinners nightly. During that season, Pisapia's "saving grace was Joyce. . . . What I was missing from the Back Porch is I didn't have partners who were driven." Finally, Fisher agreed to a buyout, and Pisapia began talking in earnest with Felton about opening an upscale restaurant on desolate Baltimore Avenue.

RENEGADE RISES

On August 29, fifty-four days following the arson, the $200,000 fire-proof Renegade reopened, but not without challenges.[7] Thompson consulted with his attorney about what had happened during the building inspector's first visit. He advised, "He thinks you're going to build a foundation right along the outside of that building and you're going to put blocks up. Then, the building is going to be *within* the setback. It's going to be illegal." Hearing this warning, Thompson simply "cut off eight inches around the building. When I rebuilt, it was *exactly* five thousand square feet." Renegade's new front area was divided into a dining room and a bar with "three white fireplaces, Victorian photos and oil paintings in ornate frames, bookcases, mirrors, sofas, and plants." The kitchen in the back section cut into the wooden dance floor with disco lights and a state-of-the-art sound system. An outside deck was used for Sunday tea dances. On Labor Day weekend in 1980, the club was mobbed.

Most people frequenting Renegade were gay men. Musician Peter Decker describes it as a "very elegant, fancy, *wow* sort of place." Compared to the Boathouse, where it was "much easier for [Decker] to make friends," Renegade felt like "a hookup place." Twenty-two-year-old Chris Yochim, who began working as a chemist for DuPont in 1980, disagrees. He and his friends found Renegade "a fun place to go" and "very welcoming." It attracted "a lot of people who were newly out." Although it was "big," there were "different areas where you could hang out. If you wanted to dance, you *had* to go to Renegade."

Over the next few years, Renegade expanded. "The plan was to do it step by step," explains Thompson. After paying off his debt to Dolly, he purchased eight wooded acres behind the property. This became the "Back 40," with room for hundreds of parked cars. He later moved the kitchen outside the concrete platform and lifted the ceiling by about ten feet, installing a mezzanine level. By the mid-1980s, there was even a swimming pool and a motel.

Originally, Thompson "was only going to operate it as a seasonal thing." After the fire, "I felt like if I did that, I was going to lose the business." He kept Renegade open to "win the locals over during the winter" and to "have a base when the spring came." The plan worked; it "killed the Boathouse."

The Boathouse owners "had a very, very bad winter. They were losing money," Thompson remembers. "They were ready to give up. All sorts of rumors were going around." Nevertheless, it reopened for the 1981 season with its new Western and Levis "Wreck Bar." Business, however, remained a fraction of what it had been before Renegade's reopening.

Declaring that he is "known to be quite the prankster," Thompson opted to have some "fun." He selected the manager of one of his DC clubs, "an overweight Italian" with a "little bit of a Mafia look. I took my lawyer . . . who had a very young Jewish lawyer look." Then, he dressed one of his bartenders with his Rolex and diamond rings "to make him look like a high-class hustler." As Thompson tells the story:

> I even rented a black town car and sent them down to pretend to buy the place. I gave Tiny, the Italian-looking guy, $100 bills. I said, "Now, you take them out to lunch and have cocktails first. Every single time you pay for something, pay with a $100 bill." I said, "You'll see June Sennabaum's eyes light up!"

His prank was taken "more seriously than I expected." The Boathouse owners held a "grand closing" at the end of February, and Philadelphia's gay paper, *PGN*, broke the news that "June and Sid [were] selling the collegiate-looking disco/restaurant to a trio of Washingtonians." The Boathouse, of course, was not sold, and it continued operating until the early morning of April 15, when it burned to the ground. Sid told arson investigators that there had been no recent problems and that employees had closed at 1:00

A.M. Curiously, the owners' German shepherd, which was always within the compound after closing, had been left to roam outside the fence.

Aside from Renegade, the only remaining queer bar in the area was Nomad Village. As the Boathouse and then Renegade sucked away their business, the Godwins listed their A-frames and eight-unit building for sale. With no buyer, they unsuccessfully sought rezoning of their 1.5-acre oceanfront site for condo construction. When that failed, the Nomad welcomed lesbians, who found Renegade far less welcoming. As Kanter describes, Renegade's first manager "hated women, was mean to women, [and] just treated us poorly."

In Rehoboth, as in DC, Thompson faced not only the reality of competition but shaky race relations. With its expanded acreage, Renegade now abutted what Whites called "West Rehoboth." During the early 1980s, this historic Black community still preferred to "keep to themselves." As in decades past, it remained a "pocket of poverty" with outhouses, "rusty Chevys on cement blocks, a trailer park with no running water, [and] windows shuttered with cardboard." A "western-style shootout on the dusty streets" in 1981 left hospitalized a pair of sixty-year-olds, who had been quarreling about a craps game. Brenda Milbourne, who grew up in the 1960s, when "it was a village," remembers that "everybody looked after each other." By the "early 1980s, life changed back here," she explains, "like a cloud had come down and, when it lifted back up," it was destroyed. "We should have been part of Rehoboth," she continues. "I wish that our parents had had enough education and enough knowledge to fight back during the situation of segregation, but they could not. . . . I would like to see all these fences knocked down, all the animosity knocked down."

West of Rehoboth, "any extensive change is doubtful without central sewage," which "Rehoboth Beach has refused," reported the *Whale*. Despite developers' interest in building low- and moderate-income housing, Mayor John Hughes opposed tapping into Rehoboth's sewage system ("It would be a serious mistake to inhale sewage into our backyard") or annexing the area ("We have primarily single-family dwellings while West Rehoboth is comprised of commercial strips [and] trailers").

Renegade folks "got along with those people," although, Thompson admits, "We didn't at the very beginning." Initially, Renegade had "trouble with West Rehoboth [residents] robbing people." He "let them know that we weren't going to let them fuck with us." Thompson hired a chief of security, Peppers, who was licensed to carry a weapon: "The word got out in

West Rehoboth, 'Don't mess with Peppers because he's crazy.'" Thompson
also met with some longtime residents—the Allens, the Duffys, the Har-
mons—who were "very suspicious until they got to know you." When he
opened his twenty-nine-room motel, he hired women from the area for
housekeeping, while their boyfriends and husbands obtained parking-lot
security jobs. Wayne Hodge, who was managing Renegade, reminded these
workers, "You tell everybody back there, 'Don't break in because your jobs
are going to be on the line!'"

In 1984, Burton Village, a subsidized housing development, opened on
the west side of the canal. Although some Rehoboth residents were disturbed about a queer dance club setting up shop across the border, another
set of impoverished Blacks—supported by the federal government—was
more disturbing to many gay and straight Whites. Situated on the main
road between Renegade and Rehoboth, gay vacationers who ill-advisedly
walked from town to the club sometimes had problems. Hodge recalls,
"Back in those days, you took your life in your hands if you did that at
night." There were risks even for those departing Renegade by car. Late-
night drivers, sometimes turning the wrong direction, swiftly arrived at
"the Corner" of dead-end Hebron Road, where they were occasionally harassed by drug dealers. Through Thompson's connection with the state
transportation department's Raymond Pusey, a "No Exit" sign was placed
on that side of the road.

BAR OWNERSHIP FOR DUMMIES

Bars and dance clubs—gay or straight—have the imprimatur of their owners.[8] Most customers, of course, pay little attention to the myriad details
contributing to a successful bar. Nevertheless, they are opinionated about
clubs they like or dislike. Thompson was a master of club design, employing
principles of interior architecture; a student of the streets, leveraging his
knowledge of behavioral psychology; an adroit businessman, creating systems of oversight and control; and a practical politico, networking with
people who mattered. Walking into a Thompson bar, a careful observer
could learn a lot about the owner, just as one can by visiting someone's
home.

The average gay bar, according to Thompson, runs about eighteen
months. Apart from his first two ventures, most of his bars, including Renegade, thrived for decades.[9] From the many clubs and bars he has owned,

often reluctantly or by seizing opportunities, he developed a few principles from which he seldom, if ever, wavered. These included the following:

Avoid partnerships. After cashing out from the Pier 9 partnership, in early 1971, Thompson ventured into his second gay club, again "reluctantly." As the onsite manager for the cavernous southeast DC club, Grand Central, he frequently was at odds with his co-partner. "Some of the investors would come in and pull his ear. Then, he'd come back and want to change what we [had] agreed to do!" Thompson concludes, "It was just impossible to do anything" and swore "never, ever, ever to have a partner!"

Never call police. When operating his Dupont Circle bars (Frat House, Badlands, P Street Station, Omega, Apex), Thompson sometimes had "problems with the police." Prior to Stonewall, police raided at whim or when bribes were not promptly paid. As homosexual bars transformed into post-Stonewall gay clubs, the relationship with local police began changing. Additionally, when city administrations changed, so did politics and practices. Regardless of who was in power, Thompson knew that "if you had one problem in the bar, but called the police, you had two problems."

Design for desire. Thompson is a student of practical psychology. "You have to understand people," he observes. "Particularly in gay bars, they love to look at other people, and they love to rub up against other people." During its thirty-two-year existence, Renegade went through several metamorphoses. It included intersections where people had to squeeze together as they passed through on a crowded weekend night. A balcony allowed customers to unobtrusively peer down at the crowd. A sedate piano lounge offered respite without a cover charge.

Watch what customers do. "People don't want what they tell you they want," Thompson insists. "What they say has nothing to do with what they think!" After the Frat House, he opened Badlands, which attracted a mostly college crowd in the 1980s and 1990s. "They would come to the door in groups. In those groups would be women and men, mostly gay, but some straight. There would be Blacks. There would be Latins. There would be Orientals [*sic*]." Although he was accused of discriminatory carding policy at some of his clubs, once bar-goers were inside, "they'd do it on their own."[10] According to Thompson:

> Over time, you would see them separate into areas. The upper level is where all the older lesbians went. The main bar is where the gay guys who looked nice went. Bar five, the back bar, is where guys who didn't look quite nice went. Right along the side of the dance floor

is where all the Black people would hang out. The backroom is where all the Latinos would go.

Be a networker. Before the Internet, accessing information about gay-owned or -friendly businesses was difficult, especially outside major metropolitan areas. At Renegade, Thompson maintained a list of such businesses and professional people: "When anybody wanted help or anything, we would tell them who to go to and who not to go to." He kept the list to himself. He knew those with influence, be it formal or informal, and avoided antagonizing them: "You make friends with the town, and when something comes up, they're going to be on your side."

Never talk politics or drink your liquor. Bar patrons generally enjoy talking and often schmooze with bartenders. Some knew who Thompson was, but only his closest friends knew his politics. Also, "bar owners too frequently get involved in drugs, drink too much, and bring their personal lives into the bar. I did none of those things. I ran it as a business."

THE RENEGADES

In his 1957 collection *Exile and the Kingdom*, Albert Camus's short story "The Renegade" depicts "a person's need for a sense of unity and order . . . when confronted by an unfathomable world."[11] This story has little relationship to Thompson or those working at Renegade. It does, however, offer insight into living within an uncertain world seemingly without meaning.

Those frequenting Renegade during the early 1980s certainly included career-tracked Capitol Hill gays, Philly professionals, and blue-collar Baltimoreans. But Thompson also welcomed Delaware homosexuals, many of whom were from or still living in small towns and rural areas. Unlike urbanites, and aside from a few students at the University of Delaware, these Diamond State lesbians and gay men had no support groups, no queer publications, no accepting religious denominations, no political organizations, and no civil protections. Some, like Camus's missionary, entered a metaphorical "House of the Fetish" for ephemeral pleasures in a futile escape from a heterosexual world devoid of love, hope, or meaning. For others, their burning emptiness, inflamed by bigotry and prejudice, evoked homosexual rage and revolt against hegemonic heterodoxies. For a few, the seductive promise of unity and order was recompense for docile cultural assimilation and rejection of the "gay agenda." All were renegades. All would soon meet up at Renegade.

6

DIAMOND STATE REFRACTIONS

I see great joy and deep sorrow and all points in between, but
more of all I see a community in progress.
—**Steve Elkins**, *The Way I See It*

On October 10, 1982, Glen Thompson welcomed Ivo Dominguez Jr. and his life partner, Jim Welch, founders of the Gay & Lesbian Alliance of Delaware (GLAD).[1] The Wilmington couple was familiar with Renegade, but they "didn't generate any notoriety or attention because we were just there to have a drink and dance." This time, they stood at the bar without drinks, but "with a bunch of papers to hand [to] people," including the phone number for their newly launched gay hotline.

It was difficult enlisting Delaware queer bars to help organize, so they were pleased to have this opportunity to introduce Sussex County gays to GLAD. "We never got total support from the bars except by calling in favors from our friends who were well known or who were bar flies," Dominguez bemoans. Typically, the couple would ask whether anyone knew someone to put in a good word. In this situation, Audra Rivers contacted her old friend, Thompson.

MURDER IN THE MIST

Ten months earlier, eight days before Christmas, Rehoboth's first murder in a decade had occurred.[2] A bludgeoned body was discovered on a Friday before dawn near the corner of 1st Street and Delaware Avenue. He was the town's first gay-identified murder victim.

Charles Krauss had lived in town for eight years. The thirty-nine-year-old managed Elizabeth Hooper's Nice & Easy restaurant in summers and her Corner Cupboard Inn during the off-season. The Baltimore native had first met the "quiet and friendly" young man when they worked at a Virginia Ramada Inn. Hooper invited Krauss to join her in Rehoboth when she bought her aunt and uncle's fifty-year-old inn. Always with a smile on his face, "he was one hell of a good guy," she mourned.

Investigators quickly focused on the town's "low-profile" gay community after discovering that Krauss "had homosexual activity in his background" and making inquiries at Renegade. Nineteen hours after the body's discovery, Police Chief Harry Maichle Jr. announced that a suspect had been detained. Thirty-five-year-old J. Hunter Clark III confessed within minutes of his arrest. Bail was set at $50,000. Commending the speedy apprehension, Mayor John Hughes decried the bond as "too low."

The *Whale* headlined that the mayor was "Begin[ning] the Crackdown on Subculture's Seamier Side." Dismissing the idea that this "isolated incident [wa]s representative of the gay community," Hughes, nevertheless, was quick to point out that the murder coupled to two arsons "[we]re crimes not familiar to this community *and* they've been gay-related." The mayor went on to link the graffiti-covered Rehoboth Avenue restroom rife with homosexual messages and "peep holes that have been cut into the partitions." Declaring that "we're not running a brothel," Hughes promised quarter-inch steel partitions and police patrols.

The assailant, a six-foot-four, red-bearded, computer-science student, had met the feather-weight Krauss at the Sea Mist, a local mixed bar near the corner of Rehoboth Avenue and 1st Street. Although they were just casual acquaintances, the pair drank together for several hours on Thursday night. Clark departed around midnight. He drove around Rehoboth in his ruby-red van before he spotted Krauss leaving the bar about ninety minutes later. He offered Krauss a ride home—just five blocks away—and tempted him with more liquor.

The pair had been joyriding around Rehoboth for some time before Clark turned to Krauss and asked, "So, what kind of sex are you into?" To which he allegedly responded, "Pain." Clark smacked Krauss across the face with the liquor bottle. He then grabbed a tire iron, crushed his skull, and dumped the body. After jury selection and opening arguments, Clark—with prior convictions for disorderly conduct, bad checks, and theft—accepted a plea bargain. He was sentenced to life in prison.

"That was a shock to everybody," recollects Thompson. After this incident, Welch recalls, "people were careful," while the public became more aware that Rehoboth was becoming "the gay summer capitol." Educator Dolph Spain, who had just purchased a summer house with his partner, Lloyd Johnson, remembers this incident as the beginning of the area's "reputation that if you told people you were going to Rehoboth, they thought you were gay." The path to Rehoboth's fame, however, had been paved by prior generations of homophile, gay, and queer activists who worked almost exclusively in the relatively less conservative Wilmington and Dover areas and at the University of Delaware, in Newark. Without these early efforts, the rise of Rehoboth's queer political community in the 1990s would have been unlikely. Any understanding of the transformation of hearts and minds of Rehoboth townsfolk and its emergence as the preeminent queer community in Delaware begins with this earlier history.

EARLY ORGANIZING IN DELAWARE

Before CAMP Rehoboth were organizations ranging from GLAD and Gays of the Diamond State to the Gay Community and Delaware Dykes Hotline.[3] Before *Letters* were publications like the *Cruiser* and *GLAD Tidings*. Before lobbying to end workplace and marriage discrimination came efforts at homosexual law reform. Before Steve Elkins and Murray Archibald were Ivo Dominguez Jr. and Jim Welch; before them were Zachary Zarr, Debbie Snow, and Richard Aumiller; before them were James R. Vane and Clark Polak. These efforts and people—among others—were unheralded at the time and now are mostly forgotten.

Beginning in the 1950s, an odd coterie of mostly men launched the "homophile movement." Largely focused on moving homosexuality from criminal prosecution to medical treatment to social tolerance, they embraced the pioneering research of publicly identified heterosexuals Alfred Kinsey and Evelyn Hooker. Some, like Franklin Kameny and Barbara Gittings, favored peaceful demonstrations by conservatively dressed protesters; others preferred a less confrontational approach. Both supported legal reform efforts, although few linked criminal reform to sexual liberation.

In 1962, the American Law Institute published the Model Penal Code. State legislatures were encouraged to modernize their criminal statutes by referring to this comprehensive framework. Six years later, four states had revised their legal codes; only Illinois had deleted the consensual sodomy statute.

Toward this end, Polak, the energetic wayward son of a Philadelphia Jewish family and an enigmatic entrepreneur, had been elected president of the lesbian-run Janus Society in 1963. The next year, under the banner of the society, he began publishing a glossy magazine, *Drum*. This so-called gay *Playboy* radically mixed news stories for "queers," while "putting 'sex' back into 'homosexuality'" through "fiction for 'perverts,' . . . [homoerotic] photo essays for 'fairies,' and laughs for 'faggots.'" Not surprisingly, its circulation grew larger than prudish homophile magazines *ONE*, *Mattachine Review*, and the *Ladder* combined. He enjoyed little support from conventional homophile leaders, who had a "purist notion," observes Gittings. Janus was expelled from the confederation of East Coast homophile organizations and abandoned by Philadelphia lesbians, who formed a Mattachine chapter.

Polak was brash, abrasive, and a lone wolf, and his sexual politics were radical yet pragmatic. He organized the country's first homosexual sit-in that occurred at a Philadelphia restaurant in April 1965 and formed the Homosexual Law Reform Society the following year. With revenue from *Drum* and his pornography-distributing Trojan Book Service, he deployed "respectability, selectively tailoring his messages for specific audiences," notes historian Marc Stein.

In early 1968, Polak allied with the more conservative Vane, who had registered as a Delaware lobbyist for the Homosexual Law Reform Society. They joined the American Civil Liberties Union (ACLU) to lobby the Delaware State Assembly on penal reform. Vane addressed the House Judiciary Committee about decriminalizing homosexual activity. This former Air Force captain and Dover native stated unequivocally that sex between "consenting adults in private should not be subject to arrest." Unlike Polak, however, Vane was careful to underscore that he was not seeking social acceptability and certainly not advocating for sexual liberation. Vane's desexualized definition of a homosexual was one "who prefers all of his *social* contacts with persons of the same sex."

Three years later, Vane was lobbying for his organization, Human Enlightenment, to inform the public of the "problems of the homosexual community." The traditionally dressed fifty-four-year-old appeared again at Legislative Hall. Speaking in favor of S.B. 356 to eliminate the sodomy statute, he testified, "I've lived with the same man for twelve years." He then declared, "What happens in a person's home, between competent adults, isn't any of the public's business."

Delaware's sodomy statute was repealed in 1972, "mainly through his efforts," lauded Wilmington's *Morning News*. That same year, the state's Alcoholic Beverage Control Commission (ABCC) quietly rescinded its prohibition of same-sex dancing in bars. In 1973, Delaware's new legal code, which decriminalized consensual sodomy for people ages sixteen years and older, went into effect. Vane held a "coming-out celebration" at a Wilmington restaurant. Few attended, and those who did objected to the presence of a reporter he had invited. Delaware homosexuals "are not ready," Vane told the *Evening Journal*; decriminalization, he realized, was not sufficient "to allow homosexuals to live their lives freely."

By the early 1970s, efforts to ban discrimination based on sexual orientation had been successful in Minneapolis, Detroit, and DC, but no state had enacted such legislation. Vane energetically set about advocating for such a law in Delaware. Its citizens and their representatives, however, were less than supportive. In September 1973, he attended a North Star Civic Association meeting. It featured a neighbor, Delaware's junior senator, Joseph Biden Jr. The senator spoke for ninety minutes to about thirty residents. Vane then "startled Biden with his sudden queries" regarding job discrimination against homosexuals in the U.S. civil service and military. "My gut reaction," responded the stunned Biden, "is that they are security risks, but I must admit I haven't given this much thought." The young Catholic politician paused. "I'll be darned!"

In June 1974, the Delaware legislature considered a bill against employment discrimination on the basis of sexual orientation. A second bill to outlaw housing discrimination had been withdrawn. It proved difficult for Vane to motivate gays and lesbians experiencing discrimination to sign statements or to testify. Just two state senators, one Democrat and one Republican, supported the bill. One Senate opponent, who demagogued that Delaware would become "a haven for homosexuals," voted "nay" in a falsetto voice.

After lobbying the legislature for seven years, Vane ended his seemingly quixotic journey. "Younger people who did not suffer as we did aren't willing to do anything for anyone else," he lamented. Content with dancing in bars, having sex, or rapping in groups, "the gay community here has no social conscience."

Meanwhile, during the late 1960s and early 1970s, homosexual organizing had moved onto college campuses.[4] University of Delaware students and nonstudents formed a private group, the Gay Community, in the fall of 1971. Zarr announced its presence in the student newspaper, the *Review*: "We have been content to shoulder straight society's definition of the homosexual as queer, effeminate, faggot; we never felt a need to break the silence of bigotry and shame." But, he countered, "We are challenging the moral order of this society, each time we come together."

They met at various homes, focusing on personal growth and self-acceptance, although also hoping to "educate the community at large." A year later, one of the programs sponsored by the group featured a documentary, *Some of Your Best Friends*. Gittings, the head of the Gay Task Force of the American Library Association, led the discussion among the sixty people attending.

In 1973, the Gay Community received university recognition. Flyers around campus proclaimed, "Sometimes the Hardest Step Is Often the Most Rewarding" and "Don't Live Your Life a Lie." There, too, was a weekly ad in the *Review* along with gay dances and rap groups. Yet aside from a Newark school speaking engagement, the group made no effort to educate the community or to engage in political issues.

A year later, Snow, a photographer and artist, along with her house-mate, Barbara, a junior high school teacher, formed the Delaware Separatist Dyke Group. Although its name "scared many women away," small weekly "social rapping" sessions were hosted at their Wilmington home.

Mostly men participated in the Gay Community. By 1975, it had about eighty members. On any given Sunday evening, several dozen would gather in a dormitory basement for camaraderie and occasional programs, including Aumiller, who had joined the group when he entered the Department of Theater's graduate program in 1972. Born into a conservative middle-class Ohio family, the gangly twenty-five-year-old also worked part-time for the university's theater. When he was appointed its director in 1974, he became faculty adviser to the student group. In July 1975, a small Philadelphia newspaper published a story about Delaware gays, quoting the boyish-looking Aumiller. The university's president read the article. "His private life," he told the provost, "*had* to be private." This concern, however, was not relayed to Aumiller, who was issued another one-year contract the following month. "By hiring me, they told me my sexual preference doesn't affect my ability to do my job," he later trumpeted in Wilmington's *Sunday News Journal*. The reporter prominently opined, "The Gay Community actively campaigns to recruit new members."

That same November week, the *Review* published a two-part, front-page story about homosexuals on campus. In the first segment, Aumiller explained that the Gay Community's goals had changed since it had formed. Touting its success "with raising our own group consciousness," now "efforts [we]re concentrated on raising the public's consciousness." The second story was a sympathetic portrayal of three students, including an urban "feminist" and a woman from a "conservative" small town. They expressed frustration that few lesbians were "out" on campus and that the scattering of lesbians at male-dominated gay bars were mostly "truck driver" types. There appeared to be little negative reaction to the articles, aside from one letter to the editor decrying the gay group, which met "on Sunday (the Lord's Day)." Appearance, however, disguised campus reality.

During this time, a few outside Delaware's ivory tower were also raising public's consciousness. Most publicly was S. Sgt. Rudolph "Skip" Keith Jr., a DC African American with seven years of service, including a tour in Vietnam. The twenty-five-year-old announced that he was gay at a race relations class held at the Dover Air Force Base in May 1975. "I really got tired" of being silent and complacent, he confessed to a reporter. "They know damn well there are thousands [of homosexuals] in the military." An investigation was launched. Keith was discharged four months later, although not before he was granted a furlough to attend New York City's gay pride march. He pledged to join an appeal with T. Sgt. Leonard Matlovich, a twelve-year veteran with a distinguished record who had voluntarily disclosed his sexual orientation at Langley Air Force Base. Both cases received national media coverage, but the New York Times observed that Matlovich's was "the more celebrated of the two cases." The husky mustached Matlovich, pictured on a TIME magazine cover, became the gay rights poster boy; Keith, a portly Black man with wire-rimmed glasses, quietly returned to his family home in DC.

THE AUMILLER AFFAIR

On Tuesday, November 4, 1974, Edward A. Trabant sat in his presidential office at Hullihen Hall.[5] Copies of the current University of Delaware's student newspaper as well as Wilmington's Sunday News Journal were on his secretary's desk. A prominently displayed photo of instructor Aumiller set adjacent to the Journal's headline: "Gays: 'There's No Need to Deny Fact' Says a Homosexual Activist at U.D." The wheels of the university began grinding.

A former engineering professor, Trabant had worked on the Manhattan Project and served on the board for the Army Nuclear Effects Research Center. At age forty-eight, in June 1968, the lanky Georgia Tech academic vice president had been chosen to serve as the University of Delaware's twenty-second president.

Given the publicity, the university provost suggested that Trabant quietly dismiss Aumiller under the guise of budget cuts. Although this action was politically expedient, Trabant believed that Aumiller was "hiding behind his academic gown to promote his own personal cause," that the university was becoming a "Mecca for homosexuals," and that theater productions had "homosexual overtones."

His office contacted Aumiller, who guessed the topic and assumed that the president simply wanted factual details. At the meeting, Trabant expressed affront at a reported poster in Aumiller's office ("Sometimes the Hardest Step Is Often the Most Rewarding"). Aumiller pointed out that the flyers and ads were paid for by the student group through university funds. Further pressed, the instructor denied that he was a "homosexual activist" or that he had solicited the Sunday newspaper interview, which he said "was misleading and inaccurate." Trabant informed him that "they were on a 'conflict course' because the majority of Delawareans did not share his views on homosexuality, nor would they in his lifetime." Aumiller then asked whether he should speak to clear the record. Trabant said that "no," it had been a "bad idea" to have spoken to the press. Comparing the university to a "small pond," he lectured that a "small wind" could make "large waves." He promised Aumiller they would meet again.

Instead, two days later, Trabant dictated a letter to the chairman of the board of trustees in which he outlined actions to "correct the situation," warning that as "an advocate and evangelist for gays, [Aumiller would] naturally attract others to the campus." Trabant acknowledged that should Aumiller sue, "the chances of the court upholding any action that I take are minimal." Still, given past experiences, he judged a legal contest to be unlikely.

On January 6, 1976, Aumiller was fired, effective immediately. In addition to being charged with "advocating homosexuality" and failing to disclose his sexual orientation, he was faulted for speaking to the press and advising a group that "meets clandestinely at nights in a dormitory basement." Word quickly spread among students. Meanwhile, Trabant openly addressed the issue in the press: "He placed himself in a position of encouraging, condoning, and sanctioning homosexuality for the undergraduates." The president further bellowed, "I resent the bedroom behavior of university employees or others being portrayed in the public press." In turn, Aumiller filed a grievance with the university. In contrast to Trabant, he "had chosen instead to work through established university channels to achieve a dignified and responsible agreement." Further, he was "not willing to argue the issue of [his] homosexuality with the president." Unlike other homosexual professors whose contracts had not been renewed by the Trabant administration, Aumiller had "no intention of leaving Newark until [he had] exhausted every source of redress."

In February, Aumiller's attorney filed suit in U.S. District Court, supported by the ACLU and the American Association of University Professors, among others.[6] That same month, homophile activist Kameny visited campus to speak on "Gay Rights: Past, Present, and Future." Kameny, with a Harvard Ph.D. in astronomy, had been dismissed from his federal position due to his sexual orientation in 1957. He had challenged it in court and, four years later, launched the Mattachine Society of Washington. In his talk, Kameny stressed how the absence of civil rights protections for homosexuals created the feeling of a "sword hanging over their heads." The headline of the state's leading newspaper read, "UD Speaker Endorses Homosexuality for All." Conservative columnist Bill Frank, who summered in Rehoboth, pointed out the paradox between Aumiller's firing for *allegedly* advocating for homosexuality and the university's funding of Kameny, who *expressly* did.

IVO'S STORY

Within this historical context, Ivo Dominguez Jr. joined the Gay Community in the fall of 1976, much to the dismay of Professor Ivo Dominguez Sr.[7] As a boy, Junior had enjoyed long walks on the beach of Rehoboth past the last lifeguard stand. On that southern end in 1971, Dominguez had found "certain kinds of guys" and, at age thirteen, intuitively knew that "those guys are queer." Already sporting a beard, he "never did anything . . . but I sure spent a lot of time looking" and witnessed "a lot of surreptitious handholding."

What is more ingrained in the youthful Dominguez's memories were challenges confronted by his Cuban-born parents. In addition to small signs in some Rehoboth restaurant windows—"No Coloreds"—his family had to navigate prejudice against Latinos. His father always made sure that restaurant and hotel reservations were under the name "Dr. Ivo Dominguez Sr.," as it "made a difference sometimes in how we were treated. . . . It was kind of like visiting White Man's territory when we went to a fancy dinner in Rehoboth."

Dominguez also remembers encountering a roped-off area on the north end of the Boardwalk. Popularly known as the "Crow's Nest," this very narrow strip of beach was "reserved" for African Americans. Seventy-two-year-old Ada Waples Burton recalls "sitting at the little space." Although discrimination was federally banned in the early 1960s, well into the early 1970s, the beach and Boardwalk remained mostly segregated. Jay Stein, who grew up in Rehoboth and operates a business directly in front of this area, acknowledges, "Even as time went on [and de facto segregation ended], Blacks would still come back to that beach." West of Rehoboth–born Burton reflects, "Now [that] you can walk the Boardwalk and go in the restaurants . . . you're *somewhat* equal."

Descending from families of wealth and privilege, Junior's parents were conservative, authoritarian, and religious. In Cuba, his grandparents had owned jewelry stores and plantations. His aunt had once dated Raul Castro, whose family owned a nearby plantation. Born in 1958, three weeks before the Cuban Revolution ousted dictator Fulgencio Batista, the Dominguez family fled to Spain. "Thinking the revolution would fail," his parents believed that self-exile would be temporary: "It didn't work out that way." At age seven, Dominguez resettled in Florida. His father, who had been a professor of Spanish literature and an attorney, returned to college to earn his degrees again. Five years later, the family moved to Newark after he accepted a professorship.

In the Diamond State, adolescent Dominguez got "really good at doctoring IDs." However, he "*only* went to the bars." He recalls a nearby queer bar, the Golden Greeks, with a "tiny dance floor in the back with a jukebox." Customers were only "allowed to dance if Stella liked you." Rumors said that Wilmington police routinely wrote down patrons' license plate numbers, despite Stella's husband being a retired vice cop with the city.

Dominguez came out to his closest friends during his first couple of years at Newark High School. During his senior year, he disclosed to "teachers who I cared about and more of my friends." This action was, in part, due to the battle royal between the university administration and instructor Aumiller during the spring term of 1976. Dominguez, who regularly read the *Review* along with the queer students' newsletter, the *Cruiser*, "felt empowered" with an urgency "to begin to step up."

Dominguez's life dramatically changed when his parents, who had been surreptitiously monitoring his mail, confronted him about a love letter. In front of his eyes, they transformed from caring parents, championing "the palest one of the whole family," their "golden child," to wrathful, contemptuous adults. "They kept me a prisoner at home," he swears. Alone for a short time one day, he escaped with a handful of belongings. He lived on the streets for two weeks before "I found a friend from high school whose mom and dad let me live with them until I could get a part-time job."

Refusing his parents' money "to change my last name and to leave the state," Dominguez was then "kidnapped off the sidewalk" and "held prisoner by a deprogrammer for a weekend." He also claims, "Mom tried to kill me twice, once with a knife and the other by poisoning me." Thirty years later, on her deathbed, he was refused a final visit. Her obituary listed only one child—his sister.

THE GAY COMMUNITY REBOUNDS

Dead to his family and living with straight roommates, Dominguez attended the University of Delaware as a first-year geology student in the fall of 1976.[8] On campus, the Gay Community was decimated and disheartened, but not disbanded: "For quite a while, I was the only guy to show up, but there were quite a few lesbians." During his first year, he received "a healthy dose of education on women's issues and feminism." A lesbian rap group met weekly at Daugherty Hall's coffeehouse, where Dominguez became "immersed into this stew of college lesbianism." Although he had no affinity with children, he often babysat their kids and socialized with the lesbians afterward: "I was basically raised by dykes in terms of understanding the community."

Within a couple of years, Dominguez had graduated from member, to treasurer, to president of what was renamed the Gay Student Union (GSU). In 1978, he brought Leonard Matlovich and Elaine Noble—the first openly gay person elected to statewide office in the United States—to campus and convinced Aumiller to return for a speaking engagement.

Aumiller was initially reluctant to accept the invitation: "I think the thing that got to him was that the group *still* existed, that we were still pushing." The April event was well publicized. "He hadn't given up. That was the biggest message," says Dominguez. Aumiller, then director of theater at Duke University, proclaimed to the fifty or so in attendance that the university's "sacrificial lamb trick didn't work."[9] He cited the continuation of the student group and his personal settlement along with payment of more than $60,000 for his attorney's fees, which Judge Murray M. Schwartz had doubled in a stinging rebuke of the university's actions, stating, "I cannot find a scintilla of evidence in any newspaper articles to support the inference that Aumiller was on a campaign to convert heterosexuals to homosexuality." Further, the judge had found "nothing" to "support the contention" that Aumiller had "abused his position" and that "no disruption [had] ar[isen] from any of the articles." In exacting punitive damages, Schwartz had judged that "President Trabant acted maliciously or wantonly disregarded [Aumiller's] constitutional rights."

That autumn, Dominguez was sitting in the GSU office when the phone rang. The owner of the Lobby Bar, "the warrior princess" Camilia Griffin, was reaching out: If GSU students could raise money for back rent, she offered to turn the bar, located in a strip mall just off Interstate 95, queer. In January 1979, it officially "turned," as Dominguez and another student walked onto the expansive dance floor. By March, several hundred were gathering on weekend nights to dance to a disco beat beneath the multicolored, flashing lights and to sip specialty drinks, such as the "flaming faggot." This spot became "the seed around which the rest came," Dominguez says. A rare potpourri of genders, ages, and races queered space for socializing—and organizing.

Undeterred, the Trabant administration sought legal ways to dismantle the GSU. Dominguez received many phone calls from the vice president of student affairs, making it feel "like high school." Chastising the students for being "too radical or too out," the administrator prohibited gay literature about the group during Parents Weekend. He later stipulated that "people who were not full-time students could not be a member of any student organization," changing the rules for all to target the gay group.

This incident was the genesis for the United Gays of the Diamond State, launched by UD alumni Marshall Gealt in 1979. Finding nonstudents to join, however, proved difficult. Welch notes, "People were afraid to come out. If they got involved in a political organization, their job would find out, or other people would." Parallel to Gealt's efforts, some lesbians hosted a Delaware Dykes Hotline to network with women who were cautious about gathering in public. Despite challenges and through these efforts, a contingent of women and men, including a handful from the Rehoboth area, journeyed to Washington for the March on Washington. In October 1979, Dominguez was accompanied by his new lover, Welch.

GLAD YOU'RE HERE

It was a chilly October Sunday afternoon in Washington. Welch walked arm-in-arm with Dominguez.[10] Together with forty-eight others, including a handful from southern Delaware, they sported burgundy shirts brandishing the United Gays of the Diamond State logo. Marching beneath a

Jim Welch (*background*) and Ivo Dominguez Jr. (*foreground*), 1987.
(Courtesy of Jim Welch and Ivo Dominguez Jr.)

buff-colored diamond-shaped flag of colonial blue, emblazoned with the state's coat-of-arms, they merged into a sea of one hundred thousand activists from nearly every state. As the crowd walked down Pennsylvania Avenue toward the White House, the Los Angeles Gay Men's Chorus sang melodies, including "Stout-Hearted Man." Welch turned to Dominguez and, with a twinkle in his eye, said, "There *is* a movement that's not just you!"

A year earlier, when Welch had first encountered Dominguez, his activist reputation had preceded him. He "was *really* out," while Welch had recently come out. However, once they met, concerns about his radicalism melted away: "I fell like a brick!" Welch recalls. During the next few months, each time they encountered one another, they danced and talked with a cluster of mutual friends, until they finally hooked up at the Lobby Bar. Once together, they broadened and deepened Delaware's queer rights movement, including by cofounding Rehoboth's first gay and lesbian organization—CAMP Rehoboth.

Between 1980 and 1982, the only queer organization in Delaware was the Gay Student Union.[11] After the demise of United Gays of the Diamond

State, "we needed to create something based in the community that was not associated with the university," explains Dominguez. "Student groups have limited credibility when talking to businesses and legislators." Once settled in their West 28th Street Wilmington home, the couple launched GLAD in 1982.

Most of the board members were from the original student group at the university. Many were Jewish or women. Members included former Diamond State founder Marshall Gealt; May Barrows, a former lesbian coffeehouse regular and women's movement activist, with her partner, Lucky; and Denise and her partner, Shawna, who continued to remain in the closet. Denise's expertise was logistics, keeping track of GLAD's mailing list on 3×5 cards. Barrows organized many of the social activities and was involved in rap groups. Gealt and Barrows were the group's nonconfrontational public faces. Dominguez explains that they "were more 'acceptable'; they weren't of color." The price these pioneer activists paid was sometimes heavy. Gealt was fired from his job. Shawna and Denise were forced to move from their apartment because of neighbors' harassment. Dominguez and Welch routinely received offensive late-night phone calls and bore the brunt of criticism from closeted or bar-oriented homosexuals.

GLAD created low-profile social spaces, such as monthly potlucks, skating night at a local roller disco, and cruising on a riverboat. Dominguez and Welch introduced themselves to local, county, and state politicians and spoke at college classes. They also developed "consciousness-raising groups" and specific questions to prompt weekly discussions. A gay hotline operated out of their basement. Although phone counselors provided basic networking information and psychological triage, they lacked the array of professional counseling necessary. Therefore, a major responsibility of GLAD's Health Committee was finding counselors, addiction counselors, and physicians "who were safe to refer [to] somebody."

This committee also worked on "broader issues," Welch emphasizes, "to make sure that health issues were pushed because of poor healthcare for lesbians in Delaware." Legal services were also needed. In the fall of 1980, a Delaware family court judge had awarded custody to a Newark lesbian mother whose grandparents had sought custody of her five-year-old daughter. This homosexual custody case was the first in the state, although other judges, including in neighboring New Jersey and Pennsylvania, had ruled affirmatively on this issue.

In 1983, Dominguez resigned his university job and, in September, the couple leased a two-story building on East 7th Street. The first floor became a bookstore, the Hen's Tooth. A commercial venture with a political venue, it was inspired by the late Harvey Milk's camera shop—"a way of organizing the community." Dominguez spells it out: "Walking into that space didn't automatically brand you as queer." Also, it was in an area that attracted unorthodox customers and was familiar to locals. Nearby were a comic bookstore, a rockabilly bar with alternative music, and two gay bars, Renaissance and Stella's.

Like James Robert Vane a decade earlier, they were greeted by homosexual apathy or animosity. Dominguez recalls, "I don't know how many times at the bar, Jim or I would get 'Tone it down, guys!'" This "tension," he says, was created because "we were 'making it harder for them' by being out . . . harder to fly underneath the radar."

Unlike Newark or Wilmington, Southern Delaware was "even more conservative, even more closeted." Consequently, the first attempt to organize in Rehoboth, at Renegade in October 1982, was unsuccessful. One of the few interested locals was Billy, a hairdresser: "Everybody knew he was queer. He drove a big old pickup truck" with "a big, bright pink parasol" in the gun rack. Many at Renegade that evening ignored them or questioned the need for activism. It was like "I don't want to think about anything serious right now," recalls Dominguez. Welch concurs: "People went to Rehoboth for vacation"; those who lived in the area "didn't want to have an organization because the locals were afraid."

BEING NOMADS

Outside Newark's Lobby Bar, just one place in Delaware was hospitable to GLAD's political and fundraising efforts: the Nomad Village.[12] "Jimmy Short was one of the first persons we ever talked to there," recollects Dominguez. Like nomads, GLAD activists visited this North Bethany Beach bar and had "some good chats" with Short before inquiring about hosting an event. "He didn't get involved with the group," notes Dominguez, "but didn't mind if we started with a little political pitch."

Short had worked at the Nomad for nearly twenty years, since convincing the more closeted Randall Godwin to turn one side of the establishment gay in the early 1960s. The two made an odd pair. Short hailed from a Georgetown banker's family, loved to chitchat, and, despite his arrest and imprisonment in 1961 for sodomy, seemed to always have a smile. Godwin hailed from a wealthier and larger family based in Roxana, in the southernmost part of the state. Often cited in the society section of the *Delmarva*

News, the family owned hotels, an auto dealership, a lumber company, and a real estate firm. Valedictorian of his high school class of 1943, he married Betty Jean Dukes from the same town sixteen years later; her mother was vice president of the Godwins' lumber company.

Being "from one of the old families," observes Thompson, Godwin "had to live that kind of lie." Michael Decker, who first discovered the Nomad in 1970 at age nineteen, confirms Godwin's sexual orientation: "One year, he had a contest, Mr. Right. He was looking for a boyfriend. You would submit applications and photos. If you were Mr. Right, you got a convertible and lived with him. It was pretty bizarre."

Short was Decker's "entrée into the adult gay world." When he entered for the first time, "there was a little guard at the door." To the right was the entrance to "the Other Room." After paying for his membership, the wide-eyed youth passed through: "The walls all had velvet paintings of Arabs on stallions and Elvis." On any weekday evening, "it was mostly empty. That was when you really met the locals." Decker remembers a mix of "fishermen, fishing captains—and lowlifes." There, too, was the local police chief, "a big bear of a man and a real cuddly guy" who arrived promptly at 11:00 P.M. each night. With just a handful of customers, Decker hung out at the bar with Short, who "always had interesting things to chat about." On weekends, the atmosphere was entirely different, as hundreds of folks from nearby Rehoboth and Coastal Virginia to Northern Delaware and DC entered the Other Room.

As a queer youth, Decker found it "a fun social time. I think it had to do with people developing a gay community and a sense of what being gay was going to be." In contrast, the older Thompson explains that affluent Rehoboth homosexuals "didn't go out to the bars. They went out early in the evening. Back then, it was the house parties . . . where they would display their wealth." He also was not particularly fond of Short, whom he considered "a dirty old man."

For Short, a former high school teacher, "the great tragedy of his life was being caught having sex," judges Decker. "They tried to pressure him to identify other gay people. He refused. Most of his friends refused. But he was betrayed by some." Although Short was open about his incarceration and sodomy conviction, he seldom disclosed the details of what he termed "the incident."

On March 6, 1961, patrolmen stopped a teenager wandering along Newark's East Main Street at 3:00 A.M. After questioning, the adolescent disclosed that he had just exited the nearby apartment of thirty-seven-year-old Vance Middleton, with whom he had engaged in "an immoral act." Presenting a court order, investigators seized thousands of male photographs, dozens of films, photographic equipment, and a diary from Middleton's apartment. After his interrogation, police then obtained a search warrant for Short's apartment, five blocks from the Middleton residence, leading to the thirty-one-year-old's arrest on charges of sixty-three morals counts.

Other suspects were rounded up, removed from their jobs without notice to their employers, and filmed during interrogations. Although the newspapers reported that many more men were under investigation, eighteen people ages sixteen or over, including eleven juveniles, were arrested. Among those not arrested were a University of Delaware history professor who fled to France, a state trooper, and, allegedly, a son of the sitting governor. Ultimately, just two men, Middleton and Short, were imprisoned. Short was released in mid-1963. His scandalized Georgetown family exiled him to Rehoboth, where he lived in a cramped converted garage apartment behind the family's huge Norfolk Street home.

After transforming the Nomad into a queer space, Short and Godwin—with Frederick Baker and Clarence Arnold—turned Rehoboth's old Stokes Hotel, at 1st and Brooklyn Streets, into a gay speakeasy. In the early 1970s, the Sandcastle "was a completely clandestine affair," according to Decker. It did not advertise, and it wasn't listed in gay guides. It "had this little porthole in the door, which had a fence over it. You'd knock, and this little gate would open. They'd look through. If you had a password and a membership card, they'd let you come in." Members entered a large open area with dilapidated furnishings and a bartender who offered mixers for the alcohol they brought. The two upper floors had a bathhouse format, with tiny rooms where "lecherous men" dwelt. And "like all gay bars here, it burned down." In October 1975, an arsonist's work left only the skeleton of the building.

By the early 1980s, with the Boathouse and Renegade open, the customer base for the Nomad had dwindled. Decker reports that Nomad folks were "somewhat embittered; they felt gays were fickle." So, as Short and Godwin got to know GLAD and saw that it attracted customers to the "dying bar," Dominguez says that his group's presence expanded. He was soon given "free rein in coming up with themes and decorating," with the owner donating the night's cover.

One of GLAD's first Saturday night events was on Memorial Day weekend in 1984, featuring "Music by Sharone," Sharon Kanter. She recounts being asked to DJ by Barrows's partner: "It got Nomad people's attention, since most people were going to Renegade." The events were so successful that Kanter passed out flyers on the beaches, promoting women's dances at the Nomad.

"Perhaps," speculates Dominguez, "because of the competition with the Nomad or the shame that a smaller and less wealthy bar was willing" to do fundraisers and to collect money for queer organizations, Renegade opened its doors wider to GLAD—and to women. Meanwhile, he and his nomadic band of GLAD activists continued to approach gay bars and gay-owned businesses for support. "Until the gay movement is in Dagsboro, Blades, and Duck Creek," Dominguez told a reporter, "people are not to going to recognize that we're a part of every American community."

7

BLOOD MOON

It was a determined effort to not feel so helpless in the wake of
the destruction that AIDS was having in our lives. I often
wondered since then what our world would be like if there was
no AIDS.

—**Murray Archibald,** *The Love Dream*

During eighteen months of working at the Back Porch Café, Victor Pisapia and Joyce Felton often spoke about developing a new type of restaurant in Rehoboth.[1] Felton explains:

People were coming from DC, Philadelphia, Baltimore, and they had
gay bars in their towns. So, when they would come to *their* beach,
that's what they wanted. I'd have dinner with these guys, and I would
see them at the Back Porch when they would come to the bar. . . . But
it was not designed and it was not promoted to be that kind of spot.

The pair earnestly started looking for a location after Labor Day weekend in 1980. A Victorian beach house was available on commercially desolate Baltimore Avenue. Pisapia, who had been adamant about this location,
now faced the reality of a large mortgage payment with a high interest rate.
He "was sitting on the fence," Felton says. "The deciding factor was my mother." Blanche told the pair, "What's the worst that can fucking happen? Sell
it! Go for it! Be passionate! You got a great concept!" Felton borrowed money
from her parents, and Pisapia sold his interest in the Back Porch along with
his car to purchase what would soon become the legendary Blue Moon.
Pisapia and Felton were champions of Rehoboth haute cuisine, along
with Nancy Wolfe, whose Chez la Mer, specializing in French country cui-

Joyce Felton and
Victor Pisapia, ca.
1987. (Courtesy of Victor
Pisapia and Jim Bahr.)

sine, had opened a year earlier on the opposite side of Rehoboth Avenue.
Together, the trio challenged beach town palates that generations of tourists had dulled by stuffing their mouths with fried fish and crab imperial,
pizza and Nic-o-bolis, cheesesteaks and salty vinegar fries. "We wanted to
be the beautiful restaurant with beautiful people," says Pisapia. "We wanted to open a kind of urbane place with a chic, hip atmosphere," Felton told
Letters readers. Longtime food critic Bob Yesbek describes their dream as a
"low-key, über frou-frou eatery with candles flickering on darkened walls
alongside a quiet bar with just a hint of soft background music." In 2004,
the *New York Times* christened the Blue Moon the "grande dame of Rehoboth's gay businesses."

The Blue Moon, though, would be far from low-key. "We didn't realize
the shitstorm that was going to ensue," Felton concedes.

JOYCE'S STORY

Felton grew up "in the fifties, where the norm was for women to wear
aprons and be housekeepers. That is *not* what happened in our household."[2]
She was attentive to "people who have less and of women's rights." Her role

model—"the first feminist I ever met"—was her mother. Blanche had wanted to go to medical school, "but there were no spots for women." Instead, she earned a double Ph.D. in marine biology and zoology, becoming a tenured CUNY professor. "She was a badass, a warrior for the rights of the underdog," Felton admiringly portrays.

The Felton family was a reformed Jewish household in Queens. She attended a Jewish primary school and was bat mitzvahed. She then chose to attend Bayside, where she organized the first Students for a Democratic Society (SDS) high school chapter in the country. Felton often protested at antiwar and women's rights demonstrations—and spent a lot of time barefoot and braless in the Village, "picking up markers and guides" while being "surrounded by people who lived, dressed, thought, and espoused what I fervently believed."

Seeking "somewhere where I was the voice that hadn't been heard," Felton enrolled at the University of South Carolina "to be an annoyance, a perpetrator, an instigator." During the late 1960s, "I felt like a stranger in a strange land." Her dorm mate had never met a Jewish person, and Felton witnessed the Black Student Union burning the Confederate flag on the quadrangle. Rather than studiously attend classes, she mostly hung out at the infamous counterculture coffeehouse the UFO, frequented by sandal-wearing hippies and war-weary Fort Jackson soldiers. "There were constant meetings at the UFO," she remembers. "It was Insurrection 101," and Felton was a "foot soldier." Traveling throughout the Palmetto State to organize, demonstrate, and agitate, she found little support for organizing campus SDS chapters. However, she abetted the antiwar movement by supporting shipments of marijuana from Vietnam in GIs' stereo speakers and opening her first business, Big Mama's Headshop and Holding Company. Predictably, two years later, this poster girl for the infamous Yankee carpetbagging troublemaker was not so politely asked to exit the university—and the state.

One day, while Felton was hitchhiking, a hippie driving a beat-up van stopped. He was from North Carolina. Felton decided to join him and later married him. In the early 1970s, Charlotte was far from the sophisticated banking center into which it metastasized. The town included a little Haight-Ashbury pocket, known as Spirit Square, and a variety of feminist, hippie, and queer communes in the area: "I was mentored by some guys from Philly. They had a high-end sandwich shop with a wine store attached." There, she learned the restaurant business. Eventually, Felton and a lesbian friend renovated a downtown Baptist church that had "a beautiful rotunda with stained glass busted out and pigeons roosting," transforming it into a vegetarian restaurant, the Black Cat Café. Drumming circles and yoga sessions occurred when the mural-laden dining room was not in use. After a serious accident, Felton divested herself from the restaurant and her husband, returning to New York City in 1978.

A LINE IN THE SAND

Opening night on Memorial Day in 1981 was rainy.[3] The Blue Moon's maître d', dressed in a classy leather outfit, greeted reservations-only guests. Felton, dressed in an elegantly hip manner, acknowledged guests as they passed luscious floral arrangements. Pisapia worked in the kitchen, preparing nouvelle cuisine dishes from his mostly French-Japanese menu.

The renovated 1907 Sears craftsman house had "banquette seating, interesting lighting, [and] quilted fabric" from a New York designer. Felton wanted "the design to match the food. So, there was an enhanced artistic palate with an enhanced culinary palate." Felton adds, "It looked like an art gallery in addition to a restaurant." There were 1940s-styled, fabulous-looking Manhattan waiters wearing khaki shorts, sporting blue leather ties, and showing off hair coifed by DC stylists. The atmosphere was a "combo of professionalism and sexiness." The intimate restaurant was "jazzy, dark, with seamless service of really interesting food and a conviviality."

Jack Ackerman and his longtime companion, Alan Anderson, a Maryland assistant superintendent of schools, had long summered in Provincetown. They began coming to Rehoboth in 1970. It was "pretty dead" aside from the Nomad in Bethany Beach and Joss, a gift shop on the first block of Baltimore Avenue. At decade's end, the only new gay-related businesses were the Back Porch Café, Ed Conroy's and Roy Anderson's Wooden Indian, June and Sid Sennabaum's Boathouse, and Herbert Koerber's Paradise Inn.

During the late spring of 1981, change was in the air; "word had gotten out," as anticipation rippled through closeted gay circles. Knowing that it was going to be a full house, Ackerman entered with Anderson the weekend before to see what "everyone was talking about." When the couple dropped in, Felton was "setting up the tables with white tablecloths and flowers. Her waitstaff was flitting around; flirting was more apt!"

Ackerman considered them lucky "to get in" for the Moon's Memorial Day debut: "It was like a Broadway opening" with "a *very* mixed dinner crowd. There were queens screaming 'Mary' at each other" along with "refined diners. It was kind of like a 'We're in and you're out' thing. It was a gay status thing. It wasn't like Renegade." Felton and Pisapia "made an investment in a community that made an investment ten-fold in us" as the Moon "became the hub, *the* spot." She continues, "People requested certain tables; they wanted to be seen." On Friday evenings, "we were like a magnet or a Mecca."

Felton also points out that "not only gay men and women but Jews from North Shores wanted something cool and hip. They were building multi-million-dollar houses, and they didn't want to go to Snappy's." Additionally, a new breed of tourist "wanted a replication of what they were used to in city dining, but with a beach feel." Old Rehoboth, too, had lot of "hidden money" and "was very inbred," according to Pisapia. "When they saw something new like that, they all brought their friends."

One person attracted to this nascent culinary gay Mecca was a young chemist. Transplanted from Louisiana to work for DuPont, Chris Yochim had frequented Atlantic City during his first summer in Delaware. In 1979, he found New York Avenue, a "place to throw a boa around your Adam's apple and slip your man paws into a pair of stilettos," crowded with "New York and Philadelphia people." It had become a favorite gay destination after the homophobic "clampdown" in Cape May.

Glen Thompson, who had been visiting Atlantic City for years, remembers "the heyday for the gay scene" from the late 1960s through 1980. It was a "very decadent place—ahead of its time for decadence!" Prior to this time, "gays were not very welcomed." He recalls Louise Mack's Entertainer's Club, located in an unimposing house on Snake Alley just off New York Avenue, which had been a homosexual haunt since Prohibition. Dinner jackets and ties were required after 6 P.M., no-touching rules were enforced, and cross-dressing men entertained. When Mack, a onetime Ziegfeld girl, died, Thompson remembers a "funeral line miles long." Vals opened in the mid-1960s after a legal challenge to the no-touching/no-dancing ordinance. Atlantic City native John Schultz, however, "really started the movement of gay people" visiting. A hard-headed businessman, he launched the Lark, a happy-hour bar off the boardwalk, and then added a bevy of bars, clubs—and a hotel. Without him, "the gay scene would never have happened," Thompson credits. During the 1970s, New York Avenue was bustling; "at 2 A.M., you couldn't drive a car down it," recollects Schultz, as mostly gay men departed Dirty Edna's, Val's, M&M, or the grande dame Entertainer's Club for other shows or bed at the hundred-room Chester Inn. Thompson even operated a club, Bellevue, in the mid-1970s.

By the end of the decade, it was "blown out by gambling," observes Bryant Simon, author of *Boardwalk of Dreams*. The first casino hotels opened in 1978, resulting in bulldozed buildings, exorbitant lease rates, and soaring prices. This development "drove gays away," many of whom, says musician Michael Decker, ended up in Rehoboth.

Yochim recalls that Atlantic City "was really seedy" and "wasn't as friendly as Rehoboth." The next season, he summered in Rehoboth, becoming a Moon regular throughout the 1980s. He vividly remembers happy hour, "where everyone would meet and have a drink or two. You could walk to dinner and find out what parties were being held at various houses." Yochim continues, "It was a way to kick-start the weekend. By six o'clock, the place would be packed." On Saturday night, "we might go to the Moon's happy hour, but then everybody would get into the car and go out to Renegade."

The Moon "was a fun place," Yochim reminisces. He tells the story of a customer who "tried to leave a tip of loose change. The bartender took it. 'Shrapnel!' He just threw it on the floor. 'We *don't* take shrapnel at this bar!'" Yochim also "liked the feeling of community." Announcements were placed in the restaurant, and Felton routinely fielded weekday phone calls: "What's going on?" "Who's doing what?" "Get me a reservation." She underscores that the Moon "wasn't behind fences or plate-glass windows; it was a statement. It raised the hackles of a lot of people who didn't want us to be seen." In short, "it was not a restaurant but part of a movement. It was having a voice in a town where there were no rainbow flags flapping in the breeze."

The Moon was a home for artists and art lovers, for epicureans and bon vivants, for talented performers and their aficionados, for raconteurs and schmoozers, for gays and straights, for would-be entrepreneurs and fledgling activists. And, as Yochim points out, Felton was "the center of attention." Like Liza Minnelli in *Cabaret*, "she was always incredibly dressed, fashion-forward, and fashionable." She "enjoyed meeting people and getting to know them, making everyone feel welcome," says Yochim. "She absolutely cared about the community."

However, for the community of Old Rehoboth, the Blue Moon was a line in the sand. In August 1981, John Hughes was overwhelmingly elected mayor, supported by the powerful Rehoboth Beach Homeowners Association. He promised law and order, pledged planned growth, and championed family values: "We call ourselves a family resort, but silently watch the vast population of homosexuals flourish within our midst; a population which I feel is antithetical to the term 'family resort.'"

Within a month of assuming office, the mayor summoned Felton and Pisapia to his wood-paneled office overlooking Rehoboth Avenue. "Pilgrims," from a William Blake etching of Chaucer's *Canterbury Tales*, stared down at the pair. Hughes, who had been a town commissioner for six years, held out a newspaper article about the Blue Moon, "describing what he called 'gay food' in Rehoboth."

In a brash New Yorker style, Felton queried, "What exactly makes food gay?"

At first muted by anger and astonishment, Pisapia trailed, "We don't have gay swordfish."

"Are the rolls gay? What does that mean?" Felton pressed.

"It's your clientele!" the six-foot-six Hughes thundered. "There's no way this town wants a gay restaurant!"

"We are creating an inclusive, welcoming, hip, challenging, awesome restaurant. All are welcome," she countered.

The meeting was brief, but to the point: Hughes "laid the gauntlet down," recalls Felton.

The Moon's owners were broadsided. Pisapia admits, "We were really so busy with the restaurant [that] we really didn't deal with the politics too much"—until then. "We were pretty naïve [to not anticipate] that there would be such resistance," Felton confirms. "I really didn't have any idea that it would be such a contentious, us-versus-them" situation. "We didn't realize that this might be a preamble to some difficult times ahead." It was.

NEIGHBORS

Rehoboth's emerging gay scene was visible to all, alluring to many, and troubling to some.[4] The town's closeted era of a distant beach presence, same-sex summer-cottage roommates, private dinner parties, and discrete visits to distant bars was ending. The age of dance clubs and house parties, golf shirts and ripped black tights, amyl nitrates and cocaine—bracketed by the twin cataclysms of the Moral Majority and AIDS—was lapping onto the shores of this resort town.

This era marked Rehoboth's visible transformation into a nascent *gay* family resort. Three months after the Moon's opening, the state's Sunday newspaper headlined, "Gays Have Found a Refuge in Resort Town Atmosphere." This less-than-flattering portrayal warned that "male homosexuals have become noticeable." It was the kind of publicity that many locals, including long-standing gay and lesbian residents maintaining "a low profile [and] claim[ing] to understand the conservative attitudes," found gauche.

As visibility increased, so did harassment. A Blue Moon waiter, beaten twice on the same night, was told by his attackers that they "wanted to kill a faggot." Murray Archibald recalls, "It was not unusual for cars to drive up and down Baltimore Avenue and throw things at the Moon or to scream things to people on the street." Volunteering that neither he nor Lloyd "are flamboyant gays," Dolph Spain recalls the couple walking to the Moon and crossing the intersection, "when someone threw a Coke in my face." He began carrying "a rock in my hand, as I felt that much anxiety." Pisapia acknowledges, "There was a lot more homophobia that we didn't realize existed." At Renegade, four youth rushed into the bar, looking for a fight, and a hot-rodding teen nearly ran down a security guard. Roving pickup trucks of young men wielding baseball bats and hate-inspired spray-painting graffiti artists were wearisome, if not common. Wayne Hodge, who was doing Renegade's books, remembers that "they would arrive with shotguns and shoot at the property." He claims that drag queen Sophie Tucker "got on the roof and started firing back." Hodge adds, "They never fired at the bar again!"

In spite of or oblivious to these problems, a growing number of lesbians and gay men journeyed to Rehoboth. One regular visitor reminisces, "My first impression was that it was a fantasy land, not anything like the gay clubs or social life in Baltimore." As proprietors of the social hub, if not the command post for an emerging queer community, the Moon's owners worked quietly with town officials. "All Rehoboth Police really did was put out parking meter tickets, but then all of a sudden, they have a town that is erupting with all kinds of homophobia," explains Pisapia. He and Felton visited Chief Harry Maichle Jr. "to figure out how to handle certain things which were happening." They also knew, according to Felton, that "the horse [wa]s out of the barn" and that Hughes "wasn't quite aware of the reality of what was going on in his town, which was no longer 'his' town."

"Will the waves of fashion sweep over Rehoboth?" asked a *Blade* reporter. Although "it's hard to see a seed ground for the sort of Gay-linked development that dominates the other [East Coast gay] resorts," the writer continued, "it will be some time before the town becomes another Fire Island, if it ever develops." Yet, the fear of a changing Rehoboth—flanked by cruisy dunes to the north, a queer disco complex at its western doorstep, a mostly gay club overhanging Rehoboth Bay to its south, and now a bad Moon arising within its business district—intruded on many an Old Rehoboth cocktail party and bridge game. Admitting that he could "deal better when it's in the closet," one Realtor whispered to a reporter, "If they find out gays are interested in buying property next door, they do everything they can to either buy the house themselves or find another buyer."

Although the political landscape was changing, Felton and Pisapia planned to open an outside bar for their second season. This move required permits and official approvals. After the confrontation with Hughes, "it was more difficult for us to get things done. We had to play by every single rule, and sometimes those rules changed." Fallacious complaints from neighbors and competitors were so numerous that Felton was on a first-name basis with every inspector. Felton became "aware of where people's allegiances lay and their feelings, thoughts, and beliefs pretty quickly."

Neighbors Bertha and Ray Pusey enjoyed their summer home catercorner to the Moon. Yochim, like other Moon regulars, was familiar with the Puseys peering at the nightly scene from their second-floor screen porch: "You could see them. They were *always* there." He remembers "on more than one occasion, the police coming because of noise complaints. All it was was people coming and going from the Blue Moon, laughing and having a good time. From their perspective, it was disturbing."

Further, "the gay competition made things even more difficult." According to Felton, the Puseys "collaborated with the competition of ours. He [Thompson] was promoting them to be complainants." Thompson denies this accusation. Asked about the reported "bad blood" between the Puseys and the Blue Moon, he swears, "No! Never!" Sometimes, he'd visit the Puseys, and "we would sit on that screen porch and look over at the Blue Moon. Bertha would love to watch the gay boys. And her mother absolutely adored it!"

At the town level, City Manager Greg Ferrese "did all their dirty work," alleges Felton. She was less aware of his ties to Thompson, who underscores that "Ferrese had very unpleasant relations with Joyce Felton." When there were concerns and "he wasn't quite sure what to do, he would call *me*," according to Thompson.

Felton also faced resistance from or quarreled with some local gay men who, similar to Thompson, chafed at her strident feminism. One of those was Koerber, the owner of Paradise Inn, which sat nearly behind the Blue Moon. Keith Fitzgerald, who had worked with Felton at the Back Porch, also was friends with Koerber. He remembers the feud between the pair: "It started because he didn't like women, but it kept going on." One Moon happy-hour regular also remembers Felton chatting about "those Paradise guys." She considered them "really low class . . . too promiscuous." Felton disagrees, saying that it was "hard for me to judge someone else when stones are being thrown at me." Granting that Koerber "wasn't warm and fuzzy," she admits, "We didn't bond, but I give him a lot of credit for being a trailblazer. He was pretty fearless, and he wouldn't take no for an answer."

Like Koerber, the Moon's owners wouldn't back down. In their second year of operation, the new street-side, barrel-vaulted patio bar was offering, in Felton's words, "strong, good-looking drinks served by strong, good-looking people." Pisapia vividly remembers, "It was a visual experience. People would drive by and gawk. Cars would stop. It was like, 'Oh my God! What's going on there?'"

THE RIVE GAUCHE OF THE AVENUE

There was *always* something going on at the Moon.[5] "It was *never* just a restaurant," asserts Pisapia, who freely borrowed from French cuisine, and Felton, who modeled the bohemianism of Paris's Left Bank. Artwork from DC, Philadelphia, and New York along with that of Delaware artists rotated every three or four weeks. Musicians performed on the back deck, including Libby York, who had traded her interest in the Back Porch for a Manhattan jazz-singing career. Its theme parties were "outrageous. People *had* to come."

A jewel in the grande dame's crown was the 1983 retrospective of Man Ray's photography. Part of the Montparnasse set of artists, the surrealist photographer and painter portrayed such contemporaries as Salvador Dalí, Jean Cocteau, Pablo Picasso, Gertrude Stein, and James Joyce. When he died, in 1976, his muse of thirty years, Juliet Man Ray, a dance student of Martha Graham and an artist in her own right, assumed responsibility for his works. She decided that the first American retrospective would be at the Blue Moon and that she would trek to Rehoboth for a summer weekend.

"The art community was so pissed off that our little restaurant had the first retrospective of Man Ray," Pisapia touts. "That was just unheard of." Her conditions for attending the premier were "two blond gorgeous men at my side at all times, a house with a pool, and a bottle of Jack Daniels." Juliet, then in her early seventies, arrived on premier night in a Rolls-Royce Silver Shadow. Under a sky alit by klieg lights, she entered the Moon, wearing a stylish caftan and designer hosiery patterned with eyeballs.

Felton and Pisapia also recruited potential businesspeople and supported those new businesses. They believed, as Felton explains, that doing so would lead to "more reason to come down here: more boutique shopping, more interesting art galleries, more fine dining restaurants." On visits to

DC, they "talked to a few people and got them to open up design shops and clothing shops," details Pisapia. "We were re-creating the town" and "embraced everybody." He proudly claims, "We never had a Glen Thompson kind of attitude: I will win it all. Fuck all of you."

During the 1980s, several queer-owned or -friendly restaurants opened—the Palms, Astral Plane, La La Land, Square One, and Sydney's. Wilmington's *Morning News*, headlining "Rehoboth's Growing Gay Population," estimated fifteen gay-owned businesses. Delaware's leading conservative columnist, Bill Frank, queried his morning readers, "Are the gays in Rehoboth troubling you?" Once a sleepy side street, The Avenue had transformed into a commercial destination. Flanking the Moon were clothing and jewelry stores, a bakery, and an art gallery along with Terry Plowman's Front Page restaurant and Pat Whittier and Pegi Fuller's six-room Paper Nautilus guesthouse across the street.

Farther down The Avenue, a former rooming house and courtyard had been converted into eight specialty shops, ranging from Crysti's, selling women's apparel, to Elephant's Trunk, offering finely crafted toys. On the other side, toward 2nd Street, was Rehoboth Muse, a Victorian alleyway of boutique emporia partly owned by town commissioner Norman Sugrue. Here, Secrets on the Beach showcased Crazy Shirts of Hawaii. Owner Sharon Kanter—a lesbian, like many of these pioneer entrepreneurs—sometimes hosted champagne parties. Yet she dreaded visits from the lumbering Sugrue, issuing stern warnings about risqué underwear displayed in her window, or when her deceptively diminutive neighbor Bertha Pusey brought coffee served with bitterness.

Around the 1st Street and 2nd Street corners were other queer businesses. Owners Bill Sievert and John Theis, who had met at San Francisco's Stud Bar, operated Splash, an upscale casual clothing store, when Sievert wasn't working on his mystery novel set in Rehoboth. There, too, was a lesbian-owned clothing store, Norma Reeves's Whip Stitch. The Tijuana Taxi, a laidback funky Mexican joint, was opened by Pisapia and Felton in 1985. One street south, on Maryland Avenue, Bill Courville and Bob Jerome opened their upscale Rehoboth Guest House. Along Rehoboth Avenue were the End of the Line, showcasing Key West merchandise; Greybeard's of London, a tobacco and gift shop owned by gay DC bookstore pioneers Deacon Maccubbin and Jim Bennett; and, of course, the venerable Back Porch Café, now owned by Keith Fitzgerald, Leo Medisch, and Marilyn Spitz.

"We were great supporters of other people who were opening up establishments that were a step above," Felton says. Although she celebrated "this new feeling of experimentation," there was also "resistance, resistance, resistance." Hodge's boss, Thompson, and his friends, the Puseys, were part of that resistance.

WAYNE'S STORY

Hodge stepped out from a Trailways bus, a sole suitcase in his hand and hair well past his shoulders blowing with the breeze.[6] The drawn-out ride from DC to his summer destination was not uncomfortable. In 1987, along Highway 1, there were no outlet malls, no chain restaurants, no townhomes—just farmers' fields and isolated businesses, including Richard Derrickson's Midway Shopping Center.

On the town's outskirts, along the service road to his left, Hodge spotted Thompson's pale yellow and blue Renegade. He remembers first visiting the dance club and restaurant years earlier with DC friends. They had enjoyed its beachy feel, its dance floor with a low ceiling, and "a dryer hose that went around the back of the bar, with holes punched through with lights in it. It was wonderful!"

The resort town had awoken from its wintery slumber. Along Rehoboth Avenue, traditional commercial establishments, some owned by the town's old guard, were already open: Bob Derrickson's Carlton's Men's Wear, opened in 1960 by his father, State Rep. Harry Derrickson, and his cousin Don's nearby Sandcastle Motel; the Rehoboth Pharmacy, which Gene Nelson had owned since 1966; and the office of Realtor Sugrue at Lingo's, a family name synonymous with Old Rehoboth. There, too, was the incidental car sporting a "Keep Rehoboth a Family Town" bumper sticker. Its advocates, the Rehoboth Beach Homeowners Association and its posse of city officials, were frustrated. The town was flourishing with "people like us," trumpeted the *Washington Blade*.

The twenty-seven-year-old Hodge walked down Rehoboth Avenue with suitcase in hand and strolled into the Palms Restaurant. His eyes first centered on a giant palm and two ceiling lights beaming downward, situated near a huge Chinese urn with a scattering of pink flamingos. Toward the back was a piano bar with a large open-air patio for dancing. One Hawaiian-shirted waiter asked, "Who are you?" Hodge responded, "I'm the new manager."

Weeks earlier, Thompson, sitting in his cramped three-desk office above Badlands, had turned to Hodge and asked, "Do you want to go to the beach for the summer?" Hodge looked up from a spreadsheet. "To do what?"

Organizers of the PRIDE '94 Sponsors' Ball include (*left to right*) Glen Thompson, Doris Vaughan, and Wayne Hodge. (Courtesy of *Cape Gazette*.)

Thompson, with his Doberman, Ripper, resting nearby, explained, "I need someone to manage the restaurant because there's nobody there."

Hodge had been his eyes on the ground for two years. In 1985, he had quit his government job to oversee the books of this gay bar empire. So, when the Palms manager died, Hodge seemed a logical replacement.

He responded, "I've worked in restaurants, but I've never managed one."

Growing up in Portsmouth, as a teenager, Hodge had cooked at seafood restaurants in nearby Norfolk and discovered the seventies' "gay life" at the Oar House and Cue Club, meeting friends the first night. In 1981, he and several drag queen friends rented a U-Haul and moved to the DC area. Hodge landed a job at the Bureau of Public Debt, calculating non-interest payments for treasury securities notes. After his nine-to-five cubicle job, though, he worked the DC scene, barbacking, bartending, waiting on tables, and cooking. Two years later, a month into a job at P Street Station, he first encountered the forty-something Thompson: "The manager came over and said, 'The owner just came in, and he wants one of y'all to wait on him.' . . . He liked the fact that I gave him a check. I didn't just wave it off and serve it to him for free."

Recognizing the growing niche of Rehoboth's upscale dining scene, Thompson opened the Palms in 1985 at the upper end of Rehoboth Avenue.

A reviewer in the *Sunday News Journal* wrote that the restaurant's purple facade "serves as a beacon for the gay community as does the Blue Moon's bold design over Baltimore Avenue."

At the end of the 1987 season, with Renegade's manager leaving, Hodge was asked whether he wanted to stay. "I [was] ready to leave DC." He explains, "AIDS had taken most of my friends. Everyone who I knew from Norfolk was dead." During his first year at Renegade, "I had to take care of the motel, clothing store, and a dance club, plus doing the Palms." Meanwhile, Thompson renovated, raising the dance floor's ceiling and adding a second story. Hodge details:

> Strobe lights were just kind of coming into the whole gay bar scene. We put in the white-and-black checkered floor, like *Saturday Night Fever*. . . . He put a light and sound system mechanism that came through the roof. He had the spin lasers. . . . We put a large bank of mirrors on one side of the bar. He had a 1969 Spitfire hanging from the ceiling.

The Palms was also undergoing a menu "metamorphosis," from food "with a relative lack of flash" to Nouveau French cuisine. Thompson and Hodge also knew that they had "to figure [out] something" to increase bar income because "the guys were going to the Blue Moon." During this era, Felton explains, lesbians "really didn't have *their* place. There really was not a women's bar where they felt comfortable enough." Hodge agrees: "There has always been a separation," particularly at Renegade. Palms then launched lesbian Sunday tea dances at its spacious patio that became popular, especially with the gorgeous twenty-three-year-old Paige Phillips bartending.

PARADISE LOST

In February 1987, thirty-something Courville was at his Mt. Pleasant neighborhood home in DC. He opened the *Washington Blade*, which he read religiously from beginning to end. With a Ph.D. in psychology, Courville enjoyed the classifieds; they lifted his spirits after reading obituaries of gay men and news of meager AIDS funding from Ronald Reagan's administration. Sandwiched between personals and escorts were real estate listings, including a one-inch ad for a guesthouse in Rehoboth Beach.

Courville thought about his youthful days living in New Orleans and working at the Maison de Ville, a small, dusty, red, stucco-painted guesthouse overlooking Toulouse Street. There, Tennessee Williams had once lived while penning *A Streetcar Named Desire*, when not sipping Sazerac cocktails in the garden courtyard. Courville circled the ad and placed it on the kitchen counter for his life partner, Jerome, to read. The couple had met two years earlier while crossing P Street Bridge and had gradually merged their lives. He glanced at the ad.

Jerome, the more cautious of the pair, had grown up in California, attending college in Claremont and later working as a Senate staffer. Like Courville, he had a Ph.D. and traveled throughout the world before their encounter. Unlike him, Jerome had never been to Rehoboth. Courville nudged, "Let's go look at this! We will have a business and an income—and a place to live!"

The next weekend, they crossed the Chesapeake Bridge and drove to Paradise. Rehoboth was mostly shuttered, but Renegade was open at the fringe of town, as was the Blue Moon on The Avenue. Driving one street over, they arrived at 40 Maryland Avenue.

A Realtor, whose lover "Dolly" performed at the Moon, met the couple at the nineteenth-century house. "It was pretty awful," remembers Courville. The Paradise Guest House sign was washed out, and the wide front porch with its handcrafted trellis lusted for paint. The pipes were drained. There was no heat or electricity. Slivers of mirrors were glued on living room walls, a disco ball dangled from the ceiling, and 1930s overstuffed maroon chairs and yard-sale-grade furniture faced an old TV. The scent of stale cigarette smoke lingered.

As they wandered through the twenty-eight rooms, most barely wide enough for a floor mattress with a thin plastic sheet and sometimes an odd-fitting dresser, they eyed stacks of men's magazines and iconic videos (*Boys in the Sand*, *Stryker Force*) along with chests of dildos in every imaginable size. Off the living room, a narrow passageway at a left angle to the main corridor led to the first-floor bedrooms. At the end was a trap door; they didn't venture down. "Seasonal resorts like the Paradise were kind of like bars," Courville explains. "They look great at night—just don't look at them during the day!"

On their drive back, the couple chatted about the venture. Jerome explained to Courville that "if we were going to invest, he needed to run it, so we could learn the business." He knew that his income would cover their personal expenses if Courville was willing to do the day-to-day management. "We were youngish. I don't think we thought about what a massive undertaking it was."

Paradise Guest House with Herbert and Mami.
(Courtesy of Bill Courville and Bob Jerome. Artwork by Pamela Bounds.)

After they purchased the property, just a couple of months remained before the ten-week season would begin on Memorial Day weekend. Those next weeks were frantic: discarding discolored mattresses and sex toys; tearing out faux bedroom walls to restore the original fourteen rooms; buying new white wicker furniture; and upgrading the bathrooms, deck, and kitchen. Everything was thoroughly cleaned. Fresh white paint glistened on the walls, and gray-painted floors replaced piles of tattered, sandy rugs. A local lesbian contractor built sturdy outside showers, replacing a rickety wooden stall connected by a water hose and lined with reflective aluminum foil—designed more for strutting than showering.

With little time to advertise in this pre-Internet era, they did their best to explain the changes to former guests, beginning with its new name: the Rehoboth Guest House. Courville remembers one man calling a few days before, asking whether he could change his check-in to Wednesday. "No, you can't," he said flatly. "You can come Friday at two o'clock, but not one minute sooner!" More importantly, it now was open to lesbians as well as heterosexuals, and there was no smoking.

Reactions from Paradise veterans varied when Courville and Jerome discarded the blue, white, and yellow Paradise Guest House sign and its ethos of male eros. One of the new owners' early supporters was Charlie Allen, who, like Kanter, worked in the Baltimore school system but summered in Rehoboth. However, "some hardcore folks were upset," Jerome recalls. "This used to be a gay male oasis" where men could "be themselves: wearing dresses; walking around naked; having piercings everywhere. They could get out of their suits and live the lives they wanted with people like them." In an understanding tone, he admits, "That's hard to take away." The Paradise had been a safe spot not only for Philadelphia accountants, DC staffers, and Baltimore teachers but college kids enjoying summer break, career-embarking twinks, and closeted locals seeking safe harbor.

SEX ON THE BEACH

Allen was best friends with the German-accented Paradise owner Koerber and his boyfriend, Alvarado Ortiz-Benavides, whom everyone called "Mami," colloquial Spanish for "sweetheart." A gregarious man with fading hair and a reddish beard, Allen often helped Mami with housekeeping and other chores. Mostly, though, the once married gentleman with a Ph.D. from Temple just enjoyed the sexual freedom of Paradise and the camaraderie among male guests. Some returned each year for a week, others visited more frequently for long weekends, and a few stayed for the whole summer. Most guests were younger than Allen's forty-odd years, yet everyone seemed to get along.

Most of Koerber's clientele came from word-of-mouth advertising, although he ran a classified ad in summer issues of the *Washington Blade*: "Friendly guesthouse, close to beaches and bars." One of the very first media stories about gay Rehoboth appeared in the May 1980 issue of this iconic paper. It described Paradise as "utterly comfortable" and quoted thirty-eight-year-old Koerber as saying, "Tell people I can put them up—maybe even give them a discount during the week—but on weekends, after the bars close, my lobby will be packed."

Before he opened Paradise in 1979, there were no openly gay-owned and advertised guesthouses in Rehoboth. The gay speakeasy, Sandcastle, had burned to the ground four years earlier. The grand Pleasant Inn Lodge, hosted by the reclusive, debonair bachelor Peck Pleasanton and his octogenarian mother, Bessie, welcomed an occasional well-behaved "single" gentleman.

Koerber had bought the property from Elwood "Woody" Swarmer, the executive director of the Center for the Handicapped. This DC organization had acquired it a year earlier to bring a handful of clients each week to sum-

mer at the beach; Geriatric Services of Delaware had a similar house in Rehoboth for low-income seniors. However, unlike that service, Swarmer
faced neighborhood objections to the proposed designated handicap parking space and outside ramp. "We don't want that here. This is a family beach
area" was the old guard's view, recalls his niece, Michelle Greenberg. Given
homeowners' concerns, the town denied necessary permitting, leaving little option but to sell. Swarmer vowed, "I'll just recoup the money. They'll
have a house of all gay men there!"

During eight seasons, Paradise evolved, as did Koerber and Mami. The
two were an odd pair. Koerber, who swore like a sailor, was tall and thin,
with longish hair and a handlebar mustache. He was always tanned, even
though his forehead would get beet red, given his German complexion. The
much shorter Mami, whose family lived in Latin America, was soft-spoken
and sweet. Compared to the larger-than-life Koerber, he was less memorable to guests. Jerome describes him as "the German businessman. Mami
was the one-time boy toy." They wintered in Key West, operating a gift shop
and hawking such kitsch souvenirs as black velvet paintings and seashell
coasters.

Koerber monetized every aspect of Paradise, creating a sexual Disney-
land. The bathhouse's cubicle-size rooms could bed upward of fifty registered men. Their friends and friends of their friends often wandered in
throughout the night. "It was shabby and crowded, but we were young and
didn't care," one Paradise regular muses. "It *had* a reputation. It was *our*
party house."

The second floor, with an aroma of poppers and pot, was clothing op-
tional, with some toweled men cruising into the wee hours. Plywood partitions were set between rooms; guests on one side enjoyed a window, while
the other was windowless. Koerber's "summer curtains" served as doors,
allowing air (and guests) to circulate. Those with bedroom windows overlooking the sundeck could extend an invitation to a coconut-lotioned twink
or a weightlifting hunk. "*Everything* went on at the deck and in the windows
and rooms behind it," discloses a frequent guest. There were late Saturday
afternoon happy hours and skit contests. Staging was festive, if not overly
decorative, with a jerry-rigged backstage area for costume changing. A raucous backyard crowd cheered contestants. Overlooking it all were the Puseys, perched on their second-floor screen porch with its bird's-eye view of
the backside of Paradise.

Room rates were low, and backyard camping was just $5 for those
bringing tents. Campers, though, had to be late-night partiers. Before

dawn, visitors sometimes entered from the alley along a little path leading to the unlocked side gate. Nocturnal grunts, gasps, and groans harmonized to sounds of crashing waves. Back then, as one Paradise regular stresses, "Sex wasn't a taboo thing. It was like going to lunch!"

During the day, Koerber was often found in his flip-flops, T-shirt, and khaki shorts, puttering in the garden or tending to his beloved lace-cap hydrangeas. He knew everyone by their first name but didn't allow guests to reserve a specific room. One returning guest remembers phoning Herbert for a reservation and requesting a first-floor room with a door: "'Oh, honey!' Koerber laughed. 'It's just first come, first served.'"

"Herbert [had] turned every square inch of that attic into a bed-sleeping-sex area. It was masterful," Jerome lauds. "Every inch was geared toward pleasure." And, as he and Courville later discovered, there was a leather sling in the "dungeon"—a 10×12 cinder-block room accessible only from the first-floor trap door. Another section of the basement had a small room where staff bunked. Yochim will never forget arriving one weekend when Koerber could offer him only that room. "Oh my god, was that bad! You literally went through the storm cellar door to get in."

Ackerman and his partner routinely stayed at Mary's Rooming House, around the corner at Baltimore and 1st. Mary Joles preferred a closeted clientele, so "there was an undertone of a gay presence." In time, as Koerber walked by, he would entreat the couple to join him for late-afternoon drinks on his wrap-around front porch lined with rocking chairs: "There wasn't any place to have a gay happy hour, so he would invite his guests plus other people, hoping they would spread the word."

Through the mid-1980s, Paradise thrived as a money-making machine: a bathhouse on the beach. As the number of gay-owned upscale shops, restaurants, and bars multiplied along with media attention, more gay men vacationed at Rehoboth and visited Paradise, which was also under more scrutiny. It certainly didn't help Koerber's relationship with the Puseys when he hosted his infamous interracial Black & White weekend parties. He would meet Black gay friends in Philadelphia. They'd cram into Koerber's van, reeking of pot, for a journey to Paradise. After dancing at Renegade, guests returned to party naked in the backyard, often until dawn.

Koerber provided weekend shuttles to Renegade. Around 10:00 P.M., he'd drive up in his blue-and-white sixties van, hop out, and, as a regular recollects, "scream down the hallways: 'Get your asses down here!'" He shuttled guests back and forth, with the last pickup at 1:00 A.M. "I remember Herbert telling people, in his heavy accent, 'If you miss the last bus, you have to walk the fuck home!'" His gruffness masked protectiveness. "He'd warn them he was leaving, and he would even count!" Another frequent visitor remembers Koerber "as the kind of guy you'd call at three o'clock in the morning to say, 'I'm in jail.' And he'd be there."

Reports began surfacing about clusters of young gay men contacting Pneumocystis carinii pneumonia. The *Washington Blade* published a landmark front-page story headlined "Rare, Fatal Pneumonia Hits Gay Men" in July 1981. Koerber began to worry. One guest, living in New York City and volunteering as an AIDS buddy, remembers their porch conversation: "I'm not sure whether or not I'll have a clientele."

Koerber was not the only queer business owner who worried. Reflecting on those early years of AIDS, Felton comments, "What we had thought was going to be a death knell for us as a business, which had a huge gay following, was absolutely the opposite. What people wanted was a place to go to feel safe, have fun, look good, and have a sense of normalcy, promise, and hope"—away from the urban apocalypse.

For many gays, Paradise offered a rare time to be themselves and to enjoy the camaraderie and support from other men at a beach resort. Sadly, for some, time spent there was also a death sentence. Sexual desire and psychological denial coupled with governmental inaction and public apathy fueled the AIDS pandemic.

After the 1986 summer season, Koerber and Mami sojourned, as usual, to Key West. Koerber never returned. "I can remember being surprised to hear that he was ill," laments a longtime patron. "He went quickly; we had no indications he was ill."

Koerber died a week before Courville and Jerome opened their business on Memorial Day weekend. Mami was with him until the end.

BLOOD ON THE SAND

With hope and despair, gays smashed or were pushed out of their closets as AIDS emerged.[7] The first local report of a known Rehoboth case appeared in 1983. Throughout the decade, Sussex County cases increased, although not at the rampaging rate of New York, Philadelphia, Baltimore, and DC. Gay men from those localities increasingly vacationed in Rehoboth, away from daily reminders of the virus.

In 1985, Jim Welch, who a year before had been elected to a leadership position in the Delaware Nurses Association as a "feminist and openly gay male," was appointed director of the state's AIDS Program Office. Within the first four months, he had administered 450 antibody tests, counseled nearly eight hundred people, conducted seventeen training sessions for health workers, and provided fourteen educational programs to at-risk populations.

Delaware provided testing and some financial support for assisting people with AIDS, but it fell upon volunteer efforts to provide boots on the ground. The first local group, PALS, based on a similarly titled organizations, Buddies, in San Francisco, was launched in 1985—the same year Ryan White was expelled from school and Rock Hudson disclosed his diagnosis. Aside from a few poorly attended fundraisers, the group's efforts were very limited. When it disbanded eighteen months later, the number of reported county cases had risen to eighteen.

In its wake, the Sussex County AIDS Committee (SCAC) was organized under the umbrella of GLAD's Delaware Lesbian and Gay Health Advocates (DLGHA), which now had 120 volunteers and a separate AIDS hotline. SCAC would have greater visibility and access to resources, according to DLGHA's newly hired executive director, Ivo Dominguez Jr. Yet he reported that local "response is not great, there's a lack of willingness to come out of the closet." In 1987, the number of officially reported local cases stood at thirty, although Dominguez's estimate was "around 50 or 60"; the state's epidemiologist estimated that three thousand Delawareans were HIV+.

As the number of infections and deaths from the virus multiplied, so did incidents of virulent homophobia. On a Sunday afternoon in July 1987, a thirty-nine-year-old man who worked at the Library of Congress, entered Beebe Hospital, bleeding from his foot and accompanied by three friends. Orthopedic surgeon Robert F. Spicer, with thirty years of experience, was on duty. Suspecting that the victim was homosexual, given his effeminate "demeanor" and friends' gay-themed T-shirts, Spicer gruffly inquired whether the injured had been tested for the virus, repeatedly asking about any "ailments." Diagnosing a severed tendon that required emergency surgery, Spicer was "uncomfortable with what [he] perceived as a risk to [himself] and the hospital." Three hours later, a medical helicopter airlifted the patient to George Washington University Hospital. There, another orthopedic surgeon concluded that the tendon was not severed. Local activist Keith Lewis informed Wilmington's *Morning News*: "This isn't an isolated incident."

In mid-1987, the state's AIDS Advocacy Task Force completed its draft report on recommended AIDS policy for the legislative assembly. To Dominguez's dismay, much of what he had written was deleted, castigated as "preachy" and "opinionated," including Blacks' "brutal histories of neglect" and inadequate HIV information and care, nonexistent educational materials in Spanish, presumptions that "AIDS is caused by homosexual sex or too much sex," and the belief that "'good women' aren't having sex" outside heterosexual marriages. Nevertheless, the "cleaned-up version," Dominguez conceded, still "contain[ed] more than the state [wa]s usually used to publishing."

As in most places, there were reactionary responses. Rehoboth's pharmacist and former town commissioner, Nelson, shrugged, "Maybe AIDS is just part of the grand scheme of things; we haven't had a war for forty years." House Speaker Bradford Barnes blasted gay bars in Rehoboth as "East Coast distributors of AIDS," promising to reinstate the sodomy statute. William Oberle, the house majority leader, derided "the owners as the real prostitutes in this system," demanding that the Department of Health investigate businesses encouraging homosexual activities at bars. Thompson, who had reluctantly opened Renegade to GLAD years earlier, vowed, "The gay community is ready to fight."

PART III

THE STRAND

That's the place for fun and noise,
All among the girls and boys
Let's all go down the strand
—**Harry Castling** and **C. W. Murphy**, "Let's All Go Down the Strand"

I n the fall of 1987—as Wayne Hodge assumed managership of Renegade, as Glen Thompson was celebrating his fourth year with his lover Richard Verzier, as Steve Elkins and Murray Archibald were living in New York, as Ivo Dominguez Jr. and Jim Welch were renovating their Griffin Gay Community Center in Wilmington, as Sharon Kanter shut down her seasonal shop and returned to Baltimore, as Bill Courville and Bob Jerome completed their first season at the Rehoboth Inn, and as Libby York was singing at intimate New York jazz clubs—Joyce Felton and Victor Pisapia realized an opportunity to fulfill their dream of a New York–style nightclub in the heart of Rehoboth. "It was like," as Bob Dylan lyricizes, "the stillness in the wind before the hurricane began."

SMALL-TOWN FOLLIES

Since the opening of the Blue Moon in 1981 and the subsequent launch of their hip Tijuana Taxi four years later, Felton and Pisapia had been doing business with Lorens W. "Bill" Larsen Sr.[1] He operated Arctic Ice at the rear of his eighteen-thousand-square-foot building on Rehoboth Avenue, just steps from their restaurants. Built in 1931, this structure was Rehoboth's volunteer fire station, with the street level housing fire trucks along with four bowling lanes and an upstairs area for community dances, plays, and dinners. During World War II, it lodged GIs stationed at the beaches. When Larsen's father, Ejner, purchased the property in 1945, he used the downstairs for an auto shop while his three sons, including Bill, converted the upstairs into the Colony Club Skating Rink. In 1957, Rehoboth Bowling Lanes, which included pool tables and pinball games, replaced the auto shop. For decades, Larsen provided free skating lessons to children and was also known for offering a caring ear to neighbors' problems.

Just a block and a half from the beach, this historic building was part of Rehoboth's controversial entertainment tradition that had begun with illegal dancing, ten-pin bowling, and card-playing a century earlier. During the first few decades of the 1900s, on the same side of the street stood the Del-Reho Motion Picture Hall, the Royal Roller Rink, and the Silver Dollar Dance Hall, "the social center of Rehoboth Beach [where] long-gowned ladies and sport-jacketed men wearing ties would gather." These businesses were owned by Charles Horn Sr., whose dance hall pavilion on the beach had washed out to sea in the Great Storm of 1914.

Evelyn Thoroughgood remembers dancing away the summer of 1945 at the Del Reho. The twenty-four-year-old was dating the band's drummer, who was from Mississippi. One night, "a colored waiter . . . with a beautiful voice" was "recruited to sing." During a break, Thoroughgood's exasperated boyfriend whispered into her ear, "If my parents knew I was playing for *that* man to sing!" However, she confesses, "We were segregated," too. She recalls the Blue Hen Theater on Rehoboth Avenue, where she once ushered: "One side went up to the White balcony and one side went up to the Colored balcony," with a curtain "hanging down the middle that separated them." It was later sold by Horn's son to the entrepreneurial Derrickson family in 1960, which also owned the other two downtown movie theaters.

William Derrickson Sr., who had moved to Rehoboth during the 1930s, operated the Avenue Theater, beginning in 1941. He then bought the downtown Center Theatre, adjacent to Ejner Larsen and sons' skating rink, a few years later. Derrickson closed off a fire exit, complaining about "excessive noise" from the rink. He insisted that Larsen was "paying for protection by police and commissioners." The town promised to monitor the noise by using state-of-the-art sound meters. The families' feud had begun.

Larsen's bowling alley stayed open well past midnight during the summer season, catering to young people briskly moving between it and the Silver Dollar Arcade on the Boardwalk. In the 1950s, with the approval of his father and town elders, the upstairs roller rink doubled as the Surf Club, where teens danced through midnight to "record hops" and boisterous bands from DC, Baltimore, and Philadelphia. After the demise of the Zen Club in 1963, these were the only late-night options for youth. During the 1970s, Larsen's building was still a hub for youthful entertainment into the early-morning hours. Popular music, though, had changed. The record hop had morphed into an underage disco, featuring Top-40 rock 'n' roll with light shows. Yet teenagers continued to parade back and forth from the disco to the arcades. In the early 1980s, the town began a "crackdown" on "disorderly youth," some of whom littered the pathway with beer cans or trailed a faint odor of marijuana.

Occasionally, more serious matters occurred. When Lingo's Market, which had opened in 1897, was burglarized, rumors of a "cover-up" circulated. The two fourteen-year-old perpetrators, friends of the mayor's son, simply paid restitution in lieu of arrest or a court hearing. Given the intervention by Mayor John Hughes and Police Chief Harry Maichle Jr., Archie Lingo, third-generation owner of this grocery store, "felt [as] uneasy about taking the steps to reopen the case" as he "felt uneasy about the charges being originally dropped." Small-town justice is seldom blind.

Two years later, during a predawn February morning in 1984, Bryce Lingo sped down 2nd Street in a Jaguar. His ten earlier traffic violations appeared to have had little impact on his driving behavior. Arrested for speeding, he was escorted to the Rehoboth police station on suspicion of drunk driving; a sobriety test revealed a high blood-alcohol level. His brother John Lingo, second in command in the Delaware State Police, argued that the officer had targeted his brother. Bryce's father, Col. Jack Lingo, was building a real estate empire in the county and realized that his son would "be done" as a Realtor if convicted, so the colonel contacted Hughes. Promising to "look into it," the mayor then phoned Maichle, who "listened to my side of the story, as any good police chief in a small town [would]," Jack praised. The chief then summoned the arresting officer. After he "suggested"—twice—that the officer reduce the charges, he then "asked" once. They were reduced. The officer, knowing "what Bryce's record was and [that] he had received breaks for other reasons," nevertheless wrote a letter recommending license reinstatement. Maichle's actions were later rebuked by the state's attorney general.

The town's Mayberry-esque image was tarnishing in the 1980s. As concerns about the influx of homosexuals grew, residents were also dumbfounded that some R-rated films were shown downtown; commissioners debated "smutty" T-shirts displayed in shop windows and passed an ordinance against tattoo parlors. A Wilmington reporter surveyed T-shirt shops, finding that although "there were a few choice bathroom words, a smatter of bad taste, and doubtful philosophy . . . hardly anything [was] worth a brown paper wrapper."

Meanwhile, Mayor Hughes was earning nationwide newspaper attention for commenting about "the increasing numbers of gays in the community." At a membership meeting of the influential Rehoboth Beach Homeowners Association, he contended that the "family image" of the town was "bolstered by Fourth of July celebrations and sidewalk sales, not by gay bars and restaurants." Observing that there was a "trigger point" when townsfolk did "not feel as comfortable as they once were," Hughes warned, "they get nervous and move out." He explained that "gays have a tendency to scare other people away, and there aren't enough gays to fill the town."

The Homeowners Association was no stranger to Rehoboth's homosexuals. As early as 1982, activities around Prospect and Queen Streets (adjacent to Poodle Beach) had been the subject of concern among residents, including board member Jay Smith. Two years later, after he reported "no improvement," the board formed an "action committee," dragooning the city manager to command greater police presence. The following year, when Mayor Hughes spoke before the association, he acknowledged that Rehoboth's gay population had long been "an unspoken concern . . . an intense one that I hear[d] about every day of my life." Seeking reelection, the mayor warned that this "wo[uld]n't be solved if it's just ignored." The town's dilemma, however, was that gays were "great consumers" with "such incredibly good taste" and "opening some of the nicest businesses in town." He told like-minded residents, "If we're going to get the upper 2 percent of that population, fine." For Hughes, imagery trumped reality as political ambition fueled his campaign of homophobia. "I have no problem with the high-toned property owner who is gay," but "there is a seamy subculture." If heterosexual visitors "s[aw] promiscuity between gays on the beach, they w[ould] make a judgment about Rehoboth."

Like most political hyperbole, there was a kernel of truth to Hughes's diatribes. Honestly, "some people liked all of that dangerous activity," candidly admits Jeffrey Slavin, who was then in his mid-twenties. "If you wanted sex in those days, you would go to the Boardwalk—even until sunup. People would be hanging around there." Jack Ackerman remembers that it was dubbed "strolling the boards." These activities supported concerns about imagined "male prostitution rings" on the Boardwalk and daylight "fornicating" in public.

During this era, Mildred "Billie" Shields, a tireless seventy-two-year-old retired English teacher and board member of the Homeowners Association, was first elected commissioner in 1984. Known for her distaste for imprecise or crude language, she instituted an invocation before every meeting of the commissioners. In her "polite and unrelenting style," she also pressed the police chief to intimidate shopkeepers, advocating for him to enter certain shops with a "big smile" to "request" removal of offensive T-shirts.

Another town commissioner, Richard Derrickson—William's son and the owner of theaters, shopping centers, business buildings, and motels—fretted, "People are always asking me to show G movies, so they can drop their kids off at the theater." He warned parents, "I'm not going to babysit their kids!" However, when his business interests aligned with small-town morality, Derrickson advanced an ordinance effectively banning tattoo parlors.

Tattoos by the Sea opened at the corner of Wilmington and 1st, in a building owned by David DeRiemer, where his ill-fated Zen Den met its demise. Mayor Hughes visited, scolding the proprietress: "This is a Methodist community and the people won't stand for it!" A commissioner also visited, suggesting that the business name be changed due to people's associating "tattoo" with "red light districts." Later, the mayor excoriated wavering commissioners, "If it isn't obvious to everyone, they don't belong here." The ordinance, requiring an attending physician at tattoo shops, was approved 4–3. One astute reader of the *Whale* alleged that the motivation had little to do with public health and was more likely rooted in Leviticus's admonishment not to have the "print of any marks upon you." Commissioner Sam Cooper, voting in the minority, adduced that it was "totally designed to put these people out of business."

The Derrickson family also found itself in a public controversy. Richard's spouse, Norma Lee, earned a real estate commission when the town purchased the old Diamond Phone Company building. Cries of favoritism and conflict of interest erupted because Richard, as commissioner, had chaired the committee negotiating with the company. Norma Lee denied that the couple had ever discussed this issue, but mindful of appearances, the commissioners swiftly enacted a set of ethical standards, replacing the secretive Ethical Practices Committee established to deter unwholesome businesses. Self-described ethical watchdog David Deibler, a frequent critic of business-as-usual among Old Rehoboth families, sermonized, "Some people have been given opportunities because of their positions in the community." Still, "there are rules in the world that even Rehoboth has to live by."

In 1983, Larsen learned about the Derricksons' intention to raze their legacy drive-in theater, opened by their father three decades earlier on

Highway 1, to build a $2-million entertainment center with bowling and roller skating. Larsen countered by converting his father's second-floor skating rink into the Twin Cinemas. This move placed him in direct competition with the Derricksons. "I think there's room for more theater business," Larsen naïvely told a reporter.

Engineered for a five-hundred-person capacity, Twin Cinemas had an attractive brick facade with a large marquee overlooking Rehoboth Avenue. The Derricksons, so-called movie moguls of Rehoboth, complained about its illegal signage and riposted by installing a small, enclosed marquee outside their storefront that listed films playing at the seven-screen Midway Palace. Donald Derrickson also advised City Manager Greg Ferrese that Larsen's renovated building "significantly" encroached on city property, which "should require its removal." Ferrese, however, declared the four-to-six-inch encroachment "not a big deal." Larsen lamented to a *Whale* reporter inquiring about the most recent feud, "I've just been playing ball. . . . He initiated the whole business." In response, Donald Derrickson cautioned that "anytime anyone cuts into the pie, it effects similar businesses."

After Larsen renovated the second floor into cinemas, Pockets Teenage Dance Hall opened adjacent it. This 260-person capacity teen nightclub, serving nonalcoholic piña coladas and margaritas, sodas, hot dogs, and free popcorn, attracted teens dancing to DJ-spun tunes or bands jamming through a four-hundred-watt sound system. Past midnight throughout the summer and off-season weekends, 110 or more decibels (equivalent to a riveter) emanated from the building. There were no public complaints from neighbors along bordering Baltimore Avenue.

Thursday night dance contests at Pockets also provided space for poppin' and lockin' breakdancers. Adjudged "bad for business and disruptive," these dancers were banned by the town fathers from the Boardwalk. One commissioner, Walter Brittingham, explained that many were "intimidated by some of these people." The leader of the local breakdancing club, Wavemakers, responded, "Some people are prejudiced—we are not causing any problems—I'm trying to get Blacks and Whites together to be friends and the people love to watch us dance." Hughes, however, saw it as "people with boxes imposing themselves on other people. This is another way to keep Rehoboth a family resort—crack down! They have no right to impose their own tastes on a whole area."

With the town changing, his health fading, and now leasing his movie house to the rival Derricksons, in the fall of 1987, Larsen negotiated a

lease-to-own contract with Felton and Pisapia along with their new partner, Gene Lawson.

GENE'S STORY

In December 1987, Lawson hosted a grand opening for his Rehoboth's Atlantic Coast Properties on Rehoboth Avenue.[2] He had been involved in real
estate development since the age of twenty-three. A native Virginian, Lawson had been raised in Richmond during the immediate post-WWII era.
After his father, an officer in the Army Medical Corps, returned from Ko-
rea, the family moved from base to base throughout the world.

When Lawson and his family returned to Virginia a dozen years later,
they were neighbors to six of the seven original astronauts. This proximity
piqued his interest in science and engineering. He was selected to participate in a high school program for computers and math taught by Virginia
Tech staff. He also loved the arts, doing lighting and stage design for the
Virginia Museum Theater. There, "I had my first experiences with openly
gay people," he recalls. "I learned about being comfortable around those
people and them around me."

Attracted to males for as long as he could remember, Lawson found the
masculine outdoor life of the military appealing. He was particularly fond
of target shooting, discovering that "a lot of the military snipers were gay."
As the Vietnam War ramped up, his strong-willed father encouraged him
to apply to West Point. Father and son ultimately "compromised" on his attending Virginia Tech, where he agreed to enroll in the cadet corps.

Blacksburg, Virginia, in the late 1960s was somewhat removed from
the antiwar college movement. Although its student body and the town
were conservative, it was a libertarian conservatism, fitting the style of
Sen. Barry Goldwater, for whom Lawson had campaigned as a teenager.
Similarly, while he focused on engineering, Lawson didn't retreat from his
involvement with the arts. He was active in the student varsity glee club
and was technical director of campus theater productions. He involved
himself with the Young Republicans, although there was no campus homophile organization to join.

Lawson was in the wave of patriotic engineering students who were
prepared to work for company and country. "We were in the Cold War, and
the U.S. was planning on building a supersonic transport plane," he recalls.
When Boeing's Space System Division (SSD) program was abruptly can-

celed, thousands of experienced engineers were laid off. He encamped in the college town and opened an electronics store. Later, Lawson "branched out" into construction where, in the summer of 1972, he met his life partner of fifty years, Scott Sterl, an architecture student. Based on Sterl's house designs, the couple was hired by a computer science professor to build his home. Soon, they were building custom and speculative homes.

As a gay couple living together in a small college town during the 1970s, there "was sort of an unspoken acceptance," Lawson says. "Small towns tend to know people, and they know them *before* they find out their sexuality." As a business owner, he became involved in the centrist, socially oriented Gay-Straight Union that included members from the community as well as students: "It was very open and very comfortable. We didn't have any problems with [gay] bashing or anything like that."[3]

Although "we really weren't into the civil rights sort of stuff," Lawson participated in one local panel, "We Speak for Ourselves." From his perspective, "being ourselves, working hard" were the most helpful traits a gay person could demonstrate, along with "being useful and active in the community." By the late 1970s, however, it seemed to him that the national movement's focus had fragmented: "It started moving into all these letters [e.g., LGBT]. When we were in school you had 'gay people' that encompassed men *and* women. Then, suddenly, we couldn't say 'gay women' anymore. We had to say 'lesbians.'" He adds, "The transgendered stuff came in, and that confused things even more."

In 1979, they relocated to the DC area. One of Lawson's major projects was converting the 208-unit Port Royal apartment complex into condos. The couple became staunch supporters of the Kennedy Center and found themselves at home among other successful gay Republicans, including those serving in the Ronald Reagan and George H. W. Bush administrations. "They never were hiding in the closet," Lawson confides. "Most of our friends would not go to gay pride parades because they didn't feel like they needed to. It was not part of their lives."

During the summer of 1979, the couple rented a townhouse in Ocean City, Maryland, known for its beach-lined high-rises, commercialism, and homophobia. One day, they drove up the coastal road to Rehoboth and dined at the Back Porch Café. They were enamored with this small town. Returning to the beach the next summer, they lodged in Rehoboth and frequented the newly opened Chez la Mer restaurant and Renegade. Lawson and Sterl "enjoyed [them]selves," although the dance club's "lighting was poor, and the sound was poor." Like other gay men from DC during this era,

Eugene Lawson Jr. with husband, Scott Sterl, at 2013 Christmas Ball. *Left to right:* Marie Martinucci, Eugene Lawson, Pam Kozey, and Scott Sterl. (Courtesy of *Cape Gazette.*)

the couple bought a property. In 1981, they architecturally transformed their Hickman Street multiunit residential building located just a block from the beach. The first two floors became duplex-style townhouses, which they rented by the week. The small apartments on the third floor were rented seasonally. The redesigned upper floor with a roof deck was their summer retreat.

Lawson and Sterl dined infrequently at the newly opened Blue Moon, despite its "New York attitude." However, when the Moon opened its bar the next year, they frequented happy hour, and some of its staff rented their third-floor apartments. Their favorite restaurant remained Chez la Mer, which decades earlier had housed Collins General Store before being opened by former Capitol Hill staffer Nancy Wolfe. "We probably agreed more on local politics than national politics," Lawson says.

The early 1980s Rehoboth scene was far from queer-friendly, according to Lawson: "The powers that be and various real estate companies and other retail and restaurants would do whatever they could do to keep gays out. They would not treat you very nice. But they *would* take your money." He also recollects that the local "political scene was raucous and very discriminating." Mayor Hughes was "*always* talking in slurs about gay people," and "several of the commissioners were *very* open about being discriminatory. It wasn't just against the gays. It was against racial minorities as well."

Well before Lawson's time, the town's 1968 Comprehensive Plan had proposed annexing "the area west of the city generally referred to as 'West Rehoboth.'" It was never adopted. A generation later, Mayor Sam Cooper had been "dead set against" it. Lawson recalls town talk about annexing this unincorporated area, as the town had done with other neighborhoods. "One of the reasons that some of the people were against it," he judges, was simple: "Black people. It was obvious that these people didn't want to integrate" Rehoboth.

"As far as race [goes] in Rehoboth, [it] was horrible," Sharon Kanter, whose experiences with race were personal. "One of my partners was an African American woman. She always felt nervous going into anyplace since she would be the only Black. She would *really* feel it." Another lesbian, commercial artist Annette Mosiej, who also dated interracially, recalls, "We came down here for one weekend. She was totally uncomfortable."

Unlike outspoken Mayor Hughes, others chatted in racist and homophobic codes. Lawson and Sterl refused to join the Rehoboth Beach Homeowners Association. Its leaders, notably Francis Fabrizio, Jay Smith, and Mary Campbell,

> would talk about wanting to make sure that people who came in and were going up and down the Boardwalk were "our kind of people." It reminded me of [the 1947 film] *Gentleman's Agreement*. It was not said directly, but it was so indirect that you knew exactly what they were talking about.

Nevertheless, by the mid-1980s, two queer groups—gay/lesbian entrepreneurs and queer homeowners—were burrowing into Rehoboth's "family" soil. Ackerman, along with his longtime partner, Alan Anderson, had been coming to Rehoboth since the early 1970s. "We were aware" of other gay couples also becoming so-called block-busters.

In the spring of 1983, they bought into the Country Club subdivision. Soon, they met other DC gay couples who owned homes in this relatively affordable Rehoboth neighborhood, including Dolph Spain and his partner, Lloyd Johnson, who had met at a Baltimore bar in 1964. This group also included three other couples, each of whom had met their partners a year earlier: Nikomis "Jeff" Jefferson, who ran a DC sex shop, and Jim Vandergraft, a physicist and mathematician; the crew-cutted white-haired Anglo-

(*Standing left to right*) Ray Gingale and Eddie Fair, Alan Anderson, Nikomis Jefferson, Jack Ackerman, Bob, (*kneeling*) Chris "Baby" Bak, and Jim Vandergraft at his RB House, 1993. (Courtesy of Chris Yochim.)

phile Ray Gingale, who first visited Rehoboth during the 1950s while working as a Hollywood publicist, and the younger, darkly tanned, less talkative Eddie Fair, an architectural draftsman who renovated mansions near Lafayette Park; and the small-framed hairstylist Norman Turnbull and six-foot-six Bill Mulky, an engineer with the DC power company. A much younger couple who later became part of this group was Chris Yochim, whose German immigrant grandfather had opened a successful New Orleans distillery, and his boyfriend, whom everyone knew as "Baby." They bought a two-bedroom condo just outside Rehoboth for weekend junkets.

The older couples "all lived in DC, and they all knew each other for many, many years," Yochim shares. Each rotated to host intimate dinner parties with a focus on inspiring menus and eclectic conversations. Unlike Yochim, these age-fiftyish gentlemen weren't enamored with "standing in the Blue Moon or other places on a Saturday when the place was packed. They valued conversation and interacting with their own crowd."

Not surprisingly, there were fewer lesbian homeowners, especially within Rehoboth's pricey town limits. Although nationally women's real earning power narrowed by 12 percent during the 1980s, it was still 72 cents for every dollar of a man's wage. An exception was the Brazilian-born Aynda Marchant, who began visiting Rehoboth during the late 1940s while working at Dean Acheson's DC law firm. The thirty-eight-year-old met native Washingtonian Muriel Crawford in 1948. Marchant was an attorney at the firm; Crawford worked as a senior legal secretary. They became lovers, later bought a second home in Rehoboth, and retired to their Laurel Street cottage in 1972.

From the 1960s through the early 1980s, they did not search out other Rehoboth homosexuals or call attention to themselves. "You never gave someone the opportunity to ask the question," Marchant explains. "All through my working life, I had to be discreet." Like this generation of older gay men, this lesbian couple "never . . . had the habit of going to bars." They preferred to socialize among a small group and host summer Saturday late-afternoon porch salons, patterned after those of Virginia Woolf, whom Marchant greatly admired and often quoted: "Only women stir my imagination." These quiet activists, however, funded the groundbreaking lesbian publishing company Naiad Press, which they co-owned with former *Ladder* editor Barbara Grier and her partner, Donna McBride. Naiad was set to launch its first book, a romantic novel by Marchant under her nom de plume Sarah Aldridge. However, in 1974, no printer would touch *The Latecomer*, and few bookstores would stock it. It was advertised and distributed through the old *Ladder*'s mailing list. Twenty years later, Naiad was doing $1 million in annual sales, with 180 titles in print; Marchant had published fourteen titles.

By the mid-1980s, however, discretion was no longer a virtue among queers summering in Rehoboth, creating a homophobic backlash. "The antigay sentiment has come from the old-fashioned people," Marchant observes. "They don't see that gay people now have a financial stake in Rehoboth. They see them as outsiders who come in and disrupt the town."

A few younger women, such as Kanter, bought just outside town, while others, such as Libby Stiff and her partner, Bea Wagner, found homes in less expensive but far more conservative southern Sussex County—well outside Rehoboth. "The Ku Klux Klan was meeting one Saturday night a month in a field" near their home. Chapters had organized in the county during the mid-1950s, when *Delmarva News*'s publisher had opined, "We are not opposed to the Klan as an organization opposing desegregation in public schools."

Meanwhile, in 1984, Lawson embarked with Sterl on their next local project. They bought an old ten-room boardinghouse, the Sea Lodge, across the street from their summer home, installed a pool, and "spiffed it up." It became the Beach House, joining the ramshackle Paradise Inn and the more upscale Delaware House on the other side of Rehoboth Avenue. Naturally, not everyone took kindly to another openly queer business: "We would have our people sitting out there by the pool, and people would walk by and make snide remarks, antigay remarks—even racist remarks."

Nevertheless, it was evident that Rehoboth was rapidly morphing into a gay destination. "We were getting people who wanted to come over here and spend the whole summer or come every Friday afternoon and return to DC or whatever on Sunday or Monday," Lawson reflects. "It was interesting to watch the evolution of the place." The following year, Pat Whittier and Pegi Fuller opened the Paper Nautilus B&B, which Fuller managed while Whittier worked at IBM on weekdays. A couple of years later, Courville and Jerome transformed the nearby Paradise Inn into the decidedly more stylish (and less sexualized) Rehoboth Guest House, almost directly behind the Moon. Kanter's Secrets by the Beach was joined by other queer Baltimore Avenue establishments, such as Mike Saunders's Boxers & Drawers, the M-Style unisex clothing shop owned by Debby Appleby and Beth Shinn, and Jeff Williams's gem dealership, Rio Mining.

More gay-owned or -friendly shops and restaurants were also opening on Wilmington Avenue. One block to the south of Rehoboth Avenue, this business location was now the less expensive one. There, in addition to Chez la Mer, were Sweet Eileen's cafe and bakery; La La Land, with its funky new American cuisine served on linen tablecloths; and John Axelrod's garden-sourced Square One restaurant, which replaced Sydney Arzt's Side Street (she had relocated her jazz and blues restaurant to nearby Christian Street). In 1988, the *Whale*'s feature story trumpeted, "Rehoboth's Wilmington Avenue Bustling." It reported more than two dozen businesses were operating on these once-residential two blocks.

These and other mostly thirty-something business entrepreneurs were decidedly progressive and rainbow-conspicuous—unlike Lawson and Thompson, who were politically conservative and preferred to operate in the background and in the backroom. Although they supported equal rights for gays, neither found the activist tactics of Dominguez and the Gay & Lesbian Alliance of Delaware (GLAD), the community militancy of Felton, or the overt lesbianism of Kanter and her Nomad villagers attractive.

"Sometimes it's easier to be involved, like being a worm working its way into an apple, where you can do more from the inside than you can from the outside," observes Lawson.

STRANDING TOGETHER

Lawson was always on the "lookout" for investors and investment property.[4] In the fall of 1987, a real estate agent phoned him about Larsen's old building, where Richard Derrickson's lease had expired and its cinema equipment had been moved out. "He took me through it, and my mind just went in twenty different directions because so much could be done with it!" Lawson immediately spoke with Pisapia about its use as a restaurant.

Pisapia and Felton, aware of the building's vacancy, discussed Lawson's proposed partnership: "We had been talking about doing this nightclub for years and years," Pisapia thought. "Finally, *there* is a spot we can do it." It didn't take long for the trio to agree that this project was viable. "All of us were on the same page of the ultimate goal," reflects Lawson. For all that, as he foreshadows, "we probably weren't together very often about how to get there."

Nevertheless, the trio partnered. "It started off with the nightclub being the main thing we wanted to do," explains Pisapia. "But once we did a little bit of research, we realized we couldn't have the nightclub on both floors; we had to have different projects going on in order to get a liquor license because we needed to have food." He continues, "The trendy new food thing that was going on was diners. . . . We decided to take part of that complex and make it a diner, and the other part was to be a cabaret."

To outsiders, the partnership seemed odd; four decades later, it's judged a triadic tragedy. Nonetheless, as Lawson explains, "It was too big a project to take on by myself." Each partner brought something unique and valuable to the endeavor; each partner had liabilities. Felton and Pisapia "were plugged into the community, which was really good and important." Pisapia was "a local boy of sorts." Lawson adds, "Everybody loved him, and he was a very talented chef" and very "mild mannered." In contrast, Felton was "an aggressive businessperson" who for nearly a decade had been "a leader in trying to fight homophobia because it hurt her business." However, Lawson jabs, "Joyce was a typical New Yorker—and not in the best sense. She had her opinions about things, and it didn't matter the opinions everyone else had." Lawson, who was pursuing a law degree, brought two decades of construction experience, insider knowledge about navigating

Rehoboth's arbitrarily interpreted zoning ordinances, and capital. He also brought a righteous rigidity.

Pisapia acknowledges that Lawson "was an odd partner for us. He really didn't fit in with Joyce and I at all, but he was *very* steadfast. We thought with his connections and law background, he would be helpful, as there were quite a lot of hurdles." Felton adds, "There was the promise of money," and Lawson could bring "a game plan about how to get from point A to point B, which was critically important to us . . . approvals, licenses, variances." He agrees: "My basic function was to take the large piece, which was the whole building, and somehow, financially, divide it up into the different functions."

Lawson purchased the ice company directly and arranged for his sister and brother-in-law to operate Arctic Ice. A holding company held the master lease to the building, which sublet the second floor to The Strand nightclub, with two other leases for the ground-floor West Side Café and Surfside Diner.

Design and marketing were the bailiwick of Pisapia and Felton: "Everything focused on what we had seen in New York. We wanted to bring that kind of vibe to Rehoboth." The Strand, Pisapia stresses, was envisioned as "more than a DC bar because we felt like Rehoboth already had that." Both were good friends with Bruce Mailman, an East Village entrepreneur who owned the Saint, whose opening-night poster "featured a cyborg-like figure of St. Sebastian with lasers shooting out of his fingertips and eyes." The Strand, Lawson reflects, "was a place where people would now say: 'It had the most gorgeous guys you've ever seen.' And we did! It became a myth."

THE STRAND COMPLEX

What was to be the crowning achievement of the Blue Moon restauranteur duo instead became a turning point in the queering of Rehoboth.[5] It was a saga of confrontations and celebrations: historic police raids and arrests; forgotten one-night stands and cherished anniversary moments; hastily enacted ordinances and a watershed referendum; spring and fall follies; double-strand pearl parties and lavender balls; and partisan petitions and public meetings.

It was groundbreaking. The entertainment complex featured a European cabaret-bistro, a splashy 1950s diner, and a second-floor nightclub.

It was audacious. A six-hundred-person New York–style inferno set in the heart of a small-town business district.

It was glittering. State-of-the art lighting effects, designed by Richard Erskine, and veteran Saint DJs pounded out the beat as mirrored balls spun and spandex fabrics ruffled against back walls.

It was worrisome. The long-dreaded homosexual tsunami was washing a "family town" into an ocean of olden days.

It was innovative. The first-floor West Side Café featured Friday night drag karaoke, where wannabe singers first entered the backroom to choose a wardrobe matching their performer-persona.

It was flashy. The Surfside Diner was replete with jukebox, original 1950s booths and countertops, and sassy waitstaff chewing bubble gum who rejoined customers—"Hi, doll. How ya doin'?"—announced blue-plate specials, and occasionally performed dance routines on the shimmering black-and-white tiled floor.

It was a bacchanalia of uninhibited desire. Shirtless men shimmied on speakers along with "boys in briefs dancing on banquettes above the sunken dance floor."

It was shocking. A New Year's Eve party "invitation of a half-naked man lying on [a] satin sheet" riled one *Whale* reader, who declared that the town was "turning into a house of ill repute."

It was late night. Twinkly-clad men formed lines stretching down Rehoboth Avenue, awaiting the doors to open at midnight.

It was early morning. As dawn approached and the festivities ended, "a hunk clad only in a Tarzan loincloth" searched for his car; a couple, sporting cowboy boots and go-go shorts, strolled toward Bayard Avenue; and "three men dressed in combat boots, ripped shirts, and dog collars, waited patiently in line at the Cosmic Bakery."

It was infuriating. One writer to the *Whale* queried, "Who will control Rehoboth—God-fearing decent people or Satan's puppets?"

It was exclusive. A-list gays investing $10,000 or more skipped the line. Flashing their platinum membership cards, they'd saunter into the smartly furnished VIP lounge overlooking the cavernous dance floor with feather-painted walls by local artist Archibald.

It was notorious. A summer predawn raid shocked the town.

It was glamorous. The legendary lesbian-adored bartender Paige Phillips, in an Oscar de la Renta silk jacket with matching lipstick and an exquisite black satin dress, danced with her betrothed, the impeccably attired John Berdini, as admirers applauded.

It was death by a thousand cuts. Owners dealt with a building-permit moratorium, the necessity of hundreds of off-street parking spaces, petitions and protests, a ban on nightclubs and taprooms, a state law granting greater local authority over liquor permits, and a noise ordinance based on subjective standards.

It was smoke and mirrors. Were erstwhile opponents really bothered by noise and parking or fear of rampaging homosexuals or, perhaps, business competition—or one masking another?

It was angelic. At the back bar (sans alcohol), *Letters* editor Jim Bahr, wearing iridescent wings and a leather harness, served mineral and spring waters.

It was rock of ages. On Thursday nights, the "Rock Lobster" teen club was reserved for the MTV-dressed crowd dancing to techno pop and glam metalists, while Sunday mornings were set aside for MCC churchgoers singing traditional Christian hymns.

It was intimidating. Police Chief Creig Doyle's "zero tolerance policy" required officers to enforce "jaywalking, rowdy behavior, sidewalk shouting and laughing after 2300 hours"—only on the second block of Baltimore Avenue.

It was celebratory. Festivities included the Greg Myers Dance Company's "Shades of Grey" benefit, the performance of four former Miss Gay Americas, and the July 4th Glitter Ball Extravaganza.

It was fractious. One house owned by a couple leading the opposition was paint-bombed, while a gay homeowner reported that his rainbow flag was burned to a crisp.

It was calamitous. Wreckage of friendships, financial carnage, and a historical building's demolition were its ruinous legacy.

It was The Strand. It divided progressive residents from their conservative neighbors as well as closeted homosexuals from their *Queer as Folk* contemporaries. It was—and is—a Rehoboth Beach story that almost no one recounts the same way. It was iconic, from its lavish 1988 premier to its bulldozed demise seven years later.

WE JUST WANT TO DANCE

Our community has not developed this way because it was
hidden in a closet or behind a mask. When we share our lives
openly with our neighbors, the world is transformed.
        —**Murray Archibald**, *Unmasking Halloween*

Every community has its share of eccentrics and high-brows, profiteers
and prophets, old families and newcomers, power holders and power
brokers, gentry and proletariat, rabble-rousers and reactionaries. During crises, these characters often assume outsized roles—at least, this was
the case in the imbroglio between Rehoboth and The Strand. What naïvely
began as an entrepreneurial effort by well-known restauranteurs and developers to bring a high-tech dance club into the town quickly was confronted with the twin realities of small-town governance and heterosexual
privilege. It's a tale of the perennial struggle between change and constancy in small-town America.

BERTHA AND RAY'S STORY

Seventeen-year-old Sotiria immigrated from Katavothra, Greece, in 1928.[1]
That same year, she married another Greek immigrant, James N. Pappas,
who operated Candyland in Elkton. This tiny Maryland town, located between DC and Baltimore, was bustling. During the years between the wars,
it was *the* Las Vegas–like marriage destination for couples from the East
Coast who wanted (or needed) to marry quickly. Fifteen private chapels
hosted ten thousand marriages annually.

The Pappases had three children and opened other restaurants and shops. Both were active in the Greek Orthodox Church. When their only daughter, Bertha, was twenty years old, the family opened the Gem restaurant on 1st Street in Rehoboth Beach in 1955. Pappas bought a summer house around the corner at 42 Baltimore Avenue. Bertha then earned a secretarial science certificate from Goldey-Beacom College in Wilmington and found work at the Delaware Department of Transportation (DelDOT), where her soon-to-be second husband, Raymond S. Pusey Jr., worked. Upon meeting in Dewey Beach, he fell madly in love with Bertha. They married in 1968.

Although they were the same age, in contrast to the diminutive and strikingly attractive Bertha, Ray's six-foot-three husky frame towered over most gatherings. Her beauty and large diamond wedding ring, however, caught people's attention. He would lovingly watch her saunter around a room. His family hailed from Smyrna, just a few miles north of Dover. His father, Raymond Sr., was chief engineer and vice president for the town's largest company. Evelyn, his mother, was a leader in the PTA, a local Red Cross volunteer, and a member of various women's clubs while caring for their only child.

Having served in the army, Ray studied electrical engineering at the University of Delaware. Still, summers during the late 1950s were reserved for working on theater productions at Pigeon Forge. Technically minded, he handled lighting and sound. "People misjudged him completely. They always felt he was antigay," contends Glen Thompson. "His best friends were gay people when he was young."

Ray began work in the traffic division of the state highway department in 1962 while still living with his parents. The twenty-seven-year-old was assigned to the sign shop, located in a converted airplane hangar, where he replaced damaged signs and signals. Given his education and intelligence, he rose to chief traffic engineer. During the next several decades, he testified before various legislative committees, was widely quoted in newspaper articles, and was often cited in letters to the editor as well as the subject of editorials. In one newspaper story, Pusey contended, "We need a return to nineteenth-century standards of courtesy on the road—and everywhere else." He was credited with "countless advances in traffic engineering and management statewide."

Far less vocal than his spouse, Ray was seldom open about his conservative views within a state government dominated by moderates. Local good ol' boy Sam Cooper, whose mother, Gracie, was the town's matriarch, served as a commissioner before his election to mayor in 1990. Bertha Pusey "always had an opinion on everything," he once noted. "She could be overly emotional." Thompson agrees: "She would get herself in trouble by talking a little too much. . . . She was not liked by a number of people in power positions because she would be very blunt."

Bertha was active in the Dover and Rehoboth communities. Not only was she involved with various women's clubs; she also volunteered at Dover's family court, where she translated for Greek victims of domestic violence. Asserting that "no one should be abused," she was well known among children "as the woman who brought toys and coloring books to the shelters." The director of the Domestic Violence Advocacy Center recalls her "strong sense of fairness" and describes her as "an inspiration." Along with Ray, Bertha generally attended the commissioner's monthly meetings and town commissioner workshops and donated to local causes.

Thompson first met Ray during the late 1970s, when buying property in Sussex County. "I was having trouble with something and someone said, 'Call Ray Pusey.' That wasn't his section of DelDOT, but I contacted him." Over the decades, "Ray always came through for me." Although the Puseys summered in Rehoboth, their Dover Fairfield Farms house, with its vaulted ceiling and curtain-less Palladian windows, was their home. Thompson sometimes visited their two-story summer house on The Avenue for lunch or cocktails: "We would sit on that screen porch and look over at the Blue Moon. Bertha would love to watch the gay boys. And her mother absolutely adored it!" One time, Bertha "told me that, when she was a kid, she didn't dare say anything about gay people because her mother would slap her! 'That's *not* how you talk about people.'"

This view, however, is not shared by many Rehoboth gay people. "I just never met anybody like that woman. She was pure evil," declares Victor Pisapia, who seldom has a harsh word for anyone. Jeffrey Slavin, who first took a summer share at a Hickman Street house in 1985, also volunteers the word *evil* to describe the Puseys. The former gay mayor of a Maryland town continues, "I don't think John Hughes or the Puseys ever said 'bunch of faggots'; it was more in terms of keeping it 'family-oriented.'"

Joyce Felton recalls "spotty" run-ins with Bertha when she had the Moon, believing that the Puseys "had collaborated with the competition of ours. He [Thompson] was promoting them to be complainants because they lived right across the street." Thompson's right-hand man, Wayne Hodge, bitingly counters, "Anything that ever happened bad to them or their businesses was due to him or Ray Pusey." Sharon Kanter, whom Bertha had be-friended when she opened Secrets on the Beach, remembers having a talk with her as the couple's complaints escalated. She asked, "Why are you do-ing this?" Bertha replied, "Well, Sharon, I don't like the noise." Kanter says that they "drifted apart. I couldn't handle it. She had hatred and animosi-ty." However, Rehoboth Guest House co-owner Bill Courville cautions that in Rehoboth, "everyone wasn't Bertha." Hodge sighs: "It's a part of history that a lot of us who were around back then don't want to relive."

TECTONIC FAULTS

Throughout January 1988, a series of letters to the editor and anonymous "Speak Out" voice messages about homosexuality were published in the *Whale*, sparked by its profile of a local marine biologist turned blacksmith.[2] Thirty-five-year-old John Ellsworth was well known for his Civil War mem-orabilia, including an 1862 Union cannon that he boasted was "now in the hands of the rebels." Critics of the paper's fawning portrait included a read-er who had witnessed the local artisan "distributing very discriminatory flyers against the homosexual community" and another who attested to his "great deal of venom and prejudice against gay people."

Although Ellsworth did not publicly respond, his supporters denounced slanderous detractors spitting "all of those wrong things about" him. Most, however, focused on homosexuality. Decrying the "exploding" number of Rehoboth gays, one caller agonized, "It's hard to walk down the streets at night without worrying that a gay may attack me." Another chafed that the "homosexual problem" in Rehoboth was "keeping a lot of people away," leading them to instead vacation in "Ocean City, Md. or New Jersey beach-es." A third reader declared, "The homosexual population is getting out-of-hand and the council and Rehoboth residents should do something about it quickly."

Before The Strand's first permitting plans were ever submitted, word was out about a "gay dance club" opening on Rehoboth's main thorough-fare. "Anywhere you went, there was talk," recalls Thompson. Felton and Pisapia once again found themselves summoned to the mayor's office after submitting a building permit request. Although the mayor was different, the message from Kimber Vought that February, like that of his predeces-sor Hughes seven years earlier, was the same: Don't do it!

In mid-February, the board of commissioners trotted out its yellowed playbook for instituting ordinances to hamper, harass, or halt unseemly, unpopular, or unwholesome businesses. A new parking ordinance was proposed. Any new entertainment or restaurant with five thousand or more square feet or a capacity of more than 150 people must provide one off-street parking space for every three people or one spot for every twenty-two square feet. Any building permit submitted after January 15 would be put on hold.

Don Derrickson, who had submitted a permit for a five-screen movie complex on Rehoboth Avenue, was livid. He calculated that his project would require three hundred off-street parking spaces. Vacant town acreage was unavailable, and the cost to buy, bulldoze, and build a parking lot would be astronomical. "They are eliminating our ability to provide services," he exclaimed. A second pending project, Dominick Pulieri's three-story extension of Grotto's Pizza on the Boardwalk, also was put into limbo, as was the dance club project, which Felton estimated would require "several acres" of parking. This hastily submitted ordinance, specifically targeting The Strand, had the unintended consequence of infuriating two of the town's most prominent businessmen. Once again, the town's age-old tectonic faults of gentry property owners and religious conservatives would collide with secularized businesspeople and vacationers.

Editorials and letters to the editor filled the *Whale*. Milton Fried, the eccentric former Delaware Coast Press owner, penned frequent letters to the editor, signed "Uncle Miltie," which were as much discussed as reviled. He had first journeyed to Rehoboth by train five decades earlier and often perched on his dilapidated Rehoboth Avenue home porch just down from the proposed Strand. Commercialism and tourism, he argued, were an integral part of Rehoboth's heritage: "I do not wish to see our resort die from a slow strangulation due to hindering and prohibitive ordinances" supported by "anti-business, anti-growth, anti-development, and anti-transient" Homeowner Association–supported commissioners. Similarly, the liberal-minded Methodist minister Richard Hamilton, who operated a B&B, wrote, "Senior citizens, long-time Rehoboth residents, businesspeople, and yes, even homeowners, have begun to realize that the 'parking problem' is only a ruse to other ends than those openly expressed." A headline in the *Whale* spelled out the alleged motivation: "Rehoboth Mayor Vought Denies Charges That Parking Proposal Is Smoke Screen for Bias Against Gays."

Recalling these troubled times, Pisapia acknowledges that "there were some people who were genuinely concerned about noise and parking—the Old Rehoboth clan that didn't want anything to change." All the same, "there was a very strong religious right in Rehoboth at that point." Michael

Decker, a gay musician who had lived in the town since the mid-1970s, agrees:

> There were homophobic people in town who wanted to become com-
> missioners, specifically with regard to The Strand and having so
> many gays in the faces of people. I knew one woman, her son is gay,
> but she was just as hateful and homophobic as you could be during
> that era. Today, when she talks about The Strand: "Those people
> were so evil; they were criminals." And I asked, "What was so bad?"
> She said, "Oh, they had purple hair." I said, "You know, I went there.
> People like me went there!" She was like, "No! You just *think* you
> went there. It wasn't The Strand. You *wouldn't* have gone to a place
> like that!"

The *Whale*'s Trish Hogenmiller editorialized that Rehoboth was "in the throes of reverting back into a one-horse town." Her editorial castigated the Homeowners Association as a "power base without parallel in the city's history." Through its slate of commissioners and "with little public notice, the city imposed a moratorium on the issuance of building permits." A week before the March 8 public hearing, a second editorial lambasted the parking ordinance as a "strangulation measure" proposed "rather quietly and ever so coincidentally on the heels of the revelation that an upscale dinner and dance club was being planned."

One of those commissioners, Billie Shields, berated these editorials as journalistic "abuses" that "foment[ed] contention" and "community divisiveness." Writing on behalf of the association's board, Jay Smith denied that "a powerful cabal within RBHA ha[d] been masterminding a campaign to turn back the clock . . . and to impede business growth." For two decades, the association had been the town's "work horse." He gloated before feigning a hands-off approach: "RBHA does not make policy," although it "does make its views known to the commissioners."[3] Even so, photojournalist and restauranteur Terry Plowman called out the association for "its behind-the-scenes manipulation."

Despite its claim of being a nonprofit community group, the Homeowners Association routinely recruited its candidates for town office and others for committee appointments.[4] Although ostensibly the decision to endorse local political candidates rested with the full membership, these people were identified, interviewed, and selected by its board—with an even smaller executive committee calling the shots. For example, several years

earlier, when Shields was first elected commissioner, she had told the association, "Voters had voted not for a candidate but for a philosophy that 'WE'
endorse . . . to maintain the image of Rehoboth as a Family-Oriented city."

Once endorsements were made, the association routinely allocated between $1,000 and $2,500 to fund political ads and its get-out-the-vote
campaign. One writer to the *Whale* observed that association money to
elect its candidates "essentially wipe[d] out the opposition" and that its endorsement often came "without interviewing any of the challengers about
their views."

The association not only infused money into local elections but also
contributed human resources. Rear Adm. Francis J. Fabrizio commanded
these electoral efforts, adopting a multifront wartime-like strategy to support "our candidates." Tactics ranged from appointing "chairmen" to each
of the town's eighteen zones to coordinate door-to-door canvassing to
staffing several nightly "telethons" with a half dozen members using
phones at Lingo Realty. In the 1987 local election, "Breezy" estimated that
the designated candidates could "expect to get 350 to 400 votes from members" from among the 1,584 registered voters; ultimately, in that election,
1,059 people voted, with three of the four association candidates elected.

On March 8, more than 250 people attended the two-hour public meeting, with most, including the local chamber of commerce president, speaking against the parking ordinance. The Homeowners Association countered, proposing that movie theaters and skating rinks be omitted, as
"those businesses [we]re in keeping with the policy of keeping Rehoboth a
'family place.'" The commissioners put off their decision until the next
month.

Four days later, at the association's March 1988 board meeting, President Smith reported that "Glen Thompson [had] called him about looking
into getting up a petition against issuing a liquor license for the proposed
dancehall." Frank Hubbell "was appointed to a committee to look into this."

After reviewing these board minutes thirty-four years later, Thompson
flatly states, "That never happened. I would see Jay Smith a lot, but I *never*
had a conversation with him." Asked why Smith would give this false report, Thompson responds, "Jay Smith would say anything." According to
him, "It wasn't the whole board . . . but Smith was the single-most-powerful
person behind Bertha. There were other people," including Francis Fabrizio
and Mary Campbell, along with several formidable business owners: "She
fronted for them." Although Thompson doesn't remember Bertha talking

to him about the dance hall during this time, "she was the logical choice" because "she was real close" to The Strand's location and well known. Aside from being "interested in seeing where it was going to go," Thompson claims, "I wasn't that involved."

Naturally, Strand partners have a different view. Although they realized that there would be obstacles along the way, Pisapia insists, "It was really about Bertha Pusey and Glen Thompson. If Bertha Pusey didn't really come into the arena, I don't think that any of this would have happened. And I think that was fueled by Glen."

Asked whether the partners had spoken with Thompson prior to launching the project, Gene Lawson responds emphatically, "No." He maintains that Renegade's owner "would be doing underhanded stuff," such as "telling stories about you which weren't true in order to take business away from you, if he could do that." Further, Lawson alleges that Thompson "would support people who were doing things that would hurt us." Felton elaborates, "The Puseys were working with Glen Thompson"; they were "trying to wear us down." Asked what she thought was Thompson's motivation, she replies, "Glen was not happy that we opened the Blue Moon, and Glen was not happy that we were opening The Strand." Felton sighs: "The bottom line is some people just don't want competition."

The April meeting of the commissioners was the opportunity to "put their feet to the fire," asserted Shields, who had been disappointed about the postponed voting the month before. Immediately prior to that, she had suggested that licenses for new businesses be judged relative to a "valid purpose and need" and whether they "fit" into the town. Lawson excoriated, "In whose hands should the future of any new business be placed? The commission?"

A "capacity crowd" of supporters and opponents attended the meeting. They were "taken by surprise as reactions of disbelief, approval, and anger" swirled when Mayor Vought moved to withdraw the parking ordinance. Smith arose to speak first: "Where are they going to park?" Ray blasted, "To back away totally is to duck the issue. You are hiding from it!" The mayor, following the outcry from prominent business owners and residents, along with a lawsuit filed by Strand partners, countered, "I believe the commissioners owe it to the people to respond to the consensus, not just to special interest." He promised to establish a "blue ribbon panel" to consider construction of a parking garage. After the meeting, the attorney representing Felton, Pisapia, and Lawson declared, "We won. The lawsuit has become moot."

At the Homeowners Association board meeting the following week, Smith formally introduced members to Bertha. Her petition against the yet-to-be-opened dance hall, posing "noise and parking problems," had nearly a hundred signers. In addition to seeking the association's help in acquiring more signatures for her petition, Pusey encouraged "a lot of people" to attend the Alcoholic Beverage Control Commission's (ABCC's) hearing in the summer.

THE ABCs OF BIGOTRY

Rehoboth Theatre Building Group quickly began renovations at 137 Rehoboth Avenue, with the goal of opening the 1950s-style diner by June and the dance hall by summer's end.[5] No less deterred, the Puseys collected sufficient legal signatures to force an open hearing by the ABCC, citing late-night noise, congestion, parking, and a "change [in] the character of the neighborhood." Fuming, Felton groused, "They are concerned about something that hasn't even happened" and promised that "architectural and sound design" would significantly reduce noise.

According to Pisapia:

> There were many times early on when we said to Bertha, "We're going to do a nightclub behind you. We want to make sure you're happy and that we don't impose upon you. We've wrapped the nightclub in surround sound so you can't hear anything." . . . We did everything we possibly could to make her happy, but she was just never going to be happy.

Felton expands, "We went up and down the block to every single neighbor. We tried to explain with charts, information, and science the very specific actions we were working on to quell and ameliorate the fears." Despite such efforts, the Puseys "were not open to listening. . . . I don't know if it was homophobia that drove her, but there certainly was a mission and a mania that was apparent and evident."

In May 1988, at the annual meeting of the Homeowners Association, Ray, in his capacity as chief traffic engineer, spoke about the town's summer gridlock. "You will be hearing more about this gentleman," the association's newsletter promised. It also encouraged its several hundred member households to "voice your opposition to the granting of a liquor license" to a dance club that "does not fit into our organization's concept of Rehoboth as a 'Family Town.'" Members were asked to write letters to the ABCC via the association or to sign an attached form letter in response to "this threat to the quality of life in our town." By the end of June, the association had received 190 letters, which Smith swore to "personally" present at the August 19 liquor board hearing.

At the next general membership meeting, Joseph Belle moved that association members "pass a resolution stating their stand on gays." Although the motion was withdrawn after debate, Fabrizio later visited Belle at his Rehoboth Country Club home for a frank discussion on "what the City c[ould] do about the homosexuals." He reported the conversation to members, recommending, "We can fight the influx, not homosexuality, and can aggressively oppose anything not adhering to the traditional Family Resort image."

While canvassing signatures for her anti–dance club referendum, Bertha encountered thirty-four-year-old Plowman, a former Maryland journalist who had opened the Front Page bar and restaurant on Baltimore Avenue in 1984. She approached the lanky former planning and zoning commissioner. "I was asked if I would sign a petition 'against the Gay disco' on Rehoboth Avenue," Plowman wrote. "Though I am not a homosexual neither am I homophobic, as it seems some of our citizens are." Contrarily, "Bertha called and told me" of the incident, Thompson recounts. "She was upset. She said she never said such a thing!" He concludes, "Terry Plowman wasn't telling the truth, or it was misinterpreted."

Meanwhile, on another front, self-described homosexuals, variously identified as the Coalition for the Prevention of Gay Bashing and the Greater Rehoboth Community Centre Civic Association, began a public relations offensive. In July, a letter to the editor from the coalition claimed, "Since Joyce Felton and her partners have been running off at the mouth about their dancehall, gay bashing has risen dramatically." It warned, "We do not want those whose interest is profit at all costs using us." An anonymous caller, citing this group, claimed that "opposition" to the dance hall was "widespread" and challenged the credibility of those who "portray[ed] opposition to the dancehall as being simply antigay."

In response, Keith Lewis, an ally of Gay & Lesbian Alliance of Delaware (GLAD) and Ayn Rand acolyte, argued that such utterances exhibited a "blame the victim" ideology penned by those "motivated by their own self-hate," who were "willingly doing the dirty work of a homophobic society" while "buried safe in Rehoboth sand." In his letter to the *Whale*, he continued, "'I'll settle for less, so I'll be safe' is one of the primary ways by which minorities are controlled and excluded." From a distance of four decades, Slavin explains the psychology of the homosexual anti-Strand factions:

> That was just part of their generation, or their family, or where they grew up. It was better not spoken about. Having all that overt homosexuality was threatening to them. It then might raise a question within their family. "Why are you single?" or "What do you think about that?" They didn't want to talk about it!

The *Whale* tried to identify the individuals from these two supposedly local homosexual groups; it was unsuccessful. No one, it seemed, had heard of those who penned the letters. Whether they were pseudonyms or created out of whole cloth was never ascertained.

The Anti-Gay Vigilante Organization (AGVO) reared its head again. The Strand controversy, as Felton argues, "breathed life into what could have been homophobia or xenophobia, which was threatening *their* way of life." These youthful members, replete with T-shirts, included Strand-contracted "electricians and plumbers" who "would write on the studs as they were building, 'AGVO.' I was like 'What the fuck are you guys doing? I'm paying you!'"

The cost of renovations also skyrocketed. The town's board of adjustment, with two members (including its chairperson) who also served on the Homeowners Association board, ruled that the project constituted a "conversion," not a "remodeling." The cost of permitting doubled and, according to Felton, "instead of being charged a very modest assessment, we were charged $23,000 for every plumbing hookup."

In preparation for the August 19 ABCC meeting at town hall, the Puseys wrote to the state's major newspaper. They asked readers to envision "the Rusty Rudder in downtown Rehoboth," pleading, "It is your city that is on the line. Help preserve it." They deplored the "many changes [that] ha[d] taken place in Rehoboth Beach over the past several years . . . threatening our rights, privacy, and lifestyles." According to a Wilmington *Morning News* story, the couple "scoff[ed] at the suggestion that homophobia fueled their protest." Supporter Norma Lee Derrickson short-circuited the reporter's question: "I don't think that's a relevant issue."

A week prior to the hearing was Rehoboth's annual election. Three commissioner seats were open, with the incumbents (Sam Cooper, Billie Shields, and Norm Sugrue) endorsed by the Homeowners Association. Among the three challengers was Lawson, who, contrary to the association and its candidates, supported a city-owned parking garage and a bus system. The discriminatory interpretations of local zoning codes and the use of ordinances as political fodder were also concerns. He argued that town commissioners had an "obvious lack of knowledge of the pulse of the community" and, given his dual role as a local business owner and homeowner, that he had a unique perspective on Rehoboth's "schizophrenic personality."

"Uncle Miltie" Fried, who had run unsuccessfully for a commissioner's seat a decade earlier, similarly condemned those who would "retrogress to the era of our originators of the restricted Camp Meeting Association." Although he did not support Lawson, Fried pled for "mutual understanding," lest Rehoboth "become another Ocean City . . . or degenerate to the depths of Atlantic City."

Just below the surface of the proposed dance hall's presumed noise and parking problems was the common knowledge of Lawson's homosexuality: "I didn't put a sign up [being gay], but at the same time, everybody knew, and I never said I wasn't." He adds that many in town "didn't quite know how to react." Among those who signed his petition for candidacy were Rehoboth Beach House owners Bill Courville and Bob Jerome; Front Porch Café co-owner Keith Fitzgerald; Roy Anderson, who owned the Wooden Indian; and Joyce Felton of the Blue Moon.

Although Lawson did some door-to-door visits, yard signs, and flyers, these efforts paled considering the association behemoth. He was not surprised at his loss (finishing last among six candidates); he was upset about "disturbing actions" he witnessed on Election Day. As Lawson detailed to the *Whale*: "We all know that the [Homeowners Association] believes it owns and runs the city, but it was far too blatant" at the polling site. Smith, he alleged, "strutted around the building and made use of the city offices . . . all afternoon with papers and lists which could only mean they were using these facilities for the promotion of the incumbents."

COMING TOGETHER

Even by Rehoboth standards, The Strand saga was as historic as it was drawn out.[6] In the process of narrating this tale, one is reminded of the century-old fight between Rehoboth moralists and capitalists personalized in the conflict between archrivals Rev. John Quigg and William Bright. Eleven decades later, another community conflict divided religious conservatives from secular progressives, divorced business interests from those of a powerful community association, and evidenced a divergence of residents' opinions about vacationers. This contemporary struggle also separated closeted homosexuals from their *Queer as Folk* contemporaries. It was—and is—a beach story that nearly no one recounts the same way.

Homeowners, including wealthy retirees like Smith, along with those from generation-old families, such as Cooper, and mega-business owners, such as the Derricksons, entered the Rehoboth Beach Convention Hall. So did summer-only businesspeople, such as Kanter, and vacation renters, such as Murray Archibald and Steve Elkins. Also in attendance were clergy, local elected officials, and petitioners the Puseys, along with their adversaries Felton, Pisapia, and Lawson. All walked through the hall's common doors that Friday midafternoon in 1988. Outside, it was in the mid-80s, with a hint of rain; those crowding into the 250-seat auditorium knew that it would be hot, steamy, and stormy. They recognized, as did the *Morning News*, that this was "a tug-of-war over the city's future."

James Fuqua, the attorney representing the Puseys, along with Nancy Chrissinger, who represented the Homeowners Association, faced the six ABCC commissioners.[7] The Strand's attorney, Darrell Baker, squared off from the other side. At stake was whether Rehoboth's newest and largest nightspot, set to open that weekend, would be granted a liquor license for its first-floor Surfside Diner that would extend to the second-floor dance hall.

Many of those attending that day have passed away. Others have only faded memories. Thompson, though, "remembers it very well." Felton's "little group of people sat in the center, but they were way outnumbered. . . . They were very arrogant. They would make noises when someone else was speaking." At one point, Archibald stood up, shouting, "We just want to dance!" Felton also remembers the hearing "vividly"—albeit differently: "It was like an orthodox synagogue, with a line down the center. All the restaurant people were on one side, and the homeowners were on the other side." Both agree that the hearing grew heated as it moved from presentations by various attorneys to public commentary.

Attorney Fuqua, observing that the downstairs cabaret seated 106 people, while the upstairs dance club accommodated 625, said that it was a "classic case of the tail wagging the dog." He pointed out that the restaurant's liquor license application envisioned a bar as an "accessory" and that definition was "being pushed way beyond what it [wa]s intended to be." The owners, he argued, should apply instead for a taproom license, where the sale of food was ancillary, or apply for two separate licenses, adding, "I don't think there would be a major objection to the diner." Attorney

Joyce Felton, 1996. (Courtesy of CAMP
Rehoboth. Photo by Tony Burns.)

Chrissinger agreed, stating that it was the "magnitude" of the project that troubled the Homeowners Association.

When one of the commissioners asked Ray the primary purpose of the second floor, he responded trenchantly, "To call this a restaurant is incorrect." Jan Konesey, a state lobbyist for Common Cause who owned a summer house on Sussex Street, also spoke against licensing, as did Richard Derrickson. He inexplicably claimed that the entire proceeding was "moot," given that he was the legal tenant. Promising to sue, he proclaimed, "I ran the theater there last summer and I want it back!"

During the hearing, Pisapia explained that the diner and the dance hall were connected by a staircase. Attorney Baker noted that the original application, listing only the restaurant, had been withdrawn, given this stairwell. Further, the building had previously housed a skating rink and, later, twin movie theaters. Both had a similar capacity, yet no concerns had been voiced about noise or parking. Lawson also documented that the partners had paid $30,000 for an acoustical firm to soundproof the building, exceeding city code. Further, the complex was being developed with an eye toward attracting people by foot who otherwise would drive through town to dance at Renegade, creating more traffic and potentially hazardous driving situations.

No one spoke about The Strand's gay ownership or its primarily gay clientele. No one mentioned the town's history of shuttering its youth venues. No one mentioned the four-hundred-watt sound system used by late-night bands performing at Pockets just three years earlier or chronicled the building's nearly sixty-year history as an entertainment hub. "The Strand, though, was the first in-your-face, we're not going to be quiet about this" venture, Courville observes. Before, "it was okay to be there, as long as you knew your place." His partner, Jerome, sharpens the contrast: "The Strand was not small-town morality. It was late night; it was people dressed up in strange things—it was the Stonewall of Rehoboth!"

At the meeting's conclusion, the ABCC announced that its decision would be made the following week, frustrating many in attendance. Six days later, by a vote of 3–2, it denied the license because it failed to meet the criteria for a restaurant application. The commission's chairman, however, voted in favor. He volunteered, "I saw a need and a convenience factor," as Rehoboth had no single establishment exclusively selling alcohol by the drink. Pisapia promised to appeal. He told the press: "I think that the problem the board had was the fact that there was an upstairs, not just a dance club." Ray, in a celebratory mood, framed the choice as between a town of "raucousness" versus quietness. "The people," he pronounced, "wanted a quiet laid-back community instead of a party one."

The denial of a liquor license did not forestall the opening of The Strand or discourage party people from attending its inaugural opening. Patrons who paid the $10 cover and brought their liquor were provided with setups. Nonalcoholic beverages and food were available. Lawson remembers that Saturday-night gala: "If you went outside, the line for people waiting to get in went all the way to the post office, down 2nd Street, and around Baltimore Avenue, almost to the end of that block. It was like nothing I had ever seen!"

He also remembers, as do Pisapia and Felton, receiving a dozen dead roses.

SHADOW AND LIGHT

I thought a bit of the "shining city upon a hill." . . . [I]n my mind
it was a tall, proud city built on rocks stronger than oceans,
windswept, god-blessed and teeming with people of all kinds
living in harmony and peace.

—**Ronald Reagan**, farewell address

Despite its status as a vacation destination, small-town Rehoboth did
not escape the underlying angst and social ennui of the 1980s' infla-
tion-turned-recession, double-digit interest rates, threat of nuclear
Armageddon, and the "gay plague" ravaging Ronald Reagan's imagery of
America as a Pilgrim-esque "city upon a hill." Yet Reagan's vision resonated
with the majoritarian citizenry. From declaring "it's morning in America"
as he entered the presidency to championing America as "strong and true
on the granite ridge" when he departed, his portraiture of an industrious,
virtuous, and generous America—honeycombed with small, White-domi-
nated communities with commonly held Christian values—like that of
Dorian Gray, was putrescent.

Like Oscar Wilde's protagonist, some Americans in the 1980s—privileged by skin color, social class, and gender—adopted a libertarian and lib-
ertine urban lifestyle where power, wealth, and fame were the new American gods. Newly minted MBAs echoed Gordon Gekko's proclamation that
"greed is good," while club kids and cokeheads mixed with bankers and brokers at Manhattan's Limelight, clubs on DC's M Street—and The Strand.
These enclaves of decadence seemed oddly juxtaposed in Reagan's America,
although they were part of the same canvas.

It was an era of shadow and light. Through the Reagan-turned-Bush-era
looking glass, McMansions obscured homeless shelters, and agribusiness

replaced family farming. At decade's end, the Academy Award for best picture went to the racially feel-good film *Driving Miss Daisy*. Missing from the 1989 film nominees were Michael Moore's *Roger and Me*, a documentary on the economic crisis in the multiracial community of Flint, Michigan; and Spike Lee's raw depiction of racial tension and police brutality in Brooklyn's Bedford-Stuyvesant community, *Do the Right Thing*. Like the legend of El Dorado, the Arthurian tale of Camelot, or Plato's ideal state of Atlantis, the shining city upon a hill is mythos shrouded in metaphor.

DANCING OUT OF THE SHADOWS

For most of the 1980s, Steve Elkins and Murray Archibald lived in New York City, except for brief stints in Syracuse and Norfolk.[1] Elkins worked as a regional area sales manager for Lanier, whose EZ-1 word processor with printers sold for around $10,000 each. Meanwhile, Archibald pursued his vocation in the arts. He explains, "We were thinking that we would switch at some point and start going regularly to Fire Island. We had been there a good bit in the 1980s, but not as our main focus. We could *never* get away from Rehoboth."

In 1988, Elkins and Archibald celebrated their tenth anniversary on Labor Day weekend, staying at a Rehoboth home recently purchased by two friends. "We conceived it as a pool party," Archibald says, because "it had a beautiful backyard and pool." Elkins adds, "At the last minute, we decided to make it a fundraiser" for AIDS. The concept of a "Sun Dance" with money substituting for gifts emerged. "We had to do something to combat the despair, frustration, and pain we experienced watching our friends and loved ones die," Archibald recounts. On handcrafted invitations, he included a note: "In case of unkind weather, please join us at The Strand . . . ," which had opened three weeks earlier.

It rained torrentially the morning of September 4, but that didn't dampen spirits as the couple were joined at The Strand by eighteen hosts and several hundred of their guests to celebrate—and to donate. About $6,400 was raised for nonprofit AIDS organizations in DC (Whitman-Walker Clinic) and Baltimore (HERO). "Our anniversary party has taken on new meaning," declared Elkins. Given its success, the next year's "Sun-Dance" featured DJ Eric Cabrera and expanded the number of hosts sharing overhead costs. In 1990, they added an auction and enlarged the fundraiser group to one hundred individual and corporate hosts, who raised $32,000 for AIDS groups in DC, Philadelphia, and Baltimore.

Reflecting upon an event that is now in its fourth decade, Archibald observes that it "might have started as an anniversary party, but long ago, it became a celebration for the whole community." He fondly recalls "the look on Joyce Felton's face when she found out there were over a thousand people, and we were only expecting six hundred. I remember The Strand at 3 A.M. and hundreds of feet of georgette rippling over the undulating crowd. I remember faces that no longer live on the dance floor."

At the onset of SunDance, people contracting AIDS and their families and friends faced the sobering mortality rate of 95.5 percent, with more than thirty thousand deaths designated as AIDS-related.[2] By mid-1989, the Centers for Disease Control and Prevention (CDC) had reported one hundred thousand documented AIDS cases. The rate of death by HIV reached 10.2 per hundred thousand the following year (at its height, in 1995, it would be 16.2).

Sussex County PALS had disbanded a year before the first SunDance, as few locals had expressed interest in joining or in becoming an AIDS buddy. AIDS education and service efforts were subsumed under the Delaware Lesbian and Gay Health Advocates' (DLGHA's) umbrella as the Sussex County AIDS Committee (SCAC). Ivo Dominguez Jr. promised "more visibility" and "greater outreach." Although a few more people became involved, the Wilmington-based group had limited resources to devote to southern Delaware. Further, many residents in Rehoboth and the county viewed AIDS as a problem for "resort victims." However, in April 1988, the lead sentence of a page-one *Whale* story read, "Delaware is losing the battle against AIDS." The number of AIDS deaths in Delaware had nearly doubled since 1986 and would double again by 1990. Dominguez expressed disappointment: "We tried to expand our outreach and education in the beach area. . . . It wasn't enough."

There were few AIDS activists in lower Delaware. Audra Rivers, originally a member of PALS, established the John Isennock Memorial (JIM) Fund in 1986, the year of this Sussex County man's death. Headquartered at Renegade and directed by Glen Pruitt, it provided money for expenses ranging from transportation and food to medicine and funeral expenses. "Every Saturday night, she set up a raffle there and had a little quirky gift that someone had given," remembers Renegade manager Wayne Hodge. "No one bought raffle tickets for the gift"; the donating was the intent.

Another lone voice in the Rehoboth wilderness was Keith Lewis, an activist in Gay & Lesbian Alliance of Delaware (GLAD). Before moving to nearby Lewes, the thirty-year-old had met Ivo Dominguez and Jim Welch when he was a chemistry student at the University of Delaware.[3] "Keith was the quintessential artist. His flamboyant style of presentation and dress was somewhere between Quintin Crisp, Harry Hay, and King George," Dominguez recalls. He continues, "He was *always* identifiably queer," wearing eccentric body jewelry and "crazy clothing."

When Lewis moved to southern Delaware in the mid-1980s, his letters, from an openly gay man, began appearing in the *Whale*. He proposed that Mayor John Hughes appoint an "advisory board on Gay and Lesbian Concerns," defended the formation of a local fellowship of gay and lesbian Christians, and lambasted the "hateful, ill-informed, and un-Christian tirades" penned by the newspaper's readers. Along with GLAD chair John Ward, Lewis advocated for a dialogue that "would be to the advantage of both sides." Acknowledging that "the gay community can be quite stratified and uncooperative, too," the colorful partisan assumed a conciliatory position: "I don't think he [Hughes] realized the hostile nature of his remarks." In response, the mayor, "recouping from an arduous campaign," demurred in setting up any conversation. Lewis declared, "The virus is the problem, not sex." The best antidote, he prescribed, was to "just be honest for a change about sexuality and about discrimination."

Frank discussions about sexuality, however, were as sparse as discrimination against junkies, prostitutes, and queers was plentiful. In 1986, Gallup reported that 44 percent of Americans or their friends avoided places frequented by homosexuals for fear of contracting HIV. A year before SunDance, Gallup reported that more than two-thirds of Americans viewed AIDS as the most serious health problem facing the country. Another 1987 Gallup poll found that about half of the country believed that people with AIDS were to blame and that the disease was God's punishment. Further, one in five wanted AIDS "victims" quarantined. That year, President Reagan established a Presidential Commission on AIDS. Also in 1987, the Food and Drug Administration approved the first antiretroviral drug to treat the disease, zidovudine (AZT), although its cost and dosage difficulties curbed widespread use. The CDC launched a national advertising campaign, "America Responds to AIDS," but the U.S. Senate adopted (94–2) the "Helms Amendment," which required such federally funded educational efforts to stress sexual abstinence and prohibited the "promotion of homosexuality." Consequently, the multi-million-dollar CDC national ad campaign was generally viewed as political theater, diverting needed monies from local efforts. Federal and state responses fell short of what many queer activists thought necessary as the country was entering the seventh year of the "gay plague."

In 1987, New York City's Larry Kramer, whose autobiographic and polemic play *The Normal Heart* had angered many mainstream gay leaders, helped establish AIDS Coalition to Unleash Power (ACT UP). In San Francisco, NAMES Project founder Cleve Jones orchestrated fifty volunteers to assemble 1,920 6×3-foot panels of the AIDS Memorial Quilt at the National Mall during the 1987 National March on Washington for Lesbian and Gay and Rights. In Switzerland, James Bunn and Thomas Netter of the World Health Organization were planning the first World AIDS Day.

Regionally, DC's private Whitman-Walker Clinic (formed in 1973 as the Gay Men's VD Clinic) focused primarily on AIDS, providing education, outreach, and medical services. Established in 1981, Philadelphia Community Health Alternatives (PCHA), also originating as a health and STD clinic (Lavender Health), served mostly gay men with AIDS. In Baltimore, the Health Education Resource Organization (HERO), begun in 1983 as a buddy system at the office of gay physician Bernie Branson, was a national model for HIV/AIDS education and comprehensive patient services.

In northern Delaware, Dominguez had drafted the preface to the state's 1987 *AIDS Advisory Task Force Report*. As executive director of the nonprofit DLGHA, founded in 1984, he managed a staff of ten people, more than a hundred volunteers, and a $300,000 budget, offering AIDS education, support services, and anonymous testing. His partner, DLGHA President Welch, traveled throughout the state as director of Delaware's HIV testing program. From Wilmington's Griffin Community Center, they operated a hotline in the basement and the Hen's Teeth alternative bookstore on the main level. The DLGHA office was shared with GLAD and the Immanuel Metropolitan Community Church (MCC) on the second floor; the couple lived on the third story.

In southern Delaware, however, there was neither an outreach office nor a clinic. "It is criminal to have to transport people to Wilmington," Dominguez told a *Whale* reporter. Largely through Welch's efforts, in 1990, the state established Christiana Cares Wellness Clinic in Georgetown. By then, at least 160 Delawareans had perished.

Meager government AIDS funding often forced community groups, serving different racial, gender, or sexual groups, to compete for limited funds. "Those serving racial minority populations were also concerned about older organizations," which, according to historian Dan Royles, had emerged from "mostly white social networks of well-connected gay men." Because "the neighborhoods where they operated were unwelcoming—if not outright hostile—to Black gay men," alternative organizations for women and People of Color surfaced.

In DC, where half of the AIDS cases were in African American patients, the Whitman-Walker Clinic was referred to as "White Man Walker" for its cultural insensitivity and focus on White gayborhoods. The manager of ClubHouse, a long-standing Black dance spot in northwest Washington, started Us Helping Us in 1986. It began as an informal buddy system by local activist Rainey Cheeks before evolving into "a 12-week holistic program that focused on interventions through diet, cooking, meditation practices, nature retreats . . . and workshops." Philadelphia's David Fair, a leader of the mostly Black healthcare workers' union, partnered with nurse-educator Rashidah Lorraine Hassan (now Rashidah Abdul-Khabeer) who had worked with PCHA. They cofounded Blacks Educating Blacks About Sexual Health Issues (BEBASHI), doing street outreach and working through local African American churches. In 1987, AIDS Action Baltimore—under the leadership of Lynda Dee, Garey Lambert, and Pat Moran—began providing financial assistance and case management as "women and people of color started being affected by the epidemic." Dee, an attorney whose husband had succumbed to AIDS; Lambert, a projectionist at the Charles Theater; and Moran, its manager, who worked closely with filmmaker John Waters, "pushed the state to push . . . HERO to do the same."

In 1989, historian Harlon Dalton asserted, "We have to figure a way to communicate across the racial chasm," observing that "our language is the same, but our frames of reference are so different." Traditional AIDS organizations (along with health officials), he wrote, "have been frustrated to organize the black community to deal with AIDS. While the vast majority of such people and organizations are predominantly white, even black and Latino officials and activists have run into more than their fair share of walls."

Some of the White-established programs, recognizing their limitations, supported efforts to serve People of Color by fundraising jointly, developing culturally sensitive outreach programs, or co-submitting grant proposals. Some of these efforts were successful; others were not. One of these with a mixed reputation was DLGHA.

Echoing Dalton, Dominguez writes in his original preface to Delaware's *AIDS Advisory Task Force Report*, "The assumption of the superiority of the mainstream culture's way of doing things is often the major obstacle to needed dialogue and the provision of services."[4] Ironically, DLGHA was targeted by AIDS specialist Mark Fefferman, under contract with the state's division of public health. He criticized DLGHA's practice of placing emerging local AIDS groups, such as the SCAC and Wilmington's Alliance of Black and Hispanic Communities Against AIDS, within its nonprofit umbrella. Denouncing the organization as a "Gay White Club," Fefferman claimed that such emerging groups' "bid for federal money [wa]s a poorly disguised effort by the umbrella group to get more federal money for its AIDS efforts."

As the AIDS pandemic worsened, tensions grew among activists advocating for different strategies to secure more government funding, to access promising drug therapies, and to fast-track research. The most radical, the loosely organized ACT UP, splintered between science-based advocates and street activists as it anarchically mobilized across the nation. A Delaware chapter was formed in July 1990 under the informal leadership of Keith Lewis and Eric Brooks. This twenty-member chapter's first act was a summer protest at the Rehoboth home of U.S. senator William Roth Jr., who was to host a fundraiser. He had joined three other Republican senators, including Jesse Helms, in voting against the Ryan White Care Act that spring. With signs like "5000 Infected. What Will It Take!" and "Roth-Castle Have Blood on Their Hands," a couple of dozen protested while residents watched wearily from grand porches. Lewis, wearing his trademark large round-rimmed glasses, shouted, "We've come to realize we're going to be ignored until we're so loud we can't be ignored." Roth's fundraiser had been abruptly canceled after Rehoboth authorities informed the senator's office, but the die-in at Surf and Henlopen Avenues was not. Wilmington's *Sunday News Journal* quoted Lewis: "As long as it's gay people and black people dying, no one seems to care."

THE LIGHTNESS OF BEING

In 1989, the authors of *After the Ball: How America Will Conquer Its Fear and Hatred of Gays in the 90's*, psychologist Marshall Kirk and marketer Hunter Madsen, confronted homosexuals with "the unpleasant realities of the culture *they've* created" [emphasis mine].[5] Seemingly echoing the Moral Majority, Madsen opines, "Bad tendencies impoverished the quality of gay life" and "the need for inhibitions seems to have been confirmed by the outbreak of AIDS." Nevertheless, "as cynical as it may seem," write the authors, "AIDS gives us the chance, however brief, to establish ourselves as a victimized minority." Their thesis is literally straightforward: To advance on civil rights, gays must address the concerns of straight America (flamboyance and promiscuity, drug and alcohol abuse, narcissism and hedonism), market themselves through a national campaign (positive historical and contemporary portraits, victim imageries of bigotry and AIDS), and promote the coming-out of everyday people.

Their book was met by hostility within queer communities, including Delaware. Rather than trying to make themselves "more palatable," Dominguez countered, "a better approach would be to promote self-esteem and tolerance of diversity." Nevertheless, Wilmington's *Sunday News Journal*, in a prominent book review headlined "A Failed Revolution," blamed slow social acceptance and political advancement two decades after Stonewall on the homosexual. The message was clear: Disco is dead. Gays should enter sobriety, act maturely, and straighten up.

If queers read *After the Ball* while vacationing in Rehoboth, it was not evident on the beaches, in the bars, at the clubs, or between the sheets. The same weekend as SunDance, sun worshipers at Poodle Beach witnessed the second annual "drag volleyball" game.

Poodle Beach lies just east of Prospect and Queen Streets, at the southern end of the Boardwalk. It had been a lesbian/gay social space since the 1980s, and a Delaware State historical marker has been planned in recognition of its importance to the queer community. From the 1950s through the early 1980s, homosexuals had routinely played volleyball, enjoyed games of chess, and sunbathed farther south—past the Carpenters' private beach—to a jurisdictional no-man's land. Some then eventually resettled on the sands right off the southern Boardwalk from Queen Street. A story recounted by local photographer Tony Burns is that

> two gay cousins, fixtures in the thriving gay beach community, simply got fed up with walking so far past the Rehoboth Boardwalk to make camp. One day, they spread their blankets on the sand just past the Boardwalk. Soon, their friends and companions joined them.

One local gay historian recounts two possible explanations for the beach's name: Gay men on the beach were "all coiffed and groomed, much like a poodle" or "the guys walk around with their butts in the air, just like a poodle dog."

Whatever its origins, Forrest Park, who had moved to Rehoboth in the late 1970s, is credited as the originator of Labor Day drag volleyball. He and other gay men had played volleyball beyond Carpenter's Beach. "It was a long trek carrying that net," Brent Minor, one of the players, emphasizes. "At some point, like Rosa Parks, he was just too tired to move." During the mid-1980s, the town relented, allowing them to play volleyball at Poodle

Beach: "We had trouble once or twice with the police. But we got through it and were able to stay there." Other gay men soon joined them on the beach.

In 1988, the team "decided that we were going to celebrate the end of the season by doing a drag volleyball game," Park explains. After playing for a while that Sunday afternoon, he went back to the car and grabbed an assortment of women's bathing suits, ranging from pink polka dot and lime green to blue with white stripes. Players changed on the beach as others formed a square of sheets, shielding their modesty. Then, "at the spur of the moment," a team of nine lesbians propositioned them for a friendly pickup game.

Forrest Park (Flo), Mark Kimble (Myrna), Curt Leciejewski (Stella), and Brent Minor (Barbara Ann) are among the still-living original players. "We couldn't find a ninth person to put on a women's bathing suit," laughs Barbara Ann. That didn't affect the outcome; they won, 21–3. The spectacle drew a curious set of onlookers. It would be nothing compared to the thousands attending in later years, watching coverage on the TODAY *Show* or reading about it in *USA Today*. Eighty-four-year-old Flo says, "I had no idea it would grow to the size it did. But I'm so glad it did. It's something to look forward to year after year."

The second annual drag volleyball event established the Labor Day Sunday tradition of two teams, Flo's All-Star Classics (later known as the Originals) battling When'D's Holiday All-Stars (later renamed the Loyal Opposition). This 1989 game, in which Flo's team wore women's hats along with swimsuits, was a very competitive match and attracted more spectators.

The following year, the game was canceled. In addition to the continued Strand controversy, the heated summer of 1990 witnessed escalating gay harassment and assaults, more protests by the local chapter of ACT UP, and an unsettling August election. Myrna recalls, "There was so much emotion going on." Stella underscores, "It was an awful time to be down here." Yet the divas of drag returned to the volleyball net the following Labor Day weekend. Barbara Ann recollects the team concluding, "You know what? This is our beach, too! We're playing. If they want to come after us, they'll come after us."

In their 1991 rematch, both teams adopted themes. "Nobody knew them until we walked onto the beach," explains Stella. "It was the biggest secret in town!" That year, about four hundred spectators—many with pompoms and gay flags—gathered for the end-of-summer spectacle. A flyer introduced the two "team mistresses" as Flo, a "wall of buxom power," and When'D, the "capitalist bitch from hell." A news story laced with double entendres described the spectacle: "The Classics, garbed in tutus, got off to

Drag volleyball team on Poodle Beach, 1992. (Courtesy of Curt Leciejewki.)

a strong start with a combination of peerless pirouettes, high camp, and vicious pumps, rather, spikes." After a particularly "licentious routine involving an oversized squash . . . the Holiday All Stars climaxed in victory."

Victors donned nuns' habits the following year, strolling onto the beach with rulers-in-hand and singing Madonna's "Like a Prayer." As they filed onto the court, they sang a rendition of "I Will Follow Him." When Flo's All-Star Classics—dressed as 1950s debs, replete with poodle skirts, Hula-Hoops, and bouffant hairdos—began service, their opponents prayerfully chanted, "We shall inherit the serve!"

For the first ten years, Flo sewed her team's costumes, ranging from Dallas Cowboy cheerleaders to French maids. Remembering her role in the French maids, Barbara Ann confesses, "The cancan was tough. Now, we've learned to rotate one player out of the game as we go along to conserve our energy." Competitive play (several players were nationally ranked) was matched only by competition in costumes, cheers, and routines. "When you're out there playing, it is competitive," emphasizes Stella. "Adrenalin pumps like I never knew I had!" Play was also complicated by a drag volleyball rule that wigs be worn throughout the game.

Each year, the event grew in campy complexity and crowd size. It was not just the theme. "You have to have the music to go along with it, and you['ve] got to know what you can do with the theme," explains Myrna. For one Labor Day event, the Originals employed a *Sound of Music* theme. When the "von Tramp" little girl (Big Girl on the team) asked, "Where's Fraulein Maria?" Barbara Ann pointed to the dunes. Unbeknownst to the other players, Myrna had climbed up the ridge and, on cue, tumbled down the sand with a guitar case. When Myrna, as Julie Andrews, arrived on court, the guitar case opened, with bags of Doritos falling onto the seashore.

Cognizant of Rehoboth's bumper sticker about being a "family town," Barbara Ann admits, "There were double entendres, but never any cussing. We kept it pretty clean." Flo interrupts, "Except when we passed the sausage!" Then, there was the year the team greeted beach fans as the Church Ladies from the **R**ehoboth **E**vangelical **C**hurch of **T**he **U**niversal **M**artyr. Their sign, in bold letters, simply read RECTUM. "Whenever we would get a point, we'd cheer, 'Hail Rectum!'" Barbara Ann laughingly recalls.

Like SunDance, the Originals viewed Labor Day drag volleyball as a way "to celebrate our Rehoboth community." Not coincidentally, it was also an event that emerged during the most heated period of homophobia within the town. Barbara Ann continues, "It is a strong message: Just enjoy our lives. That sets an example for other people to see. They can take pride." It was also an event celebrating years (eventually decades) of friendships. "It started out as a group of friends who hung around the beach all summer long," Myrna points out. "That's what we wanted it to be." However, as crowds and publicity increased, there was some pressure to modify it as a fundraiser. "We always looked at this as the one major *free* event in town," stresses Barbara Ann, although "there were a couple of years where they tried to link it to SunDance."

Barbara Ann also recalls that some spectators would have a "house party" before walking to the game. By the late 1980s, an ever-growing number of White gay men leased homes for the season. Although there was an occasional woman or Person of Color in the group, most lesbians and racial minorities lacked the free time or financial resources for seven or fourteen summer weekends of fun.

Sharon Kanter had bought an inexpensive trailer beyond the outskirts of town that became her summer getaway and a place for vacationing lesbians to bunk: "The men did shares in houses, but the women couldn't afford it. They just stayed with other people."

RENTAL CRACKDOWN

People renting houses for the entire summer is a long-standing Rehoboth tradition and common at other beach resorts. One veteran of house rentals since the 1950s recalls ten or so friends, "a pretty typical Washington crowd," renting on Henlopen Avenue: "We had a mixed group of men and women . . . which raised a few eyebrows in 1953." By the late 1970s, more than a hundred houses were operating as seasonal rentals for mostly heterosexual singles buying summer weekend shares. In exchange for low-cost lodging and, perhaps, a sense of community, members often tolerated cramped housing and the eccentricities of their summer housemates. Bobby Van Fossan, the owner of the Summerhouse restaurant and bar on Rehoboth Avenue, published a directory of houses. House parties, too, were common, but varied by social class. Sunday brunches serving hors d'oeuvres on fine china to invited guests wandering around well-manicured lawns contrasted with well-advertised keggers with beer served in plastic pitchers or disposable cups to a herd of raucous guests. As one longtime summer resident bemoaned to the *Washingtonian* in 1978, "Group houses were much more exclusive years ago."

As gay men began visiting in greater numbers, they joined this burgeoning seasonal rental market. In the 1980s, the gay rental scene exploded. Classified ads seeking or offering Rehoboth rentals multiplied in the *Blade*. Harking back, Archibald writes, "I remember when there were only a handful of group houses and everyone knew everyone else."

A town ordinance prohibited the renting of summer residences to more than three unrelated persons. Because money flowed to homeowners and businesspersons, city officials spottily enforced it—until the election of Hughes. Homosexuals walking hand in hand and mattresses tied to the roofs of young people's arriving cars were the bane of the mayor. He promised a "crackdown" on homosexuality and group rentals.

Hughes seemed unconcerned about the substance of these issues yet understood their symbolic importance. His concern was less the number of people residing at the rental and more the nature of the group. "We're not going to arrest a cotillion for making a little noise" or those who have "one good party per year." Instead, he targeted those treating a rental house like a "wayside inn." In an editorial, the *Whale* rebuked Hughes and recommended "throwing out" the rental ordinance "in favor of more enforceable" ordinances on noise and traffic. Nevertheless, a subsequent proposition to lower the lawful noise limit from one hundred to ninety decibels between 1:00 and 7:00 A.M. failed to gain even a motion at the commissioners' meeting.

With the advent of The Strand, concerns about late-night noise changed. Homeowners Association leaders, their cabal of commissioners, Bertha and Raymond Pusey, and allied conservative gays joined forces in a dogged campaign to conserve their community values and to vanquish a plague of queer summer renters, Poodle Beach revelers and campy antics, late-night Boardwalk cruising and preening gayety. The mythos of a Wilder-esque *Our Town* enshrouded as a metaphoric "family resort" set counterpoint to The Strand's Wilde-esque imagery on Rehoboth's fabled namesake avenue. As these adjudicators of morals further journeyed into the valley of shadows, they confronted a fledgling alliance of progressive business owners, homosexuals, and residents.

THE ALLIANCE VERSUS THE ASSOCIATION

Rehoboth's discord during The Strand era seems unmatched, except perhaps a century earlier, during its founding.[6] Contention and conciliation, temerity and trepidation, hubris and humility, compassion and callousness, mercifulness and mercilessness, fervency and frivolity were the norms. From these community ruptures, Rehoboth and its inhabitants metamorphosed.

Despite their win at the state liquor board's August 1988 hearing, the Puseys and those behind them understood that their victory could be pyrrhic. Although Strand partners had already appealed the decision, they could also submit a different application altogether. The Homeowners Association's board, after discussion with the Puseys' attorney, prepared to reengage its lawyer and mobilize its membership.

Following the traditional post–Labor Day departure of seasonal shop owners and weekenders, two-term commissioner Norman Sugrue joined his elected cronies at a "special meeting" prior to their public work session. The effusive forty-six-year-old had operated his dad's Maryland Ford dealership before moving to Rehoboth in 1977. Later, he served on the board of the Homeowners Association prior to winning his city seat with the slogan "A Family Man for a Family Resort." That night, he grumbled, "Rehoboth is no longer a small town" and now had unwholesome "activity going on at 1, 2, or 3 in the morning." Sugrue then proposed a "late night booze palace" ordinance. This so-called bar ban would prohibit any future tavern or taproom, dance hall or dinner theater, café or cabaret, nightclub or after-hours club due to its "adverse impact on density, noise, and parking." Ten minutes later, without dissent, the commissioners approvingly set a public hearing at month's end. In his analysis, *Whale* reporter Paul Hughes linked the late summer's "hornet's nest of sentiment" against The Strand to the October ban, "removing once and for all any threat by entrepreneurs to obtain licenses." At the time, Gene Lawson observed the action as "an obvious attempt to quickly strike before anyone could realize what this draconian measure mean[t]."

Several days before this public hearing, few among those gathering at the Rehoboth Beach–Dewey Beach Chamber of Commerce meeting voiced agreement with the proposed restrictive business ordinance. One businessman bluntly declared it "another example of the homeowners' attitudes dominating the thinking of the commissioners." (The Homeowners Association had publicly endorsed Sugrue's amendment.)

Although merchants generally viewed it as "merely a guise to cover up other motives," Mayor Kimber Vought volunteered that the "proposed ordinance ha[d] absolutely nothing to do with lifestyle." He failed to mention that an earlier draft had solely targeted BYOB establishments—specifically, The Strand. Gay businessman John Theis acidly commented that commissioners were "not so much concerned about over development as with dictating WHO may enjoy Rehoboth Beach and HOW." Decades later, Glen Thompson discloses, "The people I talked to when it was going on" understood that "*that* was the purpose of it." He further divulges that the homeowners' cabal was calling the shots, while Sugrue, his eyes on the mayor's office, was a willing "front person." Town chatter and letters to the editor confirmed their assessments: "This is not a gay issue," one livid *Whale* reader wrote. Referring to Strand partners, the reader continued, "The handful who have divided this town are not interested in gay rights, only in greed." Another citizen exclaimed, "These bars are catering to homosexuals!"

The commissioners met at the overcrowded and overheated convention hall on the evening of October 28. Armed with data, Ray listed forty-one liquor licenses in the town (*all* tied to restaurants). "Rehoboth's already a liquor combat zone," he shouted. "Enough's enough!" After perfunctorily listening to opponents, the commissioners swiftly enacted the ordinance, 6–1. Only seventy-year-old Pittsburgh native John McTighe voted against it. Asked about the reason for his lone vote, the retired insurance broker enigmatically replied, "Because I'm not a member of *that* organization." The animus between him and association-endorsed commissioners was palpable. Despite serving two terms, McTighe had never been appointed to chair a standing committee, and his reports sat "gathering dust."

One opponent in attendance, Terry Plowman, marveling at "the speed with which it was passed," excoriated the ordinance as "a triumph of discrimination and deception over the democratic process." Another restauranteur, Nancy Wolfe, was aghast at the "generally arrogant air from the dais."

Within a week, more than a hundred people assembled at Wolfe's Chez la Mer. They formed the Rehoboth Beach Alliance for Responsible Government (ARG), "with avowed objectives of overturning" the ordinance through a referendum. Wolfe, who acknowledged that the "ultimate goal [wa]s to change the leadership of the city," was elected president, and Gene Lawson was joined on the board by Elizabeth Hooper of the Corner Cupboard Inn, restaurateurs Sidney Arzt and Keith Fitzgerald, businessman Bruce Blugerman, and educator Wayne Steele, among others.

The group soon garnered enough citizen signatures to force the commissioners to either rescind the ordinance or hold a referendum. Despite receiving more qualified signatures than required, the city rejected the petition, arguing that the accompanying affidavit "lacked a crucial phrase." Alliance leaders accused the commissioners of harboring "antigay sentiment" by employing a technicality. After ARG filed suit in superior court, city officials relented and agreed to hold a referendum at the next August election. During the interim, the town and the two civic organizations, along with the chamber of commerce, failed in their attempt to reach compromise language on the bar-ban bill.[7] Nevertheless, commissioners revised the ordinance, removing dinner theaters and "clarifying" that it did not apply to restaurants.

Meanwhile, the state liquor commission denied The Strand's appeal. In January 1989, the partners submitted a new application solely for the street-front Surfside Diner. "Hard on the heels of the filing came a resurgence of the same neighborhood opposition," reported the *Whale*. The Homeowners Association's board allocated $1,500 for legal fees to help "lower" the Puseys' costs. Despite a pledge from the Puseys' attorney at the August hearing that there would be no opposition to such an application, the Baltimore Avenue power couple forced another public meeting. "We don't think anything has changed," Ray adamantly announced. He offered no explanation, however, for how "traffic, lack of parking, and noise" could be an issue for a small restaurant with a tiny bar on the commercialized Rehoboth Avenue strip. Nevertheless, his attorney protested the application and demanded that the commission release the owners' financial documents, alleging indebtedness. At the sparsely attended March liquor board hearing, the license was approved, but alcohol could not be sold at or brought to the upstairs Strand.

Eventually, ARG targeted Sugrue's seat, seeking an "electable candidate" who would be "friendly to more diverse enterprises." Recognizing the political headwinds, Sugrue announced his retirement in April, telling supporters that he wanted to devote more time to real estate. Stating "he'll be missed," privately, association president Jay Smith fumed over the loss of its most pliable commissioner. On the other side, despite its original goal of changing the town's leadership, ARG failed to field or endorse a candidate, although two of its former board members had declared. Alliance officer Hooper candidly admitted, "We simply don't have a consensus." Rehoboth natives, fifty-one-year-old retired art dealer and publicist Blugerman and thirty-eight-year-old high school teacher Steele, ran opposite association-endorsed candidates: well-known businessman Donald Derrickson, acknowledged for his independence, and Richard Darley, a retired *National Geographic* cartographer who advocated for "traditional values of community and family."

BLUGERMAN'S BLUES: INFERENCES, INNUENDOS, AND INSINUATIONS

"There exists an ever-widening chasm and distrust between a few brokers of special interests and the citizenry" who "appear as wolves in sheep's clothing, acting and speaking for their own self-interest," Blugerman unabashedly stated when announcing his candidacy.[8] Writing to the *Whale*, he called for "awakening the people" and denounced association-supported "parking plans and business plans." He also advocated for absentee balloting to get a "fair representation in our town council." Growing up on Dodd's Lane, he envisioned a "metamorphosis" in his hometown.

Although fellow gadfly and retiring commissioner McTighe endorsed Blugerman for Sugrue's seat, the *Whale* reported that the candidate's "caustic remarks" had "enraged many people." The 1989 Rehoboth election would be one of the most acrimonious in memory. "Name calling, mud-slinging and innuendo have intensified to a level unheard of among the city's proper, cocktail party set," wrote a *News Journal* reporter.

Like Lawson, a candidate in the previous year's commissioners' race, the quick-witted Blugerman campaigned within Rehoboth's queer community. Unlike Lawson, whose homosexuality was never raised during his electioneering, a summer "whispering campaign" plagued Blugerman's efforts. There, too, were late-night anonymous phone calls, ranging from the obvious ("We're not ready for a gay commissioner") to the obnoxious ("Get out of the race, faggot!"). The 1959 Citadel graduate released a press statement "publicly and emphatically denying that I am gay" and vowing "to face the slander head-on." This move, in turn, generated more public homophobic responses: "He assumes that four crank calls are part of a campaign to discredit him publicly by labeling him gay. But if he had kept silent, the issue probably never would have surfaced."

Two weeks before the August 12 election, a "rancorous" association-sponsored candidate forum occurred. Commissioner Mildred Shields, who had retired to Rehoboth in 1962 with her husband and sat on the association's board, interrogated Blugerman. Given his "purported dislike of the entire commission," she asked, how could he possibly work with the other commissioners? He rejoined, "My job is to serve the citizens of this town, not you or your cohorts." Calling Rehoboth a "ninety-day town," Blugerman outlined his opposition to a parking garage or a park-and-ride system, arguing that the money would be better spent on improving the town's drainage and streets. The bar ban, he asserted, was an assault on "free enterprise," and he linked it to the ban on absentee voting, resulting in "the disenfranchisement of many voters." When leaving the event, he reported that Smith had "grabbed my arm and uttered some unintelligible threat." A homeowner present at the event was "appalled" by Blugerman's treatment. He was "degraded, threatened," and treated with "cruelty and venomous action."

The association and its commissioners lined up squarely against Blugerman, ignoring the soft-spoken and lilliputian Steele, who also opposed the bar ban. Association board member Frank Hubbell endorsed recently transplanted Washingtonian Darley, declaring that he had "absolutely no questions about [Darley's] character or his past." In contrast, he observed that Blugerman's "reputation [wa]s well-known" and "dubious." In response, a Blugerman supporter wrote that citizens were "fed up with your kissing cousins whom you hope to sit with as a rubber stamp commissioner." Similarly, Plowman observed that Darley "ha[d] been 'adopted' by the well-known Rehoboth Beach Homeowners Association cronies who have pushed him to the forefront to do their bidding."

Darley and Derrickson attacked Blugerman as "a clown" who chose to "bash" the town with his "confrontational attitude" and "his own manufac-

tured issues." Neither, of course, enumerated Blugerman's personal background or confronted the homophobia of some of the town's citizenry. Further, Commissioner Jack Salin addressed the "malicious criticism which
ha[d] been leveled at . . . Mr. Darley's spirit of cooperation." Commissioner
Shields coded her endorsement of Darley and Derrickson, praising "each
[a]s a devoted family man."

An anonymous *Whale* reader queried, "What must gays think of a man
who considers a suggestion that he is homosexual as 'willful slander against
my good name.'" Jack Ackerman had met Blugerman, a former ballet dancer and publicist for comedian Paul Lynde, years before at a Moon happy
hour. During late summer, he recalls that his neighbor, Jim Vandergraft,
had a Sunday afternoon yard party: "Jim said, 'Why don't I invite Blugerman to come to the party so he can kind of circulate and glad-hand?'" Ackerman adds, "When Bruce was coming in, I said, 'I'm glad you came. We
weren't going to pressure you if you didn't feel comfortable.' He said, 'No.
I'm glad you invited me. I'm walking into safe territory!'" Asked about how
this group felt about his denial, Ackerman replied, "I wasn't upset about
that. He was just playing politics; most people felt that way."

Blugerman's sexuality was not the only target. Some accused him of
"buying the senior vote" with the promise to donate his commissioner's
meager salary. More seriously, there were insinuations of culpability in the
shooting death of his twin brother, Robert, an avid bodybuilder who held
the 1977 Mr. Fire Island title. "I was so offended," Blugerman later told a
reporter, "I nearly withdrew from the race. . . . I never felt the truth would
be distorted." He added, it "illustrate[d] how brazen the power structure
can be when [its] power base is threatened."

When the polls closed on the second Saturday in August, the bar-ban
referendum was defeated by a 2–1 margin, ending an electoral campaign
that Wilmington's *Sunday News Journal* called "one of the ugliest in Rehoboth's history." The 1,086 votes cast, of course, did not represent those
property owners who lived elsewhere or long-term renters. Darley and Derrickson were overwhelmingly elected. Blugerman, finishing a distant
fourth, said, "This whole business ban was, no matter what they say, directed at the gay community. They cloak it all in this other language . . . but
anybody who knows Rehoboth knows what it is all about." In contrast,
Smith was "tickled to death," adding that there was a "common interest in
keeping this a family town."

Activist Lewis told the *Philadelphia Inquirer* that he was "surprised that
the gay community had not been more vocal in its protest against the pro-

posed ordinance" or the homophobic assaults on Blugerman. Unlike the queer activism found in the gay resorts of P'Town and Key West, he lampooned members of gay Rehoboth as mostly "Izod shirt, boat-shoe Republican gay men" who "ha[d] learned . . . to let things roll off their backs."

Although he declared, "You have not heard the last of Bruce Blugerman," within a year, he sold his Henlopen Acres home with its pink marble fireplace and moved to West Palm Beach, but not before confronting the association in one last hurrah. The bar-ban ordinance continues to this day, but its impact on the queering of Rehoboth during the 1990s was as unintentional as it was consequential. *Out & About*, chronicling Rehoboth as the new Provincetown six years later, observed that the ordinance "ha[d] resulted in the gene of a house party circus." The bar ban and referendum imbroglio also sparked embers of local queer activism. These would soon blaze after the next assault on Rehoboth's fledgling queer community.

CAMPTIME

Grassroots change takes place step by step, day by day.
—**Steve Elkins**, *The Way I See It*

F
ollowing decisive victories in electing their slate of commissioners and defeating the bar-ban referendum, Homeowner Association members were thanked by President Jay Smith for sending "the message that we like our town the way it is."[1] Unwilling to endorse and unable to field candidates for the 1989 municipal election, the Alliance for Responsible Governance disbanded. It's "a done deed," the organization's members declared. "Let's move on."

Bruce Blugerman, however, did not go gently into the night. "Perhaps, I'll author a book: *Bloodied but Unbowed*," he said in his cheeky manner. More seriously, he promised to test the bar-ban ordinance in court, reporting "a commitment from a prominent and successful businessman" to apply for a business license. He also offered an upbeat analysis of his defeat at the polls: "I am not the least bit discouraged by the outcome as it shows the Rehoboth Beach Homeowners Association is vulnerable."

No matter how one spun it, the twin electoral victories spurred more homophobia, while fears about The Strand persisted. A Philadelphia gay man, following his Labor Day week vacation in Rehoboth, wrote that he was "totally unprepared for the welcome I received." During his first few days, "I was glared, stared, jeered, and laughed at, called 'faggot' and 'queer' and had a container of soda thrown at me." He also recounted a girl, no older than six, yelling from a passing car: "I think gay people are stupid!" The Philadelphia tourist vowed "never again to visit Rehoboth" but counseled, "There is strength in numbers. Stand up and be counted!"

A *Whale* reader rhetorically interrogated this gay visitor: What "was [he] doing to attract such degrading attention? Why did the people who malign him think he was gay?" The reader then observed, "It used to be, before gays came out of the closet, that we scarcely knew of them. . . . Now, too many gays arrogantly throw it in our faces and recoil in anger when we react negatively." Another local, "furious at your disregard for decency and the sensitivity of others," penned an open letter to the "Gay Community" about its "outrageous sexual activity" at the nearby state park. Needing "to feel safe taking my children for a walk," she advocated for "banning gays from this area." A third categorically spouted, "Homosexuality degrades the family," and "its inroad in Rehoboth Beach does endanger the very concept and existence of a family beach."

Nevertheless, Smith continued to deny that antigay sentiments were behind the ban: "This is not a gay issue." Yet the *Baltimore Sun* story's next paragraph quoted a young mother: "That's what the bar ban was all about, keeping the gays out. . . . It's a good family town except for the gay population." Countering that gays "have families, too," Gene Lawson prophesized, "Sadly, I think it'll get worse before it gets better."

THE STRAND RAID

Multicolored laser lights filtered through a pair of giant sunglasses as Sleaze Rock streamed from one of the DJ's three turntables.[2] From the wrought-iron balcony, before reaching the upstairs lounge's sliding-glass doors, VIP members relished a sea of gay bodies. Shirtless men danced on the banquettes around the perimeter of the dance floor. Others, like Murray Archibald, wearing just spandex shorts and boots, were on the floor, dancing. "You could lose yourself in it"; it was "just the sheer joy of the dance." He continues:

> Back in those days, people gathered in clubs. That's where they saw their friends, where they could be themselves, where they might have to go back to work the next day where they were in the closet. At the same time, everybody was dying. Life and death were walking a very fine line.

Unexpectedly, the house lights brightened, and "the DJ, who never missed a beat," abruptly stopped: "Suddenly, the whole dance floor was surrounded by people."

Earlier that Sunday August morning of 1989, about fifteen undercover officers, wearing "trendy designer clothes," had entered The Strand, dutifully paying the $8 cover. Down the block, near the convention center, a school bus was packed with Delaware State Police and Drug Enforcement Administration (DEA) agents. Rehoboth police officers were also nearby. Inside, clandestine cops observed "open drug transactions"—as they had during past weekends of surveillance. "We had to change our ways of doing things," explained Delaware State Police Captain Gregory Sacco. "We're dealing with a [close-knit] homosexual community" and patrons who use a "buy-a-pill, take-a-pill" strategy.

An hour before dawn, sixty armed men stormed The Strand. Undercover police swiftly identified those patrons selling or buying drugs. Police arrested five for possession and one for drug trafficking. As the other revelers were escorted outside to brave drug-sniffing dogs, officers searched the premises. The harsh light of scrutiny revealed a Moroccan-like drug bazaar. The timeworn solid maple floor, once the site of roller-skating children and families, was littered with tabs of LSD, traces of cocaine, pills of ecstasy, and half-filled bottles of poppers. However, "no evidence was found to implicate The Strand in these activities," noted authorities, who seized forty grams of cocaine, sixty tablets of ecstasy, and a dozen doses of LSD.

Gene Lawson and Joyce Felton had left the club around three in the morning, but it was Victor Pisapia who received a phone call ninety minutes later. "There's police here. It's a raid! There are dogs!" He continues:

> It wasn't something that surprised me. People did more drugs because they couldn't have alcohol. . . . I used to tell them, "Take the goddamn drugs while you are going in, while you're standing outside in line." But you know what people are like.

A stone's throw away, Felton heard pounding on her apartment door: "I got dressed and tried to gather my energy." She phoned her attorney. Within a half hour, she was inside the club: "It was empty. Lights were on. It was a mess. People who worked for me were still there. They were very shaken up."

Lawson remembers that authorities "were immensely embarrassed." Not only were there only "a few minor, very minor possession charges"; but those "who were lined up in a row [included] . . . White House aides, Senate aides, House of Representative aides, other government employees." Grumbling to a reporter that "it was overkill," he questioned the overwhelming use of police power to arrest a half dozen people and to seize just ten eight balls of cocaine and some pills. Less helpful, Lawson, conceding that drug use was "the nature of late-night business," observed, "If anyone believes The Strand is the only place in the Rehoboth-Dewey area where some drug use has or is going on, they are naïve or stupid." Although he pointed out his personal opposition to drug use ("I have worked with Mrs. Reagan's War on Drugs") and The Strand's efforts to curtail it ("We have thrown out drug users"), the damage was done.

Later, the three partners issued a press release, acknowledging that the police were "always professional and courteous." Felton explains, "We were also trying to finesse our position. I held many other liquor licenses in the state of Delaware. For me, personally, to be antagonistic and adversarial was not going to gain anything."

Readers of the *Whale* were unsympathetic, if not incredulous. Letters to the Editor and Speak Out call-ins were overwhelmingly negative. These linked The Strand to "sacrificing children to drugs for your personal profit" and questioned whether its once-a-weeknight teen dance was a nefarious ruse "to hook our kids" on drugs and homosexuality. "We better get rid of these people," one anonymous caller voiced, "or Rehoboth is going right down the tubes." Although "it was unfortunate and it shook people up," Felton says that the next Saturday "was the busiest weekend we ever had there!"

Immediately after the raid, Lawson singled out an unnamed "local couple" to the media "who [we]re protesting any licensing of the complex" and who were employing "back-handed tactics and efforts to blacken our name." Reflecting on the raid decades later, Pisapia insists, "There was enough to know [at the time] that they were out to get us and this was all part of the plan." Felton agrees: "Part of their focus was to make our lives as miserable as possible, thinking that we would fold up our tents and leave." Lawson speculates that Ray Pusey, who "was not against using power to make our lives miserable," discussed The Strand "at his place of employment; the same place of employment as the state police and the enforcement people for ABCC [Alcoholic Beverage Control Commission]." Pusey denied this. "I've never been in the [Strand]," he said. "I wouldn't know what's going on in there."

Lawson also publicly identified Renegade owner Glen Thompson as another source of their troubles. Thompson freely admitted to reporters that he had filed complaints about "rampant drug use" at The Strand. Claiming that the owners "were unwilling to do anything about it," he explained, "I finally just gave up." For Strand partners, Thompson's allegations of wide-spread drug use were a pretext. "Competition to him was something that he wanted to stamp out, like a big dinosaur," Felton claims.

Thirty years later, Thompson is more forthcoming. "I got a call from my connection at the ABCC that a raid was going to happen," but it did not go according to plan. Set for around 1:00 A.M., "they had trouble getting the judge to sign off on it." He also muses about the weeks of undercover sur-veillance: "How could you *not* know that there were plainclothes men in that bar? When any of them walks into any of my establishments, I spot them like that!" He carries on, "It tells you right there that they [Strand partners] were all fucked up and totally out of it."

Thompson further informed the media that he had a "very, very strong anti-drug" policy. Backhanding The Strand, he adjudged, "You have to have somebody on the floor watching." Still enraged decades later, "That's bullshit," Lawson snaps. "He had drug and alcohol problems up here like he did in his Washington bars. . . . He was *not* Saint Glen!" However, Lawson jealously admits, "He didn't have exactly the same problems because he had a liquor license."

Wayne Hodge, Renegade's manager, acknowledges that "in '89, every-body was doing cocaine and the new drugs, MDA and Special K. All those drugs were around. You police them the best way you can." He stresses, "Glen always had been and always will be so anti-drug, he would rather close a place down than it being a drug bar." However, Jeffrey Slavin, one of The Strand's original investors who also frequented Renegade, recalls get-ting "approached by drug dealers all over the place." He wonders, "Who did Glen pay off not to have narcs at his place?" Nevertheless, Slavin acknowl-edges that drug use was similar, if not worse, at The Strand: "People were dancing and having discreet sex and doing drugs." Similarly, Pisapia, who sometimes visited Renegade, observes, "There were plenty of people taking lots of drugs at Renegade. There was no one at the front door telling you not to take drugs. These were nightclubs! That's what nightclubs did."

AFTERMATH

The Strand raid coupled with the referendum's defeat eliminated any pos-sibility of the after-hours club receiving a liquor license.[3] The state liquor commission also canceled the club's Labor Day gathering permit, disallow-ing alcohol sales for the annual SunDance fundraiser. The Homeowners As-sociation's objection to The Strand's gathering permits continued the following year, encouraging the ABCC "to make a thorough investigation into this matter," as "the charitable contribution [wa]s minimal." It failed to mention that the 1989 alcohol-free Labor Day event had raised $10,000.

Meanwhile, Strand owners were as divided as they were dismayed. The three partners had long been at odds regarding drug use at the club. Although "we were fairly together on the fact that it would not be good for business if drugs were there," says Lawson, "I was a bit more adamant about them not being a part of the regular goings-on at the club." The raid affected their visions of the future. In a story headlined, "Felton, Pisapia Say Bias Has Them Down but Won't Leave Soon," Felton declared, "We're tired of the harassment and haranguing over the liquor license. . . . We want to go somewhere we'll feel welcome." In hindsight, she confides, "Maybe it came from anger," but "Victor and I did seriously consider moving to South Beach." They put a letter of intent offer on a property on Ocean Drive, although "that predicated us selling the Blue Moon."

The reporter did reveal that the Blue Moon and the Tijuana Taxi were on the market. "We want to concentrate our forces on the Surfside and Strand until they reach complete economic success," Felton said, putting it in the best light. Years later, she explains, "Victor was setting the table for his leave-taking. So, it was either going to be here [Miami Beach] or there [Australia]. It wasn't going to be Rehoboth." Pisapia concurs, "We were pretty much done." He sighs. "I had no fight in me. Joyce was determined to hang in there for a little longer. Gene was determined to figure out another way to grab hold of all of it."

Lawson was steadfast, pledging to buy their shares "when the time comes." He later qualifies, "It was something we wished that we thought we could do." However, from the vantage point of history, "The Strand was going under in twelve different directions. People were trying to push it under in different ways." The configuration of multiple leases and owners, three exhausted and disputatious partners, increasingly disgruntled investors, a growing list of creditors, and the political power wielded by their opponents made it "a difficult time."

The trio also confronted the political realities of a nascent queer community and Rehoboth's archaic voting system. Pisapia had hoped that it "would step up a little bit. . . . [T]he gay community, even though it was on our side, a lot of them just pulled back. They didn't want to get involved." Felton disagrees:

> They supported us financially, but there wasn't anything that they could do. No one was going to save us. We were doomed without

that liquor license—and we knew it. I think it is a little childish
thinking that there was going to be a great march on the Delaware
ABCC or on city hall.

All three agree that Rehoboth's archaic voting rules favored the status quo.
"The people who were our allies couldn't vote," Pisapia explains. "The only
way you could vote on anything was if you owned property . . . and showed
up at the fire station" on a dog day in August. However, "things were changing," qualifies Felton, as there were "more like-minded people buying property and building. It was just at that cusp." At the time, it was not enough.

Pisapia contends, "If we would have gotten the liquor license, it would
have been much more successful, obviously financially, but also in keeping
out other elements that came into the club." Unable to license The Strand
itself, the partners retreated to the strategy of extending Surfside Diner's
liquor license upstairs. But they were legally stymied by Ray and Bertha
Puseys' pending court appeal against the original approval of a liquor license to the downstairs restaurants. A judge delayed The Strand's request
to extend the license to the upstairs dance club.

In limbo, the partners were hemorrhaging money. So, too, were the Puseys and their backers. Lawson attributes their opponents' doggedness to
fight expensive legal battles to "bigotry and hatred, [which] don't have a
price tag." He adds, "It's not nearly as expensive to run a hatred shop here
as it would be in the city. The lawyers are cheaper and getting people to . . .
do something against the gay people is less problematic."

SHADOW GOVERNMENT

In December 1989, Blugerman announced the formation of a new civic action association, Citizens Association of Rehoboth Beach (CARB).[4] Its immediate focus was a newly passed city ordinance mandating parking permits throughout the city, beginning at midnight and extending through
5:00 P.M. Ostensibly, it was "the latest attempt . . . to deal with homeowner
complaints about illegal parking and late-night noise." The only business
operating well past midnight, of course, was The Strand.

Arising from ARG's ashes—and before that, a group called Citizens for
Better Rehoboth—CARB defined itself as "an organization in which all citizens shall have a voice in determining the future of the community." It
advocated for the immediate implementation of absentee balloting, changing municipal voting from August to May, suspending a new water meter

tax, and incorporating West Rehoboth—policies opposed by the Homeowners Association and its mayor and commissioners. Mayor Kimber
Vought castigated CARB as "special interests," blustering that "special interests don't control this city." The association's board advised commissioners to "diffuse CARB" by postponing new water-meter installations until
after the election. Some board members also worried about absentee balloting by "property owners [who] know nothing about our problems." However, newly elected association board member Carole Cochran voiced the
puerile fears of many, warning about the "mass mailings to gays" of absentee ballots.

The new civic group quickly amassed the signatures required for a
spring referendum on parking permits. The Homeowners Association,
which publicly endorsed the parking permit ordinance, was caught flat-
footed when, to the surprise of many, the referendum was approved in
April. Rear Adm. Francis Fabrizio, telling the association's board that "we
are a weakened organization," vowed to increase membership for its upcoming twentieth anniversary. Smith, however, privately attributed the association's election losses or near losses during the past couple of years to
poor political timing by those commissioners who "we helped put into office." He continued:

> The water meter ordinance was offered at a bad time (too near elec-
> tions). . . . When the commissioners came up with the ordinance to
> restrict parking, it was bad timing again. It was really against The
> Strand, but it included too much about other types of businesses.
> . . . In the beginning the bar-ban ordinance included too much. . . .
> It caused an uproar.

In June, a slate of reform candidates was announced by the now five-
hundred-member CARB. Its candidate for mayor, sixty-three-year-old
Richard Hamilton, a part-time Methodist minister, campaigned as "the
voice of the citizen" in the wake of "a government directed by a minority in
a vacuum." Walking door to door, Hamilton challenged "hometown boy"
and Homeowners Association–endorsed commissioner Sam Cooper. The
thirty-eight-year-old four-term commissioner, a descendent of one of the
town's pioneering families, emphasized:

> The Rehoboth I have served and loved seems to be changing into
> something different and not necessarily better. The values of the

past, which have made us one of the finest communities in this country, appear a little more remote. The Rehoboth I wish to live in must change with the times, but only within the framework of its traditional values.

The Homeowners Association allocated $4,000 to support its mayoral candidate and two commissioners, along with more fundraising monies promised by Smith. Expending $5,800, its slate swept the August 1990 election with a comfortable two-thirds of those 1,200 voters who were not disenfranchised by voting qualifications or polling procedures. An "action agenda" was soon delivered to the newly elected mayor and his commissioners, despite board member Evelyn Thoroughgood's shallow avowal that "we are not a shadow government."

In September, learning that the Puseys' appeal had been denied, Smith warned his board, "We have only managed to hold off The Strand for a while." The board asked Smith, who had just completed four years as president, to "carry the ball" on The Strand's liquor extension application. He accepted wholeheartedly.

Reflecting on the adage that sometimes good can come out of bad, Lawson contends that The Strand's imbroglio "brought the business community together, separately from the gay community; it brought the gay community together, separately from everybody else; and it finally awoke some of the people in city government." Together, "it produced entities that were slowly putting aside their differences in order to work together to get something done. CAMP was one thing that got done."

TAKING A STAND

In September 1990, "clean-cut and somewhat preppy-looking" Steve Elkins stood before the commissioners at their monthly board meeting.[5] *Washington Post Magazine* continued its narrative:

> "I'm here to tell you things are going to change," he declared.
> "Sir, is that a threat?" one commissioner asked.
> "No sir, a promise."

Two weeks earlier, he and Archibald had arrived in Rehoboth with their New York City baggage in tow. Their move was unexpected. "We weren't down that much that summer. We were down for my show and that sort of

Jim Bahr and Victor Pisapia at CAMP office, ca. 1991.
(Courtesy of Victor Pisapia and Jim Bahr.)

into awareness about the political scene." That autumn, Bahr, Archibald, and Elkins conversed more deeply about the concept of "CAMP: **C**reate **A** **M**ore **P**ositive Rehoboth."

Most gays "just didn't understand" at the time, Archibald admits, "what we were trying to do or that we were serious." That was not true for Bahr, who considered it to be "a great idea." He wondered, "Why are we ghettoizing ourselves? Why aren't we just part of the greater community?" Not surprisingly, he wanted to participate in "building a community organization that was dedicated not just to promoting gay rights but [to] building a better culture within a town that was more inclusive."

Bahr was also drawn to Archibald's vision "of reaching out to a broader community through art and creativity" and their transcendent view about coming out. Archibald often reminded folks, "It is more than simply saying, 'I am gay.' It is saying, 'I am gay, and I am open to all the possibilities that come with it.'"

Bahr had become open to life's possibilities at age nineteen. Following his failed junior year of high school, he realized "I was quickly going nowhere" and dropped out of school. Eventually, with the help of several teachers, he earned a GED and then joined the Young Adult Conservation Corps.

It "was probably what I needed: a chance to get away from home" and "time and space to reflect." The adolescent concluded, "I can be who I choose to be."

One of those choices was to come out to the rest of his family. Like most queer youth, "to have the support of my mom and my family was empowering." Bahr experienced another "major turning point" when he traveled to New York City to visit his gay uncle, with whom he experienced the club scene and attended his first gay pride march. The impressionable youth "could turn around and see in both directions this sea of heads!"

During this period, Bahr's mother earned her social work degree and began working for the Division of Family Services. She also discovered Parents and Friends of Lesbians and Gays (PFLAG), which lacked a New Jersey support group. She initiated a local chapter. Attending the meetings, Bahr saw "the people who we were touching." The mother-son duo appeared on local television stations, were interviewed for news stories, and frequently spoke at college classes, culminating in the pair marching beneath the PFLAG banner for gay pride in 1981.

Bahr enrolled in a community college and then transferred to the University of Pennsylvania's psychology program in 1983. He joined the Gay and Lesbian Student Union. Soon, he became a co-coordinator and edited its annual gay supplement to the *Daily Pennsylvanian*. Graduating magna cum laude, Bahr pursued his graduate degree while working as a research assistant for the Marriage Council of Philadelphia, where he co-authored papers and attended academic conferences. Five years later, tiring of academia, he journeyed to DC to work at a policy institute.

No gay marches occurred in Rehoboth during the 1980s. From autumn through the winter of 1990, talk about organizing ebbed and flowed. There were discussions about "making the CAMP courtyard for retail space," Bahr remembers. Archibald described it as "an outside space open to the entire community [that] was a vital element in the creation of a community organization." Bahr thought, "'Wow! This is *the* place and *the* time.'"

Meanwhile, his relationship with Pisapia "went through a bit of a crisis point." Then, it blossomed. Pisapia shared his dream of moving to Australia and "wanted to know if I would be game to take a look for a move. I said, 'Yeah, sure.'" In February 1991, the couple journeyed Down Under. "It was a milestone," Bahr states. The couple began planning a permanent move to Australia, figuring out "how do we make this happen?"

Given his longtime relationship with Felton and their intertwining businesses, Pisapia needed time to divest from their partnership without losing this friendship. Predictably, Felton "felt a little abandoned. It had always been the two of us." It also "was a pretty volatile time, and I needed Victor's attention, but I wasn't getting Victor's attention." His buyout from the Moon "was doable but difficult," she affirms.

During the interim, Pisapia did not want to continue a commuter relationship, and Bahr had "no burning desire" to remain in Washington. He moved to the beach, and they started preparing. In Rehoboth, Bahr was disheartened by the absence of activism: "They were still talking about" organizing, yet "there was still nothing really happening that I could see." Experienced in writing and editing, armed with Archibald's artwork (including the CAMP logo design), and steeped in long conversations with others, Bahr put together a newsletter mock-up: "I just went away one weekend and thought, 'You know what, I'm just going to do this!'"

The first issue of *Letters from CAMP Rehoboth* was published in May 1991. In the four-page publication, Bahr observed that during the past fifteen years,

> a de facto community has formed, beginning with loose networks of friends and growing into institutions that support our needs and our dreams. But it has become obvious that this community needs to be more "formally" organized, if it is to continue to grow in the face of stubborn opposition.

Years later, Archibald queries, "If there had been no opposition . . . would we exist at all?" He explains, "The seeds of home and creativity can thrive in a soil of pain, failure, racism, bigotry, homophobia, heartache, and despair. They can also be destroyed by them, but without challenge, there is no reason to push."

Showing the newsletter around, Bahr remembers, "It was, 'Oh, wow! Let's do it!'" Archibald recalls, "The naysayers were numerous. Many times, we were assured 'that it just couldn't be done.' There was even concern among some members of our community because we were putting . . . [it] out on the streets for *anyone* to see." Although *Letters* had "limited appeal in the beginning," after reading the first issue, Felton "was thrilled. I felt a certain kind of vindication. It got a little bit lonely . . . being the machete bearer, whacking down so much resistance." Of course, thirty years later, "no one is burning down the little kiosks where the magazines are or taking them and throwing them in the ocean."

When Bahr assembled the biweekly newsletter, "there was no board; there was no one to hire me." That summer, however, Archibald and Elkins were busy establishing the courtyard. It was "a crucial part for creating some type of community space where people felt welcomed," Archibald underscores. "Early on, we hung the rainbow flags, and we had the rainbow fence." Facing the courtyard, the L-shaped part of the rear building became CAMPtown, while the CAMP Gallery fronted The Avenue. Lambda Rising bookstore was the first courtyard shop. Owners Deacon Maccubbin and Jim Bennett, who operated their flagship bookstore in DC and a specialty tobacco shop in Rehoboth, presciently argued, "The lesbian and gay community probably shares more of a common vision with Rehoboth Beach Homeowners Association than the Association would care to admit. The common denominator is . . . community."

RESISTANCE IS *NOT* FUTILE

You call us pansies and fairies and fruits. . . . To you it may be insult / no injury is made / for though you do not know it / you have praised our very souls.

—**Murray Archibald,** "Pansies, Fairies, and Fruits"

A July Sunday in 1991 was like any other at Poodle Beach. Gay men played volleyball, chatted with friends, bodysurfed in the ocean, and discreetly drank.[1] In midafternoon, a lifeguard spotted a bare derriere above the water line. The twenty-something contacted authorities, who dispatched summer police officers—about his same age—to the scene. They arrested the gay swimmer as he returned to the beach. He protested, claiming that his swimsuit briefly had been removed "to wash the sand out" while he was frolicking with friends.

As police escorted him toward the Boardwalk, word spread. Between 100 and 175 clapping and shouting gay men encircled the officers and their captive around the lifeguard stand. These "two groups, distrustful of each other, descended into a round of name calling and chanting." The hissing and hand-clapping pack was ordered to "clear the area" by officers, some of whom bandied antigay slurs. When this disbursement did not occur, they radioed for additional backup and threatened arrests for loitering. "What else is there to do at the beach?" one man quipped. Further arrests were made. The swimmer was charged with indecent exposure, while four other men, including one videotaping the incident, were charged with counts ranging from disorderly conduct to inciting a riot.

"It was a turning point for CAMP, in particular, and for the gay community," remembers Jim Bahr, who was at the beach that day. The editor of

Letters from CAMP Rehoboth was invited by the *Whale* to pen an op-ed. "It was important for me to get the tone right and to talk about shared responsibility," he stresses decades later.

"Both sides did much to antagonize the other," Bahr wrote in an exceptionally balanced column. "What was an individual mistake became the embodiment of long-held animosities," including a "no homos" sign occasionally displayed at the Poodle Beach lifeguard stand and a lifeguard who briefly wore latex gloves and a surgical mask before being disciplined. The stand sometimes brandished the international circle-backslash symbol overlaid with "AIDS," and whispering "gawkers" frequently stared or snuck "furtive glances" from the shore or Boardwalk. Queer-targeted searches for alcohol were common. Bahr called for sensitivity training of Rehoboth police and its beach patrol as well as placement of queer or gay-friendly personnel covering that beach section—long seen as an abominable "fag assignment" among the forty-odd lifeguard crew.

Following his op-ed, antigay sentiment dominated *Whale* reader feedback. Retiree Joseph Belle, who a few years earlier had met with the Homeowners Association's board to demand action against Rehoboth homosexuals, wrote a rambling essay, claiming that Bahr was an "apologist for the gay and lesbian community," where same-sex relationships were "the purest possible exemplification of hedonism." He further asserted, "Bahr's program of 'conciliator' is ridiculous. There cannot be any conciliation, in a moral society, with evil." Most opinions in the paper echoed Belle's position: "As long as these people confine their sexual activity to each other and never donate blood, they will cancel each other out with AIDS"; "Gays and lesbians can continue their vocal protest from now until doomsday, but you are still considered outcasts"; "Rehoboth has always been and will continue to be a community of straight, normal people"; and "All gays and lesbians should remain in their own states, chanting in their closets."

Apologists were few. Gene Lawson retorted, "Being gay and/or supporting gay causes are not in need of apology." Another reader observed, "Despite its religious origins and family façade, Rehoboth has never been saintly in its outlook." Harking back to the town's nineteenth-century division between the moralists and the secularists, the letter continued, "those Methodists moved on to more pristine pastures four score and a few more years ago."

The "Poodle Beach riot" marked the first public sign of gay political resistance in Rehoboth. In his front-page *Letters* article, Bahr warned, "If they think 'this town shouldn't have to deal with men kissing in restaurants' (to quote Commissioner [Jan] Konesey), they aren't ready for the battle that will ensue if they do not relax their agenda." As conflicts increased, there were other signs of resistance during the 1990s: dollars stamped with pink triangles; sidewalk glitter bombs; gay flags flurrying at houses and businesses; same-sex couples holding hands on the Boardwalk or exchanging kisses at a restaurant; a boycott against Tee Shirt Outlet for displaying shirts with homophobic designs; and biweekly issues of *Letters* freely distributed around town. There, too, were cat-and-mouse ploys between gay men and lifeguards. For instance, with waists below the ocean waves and bathing trunks held above their heads, several gay men waded toward the patrol stand, only to expose themselves wearing *other* pairs of trunks.

There also was resistance to a bumper sticker commemorating the town's centennial. In the May newsletter, Homeowners Association secretary Priscilla Smith included a thousand stickers that "reflect our particular civic philosophy." It read, "A Family Resort for 100 Years: Rehoboth Beach, 1891–1991." Jack Foreman, the co-owner with Dave Ruffo of Noah's Lark, contacted the Charter Centennial Committee. Its director then approved the purchase and distribution of the official version: "A Seaside Resort for 100 Years: Rehoboth Beach, 1891–1991."

Resistance has been an important tactic of the modern LGBTQ+ movement. Although the Stonewall riot is the most-cited historic event, other less remembered but meaningful acts of resistance include Clark Polak's sit-in at Philadelphia's Dewey's Restaurant; Barbara Gittings hosting a kissing booth beneath the banner "Hug a Homosexual" at an American Library Association convention; the 1966 "riot" at San Francisco's Compton Cafeteria, where harassed trans folks tossed dining ware, sugar shakers, high heels, and purses at police; AIDS activists cuffing themselves to the pews of Manhattan's St. Patrick's Cathedral; and national boycotts of Coors and Miller beers as well as orange juice, coupled with a pie tossed in Anita Bryant's face. Aside from these well-recorded events, no doubt there were many instances of resistance in towns and cities across the United States— including Rehoboth. Such resistance was not in vain.

PUSHING BOUNDARIES

On July 26, 1991—five days after the beach "riot"—Bahr and his friend Joe Minotto attended a meeting at city hall.[2] They met with the newly sworn-in Rehoboth police chief, soft-spoken forty-three-year-old Creig Doyle, a twenty-year veteran of the DC police force and long-awaited successor to

Chief Harry Maichle Jr.; and beach patrol captain Jate Walsh, the Cape Henlopen High School football coach who had spent twenty summers on beach patrol. The meeting led to an agreement to mandate "sensitivity training on gay and lesbian issues" for lifeguards and summer police before the next season. The charges against "the Poodle Beach Five," as they became known, also were dismissed several months later, after thousands of dollars had been spent on their legal defense.

A month before the Poodle Beach incident, the Delaware Senate had unanimously passed S.B. 92, giving towns zoning authority over restaurants serving alcohol. Far from innocuous, it had been initiated by Bertha and Ray Pusey. After losing their superior court appeal of the Alcoholic Beverage Control Commission's (ABCC's) approval for Surfside Diner's liquor license, they had appealed to the Delaware Supreme Court and wielded other government levers in their implacable campaign against Joyce Felton and her businesses. At the cusp of the 1991 New Year, the Puseys and their enablers had launched a multipronged effort to further impede The Strand and the Blue Moon.

In Rehoboth, Bertha castigated "pseudo-restaurants" as an "abuse of the people." Ally Commissioner Billie Shields lectured, "There are many, many people who are sick and tired of the noise and rowdiness." She then proposed a "patio/deck" commercial ordinance to ban all operations after 11:00 P.M. This "meat ax" approach to patio raucousness, however, was amended by Bertha. Stipulating that "a quiet restaurant like Chez la Mer" and others along Wilmington Avenue should not be penalized, she proposed that the operating hours of such "dining patios" be extended to 1:00 A.M., whereas those not serving "full meals" on the patio—like the Blue Moon—would close at 11:00 P.M., with "music and entertainment prohibited at all times."

Meanwhile, in Dover, Ray had begun lobbying to "tighten the reins" on the ABCC by granting a greater voice to towns, arguing that neighborhood residents had been "hung out to dry." He echoed the Homeowners Association's position that "the state legislature should impose tighter guidelines on the liquor licensing agency." Ray took many leaves of absence from his Delaware Department of Transportation (DelDOT) job to lobby legislators, many of whom he knew on a first-name basis. Others, such as Common Cause lobbyist and Dover neighbor Konesey, assisted. Her friend Glen Thompson emphasizes that she "had influence. Jan is the person you become friends with; Joyce Felton became enemies with her." An earlier version of the bill placed a moratorium on liquor license extensions statewide.

This version only affected The Strand, whose owners were now seeking to extend the Surfside's liquor license to the upstairs dance club.

Such efforts did not sit well with some in Rehoboth's business community, especially restaurateurs. Luther "Chip" Hearn, the president of the local chamber of commerce, reminded readers of the *Whale* that the statute "was written specifically about one restaurant." James Vandergraft, who owned homes in DC and Rehoboth, responded with "outrage, anger, and frustration" at the "self-righteous" Puseys. They "think they can waste my tax dollars by taking up so much of the time and energies of the members of city council, the mayor's office, the state Supreme Court all for the sake of their vendetta." Other homosexual homeowners viewed the matter differently: "For years, gay and straight residents got along fine side-by-side," but now "all I feel is a constant current of mistrust and fear."

The final version of the media-labeled "Pusey Bill" granted municipal governments zoning authority to reject applications for businesses serving alcohol prior to any submission to the ABCC. When Governor Michael Castle signed the legislation into law in mid-June 1991, Ray beamed: "I'm a happy man."

Within days, the Rehoboth Beach Board of Commissioners issued a thirteen-week moratorium on liquor-related applications from new or expanding facilities, and commissioners swiftly appointed a committee to draw up new zoning criteria. This seven-member Committee to Study Establishments Serving Alcohol was composed of four Homeowners Association–backed commissioners, including the committee's chair, lawyer Jack Hyde. Three non-commissioners also sat on the committee: Ken Vincent, a "disgruntled guest house owner who live[d] across the street from the Puseys"—his friends; Rod Pettigrew, owner of the Sea Horse restaurant, where the nine-hundred-member Homeowners Association had just hosted its twentieth-anniversary luncheon; and Susan Krick, the conservative owner of the Summer House restaurant. Because the committee lacked any participation from the queer or progressive communities, "the people being regulated ha[d] no voice in Rehoboth politics AGAIN," Bahr contended.

The Hyde Committee began deliberations on the eve of Rehoboth's first gay pride weekend. Konesey, a committee member and recent appointee to the board of commissioners, complained, "This town shouldn't have to deal with men kissing." She proposed a music ban at businesses after 2:00 A.M., effectively "silencing The Strand," noted Wilmington's *News Journal*. It was "a cannon to kill a mouse," contended Citizens Association of Rehoboth Beach (CARB) leader and failed mayoral candidate Rev. Richard Hamilton.

To the commissioners' surprise, their July 12 meeting was packed. About thirty opponents had been "tipped off" about Konesey's proposed music ordinance to be submitted for immediate passage. Felton questioned its legality because it had not been publicly announced. Although Konesey denied that hiding it had been the intent, she insisted that "there ha[d] to be reasonable standards." Immediately, Felton queried, "What standards are being proposed and by whom?" Konesey parried, "By 2 A.M. noise should be discontinued so people can get their rest." Businesses operating after that hour, she stipulated, had been contacted, and all had agreed. Business owners present denied both assertions.

It was "only through the swift and articulate response of the local community," observed a *Letters* writer, that "these proposals were not written into law." Attendee Steve Elkins declared it "another attempt by the commissioners to attack a part of the community that usually goes unrecognized." He asked, "Why else have the police twice come to The Strand recently? Why should we cut music off at 2 A.M. when it can't be heard beyond the property line?" He reported that police had found no noise violations. Later, in her defense, Konesey claimed that "95% of police calls were noise-related." When a *Letters* reporter tried to confirm this figure, he was informed by the Rehoboth Beach Police Department that "the figure [wa]s closer to 50 percent and often c[ame] from the same sources." Given all of this information, Victor Pisapia sarcastically warned diners against making "too much noise eating a soft-shell crab sandwich [that] just might rile up Commissioner Jan Konesey."

That same Friday, "A Weekend of Gay Pride" kicked off with CAMP Rehoboth's open house. It featured Miss Gay Delaware. There, too, was National League umpire David Pallone, who signed copies of *Behind the Mask* at the recently opened Lambda Rising bookstore. Well-wishers enjoyed CAMPtown coffee and deserts at Chris Monismith's Watering Hole and visited the street-side CAMP Gallery. Pride celebrants strolled the second block of Baltimore Avenue and dropped into lesbian- and gay-owned clothing shops, which had blossomed like wildflowers. "It's gratifying to see more and more options for both men and women now open on both sides of The Avenue," cheered Passport clothier Larry Belt.

The next day, eight miles north of Rehoboth, Thompson hosted a barbecue "country hoedown" at his Antique Village to raise money for the Sussex County AIDS Committee (SCAC). On Sunday afternoon, more than six hundred celebrants of "Pride '91" arrived at Renegade's parking lot and lis-

Hanging Spitfire at Renegade. (Courtesy of Wayne Hodge.)

tened to three hours of live entertainment. Event revelers enjoyed the
mini-carnival and crowded into his recently renovated club, sporting slant-
ed mirrors behind the back bar and a laser-eyed mannequin driving a 1956
Spitfire that hung above the dance floor.

Three weeks prior to the August 10 town election, the Homeowners Association invited its endorsed commission candidates—Jan Konesey and
Roger Pool—to speak at its annual meeting. Their opponents, CARB-sup-
ported candidates Richard Hamilton and Ellen Smith, pledging to "serve as
a bridge among often-contentious community factions," were snubbed.
Konesey and Pool made it "crystal clear they [we]ren't backing down one
iota from the Homeowners Association's iron-clad stance of maintaining
time-honored values." Konesey told the assemblage, "A lot of people want
Rehoboth Beach to be like it used to be. I do too." She promised to tighten
limits on noise while Pool, another member of the Hyde Committee, proposed enticing more "legitimate" businesses into town.

Although Wilmington Avenue was also experiencing growth of queer-
owned or -friendly restaurants, ranging from La La Land and Chez la Mer
to Ground Zero and Square One, the commissioners' concern was the second block of Baltimore Avenue. That June, the Blue Moon had celebrated its
tenth anniversary with the theme "Come Do That Voodoo That You Do So

Well." Felton, donning a swanky dress inspired by Rio's Carnival, greeted several hundred guests entering through a hulking voodoo mask designed by Murray Archibald. Inside, the Libby York Quartet performed jazz renditions from the Great American Songbook. Guests ambled through a paradise of flowers and greenery assembled by florist Gabby Beel and gazed at the walls decorated with shrunken heads and tomahawks. The evening extravaganza spilled out onto the patio and onto the sidewalk—just down the street from the Puseys' summer home.

In early July, The Strand had produced its annual Lavender Ball, followed two weeks later by the Double Pearl Party, where fashion elegance was the theme (think a "stunning Diana Ross costume, dangling strands of pearls hand-sewn on long black gloves"). The festive crowd raised $12,000 for Baltimore's Health Education Resource Organization (HERO), although, as one person observed, "The trouble with dancing in underwear and pearls is that not everything stops when you do." Bahr, working the water bar, flitted around the dance hall, wearing a "leather harness, cap, and Doc Martens high-top black boots with heavy white socks . . . and a very, very small pair of club briefs."

"Party time!" exclaimed Letters's preeminent gossiper David MacKay. It "is the byword for the Rehoboth way of life." House parties of gay men rolled through summer weekend nights (and mornings). Ivo Dominguez Jr. and his life partner, Jim Welch, went to "a lot" of these parties. "There was as much going on in people's beach homes as you'd find out in bars," Dominguez remembers. Wayne Hodge, however, considered them "competition." The attendees "were drinking cheap liquor in a plastic cup in the backyard. They weren't supporting the restaurants or the bars."

Following her sweeping August victory, Commissioner Konesey proposed that the commercial "noise-pollution" regulation be moved from 2 A.M. to 9 P.M. It included "sub-audible vibrations" (a complaint about The Strand long voiced by the Puseys), which she described as "some of the most nerve-wracking of background beats." Letters reported that her election "victory ha[d] galvanized many who [we]re tired of regressive and repressive legislation." Bill Sievert, co-owner of Splash and a refugee from San Francisco, summoned queer and progressive communities to action: "Everyone who enjoys her or himself here has a responsibility to become aware of and respond to the misguided antics of the powerful few who wish to claim Rehoboth Beach as theirs exclusively." Bahr bluntly heralded, "It's time to fight back!"

Enjoying his Rehoboth weekend condo, Chris Yochim, who had traipsed queer bars on the lower end of Bourbon Street as a teen in the early 1970s, recalls this being a time of "pushing the boundaries"—social, political, sexual:

> We were tired of being pushed around. Stonewall had happened twenty years earlier! This was a time when people were exerting their rights to be treated equally and not to be preyed upon. This is one of the valuable contributions CAMP Rehoboth started making from almost the beginning.

Boundaries would also be pushed as various visions of CAMP clashed head on with a disparate board and a freethinking newsletter editor. They, in turn, would work within variegated queer communities of skeptics and naysayers, believers and devotees, fence-sitters and vacillators.

VISION QUEST

Bahr describes the development of CAMP Rehoboth "as a snowball," although it could be described retrospectively as an avalanche.[3] The fledgling concept began with conversations, principally among Archibald, Elkins, and Bahr a year earlier, that expanded through Archibald-led workshops during the winter and spring of 1991 and was followed, as summer began, by the birth of *Letters*, initiated by Bahr, and CAMPtown, advanced by Elkins and Archibald. "We have outlined an idea and are beginning to fill in the details," Bahr editorialized in the June 1991 issue of *Letters*. "CAMP Rehoboth is a rough canvas on which any of us can paint our dreams." Throughout that summer, mostly White gay men dreamed and engaged in earnest conversations about CAMP Rehoboth's formal structure. At summer's end, *Letters* had expanded from four to twelve pages and increased the number and range of its advertisers. As editor, Bahr announced, "CAMP Rehoboth has been formed in name, mission, and structure, as a community service organization." The formal structure of CAMP was ready to be populated by individuals—distinctive in their life experiences and visions of CAMP—tasked with actualizing this dream.

Bahr was appointed to the poorly paid position of executive director while maintaining his role as newsletter editor. "Given the mission of the organization" and the desire to seek nonprofit status, the next task was to form a board. A steering committee sought "the people we need with the skills or the connections." Members reached out to those people. Bahr contacted activists Dominguez and Welch "because we wanted a broader base of support throughout the state" and "their names were known." Dominguez remembers this "cold call." He was "aware of who they were, primarily through The Strand and the broad community of people who had parties at the beach."

The call came at a fortuitous time, as Dominguez was in the process of "disengaging" from the National Gay and Lesbian Task Force board of directors. He and Welch also had recently bought a large, wooded tract downstate. Welch, whose relatives had long lived in this rural area, stresses that Rehoboth "was the *only* place that you could really pull an organization together. It was almost impossible to do anything in the central or western part of Sussex County."

Bahr recognized the challenge of bringing the couple "into the fold" because "they were activists, which would kind of lead to some tensions. . . . I think their sense was we weren't quite activist enough." They were ambivalent. "On the one hand, we wanted to do anything and everything to make sure that they would succeed," recalls Dominguez. On the other hand, "there was not yet clarity about what they wanted the organization to be."

The couple also had other reservations. There was chatter "in the broader community, among locals, that they [we]re starting a gay organization but calling it a weird name," recalls Dominguez. "It had no connection to anything that sa[id] 'queer.'" Welch adds that this trend of masking a group's identity was evident not only in Delaware but in other places: "People were afraid to be seen as lesbian or gay. AIDS was part of that."

Dominguez and Welch had started such organizations before and had served on various boards. "We had a lot of experience," says Welch, that "a higher percentage of the people on that [CAMP] board had not had." Hence, "in the earliest days, it was not a functioning board in the sense that you could create committees and produce things. It was more which individuals ha[d] the bandwidth to take on something and do it at this particular moment."

Among those with scant board experience or work with nonprofits was Lambda Rising's assistant manager, Yvonne "Babo" Janssen. A native of Cleveland, she had worked in Baltimore within the legal field for eight years before moving to Rehoboth in 1990. The thirty-two-year-old also worked at the Rehoboth Guest House. Archibald characterizes her as someone who "had great energy and played a big role in those early years" as secretary.

Yet, Dominguez says with regret, "I don't think people remember her as being important." However, "she always seemed to put a positive spin on whatever was being talked about or discussed." Further, "having someone from Lambda Rising was probably the best thing because more people were willing to flow through its doors than to flow through the doors of any [CAMP] meeting."

To the steering committee's credit, Janssen was not the only woman sitting on CAMP's first board. It also included Vicky Morelli, the manager of Lambda Rising, who would depart the following year to intern at the Human Rights Campaign Fund, and Tricia McCoy, who had worked at a Baltimore trauma unit and at a psychiatric facility. Janssen remembers that McCoy had "a temperament and humor of a medical professional" and was "very by-the-book." McCoy had first visited Rehoboth in the summer of 1987, staying at the Rehoboth Guest House. She became the innkeeper of this B&B the next summer. Co-owner Bill Courville recalls, "She was funny and smart and compassionate and caring—and she liked to have fun!" McCoy helped transition the B&B into a year-round enterprise and became "caught up in the building of CAMP Rehoboth."

This eight-member board also included Archibald and Elkins's longtime friend Randy Overbaugh, a DC-based music educator; treasurer Chris Monismith, a recent Philly transplant who had first bartended at the Moon before opening the Watering Hole; Blue Moon manager John Berdini, who served as membership chair and "provided a nice voice of reason and support," says Archibald; and award-winning freelance journalist and business owner Bill Sievert. Attending the first meeting, Dominguez "looked around the room." Seeing "people from Philadelphia, Baltimore, DC, and New York," he felt an "initial disconnect." As Welch explains, those "who wanted to come out and be seen at or be part of something like CAMP Rehoboth weren't local because they didn't want to be out."

The board enjoyed a "remarkable honeymoon period," reminisces Dominguez. "Everybody was just so happy to see other people show up and do something." Elkins, in his new position as board president, "tried to follow *Robert's Rules of Order*." Janssen engaged in the soft art of compromise, "trying to balance up the different directions that people wanted to go," lauds Bahr. He describes it as a "working board," figuring out "what was still, then, a vision."

Although Elkins was a board officer, Archibald, the original visionary, lacked any formal role. In a reflective essay, he later wrote, "I was of the naïve opinion that we could start the organization and then let someone else handle the day-to-day work." Archibald added, "I don't think, in the beginning, I ever intended to play a leadership role in CAMP." Formally, he provided graphics and some content to *Letters*. Informally, "Steve and I were on-site, present, and providing leadership, whether it was official or not. Whatever was going on, *we* were there."

In Rehoboth, most were indifferent, many were skeptical, and a few were upset, amused, or delighted with CAMP's debut. At the September Homeowners Association board meeting, President Emeritus Jay Smith discussed CAMP's "aims and intents." He laughingly recounted that even "one of its members joined the RBHA to 'straighten' us out.'" A moderate-leaning board member gingerly broached the prospect of just "accepting non-activist gays." Within gay circles, Hodge "questioned the need of [CAMP]," arguing, "They say, 'bring Rehoboth together.' I didn't see it torn apart." Renegade's manager was also at a loss as to "what the function was going to be—especially when the newsletter . . . was all about The Strand and the Blue Moon[,] . . . the people who [went] there," and most of the board. A more circumspect Thompson acknowledges, "In the beginning, there *may* have been a purpose for [CAMP]."

Bahr knew of Hodge's view of *Letters* and was well aware of the friction between Thompson and Felton: "Their initial reticence was 'Here is a Victor Pisapia–Joyce Felton mouthpiece coming out.'" Bahr crossed the canal "to try to sooth tensions," exhorting Thompson and Hodge, "Whatever else is going on, business-wise, we can put that aside and work together toward building a community."

Renegade began advertising in the third issue, which Bahr considers "a bit of a coup." Hodge, though, sees it differently: "Taking out ads wasn't to be nice. We had to do it because they were the ones reading *Letters*. So, if we didn't advertise, they wouldn't know what *we* were doing."

Hodge was not alone in viewing *Letters* as a promotional or snobbish venture. Dominguez, who was the board's president-elect, remembers exchanges about "what counted as 'news' and why certain individuals got covered as often as they did." He argued, "If it's going to be a community paper, then it has to serve the community and not your friends." From Bahr's point of view, the newsletter's goals were paradoxical: It was a publication of the queer community but intended for the entire Rehoboth community.

These conversations led to a broader discussion about oversight. Bahr recollects, "There was the tension of who we were and who we were answerable to." He understood that *Letters* was "meant to be a fundraising mechanism for the organization as well as a voice for the [queer] community and the values that were represented by it." Nevertheless, from his perspective, "We needed to maintain a little bit of distance" from the organization. In his dual role as editor and executive director, he believed that "while it was a project of CAMP Rehoboth, it wasn't the operation of the board to run it." There "were always conversations with Murray and Steve," although Bahr often "pushed back."

When it ended its first season, in October 1991, *Letters* was in debt. Although it had brought in about 40 percent of CAMP's first year's income, there was a loss of about $5,500. Elkins, unlike Bahr, was not too concerned. "Yeah, we'll get there," Bahr remembers Elkins saying. "He was always talking to people about donations and funding." By the end of the year, CAMP's balance sheet was positive. More than $12,000 of its income was from general donations, including SunDance, which, for the first time, listed two local organizations—SCAC and CAMP—as beneficiaries.

This donation addressed another of Dominguez and Welch's concerns. At the outset, most of the organizers of CAMP were "viewed by everybody who was involved in AIDS work in Delaware . . . as carpetbaggers." Dominguez continues, "You're taking money and putting it elsewhere" to support groups in DC, Philadelphia, and Baltimore. Thus, choosing to route donated money within the state was shrewd politics.

MacKay's column, self-described as a "'don't ask, just tell' style of gossip reporting," was one content area that Elkins, Archibald, Bahr, Dominguez, and Welch agreed upon. It was as problematic as it was popular. "Our innocence was shattered after the first four issues," MacKay acknowledges, crediting the board with "putting out the many brush fires the column would ignite." It confronted a conundrum. Archibald wanted "to rein in the gossip stuff a little bit. At the same time, people loved it." Similarly, Bahr "wasn't that keen on it. But I kind of knew, if you wanted a lot of people to pick [the newsletter] up, you['ve] got to have a column like that."

There, too, were objections within the local gay community. Readers criticized MacKay for "portray[ing] the community as one in which the only thing gay owners and renters want is to become a member of his A-List." Another couple asked, "How can a more positive environment . . . ever be realized . . . when all persons of every lifestyle read his tasteless bits of information?" Despite such resistance, the column continued for several seasons. "Being Scene quickly became the obituary page de jour," a delighted MacKay bragged. It also "catapulted [the people featured] into fifteen seconds of fame among Delmarva cut-throat catwalks—the Blue Moon, Renegade . . . [a]nd put them on every list for cocktail parties."

During these early years, CAMP's "focus was more on the business community and building alliances," says Bahr. In the board's minority, Dominguez countered, "There [wa]s a larger, broader community than just the businesses." CAMP business initiatives ranged from frequently published stories about local shops and those who owned them, to participation in a nationally distributed gay travel video, to the organization of the CAMP Business Council. This group of gay-owned businesses included many of Rehoboth's guesthouses and shops but was soon separated from CAMP—as was the CAMP Gallery.

Located in the storefront overlooking The Avenue, the gallery was owned and operated by Archibald and Elkins, selling upmarket paintings, handblown glass, and jewelry as well as hosting exhibits. Because the for-profit CAMP Gallery was linked in name and location to CAMP Rehoboth, "there were a lot of internal conversations about whether this [wa]s what we should really be doing." Bahr also remembers it "creating confusion." Ultimately, the gallery's name was changed to Space.

Another point of debate during these early years was CAMP's relationship to "related communities," as noted in its mission statement. What constituted a community? For Bahr, it included people who "affect or are affected by the happenings here." Therefore, he argued for the "need to build coalitions with others," notably Rehoboth's "straight community" and "West Rehoboth's black community." For Archibald, like Elkins, it was "building an organization that reached out and took part in all of the other organizations and tried to get involved in everything that was going on" within Rehoboth. By including residents West of Rehoboth, Bahr was "hoping to get some traction." Yet "Rehoboth was very segregated. The tourists as well as the in-town population was very White." Bahr's attitude, like that of some other local progressives, was "there's only so far you can push."[4] Other board members, including Dominguez, were reticent about allocating CAMP's resources West of Rehoboth, although they saw the importance of being allies. Dominguez wanted CAMP to "service specifically queer people." Elkins disagreed, arguing that CAMP "was more than a gay and lesbian organization." It would be two decades before this organization reached out to this neighboring African American community just across the canal.

THE CAMPAIGNER

During the first week of August 1991, the Delaware Supreme Court reversed a lower court's decision that had denied the Puseys' request to inspect financial statements filed by the Surfside Diner in support of its liquor license renewal application.[5] As a result, the ABCC reconsidered the application with additional public comment. Until that review was completed, Surfside would retain a temporary license. That same month, eleven Rehoboth bartenders were arrested in an undercover operation. Among the eight restaurants affected, "a disproportionate number of those arrested work in establishments that cater to gays and lesbians," *Letters* reported. Employees were charged with the sale of alcohol to minors and "offensive touching."

Meanwhile, the Rehoboth Beach Board of Commissioners was reviewing the grandfathered protection of about thirty restaurants from the Hyde Committee's proposed set of regulations. One included a 75/25 ratio between dining space/bar area. In response to the recommendations, one *Whale* reader questioned, "Why is [*sic*] the Chamber of Commerce and the Downtown Business Association putting up with this?"

Local restauranteurs quickly formed the Rehoboth Beach Restaurant Association in September 1991. Their basic concern—should they move (due to unreasonable rent hikes or loss of lease) or expand—was conforming to such regulations. Stressing the small profit margins on food compared to alcohol, the Restaurant Association sought to increase the percentage of bar space to 35 percent or to substitute the wording "patron area" for "bar space," allowing greater flexibility. Conversely, the Homeowners Association endorsed Ray Pusey's proposal to *reduce* bar space to 20 percent. A *Whale* reader echoed this view, asserting that outsiders "move here to start a business and . . . proceed to try and change it to match that dreaded place they came from. Rehoboth is the product of 100 years of slow, carefully planned evolution. This is not New York City."

Restaurant owners argued that they were in a competitive business and, just coming out of a recession, were suffering. Pressing commissioners as to their "intent," Felton accented, "We're fighting for our lives!" The Restaurant Association's secretary, Krick, who had also served on the Hyde Committee, told commissioners that restaurants like Chez la Mer would be devastated because its bar area constituted nearly half of the seated dining area.

Several commissioners approached Thompson: "They knew I wasn't going to guide them in the wrong direction the way other bar owners would." He recalls them inquiring, "How much space should you have for this and that to make an operation that cannot be turned into a bar?"

After six months of deliberation, the commissioners voted to restrict a restaurant's bar space to 25 percent of the dining area. Further, a dance floor would not be included in the calculation, and patios—closed by 10:00 P.M.—could not include a bar or provide entertainment. An existing restaurant could relocate, but total square footage could not exceed its current space. Denouncing these ordinances, Chez la Mer owner Nancy Wolfe wrote a scathing letter to City Manager Greg Ferrese, deploring "these needless restrictions and regulations [that] have been passed due to one couple's total obsession with Joyce Felton and The Strand."

That spring of 1992, *Letters* began its second CAMP season, expanding to sixteen pages. Its first cover—a photograph of five swimsuit-clad men caressing each other at the beach—was an accolade to "offensive touching." In her "Hit List" column, Janssen updated readers on the "continuing saga" of the Puseys, the ABCC, and The Strand in its "battle" to "maintain what was rightfully theirs." The feature story, however, was about scheduling two nights of "gay and lesbian sensitivity training" for several dozen police cadets and lifeguards. To be conducted by the DC-based Gays and Lesbians Organized Against Violence, CAMP would identify small-group facilitators and find lodging for trainers.

In the meantime, it was politics as usual. Richard Darley, another member of the Hyde Committee, was the sixty-nine-year-old incumbent commissioner. Because Don Derrickson chose not to seek reelection to the commission, the Homeowners Association's board quietly recruited seventy-one-year-old Warren MacDonald. He was publicly endorsed by the association a few weeks later. The retired Department of Veteran Affairs official and former American Legion executive had first visited Rehoboth in 1947. Absent any other candidate, he would join Darley as a commissioner.

Just before the June 6 noon filing deadline, Janssen submitted the required signatures to enter the race. That winter, "there [had been] nothing on my radar regarding running for council," she reveals. Then, a friend with blank signature sheets had walked into the bookstore. "We chatted," she recalls. "Get me the signatures and I will do it." Despite being an introvert, "being gay or being a woman needed representation." She spoke with the bookstore owners as well as Elkins, who simply advised her to "stay on point" and promised CAMP's endorsement.

In its coverage, the *Whale* questioned Janssen's experience. The thirty-two-year-old had been a Rehoboth resident for just fourteen months and "ha[d] never before held a political office." Initially, retired Commissioner Shields informed the Homeowners Association's board that "the group backing Ms. Janssen would not make a big push this year." However, when rumors circulated that Parents and Friends of Lesbians and Gays (PFLAG) leaders were in town to "coach her in campaigning" and that she would be "well funded," a special committee was appointed. Billie Shields, Jay Smith, and Francis Fabrizio would do the association's candidates' "legwork," with $3,000 allocated for the campaign. The *Whale* observed that CAMP "appear[ed] to be mounting an all-out effort." It was a "challenge to the local 'Powers That Be,'" Bahr publicly admitted. However, contrary to rumors, Janssen had a barebones budget, just enough to print a bookmark with her platform, "Babo's Family" with a pink triangle for the apostrophe, and an election-week radio announcement.

Janssen was the first openly queer person to run for public office in Rehoboth. Previously, Bruce Blugerman had denied his homosexuality, and Lawson, although "out," was not publicly identified as gay. Unlike in Blugerman's campaign three years earlier, the other candidates did not explicitly mention homosexuality or the community's queer population during this election. Wilmington's *News Journal* headlined, "Candidate Finds Lesbianism a Non-Issue," yet the issue lurked just beneath the surface. Candidate MacDonald, for example, promised to reduce "rowdiness, drug solicitation and usage, and activity not conducive" to Rehoboth's image.

Unlike during the prior election, the Homeowners Association invited all candidates to its semiannual meeting. "As a member of the ever-growing family of lesbians and gay men," Janssen told residents, "I will be conscious in ensuring fair and equal treatment of us all." Although it was popular with many homeowners, who had not seen a tax hike in fifteen years, she rejected the idea of imposing a beach fee to balance the town's budget as unfair: "How can you charge a fee for something that is owned by us all?"

Janssen was admittedly "a little nervous" about appearing before the association "that champion[ed] traditional family values." A reporter observed that the group "was polite." One member arose: "Please tell me, the gay community here—what do they [*sic*] want?" She responded, "We want the respect of others. . . . I don't want to be yelled at out of a car window. . . . I don't want to be beaten up. . . . That's all. Is that asking too much?" If elected, she pledged "lines of communication between various groups in an effort to develop a better understanding of each other and ultimately an inclusive community."

In mid-June, eleven adults walked into city hall for voter registration, with year-round leases in hand as evidence of their residency. "The red flags went up," Ferrese told a reporter. "When they all came in on the last day" with driver's licenses listing addresses outside Rehoboth, he phoned Thompson. In this situation, the city manager asked, "Where do these peo-

RB Homeowners candidate night, 1992.
Left to right: Yvonne Janssen, Judy Winningham, Cheryl Rice, and Tricia McCoy.
(Courtesy of Yvonne Janssen.)

ple live?" Although he "knew all of them," Thompson "talked him out of doing anything about it." Ferrese then reminded them of the penalty "if falsehoods are knowingly made." However, beyond demanding additional
documentation before the end of the business day, the city manager took
no other action. Only one would be Janssen-voter returned. Thompson
claims, "I saved the necks of some of them."

Janssen was the most visible lesbian activist in Rehoboth, although not
the only one. In addition to McCoy and Morelli, there was Natalie Moss.
She had lived in the DC Maryland suburbs, managing a discount women's
clothing store for fourteen years. Since the mid-1960s, Moss had enjoyed
private Rehoboth house parties, danced at Nomad Village, and sunbathed

on Whiskey Beach, later known as North Shores. She had also volunteered for the *Washington Blade* during the 1970s—working under the alias Natalie Ellis.

Relaxing at CAMPtown with her friends, she spotted an ad in *Letters*: "CAMP Rehoboth Seeking Accountant." They exclaimed, "Do it!" Moss had a business degree and was a licensed certified public accountant, but she only came to Rehoboth on weekends. Nevertheless, in June 1992, she met Bahr at the CAMP office, a narrow wedge of a shop in the courtyard. "There weren't any books to keep for bookkeeping because there were just a few advertisers [and] printing costs," so she could easily do the work as a commuter. Bahr remembers, "Once we engaged her, Natalie became an incredibly important part of the organization."

Although Rehoboth's queer community and its nascent leadership were largely men, women were gathering in the Delmarva Peninsula. The annual "Bonfire" had started with forty members of a women's softball team in 1985. Seven years later, they welcomed more than five hundred women on a thirty-eight-acre Eastern Shore farm, not far from the estate of the late Louisa Carpenter. Dogs and men were prohibited. It would be nearly another fifteen years before CAMP launched a women's project, building on the efforts of social worker and activist Libby Stiff.

Life was difficult in the Delaware countryside for openly queer folks. Stiff and her partner, Bea Wagner, had met in Wilmington in 1974. They moved to southern Delaware, near Dagsboro, in 1981 with their daughter: "We wanted to make life as easy for her as it could be. We were not out with her until she was in college," nor were they publicly out. As Rehoboth "was getting gayer and gayer before our eyes," they wanted to relocate, but "it was too expensive"—until the couple benefited from an inheritance. Twenty years later, they were two of the eight original organizers of Rehoboth Women's Conference, eventually attracting hundreds throughout the East Coast for an array of entertainment and workshops.

Although the distance from Dagsboro to Rehoboth Beach is less than twenty-five miles, the cultural differences spanned decades. Social mores and attitudes were more southern than mid-Atlantic; concerns for image and propriety were foremost. In rural Sussex County, change occurred more slowly than at the beach resort. Nevertheless, the zeitgeist of this earlier era enveloped Rehoboth's old guard. On Election Day, August 8, Darley and MacDonald won 80 percent of the vote. With heavy turnout, Janssen garnered 193 of the 903 votes cast. It was not a "defeat," she argued: Had she not run, two men would have been "handed the position." Her campaign, too, had generated "electricity in the air." Decades later, she explains, "It was the proverbial shot over the bow. . . . The base was put down, and we built upon it."

Four days before this 1992 election, the ABCC announced that it would not renew the temporary liquor license held by the Surfside Diner, as the owners had "provided false representation" in their application. This decision was based on the financial documents its owners had been compelled to release, which showed tens of thousands of dollars in unpaid taxes. They promised to appeal. The *News Journal* reported that "some blame[d] the decision on 'gay bashing' neighbors who have been relentless." Ray taunted, "I feel it is important people pay their taxes," adding that he was "happy to see the state enforcing the law."

Several days later, white oil-based paint bombs were tossed against the Puseys' Baltimore Avenue home, causing $1,500 in damage. They alleged other home attacks: "human excrement spread on their doorstep, their flower beds destroyed, and threatening, anonymous phone calls." A determined Bertha swore, "We will not be intimidated; we will go forward."

"This single cowardly act," editorialized Bahr, had "debased the hard work and good efforts of many people and businesses." He continued, "Fears of lawsuits, endless complaints, name-calling, and political machinations have despoiled the charms that originally attracted both sides to Rehoboth. Both sides have their fans and detractors, all of whom have had a hand in hurling the paint." Seeking common ground, Bahr opined, "Dissent not guerrilla warfare, dialogue not confrontation, and compromise not unyielding contradiction are the means to the end of **C**reating **A M**ore **P**ositive Rehoboth."

13

CAMPFIRED

We must not . . . close the closet door. Instead, it's time to
intensify our demand for equal protection.
—**Steve Elkins**, *Equal Protection, Zero Tolerance*

Resistance, however, was not futile.[1] At the September 1992 Alcoholic Beverage Control Commission (ABCC) hearing—after agreeing on payment terms for back taxes—Surfside Diner owners received a one-year liquor license. Nevertheless, the years-long campaign by Ray and Bertha Pusey, the Homeowners Association and its posse of commissioners, and a few "self-serving" homosexual residents and business owners had normalized bigoted actions against a more visible and vocal queer community. An "increasing number of same-sex couples could be seen walking along the streets and Boardwalk holding hands," according to the *Washington Blade*, and kiosks stuffed with *Letters* multiplied on town streets. In spite or perhaps because of this greater conspicuousness, the harassment, intimidation, and assault of queers escalated.

A half dozen teens assaulted an eighteen-year-old on Baltimore Avenue, breaking his collar bone. Near the Boardwalk, another gay youth was struck by a teen, as the attacker's companions scorned the victim. Gabby Beel was punched in the face by a youth who left his pickup truck to follow the florist into a pizza parlor. Drexel Davison decided not to place flowerpots outside his Wilmington Avenue hair salon, "worried that someone would throw them through the window." The restaurant manager of Ground Zero shuttered blinds, lest it be attacked. An employee of the National Gay & Lesbian Task Force and her friend were sitting on a Boardwalk bench when four men approached, asking whether they were lesbians. When they affirmed, the men "asked us to give them blow jobs . . . and said that we just needed one good fuck." After being touched, she "wrestled the man to the ground." The predators fled; nearby police were "slow to respond."

Gays began "learning to walk in groups," according to the *News Journal.* Between 1991 and 1992, the number of hate crimes reported against lesbians and gay men in the state increased by 33 percent. This category of hate crime was the largest, "making gays the most-hated minority group in Delaware." *Letters* routinely informed readers of how to report antigay violence to police, and CAMP launched its annual police-sensitivity-training summer workshop. However, *Letters* staff "never proactively went out to get the story that was happening all around." Bahr also concedes, "CAMP never got involved in trying to or having a sense that there was anything that we could even do about it, or needed to do about it, other than going through the police."

Violence and harassment against LGBTQ+ people were certainly not unique to Rehoboth Beach or to Delaware during the 1990s. A long list of murder victims included Oregon couple Roxanne Ellis and Michelle Abdill, whose bodies were discovered four days later in their assailant's pickup truck; New York City resident Julio Rivera, murdered with a hammer; Brandon Teena, a trans man raped and murdered in Nebraska; Matthew Shepard, tortured on a windswept barbed-wired Wyoming fence; and Billy Jack Gaither, placed on two torched kerosene-drenched tires in Alabama.

Such elegies to homophobic rage attest to the limits of liberalism against the backdrop of AIDS, the Moral Majority, and Don't Ask, Don't Tell. Despite the problems in Rehoboth, such dramatic episodic violence seemed well beyond the pale for this resort town. It was a harbinger.

CHAMPAGNE SERVED WITH A BASEBALL BAT

On the night of May 15, 1993, five Sussex County heterosexual youth chase a gay man down a street.[2] No one notices as they hurl objects at him. Into the next morning, the quintet roams Rehoboth. Around 2:30 A.M., on their rampage of hate, they walk southward toward the "gay end" of the Boardwalk. Near Rodney Street, three out-of-state tourists sit on a bench overlooking the ocean at Poodle Beach. The squad passes, shouting antigay slurs. Its leader, eighteen-year-old Miles Cuffee, from nearby Ellendale, turns around. He removes his shirt, exposing a black torso and an empty bottle tucked along the waistband of his sweatpants. "You want a piece, faggot?" Fifteen-year-old Donta Vickers, a red nylon case draped over his shoulder, steps alongside Cuffee. One of the gay men gasps, "Hey, man! We're leaving." As the gay men walk away, one ill-advisedly offers the finger and yells, "N*****s!"

This pungent comment exposes a "dirty little secret about the homosexual population," observed African American Keith Boykin. President Bill Clinton's openly gay special assistant, who had arranged the first meeting between a president and leaders of the LGBT community a month earlier, explained, "White gay people are just as racist as White straight people."

Cuffee grabs more bottles from a nearby trash bin. Vickers removes an aluminum baseball bat from his nylon case. The pack encircles the queers. Vickers squarely strikes twenty-two-year-old Randy Reed on his chest and again on his side. "We don't want any trouble," yells twenty-seven-year-old Jeff Coffey. Cuffee misses his target with the first champagne bottle. As Reed collapses, his friend, thirty-year-old William Cherrix, tries to break his fall. Cherrix pleads for mercy; Cuffee's second champagne bottle crushes his skull.

As the assailants flee, Reed, bruised and cut, stumbles toward the police station. A Good Samaritan assists and summons police and an ambulance. Within twenty minutes, police apprehend four of the five attackers. The fifth attacker is arrested after the adolescent details the exploits for his Monday civics class assignment, "What Did I Do This Weekend?"

Shock and disbelief settled upon Rehoboth. Anger flashed on the pages of *Letters*. One activist asked, "How many more? How much longer?" Steve Elkins reported to the *Cape Gazette*, "Certain segments of the homosexual population wanted to stage a demonstration to vocalize their anger and frustration following the incident, but opted instead to wait and give the system a chance to come through." Chief Creig Doyle responded, "My officers and I will not tolerate *any* hate crimes in our city." In his letter to Elkins at CAMP, he promised "to do everything possible to deter such acts of violence." In turn, Elkins told the press, "I am very convinced police are going to protect all the citizens." However, in *Letters*, he wrote that "Mayor [Sam Cooper] and the Board of Commissioners, on the other hand, are not known for their swift response to attacks on the gay and lesbian community."

At trial, plaintiff Cherrix, with part of his brain removed, testified in a monotone voice and slurred speech. Reed, outed to his family following the incident and addicted to antidepressants and painkillers, had lost his sales job, but testified. Coffey, "constantly looking over my shoulder," simply wanted "to crawl back in the closet." Fernando Harris, who had driven the getaway car, excused the group's action during his trial, explaining, "We weren't out there hunting for gays to beat up. We were looking for something to do and got into a bad situation that happened to be with gays." He received a two-year suspended sentence. Cuffee told the court, "I am sorry for my actions. I'm sorry for the victims." Convicted by jury of first- and second-degree assault along with weapons charges, Cuffee was remanded to prison for four years—the minimum sentence.

In family court, Vickers, fifteen years old at the time of the attack, was sentenced to two years at a youth facility, and Javaghn "Dwayne" Waples, the same age, received a suspended sentence. Elkins sat through the hearing of one of these youngest attackers. He "listened to his mother and grandmother" and recounted, "The entire courtroom felt their pain, realizing how easily a child can get in trouble. They each asked forgiveness from the victims and it was sincerely given."

In quick succession, other antigay incidents were reported to Rehoboth police. One man, "wearing men's black bikini underpants, garter belts, and cowboy boots," was approached by three youth who yelled, "You better run, faggot!" In flight, he was hit in the back with a brick. Another gay man, walking from his Renegade job at 3:30 A.M., was confronted by four men shouting antigay epithets near Rehoboth Avenue. He ran. They attacked, shoving him to the ground and striking his head. He later phoned the state police. After hearing about the assault, the desk trooper "put me on hold. I heard laughing and then a click." Elkins later underscored, "Stories about insensitive treatment toward complainants don't help" encourage the reporting of hate crimes.

The attitude of local judiciary was sometimes as problematic as that of some police. In one case, a Baltimore tourist filed a complaint against four teens. They had screeched "Homos go home! Faggots!" from the safety of their car while he was at the Blue Moon's patio. Justice of the Peace Frank Charles dismissed the case that same night, saying, "Let's not get carried away with this garbage. This is not gay bashing." The magistrate refused "to give some kids a criminal record" simply for making "some vague comments to nobody in particular."

Lambda Rising co-owner Deacon Maccubbin acknowledged that this incident "wasn't as serious as the baseball bat attack," but "that shouldn't mean courts condone such activity." Blue Moon owner Joyce Felton frankly stated, "There is not and never will be any smoky glass in our windows. We will not be hidden away in some dark corner quietly living out our lives.

We are out, visible, and celebratory in our living. People have the right to gather without fear of harassment."

A month after the attack, in June 1993, Elkins joined Jim Welch, Tricia McCoy, and four others to conduct his first police-sensitivity-training session. Admittedly, Elkins was anxious "about how I would be spending the next three hours." During the evening, his apprehension turned to appreciation and then a sense of accomplishment, "as many incorrect assumptions were listed, discussed, and disposed of by both sides." One officer, for instance, observed, "What most of you don't realize is that nearly all of our dealings with gays and lesbians come about as a result of their being in trouble with the law." Other officers described their assumptions of gays as being "spoiled rich kids who think the police are out to get them." Stereotypes of police were also shared. Elkins walked back to CAMP that night reaffirmed in the conviction that building bridges could create a more positive Rehoboth.

CAMPQUAKE

CAMP Rehoboth was "conceived as an organization dedicated to the development of a community in which we would be able to feel secure in building our future." At its 1992 annual autumn meeting, outgoing president Elkins also praised CAMP's "strong coalition" of "residents and business owners, both gay and straight."[3] He joined others, including Bill Sievert, as an at-large director. Ivo Dominguez Jr. assumed the board presidency, and McCoy became president-elect. Welch resigned to devote more time to the Sussex County AIDS Committee (SCAC), as did treasurer Chris Monismith, who was dying of AIDS. Two women—Amy Gehlert and Cheryl Rice—replaced them.

Meanwhile, Jim Bahr was wrapping up the second season of *Letters* and finalizing his move to Australia with Victor Pisapia. In his final editorial, Bahr noted that "CAMP Rehoboth ha[d] grown incredibly." Despite having "alienated some of the local 'power players'" and the group's "detractors," who thought "we don't do enough, don't do it right, and shouldn't be paid for the work we do," he was proud of the staff and board's "work of creating positive change."

The *Letters* staff also had expanded. "Local boy" Barry Price became managing editor. He had "just turned up on the doorstep one day," Bahr remembers. "For him it was a bit of a 'wow' that any of this was happening, having grown up in lower Delaware." Carol Fezuk, who recently had moved to Rehoboth after her Dover fiancé married his secretary, headed up sales, with Richie Griffin assisting. Brian Hunt, who operated a publishing business, handled design and layout. Natalie Moss assisted with bookkeeping.

In early 1993, Dominguez phoned McCoy to tell her he was resigning from the board's presidency. He had just chaired CAMP's January board meeting. At that meeting, Murray Archibald had given a formal "statement" about his "concerns and observations relating to the future of CAMP," including *Letters*. Archibald then volunteered to serve as executive director, to which the board agreed. Archibald says, "It was just an acceptance that if you're going to commit to something, you need to do it, and you can't just leave it to happen."

Price had been one of thirty or so people attending that board meeting. Aware of "rumors" about "the board wanting to take control of the newsletter," he had been quiet during much of the nearly three-hour session—until Dominguez had spoken. Blasting *Letters* as "fluff," he had sarcastically commented, "There had been stories suggested to cover, there had been people who could have been interviewed, but apparently those didn't count as 'interesting.'" After listening, Price had tried to "pacify him by saying that I was indeed interested in issues he mentioned, but had not reported on these things from lack of communication on his part."

Dominguez had exploded. He had threatened to resign, although not before condemning *Letters*'s columns as "toxic journalism." At that point, he had been met "with resistance" by other board members and "finally backed down." Price later trumpeted, "The radical faction was soon hushed. . . . Fluff reigns for the time being."

Following the January meeting, Dominguez felt, "I don't need to be here . . . Steve and Murray were in charge." McCoy assumed Dominguez's role, and Elkins was later appointed president-elect by the board. Wayne Hodge remembers Elkins approaching him about the now-open board seat: "Steve actually encouraged me to do it." Hodge "wanted another voice to be heard"—Renegade's. "As far as making everybody come together as a community, I didn't go on the board to help that," he confides. "I wanted to make sure that they didn't do too many big fundraising events," like Sun-Dance. Thus, when he learned "there was talk" about a Fourth of July "LOVE" fundraising event, he inveighed against it: "Wait a minute! You can't expect me to not battle here if you're going to take away every fucking weekend!" He told fellow board members that it "was designed not so much as a fundraiser, but as a big party weekend . . . at The Strand!"

Concerns about the relative autonomy of *Letters*, as well as some of its content, were on the mind of Archibald when he reported back to the board in March. He presented a "chain of command" that he hoped would "clarify responsibilities of individuals, define roles, and aid in the channeling of information." CAMP's executive director would now oversee the newsletter as well as future "Project Rainbow" endeavors related to "AIDS, political action, media and arts, fundraising, resources and information, and community outreach."

As the first issue of *Letters* was distributed in the spring of 1993, Bahr was ensconced at his Sydney home with Pisapia, who had just opened the Rattlesnake Grill in the city's hip North Shore. Overlooking a rainbow-painted fence that decorated CAMPtown's courtyard was an expanded CAMP office used by its new executive director. Archibald waxed poetically in this issue, "CAMP is two years old and, like two-year-olds everywhere, we are trying to maintain our balance." Price assumed editorship of the newsletter, while Fezuk was promoted to business manager, and Griffin became advertising manager. The expanded thirty-two-page news magazine boasted a new cover design and additional features, including Glen Thompson's column on antiques, Bahr's reflections on the Australian Outback, artist profiles, gardening tips, and occasional prose and poetry. David MacKay's gossip column remained.

After the Memorial Day publication of *Letters*'s fourth issue, Archibald fired Price. "The fit wasn't right," remembers Archibald, who needed to "establish that *Letters* was a program of CAMP Rehoboth, not CAMP Rehoboth entirely." Hunt agreed to assume editor duties in his new role as "publisher." Some of the board members, however, were caught off guard by Archibald's unilateral decision. In its subsequent meeting, the board requested "to be kept more closely informed" in the future.

"Feeling somewhat isolated, abandoned, ostracized by the so-called established power base on Baltimore Avenue," Price wrote to Bahr about his dismissal with "no explanations other than I don't fulfill the 'needs' of CAMP Rehoboth." He shared his sense of a "burgeoning desire from Steve specifically, and consequently Murray, to control the newsletter."

Dominguez, who remembers the backlash from the dismissal, says, "My biggest problem during the interregnum, when you had the truly awful newsletter, is that it . . . wasn't overtly political in a way to be useful and it wasn't bridge-building." From his vantage point, "Steve and Murray are the only reason that the organization succeeded. They were the shock absorbers for the organization." Archibald admits, "We made some hard decisions along in there." In retrospect, "You look back at things and say, 'Yeah, we could have handled that better.'"

Fezuk also "remembers them pushing [Price] out. There were always problems with the board, which wanted to direct what was going on." She also recognizes Price's immaturity at the time: "Barry would get really pissy and depressed. He was hard to work with sometimes. . . . He wanted things his way, and he didn't want to compromise sometimes."

Following the upheaval, Fezuk continued working with *Letters* while doing weekend gigs at Renegade. One of the first people she had met while selling newsletter ads had been Hodge. At Renegade, she found her family. She bartended at the club's video bar, hosted by the "fabulous" Gladys Kravitz. As Fezuk dressed for weekend nights, she'd think, "What am I going to wear that's not going to be upstaged by the drag queen?" She generally settled for her basic black cocktail dress. For last call, Kravitz "would call me up, and I would do 'Proud Mary' and 'Master's House' . . . shove it up the master's ass."

At the end of the 1993 season, Fezuk resigned as *Letters*'s business manager: "When Murray and Steve decided to take [*Letters*] over, I thought, 'Well, there's room for something else. Something that was a little bit more fun!'" From CAMP's original founders and board members, only Archibald and Elkins remained. *Letters* began its 1994 season more professionally laid out, with a staff of three men, led by Elkins, who assumed the role of editor; Hunt's role was limited to design. Elkins also assumed positions as executive director and president of the board, while Archibald was president-elect.

STRANDED

Before Pisapia departed for Australia with Bahr, he had returned his Strand shares to the corporate owner of the dance club and the two restaurants, Route 13.[4] These shares included those of Gene Lawson, who had relinquished them "because I had a mid-life crisis and decided to go to law school. There was no reason to stay on the *Titanic*." Bill Larsen, who owned the building, was "getting worse and worse health-wise and mentally." Lawson adds, "There comes a time in your life when you finally figure out when you're done, you're done."

As Labor Day 1993 neared, the only person who held shares in The Strand complex was Elkins. Learning of this, the Puseys gathered related documents and forwarded them to the ABCC, claiming that he was not the licensed owner; "hidden ownership" could result in revocation of Surfside's liquor license. Lawson also filed a claim against Elkins for $77,200, along with related claims from his partner, Scott Sterl, and another creditor, totaling $136,000.

Meanwhile, on an August Friday evening, with just a few onlookers at city hall and only minutes before a final vote on a revised noise ordinance, the commissioners accepted additional amendments. Spearheaded by Commissioner Jan Konesey, the amended ordinance moved the onset of reduced weekend noise to 11:00 P.M.—three hours later than she had originally proposed. The Boardwalk's Funland amusement park was exempted because, as Konesey explained, it was "a Rehoboth family institution." She and her unidentified "committee" of concerned citizens also proposed eliminating the requirement for a decibel meter reading and instead allowing an officer to judge whether the noise would offend a "reasonable person." These last-minute changes surprised Rehoboth Beach Restaurant Association leaders, who thought that they had already negotiated the final wording. In a *Letters* editorial, publisher Hunt lampooned ordinance advocates who sought to "magically transform" the town into a "fantasyland, where there is no noise, except their own; there are no people, except their kind."

Early that Saturday morning, Chief Doyle entered The Strand. He had fielded a call from Ray, who claimed that "the music is so loud in my bedroom you can sing along with it." At the chief's request, Elkins lowered the music volume. A short time later, the Puseys complained again. Doyle phoned Elkins, asking him to stop by the station when the club closed. Following a third complaint from the Puseys, police arrived at The Strand, warrant in hand. Elkins's arrest sparked headline news throughout Delaware: "Man Charged with Crime Not Yet in the Books."

"They are singling out a particular place with one particular type of music," Elkins later told a reporter. In response, Ray asked, "Is gay music different than other types of music?" Bertha chortled, "The one constant in Steve Elkins' life is *every* time I hear a boom, boom, boom, I'm going to have him arrested!" Elkins retorted, "I'm a victim of a very blatant pattern of harassment. . . . This is a gay issue!" Thompson chimed in, accusing Elkins of "using sexual orientation" to distract from the real issue. Elkins winced: "If it's not anti-gay, it's anti-me." The charge against violating the new noise ordinance—which was not yet in effect—was dropped. Elkins sued the city; he settled out of court.

In early November 1993, The Strand "suspended operations" and filed for Chapter 11 bankruptcy. Elkins told the *Cape Gazette* that, although he "expect[ed] to reopen," he would "close down permanently rather than turn control over . . . to a major creditor, Gene Lawson." Lawson, reflecting on this difficult period, sighs: "Relationships can be extinguished by lots of things, but money with a lot of zeros on it is one of the biggest things." Others, though, are less generous in their assessments of Lawson's legal actions. Jeffrey Slavin weighs his words: "I guess [Lawson's] ego or need to be right was more important than the community and his friendship with Joyce. I think it was a shame that he was willing to let all of that dirty laundry get out because it just reflected so bad on our community."

COMMUNITY VISTAS

CAMP's formative years bore internal conflicts.[5] According to Bahr, the "falling-out" occurred over "where we s[at] on this spectrum" of the social versus the political. Although all agreed that community organizing was important, which communities should be organized, for what purposes, and through what means were not.

On one end of the spectrum were those whose primary focus was organizing or attending social events (elaborate house parties, club theme nights and glittery fundraisers, happy hours and beach volleyball). Their main concern was one's social position (frequent mentions in *Letters*'s gossip column, sought-after invitations to A-list house events, VIP access to clubs). On the other end were those whose prime interest was organizing or attending political events (supporting candidates in local elections, boycotting national and local businesses). Their major focus was advocacy for one's political positions, such as gay hate crimes legislation, and the broader movement for cultural change.

Archibald and Elkins, along with their friends, fell somewhere midway on this spectrum. Archibald often "talked about how difficult it can be to walk a 'middle of the road' line as we try to listen to the needs of individuals and seek to develop and maintain a direction that works for a majority of the community." He argued that CAMP

> means that we take part in the community. It means that we find whatever ways we can to affirm one another. It means working with the city police and government to create a safer environment for us to live, work, and play. It means establishing a place where connec-

tions can be made, where issues can be discussed, where resources can be found. . . . Most of all it means celebrating, discovering and creating who we are as gay and lesbian people.

The couple's focus was on the broader community. "CAMP Rehoboth is more than a gay and lesbian organization," Elkins wrote. "It takes all kinds of people from all walks of life to really make a worthwhile community. The primary mission of CAMP Rehoboth has been, and will continue to be, working toward building a safe and inclusive community with room for all gay and straight."

Bahr sat to the political left of Archibald-Elkins, in contrast to the business-oriented Pisapia, whose "focus in Rehoboth was to create," not politicize. As *Letters*'s editor and CAMP's first executive editor, Bahr had been confrontational, routinely editorializing against the town's "official harassment," advocating for coalition building with people West of Rehoboth, supporting boycotts of unfriendly merchants, and challenging the concentration "of power into a few hands with homogenous interests." Yet like Archibald and Elkins, he wanted "to accomplish more than just to be a social hub for the [queer] community."

On the most political end of the spectrum, however, were Dominguez and, to a lesser degree, Welch. For Dominguez, "political doesn't mean legislative and it doesn't mean just local government. Political is talking about freedoms. Political is talking about why and how we insert our identities in the world of broader cultural change." Long active in queer politics and business, paganism and public health, the couple criticized CAMP as too "soft." The organization, Dominguez thought, was "headed to become something that was good for the [Rehoboth] community, but it was not the new torch bearer for progress in our [queer] community."

Archibald had a different perspective, asking:

How do we talk about making progress in a world that is always being reshaped by a current tide of politics, powers, money, religion, and trends? How do we know our efforts will make any difference at all in the world around us? The answer is—we don't.

"In those very beginning days," Dominguez reflects, "there was a lot of back-and-forth around acceptability politics." He explains, "There was this strange dynamic, that we want[ed] to help the queer community, but we want[ed] to look conservative enough so we c[ould] fit into Rehoboth."

At the spectrum's other end were former *Letters* staff members Fezuk and Price. After leaving CAMP, they formed *Rehoboth UnderGround* in 1994, focusing almost exclusively on social life within the queer community. "When I decided to go ahead and do something, it was from the social end because people were not coming here to get into the politics," Fezuk says. CAMP leaders, she believes, were just doing "what they needed to do to get more grant money and provide this service for that group. I just really thought we needed something that was a little lighter." Prior to its inaugural issue, she told a mainstream newspaper reporter, "We wanted to take a direction more toward entertainment aimed at the affluent gay community and tourists."

To their credit, neither Archibald nor Elkins viewed *Rehoboth Under- Ground* as competition. "Congratulations, Carol and Barry," Elkins wrote. "It is another sign there really is room for all." CAMP's middle-way political philosophy, epitomized by the then-current Clinton administration, was to seek common ground and avoid unnecessary conflict. Reaching out rather than fighting and collaborating rather than competing were their preferences. In word and action, CAMP under their leadership would become a positive presence in Rehoboth. When engaging another community group, an organization, or a city official, their approach was "What can we do for you?" rather than "This is what we need from you." Attending commissioner meetings, participating in local business organizations, joining the efforts in the town's Main Street project, gathering weekly for services at Epworth United Methodist Church, and supporting the Rehoboth Art League were some of the many inroads they made into the Rehoboth community.

This strategy garnered political support and bridged social divides. It did not, however, overcome hostility and suspicion harbored among some of the town's heterosexuals. One warned, in the *Cape Gazette*, "Do not come into this community with a chip on your shoulder and the mote of paranoid persecution complex in your eye." This well-known attorney also expressed his distrust, asserting "that some of you in the gay community feel the only remedy to the ostracism is to take over the city." Neither did it curry favor with those queer activists whose approach to community organizing was more akin to that of Chicago's Saul Alinsky than to Barack Obama. "Claiming leadership in an organization means that you have to buy into the vision. I had not bought into *that* vision," Dominguez says. "It's one thing to be a good neighbor," but "it's quite another to go out and ask, 'What do you need from us in this moment?'" He concedes that "there might have been some altruism there, but this is about respectability politics and buying your way into the community." From Dominguez's perspective, "there was a lot more that CAMP could have done had it not been involved in those things . . . coming-out groups . . . access to therapy, access to non-bar space for social stuff." In short, CAMP "c[ame] across as a community service organization primarily run by queer people, but not for queer people. That's why it never became home for me."

THE LAST DANCE

On the last Saturday of July 1994, the party crowd made a final club choice between The Strand and Renegade. "Following the season's pattern," most drove to Thompson's club, where DJ Jeff Harrison spun tunes for a packed dance floor until dawn.[6] Renegade's Sarong Soiree attracted more than a thousand partiers, including scantily clad "hot models," to "Fight the Right" for the benefit of the Human Rights Campaign Fund. In contrast, just a "few loyal fans" were at The Strand, which had halved its cover price. "Strand expatriates have become aimless wanderers on Saturday nights. They want to go to The Strand, but to the old Strand. Some long forgotten political nonsense haunts them and keeps them from going to Renegade." As dawn arrived, the *Letters* gossip columnist "watched from my car as the last dancers wandered home with whatever mementos of the past seven years they could carry."

At the beginning of 1994, Elkins had relinquished control of The Strand to the bankruptcy court, with the business overseen by a Philadelphia lawyer. Although Elkins had declared that he was "personally out of the management," the powers that be in Rehoboth continued to target the dance club. A new noise ordinance, proposed by Commissioner Jack Hyde, was designed to "put another nail in the coffin of The Strand" by halting all live commercial entertainment after 1:30 A.M., including televisions and radios—even if it couldn't be heard from outside. Hyde had wanted this inclusion earlier, but "Jan [Konesey] was getting so much flack," he claimed, despite noise complaints against the dance club, which "had been constant."

This latest tightening of the noise noose worried Sydney Artz, president of the Rehoboth Beach Restaurant Association, noting that it "would be very critical in The Strand's efforts to come out of bankruptcy." Hyde rhetorically asked, "If they have financial problems, should we allow them to make noise?" It also worried Lawson.

As a major creditor, Lawson was afforded the opportunity to operate The Strand as the court sorted out the financial details. Yet he, too, faced problems with town officials. In the spring of 1994, Lawson relaunched the under-twenty-one Friday-night dance club XLR-8, playing a mix of progressive/industrial/house music, and on Memorial Day weekend, The Strand reopened for Saturday nights. Although Hyde's revised noise ordinance had passed unanimously, it was not enforced, following advice from the city attorney. Nevertheless, the new Strand "got off to a rocky start." Rehoboth police visited the club on the hour, claiming past concerns about the "blatant use and sale of drugs in the facility by the former managers" and following a noise complaint by Royal Rose B&B owner Kenny Vincent.

Meanwhile, on The Avenue's second block, Chief Doyle instituted a "ticket first, ask questions later policy." After a citizen complaint by Vincent, police had issued a warning ticket to three men finishing a beer and a joint in front of his B&B. Unsatisfied, he and the Puseys attended a commissioners' workshop meeting at the end of May, requesting "more police visibility." Following a meeting with the mayor and city manager, Doyle instructed his officers to "maintain order on the block" by ticketing violators of *any* ordinance—ranging from speaking beyond a "normal tone" to jaywalking—on The Avenue. One officer was assigned permanent duty on the block, while others patrolled every half hour in marked and unmarked cars during the weekends. In one instance, around 10:00 P.M., a man was handcuffed and arrested after asking, "Hey girl! Are those Bugle Boy jeans you are wearing?" Although this quip had been directed at his friend, the police officer felt otherwise. Asked by a witness the reason for his arrest, another patrolman replied, "We're just trying to keep Rehoboth a family town."

"Is it proper," Elkins asked, "to treat people differently for violations on Baltimore Avenue than they treat them on Rehoboth Avenue?" One resident who operated a B&B on Brooklyn Avenue near Funland, which had been exempted from the late-night noise ordinance, was irate: "Three blocks away people are stopped for talking while we have people screaming at the top of their lungs!" One vacationer decried the police for "acting as a personal Gestapo for individuals with an axe to grind." Of course, the police actions resulted in a quieter street, leading Elkins to grant that "maybe it was needed."

In July, a story appeared in *Letters* chronicling a gay bashing West of Rehoboth. Two men leaving separately from Renegade had turned left on the service road and onto the dead-end Hebron Road. There, they had encountered "a group of black men who stated: 'What are you looking for? There's no fags down here!'" Both had been assaulted. A few weeks later, in a letter to the editor, a Maryland visitor took issue with CAMP's coverage, questioning "the words you use, the reasons you use them, and the effects they have on our public and myself." Why was it "necessary to include the race of the attackers," she wondered, when "the race of the victims [wa]s never mentioned?" She asked, "Is race pertinent to this case?" In response, Elkins promised to "take care to avoid any such insensitivity in the future."

Elkins, of course, was not the only gay White man of privilege whose perspective was colored by his race. Asked to reflect upon queer People of Color in the Rehoboth area, Hodge credibly comments:

> What was the gay Black and Latino life back in those times? I don't know. I had some Black friends—mostly drag queens—back in those days, but I didn't have any deep conversations about what their lives were like, being in Rehoboth. . . . To be honest, back in the eighties and nineties, those cultures didn't blend well.

Throughout July 1994, the house-party scene was hopping, helped along by the publication of *The Beach Book*. Published and sold by CAMP, it listed more than nine hundred names of mostly men sharing some 186 local houses for the season. With its publication, calling cards for seasonal residents became passé, but house T-shirts were more popular than ever. "You have to realize that there were only a few places you could go in Rehoboth where you could socialize in a bar or a restaurant," says Chris Yochim. "So, the house parties became a huge part of the social fabric."

Weekend nights were all about themed house parties. At 216 Norfolk, "Oh Say Can You See," for example, attracted three hundred partiers drinking from two bars as hundred-thousand-watt spotlights illuminated an American flag. The boys at 702 Scarborough hosted the "much anticipated South Pacific Tropical Follies," welcoming 150 guests, who were entertained by each of six houses competing in on-stage performances: "At stake was the house's reputation and position."

Writing for *Rehoboth UnderGround*, Price observed, "Women are often overlooked in Rehoboth. There are very few events opened with gay women in mind." Although more lesbians were visiting Renegade and Frogg Pond on Friday nights, many still preferred traveling to Nomad Village on a weekend night. Artist Annette Mosiej, who'd had crushes on little girls in

LETTERS

FROM
CAMP REHOBOTH

**Create A More
Positive Rehoboth**

June 30, 1995
volume 5 number 6

Cover of *"Just Chillin'" Letters from Camp Rehoboth*, June 30, 1995.
(Courtesy of CAMP Rehoboth. Artwork by Annette Mosiej.)

grade school and later connected with "beer-drinking, diesel dykes" in Wilmington's softball community, enjoyed these bars and North Beach. A self-described "ruffian," she declares, "I was never in the crowd of people who were invited to really nice parties or had really nice houses. I didn't fit."

A *Letters* columnist depicted the women's scene in Rehoboth as "often elusive and difficult to follow: house parties, ever-changing hot spots, and special events dominate[d]." Those seeking "womyn's space" at summer houses had few options. Among the 186 seasonal residences were a mere 13 female-only options—most well beyond Rehoboth's town limits—and just two lesbian-owned guesthouses. Felton underscores, "The lesbian community was disenfranchised. They really didn't have *their* place."

With some reservations, Renegade's Hodge launched a Sunday late-afternoon "Ladies Tea Dance" after being approached by drag legend Jamé Foks. "We were expecting maybe a couple of hundred people. Well, 850 people showed up!" Two years later, Hodge would have nine bartenders serving a thousand women: "By the time it ended, at 8 o'clock, we had to get them all out" to prepare for 1,500 men.

Because The Strand was closed, the seventh annual Labor Day weekend SunDance festival was held at the town's convention center, attracting more than a thousand people and clearing nearly $63,000, most of which was donated to SCAC. Elkins crowed, "The very fact that we were welcomed into the Convention Center is further evidence of the important role the gay and lesbian community plays in the economic vitality and diverse charm of Rehoboth Beach." In response, a newly arrived lesbian resident wrote *Letters*, asking:

> Is it not time for the GAY COMMUNITY to realize that we have earned the respect from the Rehoboth Beach community . . . ? Economic vitality implies to me that the Gay Community has bought their right to be in Rehoboth Beach. Are we comfortable with that?

"The 'welcome' we were afforded," Elkins responded, "is a first step toward being full-time partners in the community." The lesbian letter writer also expressed "disappointment for the lack of participation from the lesbian community." This comment highlighted a question raised the previous summer by a lesbian waitress, who had asked, "Why do we expect the heterosexual community to embrace all of our diversity when we don't do it within our own community?"

PART IV

WE ARE FAMILY

We are working together to build a safe & inclusive community
with room for all. And from the way I see it, we are on the right
track.

—**Steve Elkins**, *The Way I See It*

T wo lesbians walked into city hall on June 25, 1998.[1] The Rehoboth residents asked an employee in the Building and Licensing Department whether selling sexual paraphernalia was now legal in the town. The couple had come across the sex toys while browsing a recently opened gift shop a few houses up from the CAMP office: "Do they have a license to sell that stuff?" The startled city worker explained that no store on Baltimore Avenue could be licensed for adult entertainment because it would need to be 500 feet from any other dwelling and 2,800 feet from a church; a special business license also would be required.

The matter was referred to the city attorney, who then contacted authorities in Dover. Rehoboth plainclothes detective Keith Banks and a representative from the Office of the State Attorney General visited Wild Hearts Adventures Gift Shop several times. Subsequently, armed with a search warrant, police raided the shop, seizing more than a thousand items that ranged from dildos to leather straps. Lois Bruckno, one of the four owners, was arrested; the toyless shop remained open.

The raid on Wild Hearts, advertised as "for girls like us," had "shocked" some residents while revealing "a division in the gay community." Observing that "relations with the wider community ha[d] settled," the *Sunday News Journal* report singled out "the established gay community," which had been "attracted by Rehoboth's small-town virtues" and saw "a threat to those virtues in the more explicit sexuality of other gay resorts." Fay Jacobs had bought a Rehoboth condo and began writing for *Letters* in 1995. She recollects attending the shop's opening with her life partner, Bonnie Quesenberry. "We *were* all interested," she says, but "illegal is illegal," even if it is "erotica in the backroom of a lesbian store." She "stood by Steve [Elkins]," who opined, "I think that kind of merchandise doesn't belong in a small commercial resort town," adding, "We take pride in being a family resort." In contrast, Sharon Kanter contends that many lesbians "felt it was unfair that they targeted that place. . . . It was a very prudish area here."

A year earlier, the owners of newly opened Effxx Menswear had informed *Letters* of their "outrage" at Elkins for "censoring" their advertisement—"maybe too over-the-top for your traditional family values." The Fort Lauderdale–based owners asserted:

> It's too bad your pristine staff is of the opinion that sex never enters into the minds of your readers. . . . As gay business owners who cater to gay men and lesbians . . . we want to advertise in a vehicle that promotes *our* lifestyle, not the pristine Southern Baptist ideology you have chosen to embrace.

Elkins simply observed that the ad "was not in the usual CAMP spirit." A *Letters* reader was more direct: "There is a difference between what we do in private and what we can do in public. That is what discretion is all about and it allows us all to live more comfortably in our surroundings." The writer concluded, "CAMP Rehoboth is about inclusiveness for everyone which means discretion must consider the lowest denominator, in this case anyone who might be offended." Effxx began advertising in the *Rehoboth Beach Gayzette*, Carol Fezuk's new queer biweekly paper.

The Rehoboth Beach Homeowners Association was keenly interested in the *News Journal* story. Following a discussion at its board meeting, President Mary Campbell wrote the mayor and commissioners that the article "indicate[d] the resident gay and lesbian population share[d] the same vision of Rehoboth Beach." Campbell cautioned, "We want to avoid the extremes of excessive isolation or becoming another Fire Island." She warned, "How to define and achieve that desirable level of diversity is a significant challenge to the Community." Campbell encouraged town officials to "engage in dialog" with gay leaders "in shaping goals, objectives, and values within the framework of what Rehoboth Beach has always represented from its Christian origins."

The owners of Wild Hearts chose not to comment in the mainstream press. The *Washington Blade*, however, reported that they denied the charges. The women claimed that the shop was targeted because they and most of their clientele were lesbian. The sex toys, one owner told the *Blade*, were just a small part of the gift store's offerings and, further, the state law "applie[d] only to businesses that offer sexually oriented entertainment."

The DC and Baltimore chapters of Lesbian Avengers promised a march. Its spokesperson averred, "We want queers in Rehoboth to recognize that they're not safe and they're only sometimes tolerated." On September 6, about thirty women and a few men, many wearing "Free the Toys" T-shirts and distributing lollipops, marched on the police station. "CAMP Rehoboth did not make a moral judgment," Elkins argued in *Letters*. His concern was simply that the owners received "fair treatment." He went on, "As the gay and lesbian community in Rehoboth continues to grow and mature, the diversity within our community will . . . and that's cause for celebration." Jeffrey Slavin endorsed CAMP's position: "They didn't go out and try to defend that lesbian store on First Amendment rights" and did "not worry about this fringe stuff." He applauded, "If we had to sacrifice a few people along the way and get criticized by the Left wing, so be it."

This small-town controversy was writ large in the late-twentieth-century division among lesbian and feminist activists. Second-wave anti-pornography feminists, such as Andrea Dworkin and Susan Brownmiller, and the lesbian periodical *off our backs* conflicted with third-wave sex-positive feminists, such as Susie Bright and Annie Sprinkle, and the Eros-friendly *On Our Backs*. These so-called sex wars reflected a broader tension over homosexual desexualization in furtherance of queer acceptance. They were also evidence of the siren's lure of a shared community, despite disparate values, and the limits of identity politics within a heteronormative society.

Identity politics during the late 1990s witnessed mainstream visibility for socially wholesome lesbians. In television, Ellen DeGeneres came out on her popular ABC show *Ellen*. In sports, Ladies Professional Golf Association (LPGA) tour veteran Muffin Spencer-Devlin and Hall of Famer Patty Sheehan disclosed their sexuality. In films, the early 1990s' subtext of lesbianism (*Fried Green Tomatoes*, *A League of Their Own*) was supplanted by explicitly queer cinema, such as *But I'm a Cheerleader*. In politics, Tammy Baldwin became the first open lesbian elected to Congress. In advertising, Subaru marketed its brand with car license plates reading XENA LVR or P-TOWN and such taglines as "It's not a choice; it's the way we're built."

The limits of identity politics were apparent. For example, sociologist Peter Nardi observes that queer media characters "appear no different from everyone else in television. They are mostly white, middle class, typically desexualized, generally existing outside of any gay or lesbian social context and friendship circles, not threatening to heterosexuals, and usually free from oppression." This perception, in part, explains the unlikely convergence of interest between CAMP Rehoboth and the Rehoboth Beach Homeowners Association, evidencing the leverage and limitation of identity politics within a diversifying community.

Divergence of interest within queer communities is today's norm. Although the fluidity of sexuality has been ever present—mediated by sociocultural, economic, and historical forces—variegation within the "gay community" was first widely evident during the 1990s. Gay flags had multiplied from Gilbert Baker's 1974 original eight-color rainbow flag to the pink, purple, and blue bisexual flag; the lesbian purple and black labrys flag; the leather flag of a white striped middle surrounded by alternating black and blue dark stripes, with a heart in the upper-left-hand corner; the bear community's banner of dark brown, orange/rust, golden yellow, tan, white, gray, and black stripes with a paw print centered; the two-spirit pride flag with two feathers centered against the background of red, orange, yellow, green, blue, and purple stripes; the drag flag with a Phoenix placed in the center; and the light pink, blue, and white transgender flag. The "gay movement" experienced identity by addition and community by subtraction with an ever-expanding politicized alphabet: GL, GLB, LGBT, LGBTQ, LGBTQ+, LGBTIAQ+. Social class, gender, ethnicity, and race were major cleavages, but the movement was also refracted by religion, age, and able-bodiedness.

"It's easy to believe that since most of us have experienced some form of queer prejudice in our lives, we would be more tolerant of those who are a little different from us. Unfortunately, that's not always the case," Elkins observed. "Sometimes the homo homogenization that is taking place within our culture lets us forget to celebrate all aspects of our community—and keeps us from welcoming those who are different."

THE STRAND'S LAST STAND

At the turn of the millennium, the so-called Battle for Rehoboth had largely ended.[2] The 1999 cover of *Washington Post Magazine* depicted two White men holding hands under the title "Rehoboth Beach and Its Gay Constituency, Coming to Terms." Compared to the cover article a decade earlier, "th[is] article painted a community that seem[ed] to be coming to terms with its own diversity," declared Elkins, portraying "a town that [wa]s expanding the meaning of family."

This "coming to terms" was most starkly manifested in the demise and demolition of The Strand. Although the famed club's final dance was held in July 1994, and its restaurants were shuttered, the building's owner, Bill Larsen, leased the upstairs beginning that autumn. Channel Z, previously known as XLR-8, became the new underage weekend venue at the now threadbare Strand. There had only been one complaint (from B&B owner Kenny Vincent)—until the club organized a January 1995 East Coast rave.

When Rehoboth matriarch Evelyn Thoroughgood took her usual Sunday morning stroll, she was flabbergasted: "The whole avenue was lined with cars with out-of-state plates." The organizers had informed town officials that the twelve-hour event would begin at 10:00 P.M. It attracted more than seven hundred mostly White youth—some using designer drugs—and outraged the town. One local reporter cited "the former Strand" as continuing "to be a thorn in the side of Rehoboth Beach officials." Commissioner Jan Konesey reminded voters, "I tried to institute a curfew a couple of years ago and I was booed and hissed." As the town struggled to develop yet another ordinance, an April "hip-hop party," also at the former Strand, attracted five hundred mostly Black youth. Local police and twenty state troopers scoured parked vehicles with flashlights and hammers. One officer told a security guard, "We don't want that kind in town." At least one *Cape Gazette* letter writer echoed this sentiment: "Rehoboth is not a family town any more. . . . In the last few years it has become the playground for the out-of-state trash."

Before a new ordinance severely restricting dance halls went into effect, Ray and Bertha Pusey had repeatedly called the police to complain about noise from the dance club. When a patrolman met them outside their Baltimore Avenue home, however, "no music could be heard." Chief Creig Doyle later reported, "Until you put an ear to the door on the rear deck" of the old Strand, The Avenue was quiet. The Puseys fumed.

In July, the town declared the building "abandoned." Larsen was faced with commissioners' refusal to approve a certificate of compliance for another entertainment venue. Saddled with debt and illness, he put it on the auction block. "It's been a nightmare for way too long," muttered City Manager Greg Ferrese. When the gavel went down three months later, the "ebullient" Derrickson cousins—Richard and Robert—laid claim to the "infamous" building, ending a generations-old feud with the Larsens. Among those in the crowd was a smiling Bertha, ensconced in her lawn chair. Two years later, Mariner's Square arose "from the dust of the old 'Strand' building," with a restaurant and a half dozen shops, including Effxx Menswear. The iconic symbol of Rehoboth's gay-straight divide was history.

THE GRINNING REAPER

The story headline in Wilmington's *News Journal* read, "Truck Crushed Dover Woman in Philadelphia."[3] Around noon on September 30, 1998, Ray Pusey was driving along a Philadelphia expressway to a doctor's appointment. Bertha sat next to him, chatting about their upcoming long-dreamed-about European vacation. Suddenly, a tractor trailer swerved and flipped onto their car. Tons of construction debris rained down on the blue Buick. Ray exited the vehicle unhurt; sixty-three-year-old Bertha was mangled beyond recognition. Awaiting the arrival of a nearby Catholic priest, he sat on an ambulance's back bumper, praying. The irony that he had spent more than three decades of his life as a chief traffic engineer designing safe roads was lost on few people.

At the opening of the monthly commissioner's meeting, the room quieted as Commissioner Jack Hyde led a prayer for Bertha. Mayor Sam Cooper eulogized, "She certainly filled a niche and my first reaction when I heard about her death was 'Bertha, you can't go now!'"

There were few accolades, however, within Rehoboth's queer community. Glen Thompson remembers his phone ringing, with the caller exclaiming, "You won't believe what's going on right now!" As Thompson recalls, "When Bertha Pusey died, they popped champagne and had a party at the Blue Moon. They thought it was the greatest thing that ever happened!" He instructed the informant, "Oh my god! Don't say anything to anybody. If Ray Pusey hears that, he'll go there, and it ain't going to be nice."

In Australia, Victor Pisapia received a fax: "The wicked witch is dead!" Reflecting on the tragedy, he recalls before departing from Rehoboth approaching Bertha on her porch, spouting

> all the things I wanted to say to her over the years. She kept telling me, "Talk to my lawyer! Talk to my lawyer!" I refused. Upon leaving, I said, "All we can hope for, Bertha, is that a big tractor trailer comes barreling down and flattens you into the wicked witch you are."

A memorial fund was established by the Pusey family in her honor to assist victims of domestic violence—a cause for which the State Assembly of Delaware had given her its Volunteer of the Year award.

ROOM FOR ALL?

As gay-straight tensions lessened in the late 1990s, fractures within Rehoboth's queer community had become more evident.[4] Although lesbians were more welcomed at Renegade, where drag queens reigned, affluent White boys from DC, Baltimore, and Philadelphia continued to dominate the A-list social scene. Throughout *Letters*, mostly men were photographed and featured in its social pages. However, at the threshold of the millennium, *Letters* expanded to 112 pages to include more diverse columns, including Tricia Massella's lesbian-focused "Making Waves"; "CAMP Safe," the AIDS/HIV column by Bill Sievert; Tom Santomartino's "LeatherBeach"; and "CAMPstudent," penned by one of two local queer teenagers. The long-controversial "Being Scene" column continued to appear, as did Jacobs's humorous first-person "CAMPOut" column, which won a national Vice Versa Award.

One of the unintended consequences of the "bar ban" passed a decade earlier had been the steady expansion of the house-party circuit. Reflecting on the 1990s, "Being Scene" columnist Tom Minnuto rhetorically asked, "Who knew in 1990 that we were about to be blitzed by theme parties and bachelor auctions?" New summer-season blood was recruited at the CAMP-sponsored Beach House Rush Party each spring. Described as a "party about inclusion," well-off men plunked down $1,500 to $2,000 for weekend "shares" from Memorial Day through Labor Day. In 1999, it was held at a 14th Street DC gay men's bar, the Lizard Lounge. The hundreds of men who attended understood that "clothes, small talk, and attitude often determine who ends up at which house."

Each season built upon the one before, inspiring houses to create more elegant invitations, produce more extravagant theme parties, and encourage more brazen behaviors. For instance, the 208 Rodney squad held a "quasi" drag theme party: "Austin Powers meets the Valley of the Dolls." On this "acid trip back to the swinging 60s," some guests sported "high hair, go-go boots, bell bottoms, and wild flowered pants and shirts," joined by "medallion encrusted, smooth-chested studs bulging from their rayon shirts." Powers "showed up in his striking blue velveteen suit and go-go boots." There, too, was competition for making the "grandest entrance to a party." A Poodle Beach Award was won hands down by the Laurel Street boys who arrived in full showgirl regalia at the Viva Las Vegas party, riding atop two Rehoboth fire trucks with sirens blaring and lights flashing.

Chris Yochim recollects that what "started out in people's homes grew so big, so fast that they had to start renting out venues." Held at the convention center, the Golden Poodle Awards Gala had evolved from an early 1990s four-house progressive dinner party with themed skits. It would transform again into a CAMP Rehoboth Follies fundraiser, with gold, silver, and bronze Barbies awarded to the top three house performances. Its founder, A-list organizer Chris Riss, noted that an "important reason for producing the Follies [wa]s to create community among us." Jacobs, whose all-women troupe won several Barbies over the years, remembers that the convention center was always packed for the "full-on theatrical production that Murray [Archibald] was in charge of."

By 1999, however, the men's social scene was diversifying. The Eastern Shore Bears Club hosted its first Mr. Delaware Bear/Cub contest at John Meng and Mark Fernstrom's Double L Bar. Unlike the "Grecian gay ideal of beauty" paraded during the Blue Moon's happy hour, Bears preferred "homey bars where they can be casual and free to be themselves" and "don't need to have an attitude." With its two pool tables and outdoor patio, the Double L, located at the western edge of the canal, fit the bill. It was Rehoboth's first (and only) leather bar.

Since opening on New Year's Eve 1997, the Double L had been doing a brisk business. Each September, it hosted "Bears on the Beach" for a weekend. Participants chose to sun at North Shores rather than Poodle Beach, bunk at the Shore Inn or Ram's Head rather than either the Rehoboth or Silver Lake guesthouses, and partake in the $5 Saturday night beer blast instead of sipping cocktails at the Moon or Celsius. Mr. Bear Cub of 1999, Santomartino, remembered his earlier visits to Rehoboth, where "you had to have the right clothes, cologne, and figure to fit in" and where he found that "most people ignored me and other visiting Bears." He argued, "We gay people are persecuted enough without treating each other badly. It is time we put our differences aside." Nevertheless, two decades later, a local gay resident would observe that in this "so-called 'gay community,' there are different gradients. . . . We have an 'Upstairs, Downstairs' demographic."

Other Rehoboth visitors expressed similar sentiments at the time. Bob Shilling wrote in *Letters*, advising the local gay community of an August visit by more than a hundred queer members of the Deaf community: "The gay community is not aware as to why there are so many deaf people . . . [and] many of them (not all) seem to be uncomfortable." Another visitor,

An Evening of Amateur Skits
Saturday, July 27 , 8pm
Doors Open 7pm

To Benefit CAMP Rehoboth
Rehoboth Convention Center
Tickets $25

Preferred Seating Available • Sponsor $300 (4 seats) • Host $100 (2 seats)
Tickets Available at CAMP Rehoboth • 39 Baltimore Avenue, Rehoboth Beach • 302-227-5620

Krolewska
Vodka

FOURSQUARE

CAMP Follies 2002 postcard.
(Courtesy of CAMP Rehoboth. Photo by Tony Burns.)

after reading *Letters* for an "entire summer," wrote, "In an organization dedicated to creating a more positive Rehoboth, little was ever mentioned about the recovering gay & lesbian community (or just the non-drinking)," aside from a listing for Alcoholic Anonymous meetings. "Don't you think that is a bit sparse?" The writer concluded that the magazine put "too much emphasis on the partying and drinking crowd."

MAKING WAVES

Well into the 1990s, Rehoboth-area lesbians felt silenced, marginalized, or isolated.[5] Some gathered on Thursday evenings at Donna Gibler and Joy Reese's Sand in My Shoes, a women's B&B on the Rehoboth side of the canal. The weekly event was organized by social workers Libby Stiff and Penny LeCates, who was a CAMP board member. Stiff remembers the pair saying, "We really need to put these people together, so they have a chance to meet each other." At the time, "90 percent of the women who lived in Sussex County were closeted."

The Gay Women's Support Group, known simply as "the Group," had evolved from a handful of women gathering at various places during the late 1990s to a family of more than sixty meeting at the B&B, whose owners served coffee and cake. As it grew, more women from small towns in Sussex County "would truck across" to Rehoboth. "They didn't want to be seen," Stiff explains. "Your life would be over."

This mostly rural county offered few options for lesbians during the late 1990s: a short-lived small queer bar in Seaford; occasional weekend campouts at Trap Pond, near Laurel; informal group gatherings in Salisbury; and the distant Lesbian Community of Delaware Valley gatherings across the Pennsylvania state line. Elkins was not unaware of the situation: "Though Rehoboth is a small town, its very nature as a resort town fed by major East Coast cities makes it somewhat of an extension of those cities and their more liberal attitudes." Yet he had "no doubt that all over [Sussex] [C]ounty there are out, visible gays and lesbians." Many more, however, remained closeted.

It was not only lesbian women who confronted discrimination and recrimination based on their gender and sexuality. Queer teens, even those living near Rehoboth, felt alone and stigmatized. At Cape Henlopen High School, serving the Rehoboth area, "ultra-lesbian" Rehoboth grrrl Kristen Foery wrote about her difficulties dating during this era: "I can't think of a single teenager in this county who would be nutty enough to take a same gender date to a dance. . . . [O]urs is a world of secrets and silence." Another

RBG cover of Anyda Marchant (*left*) and Muriel Crawford (*right*),
July 23, 1998. (Courtesy of Carol Fezuk.)

lesbian teen, Kristen Minor, lived near Rehoboth, where she and her family attended the Methodist church on Baltimore Avenue. Nevertheless, she "was convinced that I was the only gay person within 50 miles." Once, she was invited by her "boyfriend" to join others for a day trip to "queer Rehoboth." Walking into Lambda Rising, "I almost passed out. There was what I had been craving." The bookstore's manager, Yvonne Janssen, recalls, "There was this imaginary wall that was set for her." She had many conversations with young persons like Minor: "Sometimes, I felt that I should hang a shingle out front!"

Eighty-three-year-old Anyda Marchant also frequented the bookstore. She recalls, "As a teen, it dawned on me I would not fit into the pattern of women who married." Although she never felt pressure from her parents, Marchant—like her lesbian heroines—practiced discretion throughout most of her adult life. She explained to a *News Journal* reporter covering the 1994 signing of her eleventh book, *Michaela*: "There are some parts so private we must hold back." She deplored those "exposing their private selves [who] [we]re doing something detrimental to themselves and turning us into voyeurs."

Meeting ninety minutes weekly at the B&B, lesbians discussed such personal struggles. "The thing that became so obvious was that many women were living positive lives," Stiff recollects. However, their families "didn't know that they were a couple, and they had no documents to protect themselves in the event that somebody died." She remembers one couple, in particular, "who had been together for four years. Both had been married to men. Both had children. They knew that if one of them died, the family would come for the inheritance."

After a brief introduction, the Group usually divided into small sets of women "to help people with problems." Stiff details:

> I put out fires, but the Group decided who wanted to start. Someone would be thinking about a problem, any problem, and would ask for advice. Then, they would work together. If there were several issues, we would break down into small groups.

Stiff, with her longtime partner, Bea Wagner, had moved to Rehoboth in the early 1990s. They met regularly with other lesbians in the area, often at Thompson's Palms restaurant, which, in 1994, was sold, becoming Cloud 9—and a mainstay of queer Rehoboth. This remodeled restaurant, across from the convention center, with its "square purple tables and flash of blue, green and pink neon on aqua walls," included a ceiling designed by Murray Archibald that gradually transitioned from "dark blue and clouds of a temperamental day to a sunrise of pastel." It was the "cool space . . . the perfect 'see and be seen' restaurant." Like that of the Front Porch Café, the menu was filled with locally sourced ingredients. Co-owners Paige Phillips Berdini and John Berdini had joined Kelley Harp along with Michael Brossette and his life partner, Aaron Flamm, who already were operating Celsius, a gourmet restaurant on Wilmington Avenue. Marketed as an upscale bistro, Cloud 9 was known for its "retro food," moderate prices, and outside patio dance floor. It was Paige, however, who was the darling of the lesbian crowd. Known for her quit wit, distinctive earrings, and flawless style, the thirty-something garnished customers' drinks with her trademark smile and charmed them from behind the bar with its cloud-shaped mirrors.

THE GRIM REAPER

The headline in the *Wilmington News Journal* read, "Rehoboth Woman, 33, Is Found Dead."[6] The Rehoboth Police Department received an emergency call on a June Sunday afternoon in 1997. Police and paramedics rushed to the rear of the Blue Moon. Joyce Felton was in her apartment, where first responders found a lifeless Paige. They were told that after bartending at Cloud 9, she had joined friends at the Moon for drinks. She had called her husband to tell him she was sleeping over at florist Gabby Beel's apartment rather than making the drive home to Lewes.

At the scene, Detective Banks noticed people moving between Felton's apartment and an adjoining one where Beel lived. Judging the death "suspicious," police returned the next day with a warrant to search both residences. They found "drugs and paraphernalia" that included cocaine, marijuana, and heroin. An autopsy and toxicology report later determined that Paige had died of cocaine, alcohol, and heroin intoxication. Felton and Beel were arrested on July 2 on several counts of drug possession. Neither was charged in her death.

"The news has paralyzed our community and left us broken hearted," wrote Elkins. "In times of tragedy, the real nature of our community comes shining through." The *Washington Blade* reported that Paige's accidental death had "rocked the town's close-knit" community. "Everybody's talking about it, but too many people are in a state of denial," one of her friends said. Insisting on anonymity, this individual deplored, "Drug use has become widespread." After listening to eulogies and talking among friends, Peter Antolini wrote in *Letters*, "I saw in the faces of many the obvious sorrow over the loss of Paige, but one could also see an array of emotions from guilt and empathy to apathy and denial." Tricia McCoy, a former CAMP board member, reported that during her ten years in Rehoboth, she had "watched our community deteriorate as the drug use increased." Like Antolini, she concluded, "Many people contributed to her death. Those who partied with her, you know who you are, as well as those who looked the other way."

This tragedy had a sobering, albeit momentary, effect on the queer community. Charges against Felton and Beel were dismissed following their completion of the state's drug court program. A show titled "Building Bridges of Love through Diversity" premiered at Cloud 9 the following year as a memorial to Paige. A local band, Red Letter Day, released a CD with the tribute song "Until Then." "She was like a princess to many of us," remembered Elkins. "When she and John were married, it was as if 200 of us were being asked to give the bride away." In lieu of flowers, mourners were asked to donate to either the Kent-Sussex AIDS Program or CAMP Rehoboth.

WE ALL HAVE A PLACE

A year or so into the Group's weekly sessions, some longtime members wanted to move the meeting time so they could gather first at one of the few local lesbian hotspots: Cloud 9, the Frogg Pond, and the recently opened Plumb Loco, located just off Baltimore Avenue.[7] Owners Pat Whittier and Georgette Schaefer advertised the new establishment as "where the girls go every night." It was a "space for women," Whittier explained, "which is so lacking." This southwestern eatery was cited by the magazines *Girlfriends* and *Curve* as one of the ten best lesbian restaurants in the country.

The only other nearby women's venue was Renegade's Sunday early-evening "Ladies Tea Dance" hosted by DJ Jamé Foks. "I think it's great," Foks said, "[that] some of the other places have stepped out and are providing more spaces for women to go in Rehoboth." During the 1980s, Foks was a "well-known on-air personality on the professional club circuit" along the East Coast. While working in Baltimore, she had journeyed to Rehoboth for her first of many engagements at The Strand. Later, Foks contacted Wayne Hodge about hosting a weekend women's tea dance at Renegade, but "he told me he'd tried it and it didn't work." Ever persistent and prescient, she offered to promote the event through her company, Party Girl Productions, and to cover her expenses. He relented.

The first early-evening weekend event, in 1991, had attracted more than eight hundred women. By decade's end, "these dances ha[d] become a ritual of summer," Foks bragged. "There were just *so many* women," remembers Fezuk, who bartended there. "Trying to get them out was like herding cats." On Memorial Day weekend in 1999, a record 1,023 women danced to high-energy music and eyed the wet T-shirt contestants before their fleeting women's space dissolved into the testosterone-rich night crowd.

"Up until about that time, CAMP Rehoboth was almost exclusively male," observes Stiff. "Steve had no problem including women. It just hadn't come up that much." In 1999, Archibald explained in *Letters*, "Over the years so much energy had been directed at surviving the AIDS disaster that we thought of little else. Now, though we cannot give up on the fight against AIDS, it is time that we broaden our efforts." CAMP formed an advisory committee that he chaired to explore projects that focused on the needs of other segments within the queer community.

Stiff and her life partner often connected socially with Maggie Shaw, another social worker and nurse, and her partner, Andrea Andrus. Discussing the issues faced by the now too successful Group, Stiff recalls Shaw say-

Cover of *"Follies" Letters from Camp Rehoboth*, July 15, 2005.
(Courtesy of CAMP Rehoboth. Photo by Murray Archibald.)

ing, "We ought to get Steve to let us have a women's fest." The foursome met at Shaw and Andrus's house along with attorney Ellen Feinberg and her partner, Lesley Rogan. They were later joined by Maggie Ottato, a "very good friend of Steve and Murray" who had served on CAMP's board, and Joan Glass, a recent retiree who "was very sophisticated and knew a lot of people." Elkins was very supportive: "We'll do whatever you want to do." Stiff continues, "Steve was the board. . . . If Steve said that it was a good plan and went to the board, the board would agree."

As CAMP sought to expand "into a full-service community center," Archibald conducted several "Advisory Committee" workshops in 2000. These were open to anyone and would serve "as our creative developing ground for new programs," Elkins explained. One of these workshops was held on a cold April day at Epworth Church. Archibald had reached out to "the women's community, which was not as actively involved back then." Those attending envisioned one program as "embracing all women in our community." The CAMP Rehoboth Women's Project "was born," Shaw recalls. Its first event was a Women's Health, Legal, and Financial Conference, held at the Rehoboth Beach Public Library in March 2001. Promoted under CAMP's umbrella, about seventy women paid $10 to attend the half-day, sold-out event.

The success of the first year's women's conference resulted in its expansion to a full day and relocation to the convention center. Several hundred women (and a few in the "men's auxiliary," including Archibald and Elkins) listened to Governor Ruth Ann Minner's keynote address. Workshops on legal issues, relationships, financial planning, career transitions, and "couple's survival" were offered during the morning and afternoon. The Women's Project Committee began organizing other events: health screenings, social events, a golf league, and a women's art show—all under the auspices of CAMP.

Retitled the CAMP Rehoboth Women's Conference Weekend, within a few years, it had become a three-day event. Sessions expanded in number and breadth, ranging from golf techniques and tai chi to household repairs and heart disease. Hundreds of participants throughout the East Coast enjoyed nationally known authors, artists, performers, and comics as well as keynote addresses from women in state and national politics and screenings of lesbian-centered films. "It was really a successful event," acknowledges Archibald, and "really crucial to some of the earlier success of CAMP because of it bringing different elements of the community together." Unfortunately, though, this gathering did not include "the men's community. If it said 'women,' men went the other way."

Stiff and Wagner remained active with the project committee during its first ten years, but increasingly, they disagreed "with the direction the program was going." Stiff says that she tried

> to open it up to people from all walks of life, not just the Washington professional group. I wanted to get the women who worked at Walmart and to reach out to other people. That didn't suit. They were most comfortable at CAMP with the Washington crowd.

The couple also pushed for bringing "lots of women to participate in the planning process. [But] at this point, Andrus was working for CAMP Rehoboth, which became more of the guiding focus through its Women's Project."

There were also disagreements about gender politics. Stiff came from an era "when we wanted to be called *women* instead of *girls* or *ladies*." She emphasizes that unlike some women's events, most notably the Michigan Womyn's Music Festival, "it was *women*, not *womyn!*" Further, unlike in Michigan, where the only males allowed were toddlers and young boys, there was room for all in Rehoboth: "We actually did have one transgender individual who participated." However, to Stiff's dismay, many women from the Group refused to attend: "They wanted to be with biological women." In contrast, like many in Rehoboth, "I believed in inclusion. Exclusion is what we've all lived with; inclusion is the answer. We all have a place."

After the first decade, Jacobs became cochair. Her committee "decided to shake things up, and we called it Women's Fest," attracting more than 1,500 women. During one festival, she remembers a small contingent of women "piggybacked" on the event: "They were women-only and anti-trans." Nevertheless, it was not until the festival's twentieth anniversary that "we had one trans woman on the committee."

A CARPENTER, A DIVA, AND A QUEEN

In 1999, a fledgling interest surfaced among some transgender persons to organize in lower Delaware.[8] One wrote to CAMP, "We know Rehoboth is becoming a gay and lesbian hot spot. There are among us some transgender people as well, but we are having a bit of trouble connecting."

A year before, Kurt Charles Brown had returned from Florida after working for a decade at Disney World. Brown's father had been a builder of spec homes in Pennsylvania. "As soon as I was old enough to hold a hammer, I was out building houses," Brown remembers. When the economy worsened during the late 1970s, his father went bankrupt, and the family moved to southern Delaware.

Brown entered Cape Henlopen High School as a sophomore, quickly establishing himself as a star athlete. He was the starting fullback and one of the top three wrestlers in the state's 155-pound class. Wrestling was a sport he had learned as a boy after being mugged for a nickel in his small town: "I had this talk with my father. He told me he didn't want people thinking I was a sissy. So, I started wrestling in fourth grade." Earlier during that school year, his mom had asked, "What do you want to be for Halloween?" Brown had replied, without hesitancy, "a girl." So, he had gone to school wearing a dress, stockings, full makeup, and a wig. "The teacher made me sit in the corner" and phoned his mother. When he was picked up, "She didn't say I wasn't supposed to do that; my mom never said that. She just never understood."

Earlier, in preschool, Brown's feelings about being differently gendered had emerged: "The boys slept in one room, and the girls in the other for nap time. So, naturally, I wanted to go to the girls' room. I didn't know I was a boy." In first grade, he was held back because "I didn't want to go to school where they made you line up boy-girl-boy-girl." Feigning sickness to stay home, he dressed as a girl. Later, while still in elementary school, he came across large rubber bands at his uncle's farm. "What are these for?" His father replied, "You put them on the nuts of a bull. In two weeks, the nuts fall off and the bull is a girl." The lad's eyes twinkled. When the family returned home, he tried them on—but just for a few moments. "They hurt, so I took them off! But that was my castration attempt."

As a high school student, Brown participated in "every sport I could" and other after-school activities: "I knew when I would go home, I would get into my secret clothes." Because "I didn't want to do that," he prayed daily: "God didn't answer my prayers, so I lost my religion. I gained it back when I realized that God had answered my prayers—it just wasn't the answer I wanted."

Brown had first visited Renegade as a salaried carpenter in 1998. After many days of working, one night, Brown "could no longer sit in the house dressed as a girl. I drove to Renegade. I sat in the parking lot; I could not walk in." Muscling up "the courage" two weeks later, he entered as she. "Two drag queens took me aside . . . redid my makeup, and that was it!" Still, it was two months before "Fantasia figured out that that carpenter who [wa]s working there [wa]s also that cross-dresser who ha[d] been coming in here. That's how I got my drag name, Kathy Carpenter." She first performed "drag" with Fezuk and other Renegade employees at the August "Ugliest Drag Queen in Captivity" event. A raucous crowd tossed quarters. "Renegade was *our* community center. It wasn't CAMP Rehoboth," jabs Carpenter.

At Renegade, she was told, "You're not a drag queen; you're a transgender." Carpenter "didn't know. I always considered myself a cross-dresser, or back then, they called us transvestites. I didn't know what transgender was!" She continues:

In the drag culture, you have a real diversity. You have some drag queens who are transgender. But a lot of drag queens are just gay men in a dress. Their motives are different from the transgender person. . . . For those drag queens, when the performance is over, the dress comes off, and the name comes off.

Howard Hicks was one such person. The native Virginian first performed in DC at age nineteen, working at the legendary Lost & Found.
Sometimes, employees dressed for a theme party. He "wore a lady's nightie"
and was given the moniker Gladys. Years later, Gladys Kravitz was hosting
drag karaoke at The Strand's West Side Café. Performing as this maven's
persona, the "Queen of Karaoke" was "campy" and a "little nosy." Hicks
adds, "Gladys is really more Howard, and Howard just knows better than to
say some of the things."

Unlike Carpenter, "rather than wanting to dress as a woman or be a
woman," Hicks donned female clothing to meet and socialize with others:
"A lot of people sitting in a bar would never come up to me as Howard."
When The Strand closed, he performed on Saturday nights during the summers at Renegade's Cabaret Lounge and at Thompson's DC bars throughout
the year: "One of the reasons why it was so popular is that it kind of filled
the void of what piano bars used to be in the gay community, where people
could come and interact with each other."

In 1999, Renegade celebrated its twentieth season with title holders
from the past two decades of the Miss Renegade Pageants. The annual Entertainer of the Year Award ceremony, hosted by Ebony James, was also
held. Carpenter won first runner-up. She recounts, "The drag queens told
me: 'Well, you're not allowed to compete in our pageants anymore.'" Although she "found a lot of support in the drag community, I found a lot of
hate there, too."

During this time, Canadian-born Christopher Peterson came out of his
"magic closet" to appear at Renegade and soon became Carpenter's fairy
godmother. He "took [Carpenter] under his wing" and "instructed me on
the differences between me and a drag queen." Identifying as an "illusionist" or an "impressionist," Peterson rejects the label "female impersonator"
because "it means you are trying to be the person."

On vacation, Thompson had first heard the illusionist singing as he entered the Crystal Room of Key West's La Te Da accompanied by his life partner, Richard Verzier: "I brought him to Rehoboth. I knew right away the show
would be a hit!" Peterson credits Renegade as "my launching pad to America."

Exchanging hand-sewn garments and wigs while sharing witty apho-
risms and seductive songs, each one-hour "EYEcons" showcased six starlets.
Without leaving Renegade's stage, Peterson transformed—through voice
and vocals, clothing and persona—into a range of divas, from Judy Garland
and Bette Davis to Marilyn Monroe and Madonna. It was always a sellout.
He returned each summer with different routines until Renegade closed.

THE OUTSIDERS

No matter my own experience as a gay man, I will never know
what it is like to be black in this country. I can imagine. I can
empathize, but I cannot know, because I am white.

—**Murray Archibald,** *Black & White*

arol Fezuk had been publishing the *Rehoboth Beach Gayzette* since 1997
after the demise of the *UnderGround*.[1] Unlike *Letters*, *RBG* was published in tabloid format. "We tried to have a little bit of content on
each page," unlike *Letters*, which often had full pages of advertising, resem-
bling a yearbook. "If you had something on each page that would draw you
in, you would tend to keep a reader there a little bit longer," she explains.

To launch *RBG*, Fezuk needed sufficient commitments for advertising
and a skilled designer. Her connection to Renegade and close relationships
with Glen Thompson and Wayne Hodge were what "made it float. I had the
backing." Although they continued advertising in *Letters*, there were still
"some issues between Renegade and CAMP," she recalls, "and my spaces
were cheaper!" With Renegade as its major advertiser, Fezuk secured other
businesses, many not advertising in *Letters*. Yet, despite competition, she
and Steve Elkins collaborated, sometimes sharing copy from overlapping
advertisers. Nevertheless, as one *Letters* writer, Fay Jacobs, contends,
"[*RBG*] was not professional. Carol was great—a great bartender and a good
friend—but it didn't take off."

Joining Fezuk in this effort was Frank Williams, whose parents had
met in Rehoboth in 1935. Frank's namesake uncle had headed the town's
meter patrol. Although he had disclosed his sexual orientation to his parents at age twenty-one, in 1974, and frequented the local queer bars over

Carol Fezuk at RBG office, 1999. (Courtesy of Carol Fezuk.)

subsequent decades, "I wasn't really out here until I joined the magazine." His responsibilities were design and layout.

In 2000, a reader wrote Elkins, faulting *Letters* for its poor coverage of "GLBT African-Americans and other minorities." He explained, "I would estimate that 99% of the photos are of Caucasians posing either leisurely, in advertisements, and/or in the form of art." Acknowledging the low proportion of residents and visitors of color, the reader advocated for more inclusive "initiatives and efforts." A year earlier, board member Bill Sievert had admonished CAMP's directors, "The African American and Latin communities" were "being ignored." He stressed, "Our community boasts room for all but is somewhat one colored." Aside from Sievert's comments and Elkins publishing this letter, there were no discernible changes in the content of *Letters*, the composition of CAMP's board, or projects directed toward these minorities.

Throughout its five years of existence, *RBG* focused on queer social life, but it also provided coverage of seldom discussed topics, such as transgender matters and race relations. In 1999, Fezuk and Williams launched a biweekly series by an African American writer about the fictionalized Rehoboth town of Summerville. *RBG* promoted it as "an exciting departure from the quaint and quiet Rehoboth" but "set in and around our own drama-filled community." Philadelphia writer Hassan Sudler wove sexuality, race, and class into a southern gothic story about rape and blackmail, revenge and redemption, love and lust, suicide and murder.

On his first visit to the summer resort, Sudler's pseudonymous protagonist, Jarvis Watson, "sat in a restaurant, walked down the streets crowded with holiday visitors . . . but he'd not seen one single African American." Sudler had had a similar experience when he first arrived in Rehoboth in the spring of 1999 to begin research for what would become a three-year serialization.

Although *Letters* and *RBG* differed in layout, content, and advertising, both covered the summer 2001 campaign for town commissioner by an openly gay Latino. Mark Aguirre had first come to Rehoboth after graduating from a Maryland high school in the late 1970s: "The first time I came was with a friend. We just hung out on the north side [beach] and didn't realize exactly where the gay beach was." Eventually, he routinely stayed for a weekend or a week at a cheap cottage or house. He remembers that as early as the mid-1980s, "things were already transitioning. Things got more and more comfortable; people didn't feel like they had to isolate themselves."

Although he worked and lived in the DC area, Aguirre bought property in Rehoboth during the mid-1990s. He also began "volunteering in the community, trying to lay the groundwork for running for office there one day." He volunteered for the newly formed film society and other community groups, including CAMP: "I knew that if I wanted to run for office there, I needed to establish a reputation and let people know what kind of candidate and potential commissioner I would be."

By the millennium, "there were a lot of newcomers to the Rehoboth community—gays and lesbians, retirees, small business owners." Aguirre also recalls that this "fairly significant[ly] sized group was somewhat frustrated about how to get involved in the community," especially town government and the Homeowners Association, which its president emeritus, Jay Smith, complained was being "invaded by outsiders." For a generation, many on the town's board of commissioners had been board members of the association, as were those appointed by the commissioners to fill various town committees. Once departing elected office, commissioners often returned to the association's board. Nevertheless, the governing hegemony of the Protestant, White, male heterosexuals was about to crumble. An exception was longtime Baltimore Avenue merchant and Rehoboth native Bitsy Cochran, who had successfully challenged the association's electoral dominance in the 1990s.

RACE MATTERS

In early 1999, Carol Fezuk, Frank Williams, Hassan Sudler, and Lee Walker, who wrote *RBG*'s horoscope column, were sitting around the kitchen table in Walker's Philadelphia Olde City apartment.[2] Fezuk had already invited Sudler to contribute to the Rehoboth broadsheet. Walker, who was one of Sudler's roommates, suggested, "Why don't you write a soap opera or serial?" Williams replied, "That's been done by Armistead Maupin." Fezuk interjected, "You could do that! Come down to Rehoboth, look at it, and write about Rehoboth." Sudler promised to think about it. Later, he proposed a mystery drama, *Summerville*, about a widowed (and closeted) gay father who, with his openly gay estranged son, operates a Maryland Avenue B&B.

Sudler arrived that spring to "this little town that I'[d] not heard of in my life." The first installment was due for the Memorial Day weekend issue. Like the fictional Jarvis, Hassan walked around the town. "It was beautiful. It was homey," he reminisces. "Swans in the lake, early sunrises, people jogging on the Boardwalk, volleyball games, bicycling, brunches, lunches, dinners." He also found "the dark side of Rehoboth," where "everyone knows everyone." Sudler explains, "You go to Rehoboth and see the people who know other people: people who work with people; people who have relations with people; people who are having sex with other people. There are *no* secrets in Rehoboth Beach."

For Sudler, the town felt like one long "conversation that you walk in on during the middle." As a writer, he knew, "If you are smart you will take a seat, close your mouth, and open your ears. You will listen: how they talk to one another; how they relate to each other; how they interact with one another. This tells you about the character of the city."

Traveling biweekly from Philadelphia to Rehoboth, Sudler began "to navigate to its rhythm." His goal, as it had been for two decades of gay men, was to arrive on late Friday afternoon at "*the* bar"—the Blue Moon:

> You get there, five or six o'clock. It is packed, flowing into the street. You can hardly get to the bar to get a drink. If you look around, the muscle guys—short-sleeve shirts, arms bulging, hair perfectly coifed—look like they do not have a blade of hair on their bodies. Those people are from New York. The conservative-looking ones— hair looks good, but not as well dressed—they're from DC. Anything in a sweatshirt is New Jersey; anything in something that doesn't match generally is from Philadelphia or Maryland.

But Sudler also noticed something else during his very first visit to the Moon: race—"There may have been two or three other Black guys in the entire bar." He wondered:

> Why does there seem to be an imbalance of races in a town that is otherwise welcoming to gays? You'd think they'd be welcoming to other communities. Is it [that] the others don't want to come here? Others aren't welcomed to come here? Others aren't invited to come here?

Similarly, his imagined counterpart, Jarvis, observed:

> Even in the gay spots around town, he could walk in and suddenly realize he was the only person of color in the room. He faced questions in all the eyes he greeted. *What's he doing here? Does he think he's one of us?* How ironic that even here in the nation's self-proclaimed "gay summer capital" he should feel unwanted, excluded.

In addition to researching the town's history at the local museum, Sudler's connection with *RBG* accorded entry into the A-list summer experience—"the lifeblood" of queer Rehoboth: "Certain things opened up to me. I was privy to certain conversations, interactions, behaviors, and settings that informed me of summer in Rehoboth." House parties, he found, were "generally all guys. Out of a group of one hundred men, ninety would be White; probably five would be something other, maybe Muslim, Latino, or Asian; the other five would be Black." Initially, he was neither ignored nor accepted. Then, word-of-mouth spread about "this guy who was writing this violent, sex-filled, scandal-laden guilty pleasure." He laughs. "I think they were shocked that a Black guy wrote it."

Like most African American males growing up in America, Sudler learned at an early age about the problematics of skin color. His mother was adopted by an African American couple living in Philadelphia after his Puerto Rican grandmother was unable to care for all nine children. Sudler remembers, at age eleven, being startled by the front page of the *Philadelphia Daily News*. In 1978, there was a "photograph of a lineup of young Black men who were suspected of being with the Black Panthers. All of them were naked from the waist down." He continues, "To see someone humiliated and disgraced, put on a cover of the newspaper, was a shock. . . . When you grow up with that, you come to realize that the world is not as sweet."

Growing up, Sudler "always knew that I was, at the very least, bisexual," although he didn't come out until he was in his early twenties, while at Temple University. After attending a gala, Sudler walked by Curt's Bar and braved entry: "I did not know what an LGBTQ community was. I went into this club, and there existed these people who all knew each other. It was a very fun place." From there, he "met some people, and the community opened up to me." Joining SafeGuards, he distributed condoms and literature about safer sex at local hangouts. Although Woody's was "the primary club where everyone went," his favorite was the Nile, an after-hours, mostly African American house-music club: "Literally, I would walk in there at one or two o'clock in the morning and not leave until the sun was in the sky. It was fun and fantastic."

Sudler welcomed "this whole other community" into his life. Like others, however, he questioned its inclusiveness:

> Why do people concentrate all the time on gay men? Lesbians are sort of like, "them, too"—an afterthought. . . . The Trans community was just laughable: a man in a dress . . . or flat-out murdered. . . . Bisexuals [were] often seen as people who are on a fence.

Being a Person of Color in the LGBTQ+ community during the 1990s, Sudler also witnessed indiscriminate racism: "I see Blacks who don't want anything to do with Whites at all within the gay community. I see Whites who will regularly use African Americans, Latinos, and South Asians as sexual fetishes." He narrates one such experience in Rehoboth, when he "hooked up" with a White man. They entered a hotel room, where "the man's roommate said, 'I didn't know you liked dark meat!' He said *that* in front of me!" Then, as the White man went to take a shower, "he turned to me and said, 'Make sure you don't steal anything.'" The White man went into the bathroom; Sudler walked out the door.

Decades later, Sudler asks, "In Rehoboth, can you see it? Yes, in the same way you can probably see it in Provincetown or at Fire Island. There is this thing that is unsaid." Longtime gay visitor Jeffrey Slavin admits that "there was a lot of racism" during this era, adding, "Rehoboth *today* is not a welcoming place for People of Color."

Another subject left unsaid was West of Rehoboth. "In all the time I spent in Rehoboth, never ever until today has anyone ever mentioned West Rehoboth," Sudler says during a 2021 interview. "No one talks about it. No one mentions it. No one discusses it." He continues, "No one from West Rehoboth comes into the town. It's almost like it's understood."

People of Color certainly entered Rehoboth in decades past. None, though, could dine at a restaurant, enjoy the length of the beach, enter through the front door of residences, or watch a movie without going to the balcony. During the summers, "Coloreds" worked in town, yet very few lived there. In Jim Crow southern Delaware, Lena Winchester had a boardinghouse on the fourth block of Rehoboth Avenue. Oscar Harmon, who had moved to the area with his family in 1921, remembered that she rented the property from a White man, who "let her and her family live there as long as she wanted." Despite raised eyebrows and whispered concerns, "the town couldn't move her." Her son, Oswald, was Rehoboth's first Black lifeguard, stationed at the segregated Crow's Nest following WWII. And there was John Winston, a heavy-set man from Maryland. He invested his savings from shining shoes into a taxicab service located near the old train station. Beginning in the 1950s, he slept there by a little restaurant on the side, run by Virgie Friend, who lived West of Rehoboth.

Those were exceptions. "No one ever talks about that," says Sudler. "It reminds me of going to the South . . . where the people constantly whisper, 'That's just the way it is.'" Fellow Philadelphian and novelist Alexs Pate, who spent boyhood summers West of Rehoboth, concurs: "For all practical purposes, [it] was as 'Southern' as a city boy could get without *going* to Mississippi."

Like Jarvis, "walking into Rehoboth as a Person of Color did not phase me." Like Sudler, Jarvis

> was used to traveling in circles where he was the only African American. But here out of familiar territory he became self-conscious of his race, his education, and the way he walked and talked, believing the citizens of Summerville would be just as mindful.

This attitude, as Sudler would later admit, would give him (and Jarvis) pause.

During Sudler's trips to Rehoboth, Fezuk often arranged a place for him to stay. One weekend, he stayed at a Renegade bungalow. He remembers that although "Renegade did have the music, which was very, very good," Thompson's club "was not really my thing. I usually just hung out at the Moon."

That weekend was memorable for Sudler. As he ambled back to his bungalow near closing time, "there was this guy who was looking at me. We passed glances, but I went into my bungalow and closed the door." After taking a shower, Sudler went to bed. He was startled by a knock on the door: "Thinking, I'm from Philadelphia and I can take care of myself, I got up and opened the door." Clad in only a towel, the man pushed him into the room. "I think you need to leave right now!" Sudler demanded. He resumes:

> He closed the door. It was just me and him in this very tiny room. I knew exactly what he wanted, but I didn't know if I would be able to get myself out of that situation. I said again, "I think you need to leave!" He pushed me on the bed. He got on top of me. He started kissing me. I yelled, "That's enough! That's enough!" I had to fight with him to get him off me and off the bed. We toppled onto the floor. I went to the door and went outside immediately. "Get out! Get out!"

Bulldozing past Sudler, the would-be rapist hollered, "Fucking bitch!" Shutting the door, Sudler muttered, "That was close!"

The Labor Day 1999 *RBG* installment of "Summerville" featured a searing rape scene, admittedly inspired by this real-life attack: "They fell on him like hungry wolves and there was no escape. All six men punched on Jarvis, beat him, slapped him, kicked him, spat on him, choked him, and worst of all, they raped him repeatedly." The lead rapist, Thom, "lifted Jarvis's shirt, and in a bold, angry move, crushed the tip of the cigarette into his chest, into one of his nipples." He spied "a fear in Jarvis's eyes," a helplessness that sparked in him an urgent sexual arousal: "I'm going to crack you open like a safe!"

In this season's final episode, "all the guys who raped him were White. That's *not* by accident," says Sudler. He was "unprepared for the reaction to that story. It was more popular and received much better than" he ever imagined. However, he also recalls an email from an avid reader who was African American: "Why did you make this happen to Jarvis? . . . Black people have been through enough." Sudler replied, "He becomes a character you're going to want to root for. I have dragged him down to the lowest point to deconstruct him and now I want to reconstruct him in the face of this horrible, horrible thing."

Having concluded the first season of *Summerville*, "I felt that I belonged in Rehoboth Beach and a part of Rehoboth Beach belonged to me."

CONCERNED MEMBERS

Thirty-five Rehoboth Beach homeowners attended the association's general meeting on Saturday, October 21, 2000.[3] Two weeks earlier, the board had unanimously approved a motion recommending that it make all future political endorsements. Although this had been de facto practice, with the Executive Committee actually calling the shots, public endorsements had occurred at the general meetings. Nevertheless, some board members had expressed "worry that this might cause some dissension." Smith volunteered to explain the board's position, if that should occur.

The meeting of members was heated. As promised, Smith intervened. Inadvertently, he acknowledged that it was already "common practice to promise RBHA endorsements to individuals *before* any interview of all candidates or votes of support by the board or the general membership." This behind-the-scenes admission "added additional fuel to the fire" for those already opposed to formally extending the board's authority. Tempers were further inflamed by "homophobia openly expressed by some board members" at the meeting, which a member claimed was "the same homophobia that many believe is one of the reasons for the founding of the RBHA many years ago." Greg Oliver, a member of the association and a gay man, recalls that the meeting "did not go as scripted. There were many new faces there, including gay and lesbian ones." He remembers Smith saying, "loud enough to be overheard, 'If we don't stop the gays, they will take over.' They clearly feared the new faces and maybe some new ideas." The board's motion was defeated by a single vote.

Although Oliver phoned Mary Campbell "about the resolution that takes our voice away, she said, 'If you don't like it, vote the board out.'" He responded, "Don't you think that's a little drastic?" He later reconsidered— "Maybe Ms. Campbell is right!" At its next board meeting, a frustrated President Campbell described October's general meeting as a "mess" and underscored the necessity to "strengthen the RBHA" by revising its bylaws. This step included prohibiting board nominations from the floor, requiring 10 percent of members' signatures for board seat petitions, eliminating the option of removing board members from office, and deleting the bylaw that subjected the board to orders of its membership. The intent was to "ward off another meeting like we had last October," Campbell explained.

Given "poor attendance not representative of our large membership," the board chose to ignore the membership's October decision. In her spring letter to members, Campbell justified the edict: "Under the old procedure, a small group of members, some of whom might have joined RBHA on the day of the June general meeting, could possibly force the organization to endorse a candidate whose election might not be in the best interests of most members."

After the letter, a dozen so-called Concerned Members requested that the board reconsider its action. Several of them attended its next board meeting. After these disgruntled members departed, an exasperated Campbell apprised her board, "We ha[ve] tried and gone out of our way to include people who have tried to tear down a 30-year-old organization." Ordinarily "proper in her own demeanor," the seventy-eight-year-old, who had served as a board member since 1983, pronounced that she "had [had] her fill of all of this."

In turn, the Concerned Members blasted Campbell and the proposed by-law revisions as an authoritarian move designed to make the association's leadership even more exclusive. Concerned member Hoyte Decker, concluding that the leadership was "attempting to wrest more control," described the board's reversal of its October membership vote as "an act of panic, brought on by fear of a potential take-over by 'outsiders.'" By late summer, the Concerned Members group had grown to more than thirty. It called upon the board to "refocus its attention to a more issue-oriented agenda rather than its emphasis on candidate endorsements."

Aguirre had attended the last three Concerned Members meetings. "I have been encouraged by what I've seen," he wrote in the *Cape Gazette*. "The free exchange of ideas is encouraged even when they may conflict with another's point of view." In contrast, the operation of the association's board "seemed so blatantly wrong. I couldn't look away or deny the fact that Mary Campbell held the most important appointed position in Rehoboth Beach government, as head of the Planning Commission, and was also President of the Homeowners Association." He continues, "There is this circular thing where she is running direct mail campaigns for the mayor who then appoints the Planning Commission." Campbell was not the only board member in key unelected town positions; eight out of twenty board members held such positions, including the city treasurer and members of the powerful board of adjustment.

When a board member resigned that summer, Campbell unexpectedly nominated Elkins, who had just joined the organization a year earlier. His appointment, as the first openly gay member of the board, was approved. "We saw that as an effort to try to quell this growing movement of newcomers," recalls Aguirre. Campbell "was getting pressure from all sides in terms of opening up who was going to be in leadership for the Homeowners Association." He derisively admits, "Reaching out to Steve was a safe choice." However, the problem for Campbell and Smith "wasn't just for gays and lesbians, it was for this larger group of new people in the community," Aguirre observes, "who had not been invited into leadership."

In September, the Concerned Members group submitted its counter-proposal for by-law changes, according to the process outlined in the association's newsletter, along with a set of eleven questions for the board to address, including "Why does the board want to endorse political candidates? Is it appropriate to spend members' money on campaigning for City offices?"; "The board has been accused of being homophobic. Why doesn't the RBHA make a concerted effort to get a better [demographic] balance?"; and "Could the board establish a committee, including non-board members, to develop a pool of candidates for city-appointed committees?"

At the 2001 October meeting, the association's board stonewalled. Its responses included "For RBHA to have any influence in the future betterment of our city and, at the same time, be completely devoid of any political participation is absolutely not possible"; "The homophobic issue is not valid. . . . Who can supply documented demographic numbers for Rehoboth Beach? . . . Include items other than sexual orientation"; and "The city code gives authority to make appointments to the elected officials. For the board to become involved in that process would be not appropriate."

Five days later, the general meeting of the association was held. The resulting firestorm of rhetoric, motions, and countermotions led to unprecedented results.

DWELLER ON THE HILL

Another leader of the Concerned Members ad hoc group was the gay B&B owner of Cabana Gardens, Gary Trosclair.[4] He had retired from the U.S. Public Health Service in 1994, moving permanently to Rehoboth, where he became active in civic groups. Trosclair had first run for town commissioner in 1999, as "the candidate for all of the citizens of Rehoboth Beach." At a Homeowners Association meeting, its members approved the board-recommended endorsements of incumbents Betty Ann Kane and Jack Hyde by a narrow vote (11–10). Despite putting up signage throughout the town and being "confident about my prospects," Trosclair ran a distant third. Noting few differences among the candidates, he promised, "I'll be back."

The following year, Trosclair ran in a three-way contest against incumbent Don Derrickson and pharmacist Kathy McGuiness, whose husband served on the Homeowners Association's board. Again, all were "in agreement about the issues most important to the city." Although Trosclair was a member of the association, it endorsed the others. Again, he ran a distant third in votes and, once again, vowed to seek election the next year. Although it was commonly known, Trosclair's sexual orientation seemed a non-issue.

In 2001, motivated by the heavy-handedness of the association and "upset" by the aborted 2000 presidential Florida ballot count, Aguirre declared his candidacy for commissioner. So, too, did incumbents Richard Sargent and Patti Shreeve, along with perennial candidate Trosclair, who later withdrew from the race due to his parents' illnesses. Before the June 2 filing deadline, Aguirre was invited by Sargent to meet. Sargent told him, "You really don't have to do this. Next year [Hyde] is not going to run for office, and it would be easier for you to win." Campbell also approached Aguirre, telling him, "If [he] chose to run next year, [he] might get the Homeowners Association endorsement." He had already announced his intentions and, more importantly, "it just didn't feel right. It felt behind closed doors." But "I knew it was not going to be easy," Aguirre acknowledges. "I was running against two of the most entrenched candidates, who were joined at the hip."

Sargent, a thirty-five-year-old computer software consultant, had run unopposed three years before. Part of the old guard, he had served on the beach patrol as a teen and was now seeking his third term as commissioner. Yet Sargent "was surprised by what was developing" in the town. Aguirre also remembers "a prominent couple, part of the newcomers, [being] very upfront with [Sargent] that they were not pleased with what he did with his time there."

Aguirre officially announced his campaign at the CAMP Rehoboth courtyard, declaring, "We need to bring more people and new ideas to the table." He promised to be "a good team player who will work hard to build consensus." Citing his various volunteer activities in Rehoboth and DC, Aguirre told the press, "I think that it is important that the gay community give to the larger community. We all should be working together."

One of Aguirre's volunteer roles was chairing the annual LOVE fundraising dance event at the convention center. Created by George Domurot in 1995, it had raised thousands of dollars for mid-Atlantic organizations. In 2000, Aguirre reached out to the Rehoboth women's community, saying that he wanted to donate "some of the proceeds from the LOVE event to a women's group, if there was one." Additionally, CAMP's board considered designating New Beginnings of West Rehoboth as a beneficiary. Ultimately, the $42,000 raised from the thousand mostly gay men attending was split among the Women's Project, Rehoboth Elementary School's technology center, the Sussex County AIDS Committee (SCAC), and CAMP.

Candidate Aguirre, like Yvonne Janssen a decade earlier, fully embraced the queer community. "There have been gay candidates in the past, but the difference with me is that people are energized by my ideas," he told the *Cape Gazette*. Arguing that queer community members often served as "trend-setters," he advocated that city officials "look toward the gay community." Aguirre systematically canvassed votes, knocking on doors. Although he was received positively by most residents, he remembers that "there were people who told me to my face that they would not vote for me because I was gay."

Throughout his campaign, Aguirre emphasized the importance of giving back to the community—a value stressed while growing up as a fourth-generation Mexican American in south Texas and Maryland. Both of his parents "felt very strongly that you are to leave your community better than you found it. I've carried that through my life."

Aguirre was as conscious about his ethnicity as he was his sexuality. He proudly noted that his surname originates from the Basque region, meaning "dweller on the hill," "which sounded noble." Mark's parents taught him "to be proud of the fact that I'm Mexican American. Even though they didn't say this, for me, that meant I should be proud [of] being gay as well."

During the early 1980s, the twentysomething became involved in the local gay pride organization, where Mark learned "what it's like to volunteer and sit on a board." He was soon in charge of sports events, which preceded the June celebration, including softball: "I put together a women's division because I wanted more diversity in the organization. I reached out to People of Color and went to African American bars to solicit more involvement from various communities."

Throughout his undergraduate and graduate schooling, Aguirre had to work. He bartended at Thompson's Fireplace and, later, Badlands, where he met his future husband, Wayne Gleason. "I often thought I should transfer out to Renegade," Aguirre reminisces. After graduate school, he landed a full-time marketing position at the Kennedy Center, then at IBM, and ultimately at AOL.

At Elkins's first Homeowners Association's board meeting, in July 2001, he voted with the majority (8–7) not to endorse any of the three commissioner candidates. Shreeve, a fifty-one-year-old artist and muralist who had moved to Rehoboth in 1990, regretted their decision: "They stand for what I stand for and I'm sorry about how some board members, who are very dedicated people, have been treated."

A near-record number of voters cast ballots for the board of commissioners on a mid-August day, as storms slammed into Rehoboth and a waste spill shut down the Chesapeake Bridge. Aguirre lost to Sargent by a mere nine votes; Shreeve coasted to an easy victory. "Of course, I wanted to win," Aguirre told a reporter, but bragged, "Voter registration was up, absentee voting was up," largely due to his campaign's efforts. "I ran openly," Aguirre wrote in *Letters*, although "I didn't campaign on gay issues; I campaigned on broader community issues." Despite Shreeve's concern about the "negativity that came out near the end of the race," Aguirre knew that he would run the following year.

Each September, following a town election, the mayor recommended city committee appointments to the board of commissioners. Aguirre had requested appointment to the Planning Committee, which in years past would have been routine, given his narrow loss. Mayor Sam Cooper, however, refused. Commissioner Cochran, who had owned Monograms Unlimited since 1981, took the commissioners and mayor to task: "I think it's criminal that Mark wasn't asked to sit on a committee." Stan Mills, one of the Concerned Members, agreed: "If anyone deserves it, it's a commissioner candidate who received one-third of the votes in the last election." Cooper volunteered that he had "asked Mark to come in and talk to me, which is the first time we've ever sat down. I didn't find that he had any passion for city related affairs." Similarly, Commissioner Shreeve said that "after the campaign was over, I told him I was very disappointed with his negativity and he was rude to Mary [Campbell]." She emphasized, "I think people should sit back a bit and really get to know the people and the issues before trying to tear them down."

THE NEW GUARD

On the morning of Saturday, October 20, 2001, the Homeowners Association general meeting convened at the All Saints' Parish Hall.[5] Unlike previous sparsely attended meetings, more than one hundred members gathered. As during the summer 1879 meeting of the Rehoboth Beach Association at the Grove, two slates of board members with competing visions of the future would collide. Aguirre observed, "Just as the RBHA

Board had boldly moved to disregard its members' wishes," the other side was as determined, "just as boldly, to push for reform."

Several dozen attendees milled around the church's perimeter as Concerned Members distributed flyers with their slate of board candidates. Those entering the hall viewed an easel board with photos of the six reformist candidates, including Trosclair and Mills. Bespectacled Smith, wearing his signature V-neck sweater, was outside, too. He directed members entering to sign in and complete official ballots provided by his spouse, secretary Priscilla Smith. These, however, listed only board-endorsed candidates, including Elkins and Howard Butler, who was the only member appearing on both slates. Unlike at previous meetings, homeowners seeking to join the association that day were refused.

"The air was thick with anticipation," observed a *Cape Gazette* reporter, "a lesson in grassroots democracy." Uncharacteristically, Campbell was silent as members of the Nominations Committee and its nominees were introduced. Bill Bahan, a seventy-one-year-old retired IBM executive and former board member turned Concerned Member, was recognized. He nominated the competing slate. Another member moved to adopt the revised ballot listing all nine candidates. The chair permitted its distribution "for informational purposes only" because about two dozen members had already voted and departed. Another Concerned Member rose to be heard, arguing that parliamentary rules prohibited any ballots from being accepted until nominations were closed. After rancorous debate, a motion was made to use the ballot with names from both slates and to discard any ballots submitted prior to the close of nominations. Those who had already voted, however, could cast a new ballot. The motion was approved by an overwhelming hand vote. A motion to suspend the process and reschedule the meeting was soundly defeated.

While revised ballots were tallied, former commissioner and board member Jack Salin crisscrossed the hall, muttering, "These rabble-rousers are destroying every effort we made!" Thirty minutes later, the results were announced. From the board-nominated slate, only Elkins was elected; four from the Concerned Members' slate were elected, including Butler, who was on both slates. Immediately, Aguirre moved to end political endorsements. The motion was approved overwhelmingly.

Afterward, Campbell, wearing a pink turtleneck sweater accented by a gold pendant, spoke to a reporter. She emphasized her plans to continue as board president: "I'm of the philosophy that if you believe in something and feel it's worthwhile, then you stick to it!" She disputed press coverage that depicted the "general membership" as speaking against the current board. Ignoring the history of low meeting attendance, she groused that it "did *not* speak. Approximately 850 members were not present."

Six months passed. The association's by-laws were changed, incorporating most of the issues raised by the Concerned Members group. Board meetings were opened to the membership. Additional committees allowed participation by non-board members, and candidate forums replaced candidate endorsements. At its June 2002 general meeting, these changes were approved, 79–7. President Campbell resigned from the board. So did its secretary, Priscilla Smith, as well as the treasurer. Within a year, most of the old guard were no longer board members, having been replaced by reform-minded individuals, such as Decker and Libby Stiff.

A QUEER CONVERGENCE

We are more and more being integrated into the culture around us. . . . We might have to reinvent our cultural niche as we go forward—or that it simply no longer matters.

—**Murray Archibald,** *Reflections on a Rainbow Theory*

n 2001, Steve Elkins reflected upon the past two decades, when he and Murray Archibald had visited and later lived in Rehoboth:[1] "We've watched Renegade and the Blue Moon pass their twentieth anniversaries. We watched the rise and fall of the now legendary Strand. We've seen businesses come and go. We've danced and laughed and cried and buried friends and made new ones." In the process, Rehoboth experienced a remarkable transformation.

COWARD OF THE COUNTY

Mark Aguirre kicked off his second run for town commissioner again at the CAMP courtyard, in mid-May 2002.[2] As a candidate, he later spoke before the commissioners about voter registration, asking them to extend it, thus allowing voters to first know who would be on the ballot. Commissioner Richard Sargent interrupted, protesting this "political speech." Aguirre left the chambers and, at the steps of the building, lampooned, "One might think that the city is trying to discourage its citizens from becoming involved in their civic duty." Sargent, who had bested Aguirre by just nine votes a year before, followed him outside, telling the press, "This isn't about voter registration—it's about getting elected."

Pledging to be a "catalyst for change" and the "hardest working elected

Aguirre's campaign for town commissioner.
(Courtesy of CAMP Rehoboth. Photo by Tony Burns.)

official Rehoboth has ever had," Aguirre promised to fight for passage of
the state's pending gay civil rights bill (HB99) and to pursue similar changes to Rehoboth's city code. At the chamber of commerce forum, he declared,
"It's time for Rehoboth Beach to abandon the 'us versus them' attitude,"
encouraging members to "look at every face we see in Rehoboth as a potential new neighbor." At the Homeowners Association's candidate forum,
Aguirre was questioned about his ability to "work with the 'Old Guard,' as
a 'new man on the block.'" He responded, "I am confident that I can work
with most of the commissioners." Hoyte Decker and his wife were so "im-
pressed with Mark's level of sincerity and willingness to listen and to act
on what people are interested in," they became campaign volunteers.

In a three-way race, Aguirre took second, with nearly 60 percent of voter support. His election, he observed, made him the "first successful politician in the state of Delaware to run a campaign for office while being an
openly gay man" and the first Latino elected in the county: "My election

proves that what matters most to voters is what a candidate can do for the city, not personal differences." Longtime homeowner Dolph Spain, however, admitted, "I voted for Mark because he's gay. Rehoboth has a large gay community and it's time we were represented." He remembers thinking, "Maybe it is our town after all."

Although Delaware had passed the antigay hate crime bill in 1997, it and thirty-seven other states had yet to protect queer citizens against discrimination. As promised during the campaign, Aguirre lobbied for support of HB99. This bill to outlaw discrimination based on sexual orientation was first introduced in 1998. By 2001, it had passed the House (21–20), only to die in the Senate. In 2002, the Human Rights Campaign Fund and the American Civil Liberties Union (ACLU) surveyed Delawareans and found that most (nearly seven out of ten) supported it.

Aguirre went to Commissioner Kathy McGuiness, the local pharmacist and a native of Rehoboth, with what he had drafted in support of HB99: "She was immediate in saying, 'I will support this in any way I possibly can.'" He then spoke individually to other commissioners, asking each—outside the board of commissioners' meeting—for support of this statement: "I was pretty much told no—not that there were perhaps ways it could be rewritten so they could support it." Some believed that it was not the role of the board to lobby the legislature. Surprisingly, those commissioners who were "supportive of gays and lesbians in Rehoboth" also declined. Eventually, the commissioners agreed on "compromise language" and unanimously approved a policy statement, submitted by Commissioner Sargent. Although not endorsing HB99, "for actions within our authority, the City of Rehoboth Beach will prohibit discrimination on the basis of sexual orientation." Many attending the meeting greeted the outcome with a standing ovation. Aguirre later observed, "Only by acknowledging that there are issues that particularly affect the gay and lesbian community can we move beyond that point." It would be seven years, however, until HB99 was signed into law.

Despite their collaboration on the city's antigay discrimination policy, Aguirre and Sargent often found themselves at odds. Toward the end of Aguirre's first term, a March 2004 workshop "almost ended in blows" following a debate about enforcement of a sidewalk ordinance. Aguirre recommended that the ordinance be returned to committee, chaired by Sargent, for further review. "The buck stops here," declared Sargent. "Going back to the committee is the coward's way out!" Leaning forward and pointing his finger, a red-faced Aguirre responded, "All you know is how to avoid doing work!" Commissioner Patti Shreeve intervened, saying, "This is inappropriate." Glaring at Aguirre, she added, "I am calling *you* inappropriate." He countered, "It's inappropriate for a commissioner to call someone a coward." After Mayor Cooper adjourned the meeting, Aguirre confronted Sargent. The two stood nearly nose-to-nose. "Get out of my face," Sargent said. "Do you want to take this outside?" challenged Aguirre. Cooper inserted himself between the two to de-escalate the ruckus.

"Mark lost his temper and he has to deal with that," Sargent said later. "To physically intimidate another elected official is completely inappropriate." Asked in a *Letters* interview about being "contentious" in his work as commissioner, Aguirre reflected, "I ran for office as someone willing to work as an agent of change," adding, "Challenging the status quo . . . has never been a problem for me." Decades later, when asked about the incident, Aguirre appeared upset, perhaps remembering the diminutive, brown-skinned, bullied grade schooler or the young man for whom family honor and personal reputation were of utmost importance: "When a man calls a man or woman a coward, those are fighting words!"

WEST OF REHOBOTH MEMORIES

By the early 2000s, high-end residential development had crossed the canal.[3] Townhouses and condos had been built; outlet malls and fast-food restaurants mushroomed along Highway 1. On either side of the end of Hebron Road, dead-ending into the heart of West Rehoboth, were about a hundred properties, mostly owned or rented by African Americans. In 2003, a luxury home developer extended the street to the old Dodd's farm. Trucks hauling concrete and dirt passed through daily, further destroying an already decrepit road. At the completion of the first phase of Canal Corkran, where lots sold for $200,000 or more, the developer closed the road, and, as the *News Journal* reported, "walls were built to block the black community from view." One resident wondered, "Is it possible for anyone in America today to block streets and create dirt walls just because they don't like the color of people on the other side?"

A community land trust was established in 2005 by residents to retain their historic lands as "many families [we]re being forced out . . . because of rising costs and the push to sell land." Where once farmland and woodland stretched past its northern and western borders, million-dollar homes arose. "Where a developer might envision luxury condominiums, we envision children playing in front of modest new homes," declared the land trust director.

Meanwhile, the decade-old West Side New Beginnings, a grassroots community-based organization, had built its center and children's playground. Financial support came from the Lewes-Rehoboth Association of Congregations and local fundraisers organized by Rehoboth businesses, such as the Back Porch Café. "A bunch of civic-minded White people decided to get together and help the Black community in West Rehoboth," Wayne Hodge lauds. "Police started doing the right kind of policing back there instead of harassing them."

One summer day in 2003, Brenda Milbourne, who had grown up on Duffy Street and was raising three children, spotted a youngster just after dawn riding a bike in his pajamas. Despite the progress in the community, she knew that he was working as a drug courier. This woman of "presence [whose] eyes convey such a depth of strength and integrity" before long had launched a half-day summer program at New Beginnings with tutoring, field trips, and clean-up campaigns. It also provided after-school tutoring for children in this community, who composed 60 percent of its residents.

Nearly two decades after Jim Bahr had proposed that CAMP help this "forgotten community," CAMP Rehoboth Women's Golf League donated some of its tournament proceeds to New Beginnings. The league's codirector, Barb Thompson, had been teaching the sport to children in Milbourne's summer program. During the ceremony, Thompson teared up, explaining her childhood struggles in an orphanage and the present difficulties in transporting these Black children for such activities. One golfer spontaneously pledged $5,000 toward a vehicle purchase. Within minutes, $11,000 had been donated. Soon, New Beginnings had a royal blue Chrysler van. In accepting the donation, Milbourne reminded the audience, "We must not lose sight and remain focused on our traditions and rich diversity that gives our community much of its strength and resilience."

Renegade backed up against this community's western border. During the summer of 2002, rumors swirled that Thompson's dance club was on the market. Although untrue, they sparked one Realtor's interest. She visited, asking him to name a price. Thompson tossed out a figure of $6 million and forgot about it. Several days later, she returned with a cash buyer. Thompson accepted: "I saw the writing on the wall."

At the time, Hodge explained, "20-year-olds don't have the money to come and stay at the beach like they used to." Years later, he appends, "The twenty-five-year-old, 1984 gay person was still coming here twenty years later, but now he was forty-five or fifty! He didn't want to stand up, drink out of a plastic cup, or dance." Thompson agrees, noting that customers were fewer and the use of heavier drugs more frequent. Further, nearby up-scale residents were organizing against the bar. "We were getting more noise complaints because of the dance club music," reports Hodge. "And to be honest, dance clubs—their time had come and gone." Additionally, the social divide had narrowed. "It got to the point that most gays and straights were mixing together," he says. "We weren't the only place people could go to feel comfortable anymore."

Renegade closed in mid-February 2003, but its big farewell party oc-curred on New Year's Eve 2002. Elkins told a reporter, "It's going to be hor-ribly missed." Although many people shared his feelings, some were am-bivalent about Thompson's departure from the local gay scene: "I'm sure that Glen Thompson is proud that he created these safe spaces in our com-munity. . . . I give him credit for that." However, Jeffrey Slavin "never knew him as any kind of nice guy," adding, "I don't think Glen Thompson has any philanthropic gene in him."

Longtime CAMP board member and Rehoboth businessperson Bill Sievert wrote that Renegade's passing was "a victim of the 'new' Rehoboth economy" that had turned the sleepy beach town into "South Hampton." In his "older memories," Sievert recalled "when the gay community could choose between two large dance clubs . . . both of which flourished in peace-ful coexistence, (or could my memory be sketchy . . . ?)," and when one en-joyed "splendid meals at the Blue Moon and the Back Porch, when an entrée would set you back about $10 . . . maybe $15." He opined, "That's the great thing about memories. They're whatever we want them to be." Similarly, Hodge observes that Renegade regulars "miss the *memory* of it; no one misses it actually being there. We miss how we *felt* when we did go there in our twenties and thirties."

Two months later, after the restaurant equipment, motel fixtures, and light/sound equipment had been auctioned, developers bulldozed the "pow-der-blue block walls and pink roofs that w[ere] Renegade's trademark." Be-fore it was even demolished, however, more than two hundred prospective buyers joined a waiting list, hoping to snag one of the fifty-four condos and thirty-nine townhomes awaiting construction, listing for at least $250,000. Meanwhile, Thompson and his life partner since 1983, artist Richard Ver-zier, focused on reconstructing a 1907 Lewes home. When completed, the formerly 2,200-square-foot house had nearly doubled in size, now surrounded by seven front-porch columns, each topped with an intricate carved face representing one of the seven deadly sins.

The *Rehoboth Beach Gayzette* ended its publication a year before the closing of Renegade. Distributed throughout the mid-Atlantic, under the editorship of Hassan Sudler, it had become more diverse in stories, covers, and advertising. Many articles focused on lifestyle topics, ranging from clothes to cooking. It also addressed such subjects as "Antiracist Diversity," in which its author pointed out: "White activists need to stop trying to fit People of Color into our vision of the movement—and then wondering why the staffs and boards of directors of gay organizations remain mostly White." *RBG* covers, in 2002, included two shirtless thirty-something men, one Black and one White, leaning against a tree, while another featured three divas—two Women of Color, one White. Sudler, too, published a feature interview with Lambda Literary Award finalist and author Reginald Harris. His book of poetry, *Ten Tongues*, showcases verses on race and sexuality, musing on racialized sexual relations, family secrets, and AIDS. Sudler's final *Summerville* chapters also appeared. Readers witnessed Jarvis Watson, Sudler's doppelgänger, confessing to Denver, the gay son of the B&B owner, "I couldn't get beyond this. I tried! The rape." Standing on the roof of Cedar House, he cries, "I wish I could be rid of this PAIN." Stepping backward, he falls two stories to the ground. Denver "never saw Jarvis look so peaceful in his life."

Before what would have been its seventh year, *RBG* was sold to the commercial publisher of *EXP Magazine* in St. Louis. Carol Fezuk recalls that the beginning of the end was when Frank Williams accepted a job in New York City: "It was right at the start of digital printing." In the emerging Internet era, clients asked, "Why should I have to spend *x* amount of dollars on an ad when I can advertise on the Internet for free?" Fezuk continued as co-publisher for the renamed *EXP Gayzette*. The first new issue was published in April 2003. She departed before the end of the season.

THE GREAT CONVERGENCE

Aguirre was not the only gay or lesbian person involved with Rehoboth governance.[4] For six years, Patrick Gossett had served on the Planning Commission, arguably the most important town committee. In 2004, he ran for town commissioner, winning the most votes in an uncontroversial race. "A lot of people were saying there [wa]s no big issue this year," acknowledged Sargent, who won his fourth term. "There was a major issue about preserving Rehoboth Beach's charm, it's just that all three of us agreed." That issue was the Comprehensive Development Plan (CDP), shepherded by Gossett's committee a year earlier and submitted to the board of commissioners.

A disparate set of voices endorsed Gossett. Slavin "passionately" wanted to see him elected, writing that "his election [wa]s of the utmost importance to the future." Mary Campbell, citing the "rampant and uncontrolled development . . . driven by greed with no regard to the past and no interest in the future," also endorsed him. Similarly, former commissioner Jan Konesey wrote, "During his tenure, [Gossett's] leadership focus and attention to detail have been a guiding influence on everything we've done, from the CDP to the routine planning issues." In a full-page ad in the *Cape Gazette*, several dozen local names appeared as endorsers. These included other old guard former commissioners Patti Shreeve and Richard Darley; lesbians and gay men, such as Libby Stiff and Rich Barnett; and CAMP stalwarts Murray Archibald and Steve Elkins.

In his remarks to *Letters*, Gossett stated, "We have gone from a marginalized minority, to a respected voice in our city, to a position of leadership in remarkably few years." He continued, "The major issues in Rehoboth Beach today aren't gay or straight issues; they are issues that affect everyone's quality of life." Aguirre echoes these sentiments: "As gays and lesbians got more involved with the community, we were moving with issues that put us in a position of having power and moving to issues that involved the entire community."

Like Aguirre, Gossett had been coming to Rehoboth for decades, had bought a summer home in Rehoboth during the 1990s, had a life partner of more than two decades, had been endorsed by a national gay rights organization, had a forward-thinking world view, and was active in CAMP and the Homeowners Association. Yet, as Aguirre underscores, "There were differences which set us apart within the gay/lesbian community." Noting that "Patrick was pretty clued in to the status quo," Aguirre acknowledges that the pair were in "different camps." From his perspective, Gossett was allied with "the group that I felt needed to move on."

Unlike Aguirre, Gossett—friends with the old guard and former "Outsiders," and praised by Mayor Sam Cooper as "level-headed with the right temperament to be commissioner"—informed the *Cape Gazette* that he "never considered himself a representative of the gay community" or was its "for-sure vote." He championed the CDP-inspired ordinance that restricted the floor–land area ratio of residential and commercial buildings. Designed to retain the town's architectural character, the controversial measure was approved, 4–3, in 2005, with the mayor casting the deciding vote along with Commissioners Patrick Gossett, Richard Sargent, and Henry DeWitt. Homeowners Association President Stiff also endorsed the ordinance. Commissioners Betty Ann Kane and Kathy McGuiness joined Aguirre in opposing it. The opposition's cited concerns about restricting property rights and unintended consequences, such as encouraging boxlike houses to maximize living space, "b[ore] out as houses simply got bigger," observes Aguirre.

Although Gossett did not view himself as a "representative of the gay community," he and his life partner, Howard Menaker, were very active in it. They had joined the Founder's Circle Capitol Campaign when it launched in 2001. Its $1-million goal was to purchase and renovate the 39 Baltimore Avenue property that housed CAMP Rehoboth. By mid-decade, that goal had been reached, resulting in the property's purchase and renovation. CAMP also bought the adjacent house.

Bookkeeper and board member Natalie Moss laments, "Prices were really high back then; we really overpaid." Nonetheless, "when future generations look back on the history of CAMP Rehoboth, the fall and winter of 2007–2008," observes Archibald, "will stand out as a pivotal moment." Phase II began with a new Development Advisory Board and the groundbreaking for an adjoining community center—a $1.4-million building that would provide a large multipurpose room for exhibits, performances, lectures, and the like. Its purpose, as Archibald pointed out at the time, was not

> so we can keep doing the same things we have always done, but rather so we will be ready and able to create a future community that can handle the needs, creativity, and inventiveness of the generation who will follow in our footsteps.

"The fundraising for a project of this magnitude is, of course, endless," Archibald acknowledged. "I know that I'm not the only one in our community to be experiencing fundraising fatigue." Nevertheless, funds were raised, and the center, whose atrium was later named in honor of Elkins and Archibald, had its grand opening on Memorial Day weekend in 2009, which was attended by more than 250 persons. Elkins remembered it as a "beautiful day" that recognized "the many people of our community who have worked to make the dream of the Center a reality . . . a space to be the 'heart of the community.'"

A month later, the Sussex County AIDS Committee (SCAC) closed its doors after nearly twenty-five years of operation. Glen Pruitt, its associate executive director, explained that the board's decision was due to "fiscal challenges." With SCAC a longtime co-beneficiary of CAMP Rehoboth's fundraisers, such as SunDance, Pruitt extolled, "If it weren't for CAMP there wouldn't have been a[n] SCAC." Nevertheless, the organization that had initiated and funded it, Delaware Lesbian and Gay Health Advocates (DLGHA), was forgotten or ignored—as was its first executive director, Ivo Dominguez Jr. He and his partner, Jim Welch, were living on their hundred-plus-acre property in Sussex County. In the summer of 2007, Dominguez, an elder in the Assembly of the Sacred Wheel, consecrated their open-air temple in a ceremony on Pagan Pride Day with six hundred co-celebrants.

Meanwhile, "it was a chaotic time" at the Blue Moon, reported the *Cape Gazette*. "[Joyce] Felton was distracted from day-to-day operations," now overseen by a new chef, Lion Gardner, and his wife, Meghan, along with former Salisbury business owners Tim Ragan and Randy Haney. Ragan believed that "the days of the 'meat market' bars were giving way to the Internet," so he expanded the Moon's entertainment activities. These included Martinis with Mona emceeing drag show performers; vocalist Pamela Stanley's piano show; and limited performances, such as Leslie Gordon's one-man show, *My Trip down the Pink Carpet*. After a couple of years, the foursome approached Felton about plans to open their own restaurant: "She sensed how much they loved what she had created. Her reaction? 'Make me an offer.'" Thirty days later, in 2008, the Blue Moon had a new set of owners.

When queer visitors returned to Rehoboth, not only had the Moon's ownership changed; there was also no Beach Book with hundreds of names and phone numbers of queer summer renters. Elkins simply explains, "Everyone now has cell phones." Too, Mayor Cooper, during his campaign for an unprecedented seventh term, offered, "The gay and lesbian community brings much to this City—economically, cultural, socially, politically." No longer following the old-guard ghosts of Rehoboth past, he parroted the new mantra: "CAMP Rehoboth truly serves as 'the heart of the community,' and is a welcome partner in all we do."

This sea change of public attitude already had been visible at the turn-of-the-twentieth-century, when one *Letters* aficionado crowed, "In the time that Rehoboth Beach has become a popular destination for gays and lesbians, while maintaining its appeal to heterosexuals and, in particular, families with children, the town has gentrified, property improved, and the economy has expanded to the envy of our neighbors. We have renovated, maintained, and improved our homes." Eight years later, *Letters* observed, "The town is at this moment both what the old guard fought to preserve and what the gay community wanted to create—a mix of small-town tradition and beach-town tolerance, a place where hand-holding men in sandals coexist with baby strollers and kiddie rides."

Gene Lawson, his law degree in hand, now represented gay clients for million-dollar-plus Rehoboth homes. He remembers telling Homeowners Association president Jay Smith, "You know, you can do what you want to, but we're going to win because we are going to outlive you!" Lawson continues:

> That's what has happened around here. The old curmudgeons are dying off or did die off. We actually got gay people elected to the City Commission, gay people appointed to the Planning Commission, and gay people active in other things. We never quit; we just kept going. We were *not* going to let our lives be dictated by a bunch of morons.

Reflecting on this generational change, Slavin quips, "The irony today is that the Rehoboth Beach Homeowners Association, which was homophobic back then, now it's basically run by these conservative gays who want to keep it the way it is *now*." And like some other older gay men, he is ambivalent about what was gained and lost in the Great Convergence: "In some ways, it was nicer when we were segregated and developed a community with each other. But now that we're integrated everywhere, it's totally different." Is there any bitterness about Rehoboth's history of queer discrimination, harassment, and violence? "Certainly, I don't have any regrets that we *had* to live that way. The sense of togetherness and the creation of common values with a common mission *led* to the progress that has been made." Wistful, Slavin riffs, "I'll always miss the old days."

EPILOGUE

REHOBOTH REFLECTIONS

Three years have passed since Luis and I encountered the gaze of Delaware State troopers at a Rehoboth Avenue restaurant. Now, we are more mindful that although many businesses display gay flags and most local government officials are queer-friendly, if not queer themselves, such tolerance diminishes as one travels farther from Rehoboth—and those traveling into Rehoboth may not share the town's open-mindedness.

Letters published several short articles based on my early historical research for its thirtieth anniversary—but it never published the story of our restaurant encounter. Although *Letters* and SunDance continue, Murray Archibald no longer lives in the apartment overlooking the CAMP courtyard that he shared for decades with Steve Elkins. Meanwhile, David Mariner resigned as CAMP's executive director after serving fewer than three years. His replacement, a former university administrator and cisgender lesbian, Kim Leisey has promised to "honor the important and beautiful legacy of Steve Elkins and Murray Archibald." She joins a steadily growing number of queer immigrants to Sussex County. Delaware trails only Hawaii as the highest state per capita for gay and lesbian households, and Rehoboth Beach is the fourth-ranked small city (after Provincetown, Wilton Manors, and Palm Springs) for same-sex couples.

Unraveling and intertwining an experiential cacophony of Rehoboth voices, living and dead, queer its history.[1] However, their textual translation imbues meaning, which I view from two interpretive perspectives. One, *transformationist*, is geographic, demographic, and political change. This perspective also encompasses the transformation that occurs during the various interactions of individuals and groups, particularly evidenced in the transformative uses of *camp*. Finally, there is spiritual transformation, as individuals recognize their soulful interdependence and transcend constructed identities. Second, the *commutarian* perspective begins with the key concept of a community of believers—be they ministers and congregants, developers and speculators, homeowners and summer renters. Small towns often celebrate the bonds of communal beliefs, even if they are illusory or suffocating. The townsfolk, similarly, may reject "outsiders" or "agitators" who challenge either the area's fancied image or unmask its seamy side.

Every community experiences change. Perhaps Rehoboth has transformed more than most small towns, certainly from the mid-1970s through the early 2000s. The story of Methodist moralists of the 1880s who succumbed to modernism may have seemed quaintly irrelevant to my tale of activists challenging the town's provincialism a century later. Sexual troublemakers, such as Joyce Felton, Jim Bahr, Steve Elkins, and Murray Archibald, aligning with progressive business owners, such as Nancy Wolfe and Terry Plowman, were simply the latest incarnation of secularists to cross swords with those Christian traditionalists and conservative property owners defending Rehoboth as a "family town." It's difficult not to see the spirit of Rev. J. B. Quigg in the actions of Raymond and Bertha Pusey or the Rehoboth Beach Camp Meeting Association reincarnated as the Rehoboth Beach Homeowners Association. Neither is it a stretch to connect across generations from the self-made, financially shrewd, and politically savvy William Bright to Glen Thompson or the strict discipline of nineteenth-century Methodism to the fundamentalism of the Moral Majority. The concerns about daily "excursionists" carried by a newly constructed railway, dancing at Bright House, or drinking at the Douglass Hotel easily juxtapose with modern-day weekenders and "day trippers" crossing the Bay Bridge for a holiday of amusement and intemperance. And, of course, racist attitudes and Jim Crow's sinewy fingers extend from the unheralded heroism of a Black man who saved countless lives in the 1879 Surf House fire to the segregated Crow's Nest and the town's unwillingness to incorporate West of Rehoboth, even as it relied on its residents for cheap labor or illicit drugs.

Commercially, Rehoboth morphed into postmodern eclectic chic: an ocean boardwalk of arcades, saltwater candy shops, pizza parlors, and T-shirt vendors set crosswise to cobblestone alleyways and tree-lined streets boasting savory gourmet restaurants, edgy art galleries, and trendy boutiques. Heterosexualized spaces also transformed. Gay flags along Rehoboth Avenue displaced "Keep Rehoboth a Family Town" bumper stickers. Beach areas jealously protected by generations of young men guarding heterosexual lives became spaces for drag volleyball and same-sex weddings. Baltimore Avenue—once the site of camp meetings and Bishop Levi Scott's chapel—is now the "heart" of the queer community. The Boardwalk—once the dead-of-night spot for trysts and terror—is simply deadly tranquil.

These changes were accompanied by a demographic transformation, especially among the LGBTQ+ community. According to a Rehoboth gay writer, "we see . . . more grey hair in the bars. . . . Younger gays can't afford the town." Nevertheless, the number of same-sex couples in Rehoboth increased from thirty-four to eighty-one from the 2000 to the 2010 U.S. Census. According to UCLA's Williams Institute, Rehoboth was the fourth ranked city per capita nationwide housing same-sex couples. Those gays who helped transform the real estate market in Rehoboth, however, were more demographically similar to their heterosexual neighbors than to many within their queer family.

Political transformation was cause and consequence of these changes. A turn-of-the-twentieth-century Christian campground barricaded by Methodist moralism had been converted into a twentieth-century secular beach resort grounded in traditionalism. Yet at the turn of the next century, it was outwardly queered by a CAMP congregation seeking common ground and promising inclusion for all. As Rehoboth transformed, those who ostensibly exercised the levers of political power glacially evolved from a small clique of Methodist men of means to a varying mixture of men and women, Christian and Jewish, straight and gay, Anglo and Latino. Yet to what degree was the town truly welcoming of inclusivity?

Colored visitor faces have increased marginally, although not without acrimony. In 2020, a Rehoboth police officer demanded that members of an Indian American family produce their rental agreement after a neighbor phoned an acquaintance at the police department about "strange and bizarre behavior." The father of the family, a DC federal prosecutor, later stated that the intent was "to send a message to us that we did not belong there and the police were more than willing to deliver the message." The membership of the Homeowners Association, now led by a gay gentleman, has preserved its Whiteness. On the eve of its thirtieth anniversary, CAMP, in conjunction with the Southern Delaware Alliance for Racial Justice, held its *first* Black History Month celebration at its community center. It featured a lecture on Delaware's racial history and showcased African American artists in the Elkins-Archibald Atrium. The only references to the event in *Letters*, however, were several photos sprinkled between shots of people at other venues and a thank-you note elsewhere from a participant. The next year, 2020, *Letters* included an announcement of the upcoming event and several photos the following month. No article or column detailing the event and the celebration's importance or discussing the history of the unincorporated area West of Rehoboth appeared in either year.

CAMP also began initiatives to integrate its board and staff. Mariner, installed as executive director in late 2019, explained, "One of the things I kind of stressed [to the CAMP board] was to have people of color and trans folks on our board of directors. . . . But it is not necessarily something that happens overnight." However, Kathy Carpenter, the founder of Trans-Liance, a southern Delmarva group independent of CAMP, insists that "the 'T' is often silent" and that progress at CAMP has been minimal: "They [Mariner and the board] gave us the right to nominate people to the board." However, after nominating "a trans Woman of Color with extensive experience in LGBTQ community centers, David said she must first work on committees and volunteer; they chose a Realtor."

A decade earlier, Carpenter had cofounded TransTalk as a program of CAMP. However, she departed on poor terms after claiming that the cisgender health coordinator repeatedly "interjected himself into our conversation." The trans group "wanted to talk about gender," not his focus on sexuality. Despite these ill feelings, she credits CAMP with helping her come out to her father and "shine light on parts of my soul that once stood in darkness."

As my restaurant anecdote suggests, the controlling gaze of entitlement—heterosexual upon homosexual, male upon female, White upon People of Color, cisgender upon transgender—transforms the other into what *we* choose to see; the other becomes an object of *our* representation. Such representations, however, can change—as this chronicle of one small town demonstrates. CAMP was an important vehicle to represent *some* of these others as well as a dynamic mirror in which to see how the gaze shifted from subject to object.

At the turn of this century, the spiritually minded Archibald produced a series of seventeen acrylic paintings of butterflies titled *Transformation*. In one, the viewer's gaze is drawn to a large butterfly with overlapping colorful geometric designs that created "more colors. In all of this playful swirl, the butterfly flutters its colors and shapes altered by the others." He decoded the artwork as "addressing the way our lives are changed by our environment, by the world around us."

The first issue of *Letters from CAMP* enumerated several uses of *camp* deployed as its acronym: "traveling about . . . [to camp] unencumbered by the accumulated trappings of daily life . . . ; a 'summer camp' . . . where roaming is highly restricted . . . ; a blend of sarcasm and wit, humor and pathos . . . considered uniquely and universally gay." These camp conceptions were drawn from Archibald's artist-mind that created the CAMP acronym well before the first issue of *Letters* was published or the first dollar for CAMP was donated.

The history of camp extends at least three-and-a-half centuries, from Molière to Madonna. Transformative uses of camp are as various "as a theory of æsthetics and style; as coded communication and performativity; as a site of humor and parody; as provocative social commentary." Susan Sontag, in her groundbreaking 1964 essay, provided a wealth of examples of camp, including Tallulah Bankhead's mannish acting style, Noël Coward's plays, and Oscar Wilde's epigrams and dandyism. She argued that the homosexual was in the "vanguard" of camp sensibility, which served as a "solvent of morality."

Various camp personae represented in *Queering Rehoboth Beach* include not only the burlesque fan dancer Murray Archibald but the tuxedoed socialite Louisa Carpenter and the mirrored images of Kurt Brown/Kathy Carpenter. It was also evident in Renegade shows of Christopher Peterson and drag karaoke at The Strand, found in the leather/bear camaraderie at the Double L counterpoised with the Moon's glitter boys' aloofness, and Labor Day drag volleyball nets on Poodle Beach. The catty tête-à-têtes between gossip columnists and their readers in *Letters* and its rival *Rehoboth Beach Gayzette* also were public performances of camp.

Camp is part philosophy, part performance, part parody, and part provocation. As a grade schooler cast as young Patrick Dennis in the play *Auntie Mame*, Archibald understood camp's power in "breaking the rules." This sissy son of a southern minister argued that being queer "is already the worst thing that some people can think of to call us. Therefore, by embracing who we are, we are set free from the boundaries that our society would use to enslave us." Camp is a form of resistance.

Queering that gaze of entitlement—its objectification through the heterosexual lens—transforms this imagery into psychological agency and political empowerment. By staring into the face of the gazer, one refuses to submit to its gaze. CAMP activists dropped "glitter bombs" in front of ho-

mophobic shopkeepers and on the front curbs of residential homophobes.
They removed their swimsuits just below the surf and then surprised beach
police as they strolled out wearing a second set of trunks. They confronted
town commissioners trying to close The Strand by wearing over-the-top
outfits, interjecting catcalls, displaying exaggerated mannerisms, and sati-
rizing proponents of the dance club's ban.

"The most powerful human forces are found in the meeting of the face
and the gaze," observed Norwegian novelist Karl Ove Knausgaard. "Only
there, do we exist for another." Similarly, in her incisive *Washington Post
Magazine* story about Rehoboth's "days of reckoning," journalist Donna St.
George wrote, "Social tolerance comes in a thousand personal reckonings—
disparate moments when something in a mind or heart is shifted, unlocked, re-envisioned." The battle for Rehoboth was less a struggle over
ordinances than a contest for hearts and minds.

Queers—refugees from heterosexist families, small-town mindsets,
heteronormative schooling, and homophobic houses of worship—washed
themselves in Rehoboth's waters in a sort of spiritual transformation
(טרנספורמציה). Here, the perspective changed from self to community as
many townsfolk and queers grasped their interconnectedness with the
Other, transcending constructed differences. In 1997, Presbyterian preacher John W. Dean sermonized on acceptance of homosexuality after
nearly thirty years of ministering and being just "as prejudiced as the next
person." Archibald and Elkins traded happy-hour croquet mallets for a
Sunday pew at the Methodist Episcopal Church. It would be the homosexual—outcast from the straight man's community—that, like Job's son,
returned to strengthen God's community. William Oberle, the state's
House Majority leader who linked AIDS with gay bars in the 1980s, after
a soul-searching dialogue with his Episcopalian minister, was one of the
two cosponsors for Delaware's queer-rights bills in later decades. John
Hughes, who had publicized the Battle for Rehoboth and championed the
infamous family bumper sticker, later called for a new one: "Keep Rehoboth a Diverse Town."

The *idea* of Rehoboth emerged from a vision of Rev. Robert Todd's evan-
gelical experience, possible only within a community of believers.[2] Although the camp meeting experience was short-lived, the belief *in* Rehoboth as a community of common values was not. Throughout its history,
many of the town's struggles were between those believing that community is based on the free association of individuals versus those seeing the
community as what shapes the individual. Although many Americans

would say that community is the former, their historic support for traditional institutions of socialization—schools, churches, civic organizations,
media—suggests the latter. This invisible social bond of shared beliefs,
what the father of modern sociology, Émile Durkheim, called "mechanical
solidarity," defines Rehoboth-like small towns as characterized by face-to-
face contacts, close family ties, and shared understandings.

Throughout the twentieth century, scholars have documented change
and constancy in small-town American life. The twin "Middletown" studies,
before and during the Great Depression, detailed the persistence of traditional values in a Midwestern town dominated by a few powerful families.
And a study of "caste and class" in a southern town chronicled how "whites
and whiteness" were "inseparable" from Blacks and Blackness. A mid-century
ethnography of "Springdale" portrayed citizens still "living in an imagined
nineteenth century town that was maintained by collective illusions and personal dreamworlds." Near the twentieth century's end, there was reportage
of two Michigan towns, literally separated by a river of long-standing fears
and shaped by "twisted and knotted" relations between races.

In a dreamworld beach town dominated by century-old families, honeycombed with secretive transgressions, and shielded by protectors of history,
1st Street never impales 2nd, while Queen refrains from touching Rodney.
Yet community life flourished, evidencing a social bond among families,
straight or gay, living *within* the boundaries of these constructed avenues.
Rehoboth's history, bleached of its blemishes, is mostly read from the vaulted archives of privileged memories or in whimsical stories masquerading as
history. These community portraits often resonate more with readers' *remembered* experiences. One longtime commissioner whimsically recalled
Rehoboth as "a close-knit community with adequate parking; businesses
came back year after year to the same location, and a summer population of
mothers and children [we]re joined on the weekend by commuter fathers."
Yet in another Rehoboth, an undertow of resentment persisted, waters of
acceptance were shallow, and waves of bigotry were overpowering.

Post-Stonewall business interlopers and summer transients generally
displayed little inclination for settling within Rehoboth's normative boundaries or respecting its code of deference, decorum, and discretion. Hardly
surprising, residents—including submissive homophiles—expressed grave
concerns about "deviants" who sought to change Rehoboth from a family
town into a more diverse and accepting community. The conflict that ensued
was between those who feared the breakdown of social norms (what Durkheim termed "anomie") and those who rejected the body politic's control of

queer bodies (what the French philosopher Michel Foucault termed "bio-power"). Although no one interviewed for this book expresses the conflict in such academic terms, it is a more useful analytic frame than the psycho-political trope of homophobia.

In the classic work *Identity Politics: Lesbian Feminism and the Limits of Community*, Shane Phelan penned, "The construction of a positive identity requires a community that supports that identity. Building such a community requires both a withdrawal of support or belief in the values and structures of the prior community or culture and the creation of new values and structures." However, Phelan cautioned, "The extent to which and the ways in which the values and structures will be 'new' cannot be assumed from the beginning; often, they can change their surface to meet the new needs without undergoing a basic change." Arguably, this was the case for our restaurant experience and, more generally, modern-day Rehoboth. Elkins's sexual Puritanism and assimilationist actions allied with Methodist morality and Rehoboth's old guard. Commissioner Patrick Gossett was more likely to vote with Mayor Sam Cooper's majority than with Mark Aguirre's trio of progressive lawmakers. The 2020 mayoral election and the zoning controversy about relocating a beloved community theater have further split Rehoboth's landed queer gentry.

Queer theorist Joshua Gamson has argued that sexual-identity politics pose a "queer dilemma": organizing individuals based on nonnormative gender/sexuality while understanding that gender/sexual identities are socially constructed. Within a liberal democratic framework, interest-group recognition is pragmatic, yet it inevitably leads to assimilation and reification of normative categories through the state's control of the body.

Longtime gay resident Michael Decker, who was in the Founders' Circle of CAMP Rehoboth, had a few acquaintances who believed that CAMP "represented a sanitized version—a politically acceptable version of homosexuality. They felt it was largely desexualized . . . a sort of whitewashed reality." Further, Libby Stiff acknowledges that CAMP Rehoboth "mostly stayed a Rehoboth-Washington-centered organization [because] that's where the money was." Moreover, as Ivo Dominguez Jr. observes, "CAMP did not create the legislation . . . or cause the legislative changes to occur in Delaware," which was done by activists "not directly affiliated with CAMP."

Whatever criticisms people have of CAMP's thirty-year history, certainly it was beneficial to and a benefactor of queering Rehoboth. As an assimilationist-oriented organization, CAMP was undoubtedly influential. Dominguez acknowledges that CAMP had an "impact and bearing on how

Murray Archibald and Steve Elkins at CAMP Rehoboth.
(Courtesy of *Washington Blade*. Photo by Michael Key.)

people perceive things." Its "mere existence allowed people in the straight community to know there's enough people with power and money to create an infrastructure. Therefore, there's a real constituency." Also, few question the integrity of its founders, and fewer doubt the commitment of Elkins and Archibald to Rehoboth and gay rights. In the mid-2000s, Archibald wrote, "One of the most important things we have done is to create that focal point—a place that connects people by its very presence." Dominguez judges that although CAMP "in it itself [wa]s not an activist organization, it create[d] an environment in which that [wa]s possible."

Stiff admits, "CAMP wasn't perfect, but damn, it made a difference in southern Delaware!" Jim Welch agrees, "CAMP was important for the Rehoboth area and for the eastern Sussex County area"—a position that Archibald, and no doubt Elkins, shared. "Is it perfect? No," wrote Archibald at the time. "All we've achieved we have done the old-fashioned way—by getting to know our neighbors. It wasn't rioting or legislating—it was sitting down and just talking." In 2007, with his mind's eye bending to the past, but eyes affixed toward the future, he observed, "Time has a way of changing our perspectives of the past. . . . All of life takes on a compressed quality as we live through it. The past is the present and therefore the future as well—and we are all that we have ever been."

INTERVIEWS

SEARS INTERVIEWS

Note: All audio/video interviews are archived in Sears Papers and at RBHS.

Jack Ackerman. I: June 18, 2021; II: July 13, 2021; III: July 27, 2021; IV: March 23, 2022

Mark Aguirre. I: July 12, 2021

Murray Archibald. I: July 8, 2020; II: October 10, 2022; III: June 18, 2022; IV: September 7, 2022

Jim Bahr. I: August 8, 2020; II: September 12, 2020; III: September 21, 2020; IV: October 27, 2020

Kathy Carpenter. I: June 29, 2021; II: July 6, 2021

Bill Courville and **Bob Jerome.** I: May 16, 2021; II: May 24, 2021; III: May 28, 2021

Michael Decker. I: November 10, 2020; II: December 10, 2020; III: December 18, 2020

Ivo Dominguez Jr. and **Jim Welch.** I: November 14, 2020; II: January 14, 2021; III: March 9, 2021; IV: March 30, 2021; V: May 14, 2021; VI: May 24, 2021

Joyce Felton. I: July 29, 2020; II: August 20, 2020; III: August 22, 2020; IV: June 11, 2022

Carol Fezuk. I: January 26, 2021

Patrick Gossett. I: January 18, 2021

Michelle Greenberg. I: August 25, 2021

Wayne Hodge. I: August 2, 2020; II: October 17, 2020

Fay Jacobs. I: November 12, 2020; II: November 19, 2020; III: November 21, 2020; IV: November 24, 2020

Yvonne "Babo" Janssen. I: September 10, 2022

Sharon Kanter. I: August 6, 2020; II: September 7, 2020
Eugene Lawson Jr. I: December 4, 2020; II: December 5, 2020; III: December 12, 2020
Ronnie Mosiej. I: January 18, 2021
Natalie Moss. I: August 1, 2020
Forrest Park, Mark Kimble, Brent Minor, and Curt Leciejewski. I: January 23, 2021
Victor Pisapia. I: August 17, 2020; II: August 20, 2020; III: August 24, 2020; IV: August 30, 2020
Victor Pisapia and Jim Bahr. I: August 1, 2020; II: November 22, 2020
Mark Saunders. I: June 14, 2021
Jeffrey Slavin. I: November 28, 2020
Lloyd Spain. I: December 30, 2020; II: January 8, 2021; III: January 11, 2021
Neil Stevenson. I: December 19, 2020; II: December 28, 2020
Libby Stiff. I: November 16, 2020; II: November 23, 2020
Hassan Sudler. I: May 9, 2021
Glen Thompson. I: November 5, 2020; II: December 2, 2020; III: December 10, 2020; IV: December 17, 2020; V: January 7, 2021; VI: January 17, 2022; VII: April 1, 2022
Robert Thompson Jr. I: January 25, 2021; II: February 8, 2021
Frank Williams. I: April 26, 2021; II: May 18, 2021
Jake Williams. I: June 25, 2021
Teresa Williams and Jo Deutsch. I: June 11, 2021; II: June 19, 2021
Chris Yochim. I: August 25, 2020; II: September 3, 2020; III: September 10, 2020; IV: September 17, 2020
Libby York. I: August 22, 2020; II: September 3, 2020; III: September 5, 2020

OTHER INTERVIEWS

Roy Anderson and Ed Conroy, August 5, 2009, conducted by Violet Chilcoat. RBHS.
Murray Archibald and Steve Elkins, November 2, 2010, conducted by Violet Chilcoat. RBHS.
Ada Burton, July 16, 2009, conducted by Violet Chilcoat. RBHS.
Keith Fitzgerald, May 13, 2021, conducted by Tom Kelch. Sears Papers.
Barbara Gittings and Kay Lahusen, February 2, 1993, conducted by Marc Stein. https://outhistory.org/exhibits/show/philadelphia-lgbt-interviews/int/barbara-gittings
Walter Harmon and Waynne Paskins, July 10, 2009, conducted by Violet Chilcoat. RBHS.
Eugene Lawson and Scott Sterl, October 23, 2014, conducted by Carman Bolt. (MS2015-007). Special Collections & University Archives, University Libraries, Virginia Polytechnic Institute and State University, Blacksburg, VA.
David Mariner, June 18, 2021, conducted by Jane Therese. Sears Papers.
Brenda Milbourne, September 17, 2007, conducted by Violet Chilcoat. RBHS.
Natalie Moss, August 19, 2019, conducted by Robert Thompson. RBHS.
Henrietta Pierson, September 17, 2015, conducted by Nancy Alexander. RBHS.
Evelyn Thoroughgood, October 23, 2007, conducted by Violet Chilcoat. RBHS.

NOTES

NOTES ON LANGUAGE USE

1. American Psychological Association. (2020). *Publication Manual* (7th ed.), p. 131. Author.

PREFACE

1. Materials used to develop this section are Friedman, J., & Johnson, M. F. (2022 May). *Banned in the USA*. PEN America. https://pen.org/banned-in-the -usa/#; Kacsmaryk, M. (2015, June 24). The abolition of man. And woman. *National Catholic Register*. https://www.ncregister.com/news/the-abolition-of-man -and-woman-tpnrdgjq; Kleinberg, E., Wallach Scott, J., & Wilder, G. (2018, June 25). Theses on theory and history. *Wild on Collective*. https://www.versobooks.com /blogs/news/3893-theses-on-theory-and-history; McCullough, D. (n.d.). David McCullough Quotes. BrainyQuote.com; Munslow, A. (1997). Review of *What Is History? Reviews in History* (no. 41a). https://reviews.history.ac.uk/review/41a; Peters, R. (2021). The spinning silkworm: Benedetto Croce's history as the story of liberty. *Journal of the Philosophy of History*, 15, 305–322; Portelli, A. (1991). *The death of Luigi Trastulli and other stories*. State University of New York Press; Sears, J. (1998). *Curriculum, religion, and public education: Conversations for an enlarging public square*. Teachers College Press; Takaki, R. (1998). *A larger memory: A history of our diversity*. Little, Brown; Williams, P. (2022, September 23). Revealed: Hillsdale president says racism is like sexuality—neither should be discussed in classroom. Channel 5 [Nashville, Tenn.] Investigative News. https://www.newschannel5.com/news /newschannel-5-investigates/revealed/revealed-hillsdale-president-says-racism -is-like-sexuality-neither-should-be-discussed-in-classroom; Zinn, H. (1970). *The politics of history*. Beacon Press.

INTRODUCTION

1. Materials used to develop this section, including interviews, are Harris, B. (1872). *The doctrine and discipline of the Methodist Episcopal Church*. Nelson and Phillips; Meehan, J. (2000). *Rehoboth Beach memoirs: From saints to sinners*. Harold Dukes Jr.; Morgan, M. (2009). *Rehoboth Beach: A history of surf and sand*. History Press; Quigg, J. B. (1878, November 14). Methodist discipline. *Every Evening*, p. 1.

2. Materials used to develop this section, including interviews, are Christy, M. (1986, September 17). Bauman's new life. *Boston Globe*, p. 38; Cullen, V. (1962, March 9). Storm heaviest to hit Rehoboth. *Evening Journal*, p. 1; Forney, D. (1997, August 15). A chapter of Rehoboth Beach Afro-American history headed for auction. *Cape*, p. 7; Hogenmiller, T. (1982, March 31). West Rehoboth: Glimpses of the past, Pt. I. *Whale*, pp. 7, 26; Lynda Bird joins beach outing. (1967, July 3). *Journal Times* (Racine, WI), p. 6; Murray, M. (1982, April 17). Resort town drops racial restrictions. *News Journal*, p. A1; Nuzback, K. (2012, January 30). Court denies Michael Scanlon's appeal. *Cape*. https://www.capegazette.com/article/court-denies-michael-scanlon's -appeal/22278; Pate, A. (2001). *West of Rehoboth*. Morrow; Pringle, B. (1984, June 24). West Rehoboth has new view. *Sunday News Journal*, p. B3; Shister, N. (2014). *Revealing Rehoboth*. Mulberry Street; Sussex County Online. (2021). Henlopen Acres Delaware. http://www.sussexcountyonline.com/towns/henlopenacres.html; Terrell, D. (1980). *Room for one more sinner* (2nd ed.). Duck Press; Ward, J. (1993, June 11). Charles Mills, well-known farmer, community leader in Sussex, 91. *News Journal*, p. B4; Williams, R. (1971, September 8). Sussex sketches. *Evening Journal*, p. 39. Interviews: Burton; Felton I; Harmon & Paskins; Thompson III.

3. Materials used to develop this section are Houdek, M., & Phillips, L. (2017, January 25). Public memory. *Communication*. https://doi.org/10.1093/acre fore/9780190228613.013.181; Steinbeck, J. (1962). *Travels with Charley: In search of America*. Curtis; Thelen, D. (1989). Introduction to a special issue, "Memory and American History." *Journal of American History*, 75, 1117–1129; Young, A. (1978). *The shoemaker and the tea party*, pp. xii, xiv. Beacon Press. Interview: Slavin I.

CHAPTER 1

1. Materials used to develop this section are 14 Del. Laws, c. 392 (1873) [pp. 360–363]; After more than a year's illness. (1898, May 7). *Denton Journal*, p. 3; Beginning of Rehoboth Beach. (1873, July). *Rehoboth Beacon*; Brooks, V. W. (1915). *America's coming of age*. Huebsch; Carter, D. (1976). *History of Sussex County*, p. 27. Community Newspaper Corp; Death of J. B. Quigg. (1898, August 1). *Daily Republican*, p. 1; Death of R. W. Todd (1906, January 31). *Morning News*, p. 1; Excursion. (1873, May 5). *Delaware Republican*, p. 2; Excursion of stockholders and lotholders to Methodist camp meeting ground at Rehoboth Beach. (1873, May 3). *State Journal*, p. 3; Local affairs. (1873, April 11). *Daily Commercial*, p. 1; Meeting of the Executive Committee. (1873, May 19). *Every Evening*, p. 4; Numerical order in which the stockholders are entitled to make choice of lots. (1873, April 24). *Daily Commercial*, p. 4; Please with Delaware. (1873, May 3). *Daily Commercial*, p. 3; Rehoboth Camp Meeting Association. (1872,

December 13). *Daily Commercial*, p. 1; Rev. R. W. Todd dead. (1906, January 29). *Baltimore Sun*, p. 14; Santayana, G. (1905). *Life of reason*. Scribner; Speculating. (1873, April 5). *Delmarva State Journal*, p. 3; Todd, R. W. (1886). *Methodism on the peninsula*. Methodist Episcopal Book Rooms; Visit to Rehoboth. (1874, May 14). *Daily Republican*, p. 3.

2. Materials used to develop this section are Bright, W. (1873, July 18). From Rehoboth. *Daily Gazette*, p. 4; Enquirer. (1873, April 22). *Every Evening*, p. 3; For Rehoboth Camp. (1873, June 19). *Daily Gazette*, p. 1; Johnson, C. (1873, July 18). From Rehoboth. *Daily Gazette*, p. 4; Lesley. (1873, July 10). From Rehoboth. *Daily Commercial*, p. 1; Local Affairs. (1873, May 6). *Daily Commercial*, p. 1; Meeting of the Executive Committee. (1873, May 19). *Every Evening*, p. 4; Preachers vs. Barnum. (1878, April 22). *Every Evening and Commercial*, p. 3; Rehoboth Beach Camp-Meeting. (1873, July 7). *Daily Commercial*, p. 1; Rehoboth Beach, C.M.A. (1873, July 26). *Daily Gazette*, p. 1; Rehoboth Camp. (1873, July 21). *Daily Commercial*, p. 4; Sale of lots yesterday. (1874, May 13). *Every Evening*, p. 3; Terrell, D. (1980). *Room for one more sinner* (2nd ed.). Duck Press; Todd, R. (1873, June 11). Need for more boarding houses. *Daily Commercial*, p. 1; Visit to Rehoboth. (1874, May 14). *Daily Republican*, p. 3.

3. Materials used to develop this section are Annual Meeting of the Association. (1875, July 23). *Every Evening*, p. 4; Annual Meeting of the Association. (1878, July 18). *Daily Gazette*, p. 1; Beach notes. (1876, April 6). *Daily Gazette*, p. 1; Directors meeting. (1876, April 6). *Early Evening*, p. 3; Fourth of July at the beach. (1878, July 6). *Every Evening and Commercial*, p. 3; Local affairs. (1873, April 11). *Daily Commercial*, p. 1; Maull, D. W. (1877, April 5). The Rehoboth Beach. Paper commissioned by the Rehoboth Beach Camp Meeting Association. *Every Evening and Commercial*, p. 1; Meeting of the Camp Meeting Association. (1876, April 6). *Daily Gazette*, p. 1; Murray M. (2001, August 20). Wave upon wave of change by the seaside. *News Journal*, pp. E1–E2; New hotel at Rehoboth. (1875, September 29). *Daily Commercial*, p. 1; Rehoboth. (1878, May 26). *Morning Herald*, p. 1; Rehoboth Beach enterprise. (1876, February 10). *Delaware Tribune*, p. 1; The Rehoboth Camp. (1875, July 22). *Delaware Tribune*, p. 1.

4. Materials used to develop this section are Annual Meeting of the Association. (1878, July 18). *Daily Gazette*, p. 1; At Rehoboth Beach. (1878, July 19). *Every Evening and Commercial*, p. 1; Libel suit: Last day's proceedings. (1880, December 9). *State Journal*, p. 1; Rehoboth Camp. (1878, July 18). *Every Evening and Commercial*, p. 3; Ryan, T. (2012). *Essays on Delaware during the Civil War*. Civil War Learning Associates; Stockholders in annual session. (1876, July 24). *Morning Herald*, p. 1; Terrell, D. (1980). *Room for one more sinner* (2nd ed.). Duck Press.

5. In 1876, the association sought to remedy this by entitling anyone who owned a lot *and* a building on it to one share.

6. In his position as president, Bright was accused of fraud in a series of articles between 1877 and 1880 in Wilmington's *Every Evening and Commercial*. He sued the paper and its publisher, William Croasdale, for libel. In this case, which dominated the city's headlines in late 1880, the jury deliberated for five hours before ultimately holding that the newspaper and its publisher did not use words that "were entirely too harsh and ought in some way to be rebuked."

7. Materials used to develop this section are At Rehoboth Beach. (1878, July 19). *Every Evening and Commercial*, p. 1; Bright House Dancing. (1878, August 10). *Times* (Philadelphia), p. 4; The Rehoboth Beach Association. (1878, July 31). *Every Evening and Commercial*, p. 1; Rehoboth dancing and card playing question. (1878, August 19). *Daily Gazette*, p. 1; Rehoboth dancing question. (1878, August 14). *Every Evening and Commercial*, p. 3.

8. Materials used to develop this section are Hops. (1878, August 19). *Daily Gazette*, p. 2; Methodist discipline. (1878, November 14). *Every Evening*, p. 1; Preachers' meeting. (1878, October 14). *Every Evening and Commercial*, p. 3; Preachers' meeting. (1878, December 16). *Every Evening and Commercial*, p. 3; Rehoboth Association. (1878, October 3). *Every Evening and Commercial*, p. 3; Rehoboth Beach Association. (1879, January 9). *Every Evening and Commercial*, p. 3; State sentinel. (1889, August 19). *Every Evening*, p. 3.

9. Lemuel "Ely" Quigg, like his father, was a gifted orator. Graduating with honors from Boys High School in 1878, he had hoped to attend Dickinson College. But despite raising money over the next few months through paid recitations, the younger Quigg entered into journalism. In 1884, he was on the editorial staff of the *New York Tribune*. He eventually went on assignment to the West, writing a series of articles on various towns, published in 1889 as "New Empires of the Northwest." The following year, he published a "racy volume of sketches" of the "Bohemian Classes" in *Tin Types Taken in the Streets of New York*, under the pseudonym O. M. Dunham. In 1894, he was the underdog Republican candidate for the Fifteenth Congressional District in New York City. Serving three terms, he was active in Republican politics and admitted to the New York bar in 1903, where he worked until his death in 1919.

10. Materials used to develop this section are Annual meeting of the association yesterday. (1880, July 23). *Daily Morning News*, p. 1; Association directors recommending important changes. (1881, February 3). *State Journal*, p. 1; At Rehoboth. (1880, July 23). *Daily Gazette*, p. 1; A branch railroad. (1880, August 9). *Every Evening*, p. 3; Dancing question settled. (1879, July 18). *Daily Republican*, p. 4; Delaware's summer resort. (1879, June 24). *Daily Republican*, p. 1; Full report of the meeting at Rehoboth yesterday. (1879, July 17). *Every Evening and Commercial*, p. 3; Letters from Rehoboth. (1879, July 18). *Daily Republican*, p. 1; Rehoboth Beach Association. (1881, January 27). *Daily Morning News*, p. 4; The Rehoboth fire. (1879, August 23). *Every Evening and Commercial*, p. 3; The Rehoboth fire. (1879, August 30). *Daily Gazette*, p. 3; A Rehoboth purchase. (1880, January 12). *Daily Gazette*, p. 1; R. H. G. (1880, June 1). [Letters to the editor]. *Daily Gazette*, p. 1; To dance or not to dance. (1879, July 15). *Daily Gazette*, p. 3.

CHAPTER 2

1. Materials used to develop this section, including interviews, are 2 jailed, 4 fined for vice. (1961, December 2). *Morning News*, p. 1; Aguirre, M. (2004, July 2). A chat with Libby Stiff. *Letters*, p. 48; Announced for June 3 at shore. (1937, June 7). *Morning News*, p. 13; Barnett, R. (2005, July 29). Fancy house and fabric.

Letters, p. 40; Barnett, R. (2005, August 29). The DuPont, the torch singer and the tobacco heir. The Go Cup. https://thegocup.com/2005/08/29/the-du-pont-the-torch-singer-and-the-tobacco-heir/; Barnett, R. (2005, October 14). When did Rehoboth go gay? *Letters*, p. 40; Barnett, R. (2008, April 4). For the lovers and the sniffers. *Letters*, p. 40; Camp forum. (2004, July 30). *Letters*, p. 8; Dahn, F. (1876/2010). *A struggle for Rome*. [L. Wolffsohn, trans.]. Quality Classics; Davis, N. (1964, July 23). Get-tough policy faces beach scofflaws. *Morning News*, p. 1; DuPont heiress, pilot, friend die in crash. (1976, February 9). *Daily Times* (Salisbury), p. 1; Elkins, S. (2005, August 12). The way I see it. *Letters*, p. 3; Faderman, L. (1991). *Odd girls and twilight lovers*. Columbia University Press; Graham, T. (1994, August 12). Remembering Rehoboth. *Blade*, pp. 45, 47; Higgins, A. (Ed.). (1978–1979). Mary Wilson Thompson memoir. *Delaware History*, *18*, 43–62, 124–151, 194–217, 236–266; Hoffecker, C. (1983). Delaware's women's suffrage campaign. *Delaware History*, *3*, 149–167; Hughes, J. (1981, August 5). Obvious differences in our platforms. *Whale*, p. 5; Iskioff, M., & Springer, A. (2015). *Uniquely nasty: The U.S. government's war on gays*. [Video]. YouTube. https://www.youtube.com/watch?v=Ouj-95lNF8M; Jacobs, F. (2002, June 28). Still searching for the Tallulah connection. *Letters*, p. 56; Jacobs, F., & Stiff, L. (1999, September 17). The birth and brief life of the Boathouse, Rehoboth's first gay dance club. *Letters*, p. 70; Jacobs, F., & Stiff, L. (2000, February 4). If the Nomad's walls could talk! *Letters*, p. 16; Jacobs, S. B. (2006/2007). Not quite White. *Jewish Quarterly*, *204*; John Hughes for mayor [political advertisement]. (1981, July 29). *Whale*; Kantor, E. (1989, August 5). The battle for Rehoboth: Why Washington's favorite beach town is at war with itself. *Washington Post Magazine*, pp. 12–19, 34; Keen, L. (1985, July 5). Perceiving gays. *Blade*, p. B5; Langer, E. (2014). Bob Gray: Influential Washington lobbyist and founder of Gray & Co., dies at 92. *Washington Post*; Letter to Delaware Board of Pardons from Elizabeth B. Stiff. (2002, October 10). Sears Papers; Mannish. (1925, November 28). *Morning News*, p. 14; Marks, J. (1980, May 29). Rehoboth has most of the bureaucrats. *Blade*, p. 14; McGuiness, K. (2018, April 6). Steve Elkins: His voice is still heard. *Letters*; Milford, M. (2013, July 11). Beach cottage exudes a magic elegance. *News Journal*, pp. B4, B12; Miss Carpenter charming "bud." (1925, December 19). *Evening Journal*, p. 20; Miss Louisa Carpenter to wed J. K. Jenney. (1929, June 24). *Every Evening*, p. 10; Morgan, M. (2020, September 23). The woman who beat 19th Amendment in Delaware and mosquitoes in Rehoboth. *Delmarva Now*. https://www.delmarvanow.com/story/news/local/delaware/2020/09/23/woman-who-beat-19th-amendment-del-and-mosquitoes-rehoboth/5797628002/; Reese, L. (1977). *The horse on Rodney Square*. News Journal Co.; Rehoboth fears harm to resort image. (1964, July 28). *News Journal*, p. 4; Royle, C. (1985, July 7). Rehoboth's growing gay population. *Morning News*, pp. B1, B3; R. R. M. Carpenter at brilliant affair. (1925, December 19). *Morning News*, p. 7; Scheper, J. (2021, June 23). Libby Holman. *The Shalvi/Hyman encyclopedia of Jewish women*. https://jwa.org/encyclopedi/article/holman-libby; Sets new riding habit. (1925, November 24). *Evening Journal*, p. 15; Start work on the new streets in Rehoboth. (1925, July 23). *Every Evening*, p. 20; St. George, D. (1999, August 29). Days of reckoning: Rehoboth Beach and its gay constituency, coming to terms. *Washington Post Magazine*, pp. 7–11, 20–22; Sublett, S. (1981, August 21). Rehoboth natives are nervous. *Blade*, p. A4; Vernon, T. (1998, January 23). Rehoboth chamber honors. *Cape*, pp. 40, 42, 44; Vernon, T. (2001, September 21). Joss doors close. *Cape*, pp. 48, 50; Warren, W. (1970/1988). *Jim Thompson: The unsolved mystery*. Archipelago; Wilson, W. (1966). *The papers of Woodrow Wilson*. Princeton University Press; Interviews: Anderson-Conroy; Felton I; Thompson II.

CHAPTER 3

1. Materials used to develop the first two sections, including interviews, are Archibald, J. (2018, April 6). Everyone in Rehoboth knew Steve Elkins. *Letters*, p. 6; Archibald, J. (2018, April 6). Stephen Wade Elkins. *Letters*, p. 16; Archibald, M. (2017, May 5). The people of CAMP. *Letters*, p. 6; Beagle, C. (2018, April 6). Looking to the days ahead. *Letters*, p. 14; Beemyn, G. (2014). *A queer capital: A history of gay life in Washington DC*. Taylor and Francis; Burke, J. (1975, November 26). Raleigh woman is working on Carter team. *Rocky Mount Telegram*, p. 3; CAMPgrounds. (1991, June 6). *Letters*, p. 1; CAMP Rehoboth: An introduction. (1991, May 23). *Letters*, p. 1; Dahlquist, D. (1977, November). The White House delegation. *Blade*, p. 11; DC observes gay pride day '75. (1975, June). *Blade*, p. 1; Elkins, S. (2000, February 4). The way I see it. *Letters*, p. 4; Hogenmiller, T. (1981, February 20). RBHOA sets goals for 1981. *Whale*, p. 1; Hogenmiller, T. (1981, July 15). John Hughes: Seeking to place "a strong hand at the helm." *Whale*, p. 9; Hughes, J. (1981, July 22). Hughes answers critics on past actions [letter to the editor]. *Whale*, p. 15; Murray, M. (1984). "Homeowners" group urges vote in Rehoboth. *Morning News*, p. 4; RBHOA's dedication now bearing fruit. (1988, February 24). *Whale*, p. 4. Interviews: Archibald I; Archibald and Elkins; Thompson II, III, IV.

2. Materials used to develop this section, including interviews, are Archibald, M. (2018, April 6). The way I see it. *Letters*, p. 3; Denture maker arrested. (1974, July 1). *News Journal*, p. 1; Disco drive is opening in West Rehoboth. (1979, April 25). *Whale*, p. 25; Frank, B. (1981, July 22). Image is issue in Rehoboth Beach. *Morning News*, p. A1; Hogenmiller, T. (1981, July 15). Eleanor Lynam: Plenty of time to bring good will and harmony. *Whale*, p. 9; Jacobs, F., & Stiff, L. (1999, September 17). The birth and brief history of the Boathouse. *Letters*, p. 70; John Hughes for mayor [political advertisement]. (1981, July 29). *Whale*; Leigey, D. (1999, October 15). Speak out. *Letters*, p. 5; Merriweather, J., & Jackson, R. (2007, April 22). Gay rights advocates have fresh optimism. *Sunday News Journal*, p. 10; Murray, M. (1982, May 9). "Hizzoner" stirs up Rehoboth. *News Journal*, p. A15; Short, M. (1990, September 29). John Hughes: From baboons to bureaucrats. *Whale*, p. 7; S. M. Sennabaum [obituary]. (1988, September 2). *News Journal*, p. 16; Soulsman, G. (1981, July 16). Gays have found a refuge in resort town atmosphere. *News Journal*, p. 7; Sublett, S. (1981, August 21). Rehoboth natives are nervous. *Blade*, p. 4; Vote for Eleanor Lynam [political advertisement]. (1981, July 22). *Whale*. Interviews: Archibald and Elkins; Kanter I; Spain III; Thompson III.

CHAPTER 4

1. Materials used to develop this section, including interviews, are Davis, V. (1988, September 3). Dinner Bell Inn continues 50 year tradition. *Whale*, p. 7; MacMillan, M. (2014, October 29). Fine-dining pioneers reunite in Rehoboth. *Cape*. https://www.capegazette.com/article/fine-dining-pioneers-reunite-re hoboth/73500; Vernon, T. (1995, May 26). Dinner Bell restored to former grandeur. *Gazette*, pp. 72–73. Interviews: Pisapia I; York II.

2. Materials used to develop this section, including interviews, are Powers, A. (1982, November 10). The celebrated Zebra Room. *Washington Post*. https://www .washingtonpost.com/archive/local/1982/11/10/the-celebrated-zebra-room-24 -pizzas-on-the-wall/d7c25134-bdf7-465f-8439-0bf7df01a2a5/. Interview: York I.

3. Materials used to develop this section, including interviews, are Baldwin, B. (1981). The cakewalk. *Journal of Social History*, 15(2), 205–218; Crow's Nest. (1873, January 23). *Wilmington Daily Commercial*, p. 4: Davis, N. (1964, July 23). Get tough policy faces beach scofflaws. *Morning News*, p. 1; Down at Rehoboth. (1899, August 19). *Daily Republican*, p. 7; Firemen's minstrel staged. (1935, June 7). *Coast Press*, p. 1; Five hurt as 100 fight on Rehoboth sands. (1964, July 20). *Morning News*, p. 1; Goethem, L. (1964, July 21). Brawl spurs beach force, curfew plan. *Morning News*, p. 1; Greto, V. (2007, September 2). Erasing the line. *Sunday News Journal*, pp. 1, 11; Hogenmiller, T. (1981, September 1). Whiskey Beach: The golden era of beer kegs, body paints. *Whale*, p. 37; Pate, A. (2001). *West of Rehoboth*. William Morrow; Rehoboth fears harm to resort image. (1964, July 28). *Evening Journal*, p. 4; Rehoboth's fine prospects. (1900, August 9). *Delaware Gazette*, p. 7; Teen spot owner denies riot link. (1964, July 23). *Morning News*, p. 14. Interviews: Burton; Decker II, III; Harmon and Pashkins; Pierson; Stevenson I, II; York I.

4. Materials used to develop this section, including interviews, are Murray, M. (1988, November 20). DeRiemer, you can't fight city hall. *Sunday News Journal*, pp. A1, A4; No funds, Rehoboth puts youth center up for sale. (1954, August 27). *Morning News*, p. 12; Police raid teen club. (1963, August 24). *Evening News*, p. 18; Rehoboth closing of Zen Den barred. (1963, July 23). *Morning News*, p. 9; Rehoboth fixes fines for noise. (1963, January 29). *Evening Journal*, p. 25; Rehoboth truce OK's teen club. (1964, June 9). *Morning News*, p. 15; Resort bars teen-agers' night spot. (1963, February 18). *Morning News*, p. 16; Surprise in Rehoboth. (1962, June 29). *Evening Journal*, p. 21; This time as Sea Horse. (1964, January 29). *Evening Journal*, p. 32; What's wrong with the Zen Den? (1963, August 31). *Evening Journal*, p. 16; Zen Den done, city plans own. (1964, January 25). *Evening Journal*, p. 18; Zen Den makes the scene. (1963, July 2). *Morning News*, p. 24; Zen Den yen is stay; 60 at resort say no. (1962, September 10). *Evening Journal*, p. 20; Zen may reopen at beach. (1964, January 29). *Morning News*, p. 10. Interviews: Stevenson I; York I.

5. Materials used to develop this section, including interviews, are Carroll, C. (2016, September 29). Back Porch Café: Four decades of cutting-edge cuisine. *Delmava Now*. https://www.delmarvanow.com/story/life/food/2016/09/29/back

-porch-Café-rehoboth/90874000/; George, P. (2014, May 19). Exploring our culinary coast. *Delaware Today*. https://delawaretoday.com/life-style/exploring-our
-culinary-coast/; Mavity, R. (2014, May 5). Back Porch Café celebrates its 40th anniversary. *Cape*, p. 37; Spitz, M. (1992, August 6). The Back Porch Café. *Letters*, p.
13. Interviews: Pisapia II; Pisapia and Bahr I; York II, III.

6. Materials used to develop this section, including interviews, are Dode, L.
(1999). *Gay Key West*. Arate; Hogenmiller, T. (1978, June 28). Gay life at the coast:
Lifestyle reflects new openness. *Whale*, pp. 1, 6; Hogenmiller, T. (1978, July 4). Gay
life at the coast: A niche socially, financially. *Whale*, pp. 1–2; Laurie, E. R. [letter to
the editor]. (1978, July 4). *Whale*, p. 4; VanDyne, L. (1978, July). Greetings from
Rehoboth. *Washingtonian*, pp. 84–92; Wilding, N. (1978, June). Vacation: A delight-
ful oasis. *Blade*, p. 17. Interviews: Pisapia II; York I.

CHAPTER 5

1. Materials used to develop this section, including interviews, are Archibald,
M. (2016, May 20). Memorial Day weekend. *Letters*; Davis, V. (1986, November
26). Harry Maichle: Uniformed life agrees with the chief. *Whale*, p. 7; Forney, D.
(1980, August 13). Intense investigation dogging resort arsons. *Whale*, p. 1; Go-
vert, G. (1980, July 13). Arson at Rehoboth gay bar leaves ruins—and questions.
Philadelphia Inquirer, pp. 1-B, 3-B; Guthrie, J. (1980, September 4). 2nd Rehoboth
disco torched. *PGN*; Hogenmiller, T. (1984, February 13). Gay, lesbian Christian
group forming. *Whale*, p. 6; Renegade returns to fold. (1980, September 18). *PGN*;
Severson, J., & Sexton, A. (1980, August 17). Gay bar blazes still mystery in Rehoboth Beach. *Philadelphia Inquirer*, pp. 1-B, 4-B; Smith, G. (1980, July 3). Fire levels
Rehoboth restaurant. *Evening Journal*, p. 6; Smith, G. (1980, July 4). Pre-dawn fire
destroys night spot in Rehoboth. *News Journal*, p. 4; Smith, G. (1980, August 7).
Arson suspected in blaze at 2nd resort area gay bar. *Morning News*, p. 29; Smith, G.
(1980, August 13). Arson seen in gay bar fire; rumors ignited. *Morning News*, p. 17;
Smith, G., & Manning, A. (1980, August 7). Arson "possible" in gay bar fire. *Morning
News*, p. 6; Soap opera. (1980, July 27). *Philadelphia Inquirer*, p. B1; Studio 1 clones.
(1980, July 9). *Whale*, p. 17; Terrell, D. (1981, January 7). Year of fires. *Whale*, p. 7;
Vandalism, violence plague. (n.d.). *PGN*, p. 7; Ward, J. (1985). Whale commended
for fair treatment [letter to the editor]. *Whale*, p. 4. Interviews: Kanter I; Stevenson
I; Thompson III, IV.

2. "We switched ownership of different things," Thompson explains. For example, he would later buy the building for the Palm Restaurant in Rehoboth, but
the restaurant was under Pong's name.

3. Materials used to develop this section, including interviews, are Bodine, A.
(1961, April 30). Picturesque as storybook imaginings. *Baltimore Sunday Sun Magazine*, p. 12; Harrison, G. (1958, May 6). She'll start "interview" at airport. *Miami
Herald*, p. 17; Perry, H. (1983). *Libby Holman: Body and soul*. Little, Brown; Picturesque as storybook. House garden tour May 5 will center on Chesterton. (1961,
April 15). *News Journal*, p. 6. Interviews: Thompson I, II, III.

4. Materials used to develop this section, including interviews, are Aguirre, M.

(2005, June 17). A chat with Leo Medisch. *Letters*, p. 28; Carroll, H. (2016, September 29). Back Porch Cafe: Four decades of cutting-edge cuisine. *Delmarva Now.* https://www.delmarvanow.com/story/life/food/2016/09/29/back-porch-cafe-re hoboth/90874000/; Hogenmiller, T. (1979, July 11). Nine file for Rehoboth race. *Whale*, pp. 1, 8; Hogenmiller, T. (1979, August 15). Howard, Welborn, Lankford, Nelson win. *Whale*, p. 1; Hogenmiller, T. (1984, September 19). Miriam Howard: Life out of the limelight. *Whale*, p. 7; Mavity, R. (2014, May 2). Back Porch Cafe celebrates its 40th anniversary. *Cape*, p. 37; McDang, C. (2010). *Principles of Thai cookery.* Author; Rehoboth Homeowners group forms committee. (1979, June 20). *Whale*, p. 3; Terrell, D. (1981, July 22). Miriam Howard reminisces. *Whale*, pp. 1, 6. Interviews: Felton I; Pisapia II, III; Thompson III; York II.

5. But, a woman, even a conservative one, did not sit particularly well with those running the Rehoboth Beach Homeowners Association, whose members resented Howard's willingness to work even-handedly with the business community. For the summer 1979 election, it "drafted" William Melson, who had never served in any town office or committee. But the retired dentist and army veteran, who had been visiting Rehoboth since 1918, was someone like them. As in past years, the association's formal endorsement followed a candidate forum. The fifteen members who attended seemed content with its decision, although it was *preceded* two days earlier by newspaper ads authorized by the nomination committee, on which Melson served. Howard defeated Melson by a 3:1 margin.

6. Hoosier-born Leo Medisch, for instance, visited Rehoboth in 1979. Planning to head to New York, he fell in love with the sand and sea—and later with local artist Tom Wilson, a former New York fashion model. Medisch successfully applied for the sous-chef position at the Porch. Another, Sirichalerm Svasti, born into Thailand's royal family, was studying at Georgetown University. During a summer break from college, he visited Rehoboth and joined the Porch as its daytime chef. He later became known as Chef McDang, Southeast Asia's most famous celebrity chef and author of *The Principles of Thai Cookery.*

7. Materials used to develop this section, including interviews, are Fire razes Boat House restaurant. (1982, April 15). *Evening Journal*, p. B1; Forney, D. (1981, May 13). West Rehoboth shootout leaves wounded adversaries. *Whale*, p. 2; For sale Nomad Village [advertisement]. (1981, November 11). *Whale*, p. 25; Hogenmiller, T. (1982, March 31). Shacks, neat dwellings share space, but residents keep to themselves. *Whale*, p. 7; Hogenmiller, T. (1982, April 7). West Rehoboth: Optimistic or pessimistic future? *Whale*, p. 7; Nagengast, N. (1982, May 20). Dewey Beach nightclub fire ruled arson. *Evening Journal*, p. B1; *PGN*. (1982, March 5). Insert. p. 5; Pringle, B. (1982, July 21). Rezoning plea shelved. *Morning News*, p. 5; Soulsman, G. (1981, July 26). Gays have found a refuge in resort town atmosphere. *Sunday News Journal*, p. 7. Interviews: Decker II; Hodge II; Kanter I; Milbourne; Thompson III, IV; Yochim III.

8. Materials used to develop this section, including interviews, are Bost, D. (2019). At the club: Locating early black gay AIDS activism in Washington, DC. *Occasion, 10*, 1–9; Chibbaro, L., Jr. (1983, October 14). Badlands discrimination complaint is settled. *Blade*, p. 5; DiGuglielmo, J. (2013, January 1). Several factors con-

tributed to Omega closing. *Blade*. https://www.washingtonblade.com/2013/01/01
/several-factors-contributed-to-omega-closing/; Grand Central: A review. (1975,
September). *Blade*, p. 6; Grand Central vs. Title 34. (1975, May). *Blade*, pp. 1, 7;
Michaels, D. (1977, March). 'Catch-22' in bias case. *Blade*, p. 4; Rainbow History
Project. Retrieved August 20, 2020, from https://www.yumpu.com/en/document
/read/7701878/the-rainbow-history-project-places-spaces-clubs-bars-; Rule, D.
(2011, April 14). The Omega man. *Metro Weekly*. Interviews: Thompson II, III, IV.

9. Thompson had "fallen into" the business when a Cuban co-worker, Carlos
Cortinez, suggested that they open a gay club. "I had absolutely no interest in opening a bar," but after constant badgering, the pair along with a dozen stockholders
opened Pier Nine in April 1970, the second mega dance club in the district. DC's
Rainbow History Project lists Pier Nine's original owners as Donn Culver and Bill
Bickford. Thompson differs: "It went through several hands before they bought it."
Yet for many Black gay Washingtonians, racial discrimination in White gay-owned
establishments was not an issue, because the majority of Black gay social life existed outside these clubs and bars.

10. Badlands, for example, was the site of DC's Black and White Men Together's
complaint about the bar's practice of carding to limit African Americans and other
minorities. Although Thompson denied any such practice or policy, he agreed to
contribute $5,000 to the National Gay Task Force's nondiscriminatory response
system and post nondiscrimination notices prominently at the entrance, among
other concessions. Following the settlement, Thompson said that he hoped it would
"advance race relations." The Grand Central had had similar issues the decade before. A suit was filed in 1974 against Interco, the club's corporate owner, through
the city's Human Rights Commission. Thompson, president of Interco, promised
a court fight, citing the unconstitutionality of the DC code. On January 31, 1977,
damages of $6,250 were levied in favor of the remaining eight complainants.

11. Materials used to develop this section are Birdsall, W. (2015). Albert Camus's *The Renegade*, or a confused mind: What confusion? What terrorism. *Academia*, p. 3; Camus, A. (1957). *Exile and the kingdom*. Vintage; Neimneh, S., & Madi,
A. (2014). Existential revolt in Albert Camus' "The Renegade." *International Journal
of Academic Research*, 6(5), p. 118.

CHAPTER 6

1. Materials used to develop this section, including interviews, are Elkins, S.
(1997, November 21). The way I see it. *Letters*, p. 3. Interview: Dominguez and
Welch IV.

2. Materials used to develop this section, including interviews, are Caddell, T.
(1981, December 20). Slaying suspect arrested. *Morning News*, pp. B1, B3; Charge
changed to first-degree murder. (1982, January 26). *Evening Journal*, p. C1; Forney, D. (1981, December 23). Hughes praises murder investigation: Begins crackdown on subculture's seamier side. *Whale*, p. 5; Forney, D. (1981, December 23).
Rehoboth slaying rocks resort holiday. *Whale*, p. 1; Hager, J. (1981, December 19).
Police seeing clues to murder in beach resort's gay community. *Morning News*, p. D1;

Kraus Services. (1981, December 21). *Evening Journal*, p. C7; Pringle, B. (1982, May 25). Plea bargain results in life sentence. *Evening Journal*, p. B1; Reduced bail denied for murder suspect. (1981, December 24). *Morning News*, p. C1; Rehoboth murder charge may be raised to first degree. (1981, December 30). *Whale*, p. 7; Slaying suspect plea bargains, gets life. (1982, May 25). *Evening Journal*, p. B1. Interviews: Dominguez and Welch III; Spain III; Thompson IV.

3. Materials used to develop this section, including interviews, are ACLU, churches ask end to hanging. (1968, February 8). *Evening Journal*, p. 6; Air Force discharges homosexual sergeant. (1975, September 25). *New York Times*, p. 21; Art briefs. (1973, October 30). *Morning News*, p. 30; Art briefs: UD play. (1975, November 11). *Morning News*, p. 4; *Aumiller v. University of Delaware*, 434 F. Supp. 1273. (D. Del, 1977); Beemyn, B. (2003). The silence is broken: A history of the first lesbian, gay, and bisexual college student groups. *Journal of the History of Sexuality*, *12*(2), 205–223; Bullough, V. (2002). *Before Stonewall*. Harrington Park; Conjugal visits at prison urged to cut sex assaults. (1972, June 10). *Evening Journal*, p. 40; Cutler, H. (1973, July 3). Homosexual set here isn't ready for publicity. *Morning News*, p. 7; Cutler, H. (1973, September 25). Gay activist gets Biden's "gut reaction." *Morning News*, p. 12; deBlieu, J. (1975, November 2). Gays: There's no need to deny facts. *Sunday News Journal*, p. 10; Dibell, K. (1968, January 8). Lobbyist asks easing up on homosexuals. *Evening Journal*, p. 1; Dover sergeant admits he's "gay." (1975, July 24). *Morning News*, p. 6; Dubber, M. (2015). *An introduction to the Model Penal Code*. Oxford University; Florio, G., & O'Shea, T. (1975, November 4). Gays seeking campus acceptance. *Review*, p. 2; Florio, G., & O'Shea, T. (1975, November 7). Gays discuss social relationships. *Review*, pp. 1, 12; Forens, J. (1972, November 21). Gays find false support. *Review*, p. 5; Gay activist fights for job at U. of Del. (1976, January 18). *Philadelphia Inquirer*, pp. 1, 7; Gay airman fights ruling. (1975, July 24). *Evening Journal*, p. 36; Gay community. (1971, November 9). *Review*, p. 5; Hodierne, R. (1973, July 2). Gay's OK—not just in the light of day. *Evening Journal*, p. 3; Homosexuals hit sodomy bill. (1971, November 4). *Morning News*, p. 2; Kelly, R. (1975, November 17). Paradox at UD [letter to the editor]. *Morning News*, p. 6; Loughery, J. (1998). *The other side of silence*. Henry Holt; Moyed, R. (1974, June 5). Senate rejects measure on homosexuals. *Morning News*, p. 16; Sandza, R. (1975, September 24). Gay airman plans appeal of discharge. *Morning News*, p. 3; Schmadeke, J. (1973, February 6). Homosexuals' rights concern lobbyist. *Morning News*, pp. 7, 14–15; Sears, J. (2006). *Beyond the mask of the Mattachine*. Harrington Park; Service under stress. (1975, October 13). *New York Times*, p. 24; Soulsman, G. (1985, November 4). Aumiller looks back without anger at UD ouster. *Evening Journal*, pp. B1, B4; Stein, M. (2004). *City of sisterly and brotherly loves: Lesbian and gay Philadelphia, 1945–1972*. Temple University Press; Steinbrook, R. (1975, July 1). Gays battle prejudices, keep low profiles. *Sunday Philadelphia Bulletin*; A step backward. (1974, June 13). Editorial. *Delmarva News*, p. 4A; Walz, S. (1975, September 11). Gay airman may lose job. *Morning News*, pp. 1–2; Zarr, Z. (1971, October 12). Gay power to gay people. *Review*, p. 5. Interviews: Dominguez and Welch IV; Gittings-Lahusen.

4. The Student Homophile League was charted at Columbia University in 1967. Other colleges, such as Cornell, New York University, and Stanford, soon followed,

often more radically named as Gay Liberation Fronts. However, students, particularly in the South and rural areas of the country, found resistance from school administrators. These resulted in a series of legal battles, which ultimately established the right for such campus student groups.

5. Materials used to develop this section are Antonelli, D. (1976, February 24). Activist speaks out for gay rights. *Review*, pp. 1, 4; Associated Press. (1976, January 14). Homosexual professor dismissed. *News-Item* (Shamokin, PA), p. 7; Aumiller raps UD's president. (1976, January 15). *Evening Journal*, p. 5; Aumiller, slate clean, gets new job. (1977, August 2). *Evening Journal*, p. 1; *Aumiller v. University of Delaware*, 434 F. Supp. 1273. (D. Del, 1977); Burroughs, B. (1968, June 10). Prexy is named by U of D. *Morning News*, p. 1; Faculty unit forces review for reinstating of Aumiller. (1976, March 16). *Evening Journal*, p. 3; Florio, G. (1976, February 23). UD speaker endorses homosexuality for all. *Morning News*, p. 4; Frank, B. (1976, March 7). College daze. *Morning News*, p. 13; Frank, W. (1979, March 8). UD loses appeal, ordered to pay Aumiller lawyers. *Evening Journal*, p. 3; Fund set up for fired UD teacher. (1976, March 1). *Evening Journal*, p. 5; Gay prof link firing to story. (1976, September 14). *Evening Journal*, p. 4; Greer, T. (1976, September 14). Former U. D. gay claims publicity caused dismissal. *Morning News*, p. 1; Judd, W. (1975, January 13). UD fires an avowed homosexual. *Morning News*, p. 2; Judd, W. (1976, January 31). Summer theater canceled by UD. *Morning News*, p. 3; Judd, W. (1976, February 21). Homosexual theater chief sues UD over dismissal. *Evening Journal*, p. 3; Judd, W. (1976, March 16). Reinstate gay, grievance student group at UD advises. *Morning News*, p. 3; New campus concept asked. (1968, September 17). *Morning News*, p. 11; Powers, J. (1976, September 15). Travant tells how he feared for "gay haven" image at UD. *Morning News*, pp. 1–2; President chosen for U. of D. (1968, June 10). *Evening News*, pp. 1, 3; Wallace, A. (1976, September 19). U. of Del. president takes hard line on gays. *Philadelphia Inquirer*, pp. 1, 4.

6. The Faculty Grievance Committee gave the university administration seven days to reconsider Aumiller's dismissal due to its failure to notify him before December 15. Further, it found no evidence that he had advocated for his "lifestyle," asserting that even if he had, the administration's actions were "without justification." Given this faculty finding, the college dean, who had originally refused to reconsider, stated that she was willing to rehire Aumiller, if it was approved by the president's office. It wasn't. The university senate concurred with the grievance committee and recommended to the board of trustees that Aumiller be reinstated. He wasn't.

7. Materials used to develop this section, including interviews, are Carmen Dominguez [obituary]. (2005, August 15). *Evening Journal*, p. 16; Greto, V. (2007, September 2). Erasing the line. *Sunday News Journal*, pp. 1, 11. Interviews: Burton; Dominguez and Welch II, III.

8. Materials used to develop this section, including interviews, are *Aumiller v. University of Delaware*, 434 F. Supp. 1273. (D. Del, 1977); Manning, A. (1979, March 18). Gay pride emerges in state, hand-in-hand with caution. *Morning News*, p. 1; McCave, M. (1978, May 1). Fired prof descries UD bias on gays. *Morning News*, p. 4;

Soulsman, G. (1985, November 4). Aumiller looks back without anger at UD ouster. *Evening Journal*, pp. B1, B4. Interviews: Dominguez and Welch I, III, IV.

9. A decade later, Aumiller reflected from his New York apartment. "I guess I was the right person to pick on," he told a reporter. "I was single. I didn't have any family. I was young. . . . [M]y nose was clean." In an invited essay for the *Delaware Lawyer*, Aumiller wrote, "Any little gain you make, turns out to be a surprise. . . . Powerful institutions and individuals in this country, especially if they have enough money, can pretty much do as they please." As evidence, the chair of the board for the *Delaware Lawyer*, who had invited Aumiller to write for it, later informed him that "all hell broke loose" when the full board learned of Aumiller's article, which was then rejected.

10. Materials used to develop this section, including interviews, are Manning, A. (1979, October 11). Delaware gays to join rally in DC. *Morning News*, p. 17; Thomas, J. (1979, October 15). 75,000 march in capital in drive to support homosexual rights: "Sharing" and "flaunting." *New York Times*, p. A14. Interviews: Dominguez and Welch II, III.

11. Materials used to develop this section, including interviews, are Kirk, M. (1980, November 2). Judge's ruling reflects a growing national trend not to discriminate against gay parents in custody cases. *News Journal*, p. 21. Interviews: Dominguez and Welch III, IV.

12. Materials used to develop this section, including interviews, are 2 jailed, 4 fined for vice. (1961, December 2). *Morning News*, p. 1; 15 arrests in morals case end state's investigation. (1961, June 15). *Evening Journal*, p. 24; Cunningham, E. (1961, April 6). "Sessions" drew from six states. *Morning News*, pp. 1–2; Fire marshals smell arson in Rehoboth hotel. (1975, October 19). *Sunday Morning News*, p. 2; Grant, F. (1961, April 15). New morals action near on "parties." *Morning News*, pp. 1, 3; Grant, F. (1961, June 13). Police say immoral case finished. *Morning News*, p. 14; Jacobs, F., & Stiff, L. (2000, March 10). Rehoboth's gay history. *Letters*, p. 58; *James M. F. Short v. the State of Delaware*, 54 Del. 532, 181 A.2d 225 (1962). Del. LEXIS 118; Letter to Hon. Matthew Denn, president Board of Pardons, from Elizabeth B. Stiff, October 10, 2012, Sears Papers; *Mattachine Review*, 7(4). (1961, July), p. 4; More arrests loom on morals crackdown. (1961, April 7). *Morning News*, p. 29; More men arraigned on morals. (1961, May 13). *Morning News*, p. 21; Newark vice charges draw 2 guilty pleas. (1961, May 5). *Evening Journal*, p. 14; Soulman, G. (1986, June 23). Sharing a case, a home and a love for each other. *Morning News*, p. D6; Two file pleas in Newark moral case. (1961, May 12). *Evening Journal*, pp. 1, 2. Interviews: Decker I, II; Dominguez and Welch IV; Kanter I; Thompson II.

CHAPTER 7

1. Materials used to develop this section, including interviews, are Archibald, M. (2014, August 22). The love dream. *Letters*; Ault, A. (2004, July 16). Journeys; 36 hours, Rehoboth Beach, Del. *New York Times*, p. F5; Jacobs, F., & Stiff, L. (2000, April 7). Once in a blue moon. *Letters*, p. 16; Yesbeck, B. (2013, February 12). Re-

hoboth dining: It all started with Vic and Joyce. *Cape.* https://www.capegazette
.com/node/41349. Interviews: Felton II, Pisapia III.

2. Material used to develop this section is Felton Interview I.

3. Materials used to develop this section, including interviews, are Bryant,
B. (2002). New York Avenue. *Journal of Urban History, 28*(3), 300–327; Bryant,
B. (2004). *Boardwalk of dreams: Atlantic City and the fate of urban America.* Oxford;
Doyle, C. (1985, July 7). Rehoboth's gay population growing. *Morning News,* p. B3;
Frank, B. (1981, July 22). Image is issue in Rehoboth Beach. *Morning News,* p. A10;
Jacobs, F., & Stiff, L. (2000, May 5). Once in a blue moon, part II. *Letters,* p. 16;
Kolson, A. (1982, November 10). Quiet descends on an avenue once made lively by
gays. *Philadelphia Inquirer,* pp. 1E, 4E; Murray, M. (1982, May 9). 'Hizzoner' stirs
up Rehoboth. *Sunday News Journal,* p. A15; Sachs, A. (2011, April 8). Atlantic City:
This is your life. *Washington Post;* Sublett, S. (1981, August 21). Rehoboth natives
are nervous. *Blade,* p. 4; Wolf, A. (1993, August 3). In Atlantic City, the alternatives
for gay nightlife have dwindled. *Philadelphia Inquirer,* p. S9. Interviews: Ackerman
II; Felton I, II; Pisapia II, III; Thompson VI; Yochim II, III.

4. Materials used to develop this section, including interviews, are Jacobs, F., &
Stiff, L. (2000, March 10). Rehoboth's gay history. *Letters,* p. 58; Marks, J. (1980,
May 29). Rehoboth has most of the bureaucrats. *Blade,* p. 13; Marks, J. (1982, June
11). Rehoboth: The "last" resort. *Blade,* p. 9; Smith, G. (1980, August 7). Arson sus-
pected in blaze at 2nd resort-area gay bar. *Morning News,* p. C1; Smith, G. (1981,
March 1). Quiet, loud, fancy or plain nightlife spots are all over. *Morning News,* p.
J3; Soulsman, G. (1981, July 16). Gays have found a refuge in resort town atmosphere. *Sunday News Journal,* p. 7; Sublett, S. (1981, August 21). Rehoboth natives
are nervous. *Blade,* p. 4. Interviews: Archibald I; Felton II, IV; Fitzgerald I; Hodge I;
Pisapia III; Saunders I; Spain I; Thompson III, IV; Yochim III.

5. Materials used to develop this section, including interviews, are Frank, B.
(1986, July 28). A nice nearby place. *Morning News,* p. 6; Royle, C. (1985, July 7).
Rehoboth's growing gay population. *Morning News,* p. 15; Williams, J. (2013, April).
Memories of Juliet: When an art world icon visited Rehoboth Beach. *Delaware
Beach Life,* pp. 26–28. Interviews: Felton I, II; Pisapia III.

6. Materials used to develop this section, including interviews, are Emergy, K.
(1989, July 29). The Palms offers new menu. *Whale,* p. 16; Kelly, J. (1981, July 10).
Rare, fatal pneumonia hits gay men. *Blade,* p. 1; Marks, J. (1980, May 29). Rehoboth
has most of the bureaucrats. *Blade,* p. 14; Mascitti, A. (1986, July 27). The Palms:
An eclectic oasis for laid-back meals. *Sunday News Journal,* p. J5; McLaughlin, J.
(1985, July 5). Rehoboth: An irresistible draw for "people like us." *Blade,* p. 5; Sul-
livan, P. (1978, July 16). Beach vacations for Delaware's older citizens. *Sunday News
Journal,* pp. C1, C12. Interviews: Ackerman I; Courville and Jerome II; Felton I, II;
Greenberg I; Hodge I, II; Pisapia III; Saunders I; Yochim I.

7. Materials used to develop this section are AIDS may have reached resort.
(1983, November 23). *Whale,* p. 2; AIDS program grows. (1986, August 15). *Evening
News,* p. B3; Brown, R. (1986, September 23). State AIDS program gets $86,519
federal grant. *Morning News,* p. B4; Davis, V. (1987, April 29). AIDS uproar. *Whale,*

p. 1; Davis, V. (1987, September 26). AIDS support under new auspices. *Whale*, p. 1; Dominguez, I., Jr. (1987). *AIDS and human relations concerns. Second draft to the AIDS Advisory Task Force Report*, pp. 2–3, 6, 8. Sears Papers; First gay, male nurse elected to cabinet. (1984, July 4). *Morning News*, p. 37; Forney, D. (1987, July 8). AIDS: Locally, more and more precautions are being taken. *Whale*, p. 5; Gilligan, E. (1986, March 13). Concern brings legislative action. *Evening News*, p. 1; Gilligan, E. (1987, September 13). 32 Delaware AIDS patients have died. *Morning News*, p. 35; Gilligan, E. (1987, September 13). AIDS Task Force report opens rift. *Morning News*, p. C3; Harriman, J. (1985, May 15). Blood test on exposure to AIDS virus is offered. *Morning News*, p. B1; Harriman, J. (1985, September 16). State looks for funds to continue AIDS testing. *Morning News*, p. A1; Harriman, J. (1987, August 16). Volunteer agency supports victims through "buddy" system. *Morning News*, p. B8; Hogenmiller, T. (1988, February 19). PALS benefit concert for AIDS research flounders. *Whale*, p. 1; Montgomery, J. (1987, April 28). Health official: Easy answers won't stop AIDS. *Morning News*, p. A1; Murray, M. (1987, July 1). Doctor's fear of AIDS slows care for patient. *Morning News*, p. 1; Murray, M. (1987, July 3). Gays see doctor's refusal as prejudice. *Morning News*, p. B1; Murphy, M. (1988, October 15). Sussex County AIDS Committee provides support for resort victims. *Whale*, p. 7; PALS: Group forms in Sussex. (1985, December 18). *Whale*, p. 1; Wagner, L. (1987, July 1). Visitor says Beebe denies treatment due to fear of AIDS. *Whale*, pp. 1–2.

CHAPTER 8

1. Materials used to develop this section, including interviews, are Bradley, K. (1989, April 19). Midway renovating. *Whale*, pp. 23, 26; Cook, D. (1985, July 10). Pockets filled. *Whale*, p. 37; Diebler feels commission unfair. (1983, June). *Whale*, p. 2; Forney, D. (1979, April 4). From dance halls and theaters to a hot resort property, a saga. *Whale*, p. 7; Forney, D. (1982, March 17). Would a juvenile offender policy help Rehoboth? *Whale*, p. 4; Forney, D. (1984, June 6). Rehoboth sets new policy in wake of AG rebuke. *Whale*, p. 1; Gays pose family image problem in Rehoboth. (1985, July 9). *Evening Sun* (Baltimore), p. 30; Hamilton, G. (1985, April 24). Rehoboth Avenue center for under 21 opens. *Whale*, p. 37; Hogenmiller, T. (1981, April 8). Rehoboth police crack down on disorderly youth. *Whale*, p. 7; Hogenmiller, T. (1982, February 10). Rehoboth disbands secret ethics committee. *Whale*, p. 1; Hogenmiller, T. (1982, June 30). No welcome wagon out for resort tattoo parlor. *Whale*, pp. 1, 8; Hogenmiller, T. (1982, July 28). Tattoos. *Whale*, pp. 1, 6; Hogenmiller, T. (1983, April 19). Rehoboth commissioners pass ethical standards. *Whale*, p. 4; Hogenmiller, T. (1983, June 22). Movies will return to Rehoboth next month. *Whale*, pp. 26, 28; Hogenmiller, T. (1984, May 23). Dave Deibler: The devil's advocate. *Whale*, p. C1; Hogenmiller, T. (1984, June 20). Creating indigestion in Rehoboth Beach. *Whale*, p. 1; Hogenmiller, T. (1984, July 18). Breakdance. *Whale*, p. 1; Hogenmiller, T. (1984, July 25). Bowling and movie feud. *Whale*, p. 6; Hogenmiller, T. (1985, June 22). Rehoboth's Hughes ponders growing influence of gays. *Whale*, pp. 1, 9; Hogenmiller, T. (1986, April 23). Billie Shields: Petite pillar of

strength. *Whale*, p. 7; Homosexuals, resort town's mayor at odds. (1985, July 13). *Santa Cruz Sentinel*, p. 44; Lecato, S. (1982, July 14). Rehoboth deserves equal business standards [letter to the editor]. *Whale*, p. 4; Lewis, C. (1986, June 15). T-shirt smut or T-shirt wit? *Sunday News Journal*, p. C1; Lewis, C. (1987, April 28). Getting it off their chests. *Morning News*, p. 3; Mooed, F. (1984, May 28). Oberly questions quality of mercy at the shore. *News Journal*, p. B1; Murphy, M. (1988, August 10). *Whale*, pp. 27–29; Murray, M. (1982, July 10). Rehoboth passes law to shut tattoo parlor. *News Journal*, p. 3; RBHA to honor resort resident Billie Shields. *Cape*, pp. 50–51; RBHA board minutes. (1982, November 29); RBHA board minutes. (1984, July 20); RBHA board minutes. (1984, August 17); RBHA general meeting minutes. (1985, June 21); Rehoboth twin cinema to open within the week. (1983, November 16). *Whale*, pp. 20–21; Resort probes rink noise. (1948, January 26). *Journal-Every Evening*, p. 17; Theater owner appeals verdict. (1949, January 25). *Morning News*, p. 6. Interviews: Ackerman I; Lawson and Sterl; Slavin I; Thoroughgood.

2. Materials used to develop this section, including interviews, are Aguirre, M. (2002, August 23). The view from Laurel Street. *Letters*, p. 64; Aguirre, M. (2004, July 2). A chat with Libby Stiff. *Letters*, p. 48; Albelda, R., Badgett, L., Schneebaum, A., & Gates, G. (2009). *Poverty in the lesbian, gay, and bisexual community*. California Center for Population Research, UCLA; Davis, V. (1988, May 25). Rehoboth's Wilmington Avenue is bustling. *Whale*, pp. 29, 39; Francis, R. (1998, July 23). A quiet and courageous life together. *Cape*, p. 22; Gay liberation front affirms existence at tech. (1971, January 20). *Collegiate Times*, p. 2; Graham, T. (1994, August 12). Remembering Rehoboth. *Blade*, pp. 45–47; Grapperhaus, R. (1957, December 5). The Ku Klux Klan. *Delmarva News*, pp. 1–4; Hansen, P. (1981, July 10). Naiad Press. *Blade*, p. B4; Jacobs, F. (2003, Apr. 4). Rehoboth author to publish 14th novel. *Letters*, p. 12; Lamb, L. (2006, February 7). Aynda Marchant: Author, publisher. *Washington Post*; Marcus, E. (1999). *Together forever*. Doubleday; Neighboring editors. (1972, December 16). *News Journal*, p. 18; Rehoboth planners seek more annexation info. (1997, February 7). *Cape*, p. 4; Shickle, R., & West, D. (1971, February 3). Letter to the editor. *Collegiate Times*, p. 2; Soulsman, G. (1994, June 16). The coming out of Anyda Marchant. *News Journal*, p. D1. Interviews: Ackerman I; Lawson I, II; Lawson and Sterl; Mosiej I; Stiff I; Yochim III.

3. There were antigay incidents on campus, however. In 1971, for example, a "gay student was enticed and attacked" at a residence hall. One student wrote that the attack was due to a "gay fellow" entering with "the intent to have sex." What else, a writer asked, "can the Gay Liberation Front be other than a dating service for lonely queers . . . ?"

4. Materials used to develop this section, including interviews, are Lawrence, T. (2013). The forging of a White gay aesthetic at the Saint, 1980–84. *Dancecult*, *3*(1), 1–24; Interviews: Lawson II, III; Pisapia IV.

5. Materials used to develop this section are Barth, B. (1992, August 20). Legions of youth. *Letters*, pp. 9–10; Bradley, K. (1989, February 22). Under 21 only! *Whale*, pp. 7–8; Chibbaro, L., Jr. (1994, July 15). Gays raise a racket over noise ordinance. *Blade*, p. 1, 5; Combs, W. (1991, June 6). Do you want to dance? *Letters*, p. 2; MacKay, D. (1992, June 11). Being scene. *Letters*, p. 8; MacKay, D. (1992, Octo-

ber 1). Being scene. *Letters*, p. 18; Ryan, T. (1988, December 28). Who will control Rehoboth Beach? *Whale*, p. 5; What's Rehoboth coming to? (1988, December 31). *Whale*, p. 4.

CHAPTER 9

1. Materials used to develop this section, including interviews, are Archibald, M. (2014, October 10). Unmasking Halloween. *Letters*; Bertha P. Pusey [obituary]. (1998, October 9). *Cape*, p. 34; "Bulls-eye" means Bob for sign shop. (1962, April 16). *Morning News*, p. 1; Burden, M. (2002, February 13). Elkton marry-land. *Washington Post*, p. C2; DelDOT promotes Pusey to operations director. (1993, September 10). *Cape*, p. 36; James Pappas [obituary]. (1972, November 15). *News Journal*, p. 12; Jobless direct fire hoses as plant ruins smolder. (1948, July 15). *Journal-Every Evening*, p. 29; Kester, K. (2000, February 18). Rehoboth's Pusey leaves legacy to fight against domestic violence. *Cape*, p. 25; Okonowicz, E. (1979, August 19). Uneasy rider. *Sunday News Journal*, p. E1; Pusey mass. (1998, October 3). *News Journal*, p. B2; Raymond S. Pusey [obituary]. (2018, March 2). *Cape*, p. 34; Sotiria J. Pappas [obituary]. (1998, January 21). *News Journal*, p. B4; Vernon, T. (1998, October 9). Community activist Pusey dies in crash. *Cape*, p. 14; Volunteer of the week. (1998, February 7). *News Journal*, p. B3; Interviews: Courville and Jerome II; Felton II; Hodge II; Kanter II; Pisapia IV; Thompson IV.

2. Materials used to develop this section, including interviews, are Another viewpoint on gays. (1988, January 30). Speak out. *Whale*, p. 4; Atkinson, J. (1988, August 13). Rehoboth's incumbents in RBHA's pocket [letter to the editor]. *Whale*, p. 4; Davis, V. (1987, August 12). Vought takes Rehoboth mayor's seat. *Whale*, p. 1; Davis, V. (1988, February 24). Major building permits at a halt in Rehoboth. *Whale*, pp. 1, 3; Davis, V. (1988, March 12). Opponents blast resort's off-street parking proposal. *Whale*, pp. 1, 6; Davis, V. (1988, April 2). Plan tops Monday workshop. *Whale*, pp. 1, 3; Davis, V. (1988, April 6). Discrimination? Rehoboth Mayor Vought denies charges that parking proposal is smoke screen for bias against gays. *Whale*, p. 1; Davis, V. (1988, April 13). Rehoboth dashes off street parking plan. *Whale*, pp. 1, 2; Ellsworth portrait draws more ire. (1988, January 16). Speak out. *Whale*, p. 4; Fried, M. (1988, March 16). Shepherds are leading resort astray [letter to the editor]. *Whale*, p. 5; Hamilton, G. (1982, April 21). RHOA plagued with dwindling activity. *Whale*, p. 5; Hamilton, R. (1988, March 23). Proposed parking plan for Rehoboth [letter to the editor]. *Whale*, p. 4; Hogenmiller, T. (1979, August 10). Chichester threatens suit of RBHOA over comments "detrimental" to his character. *Whale*, p. 2; Hogenmiller, T. (1988, February 24). RBHOA's dedication is now bearing fruit. *Whale*, p. 4; Hogenmiller, T. (1988, March 2). Off-street parking plan a strangulation measure. *Whale*, p. 4; Lawson, E. (1988, April 9). Reader comments on parking issue [letter to the editor]. *Whale*, pp. 4–5; Murray, M. (1988, April 9). Rehoboth commission curbs parking proposal. *News Journal*, pp. 1, 7; Personal communication with Glen Thompson, February 9, 2022; Plowman, T. (1988, March 2). Commending *Whale* editorial on RBHA [letter to the editor]. *Whale*, p. 4; RBHA board minutes. (1984, August 17); RBHA board minutes. (1984, September 12);

RBHA board minutes. (1987, August 4); RBHA board minutes. (1988, March 21); RBHA board minutes. (1988, April 18); RBHOA. (1980, August 13). *Whale*, p. 2; Shields, B. (1988, March 2). How to measure responsible editorials? [letter to the editor]. *Whale*, p. 4; Smith, J. (1988, March 2). Editorial was community disservice [letter to the editor]. *Whale*, p. 4; Speak out. (1988, January 9). *Whale*, p. 2; Students come to Ellsworth's defense. (1988, January 23). Speak out. *Whale*, p. 4; Wagner, L. (1987, December 30). John Ellsworth gets a bang out of Lewes. *Whale*, p. 7. Interviews: Decker I; Felton III; Lawson III; Pisapia IV; Thompson VI.

3. Established in July 1971 in opposition to high-rise condo development, parking, and group rentals, the association successfully elected like-minded commissioners. By the end of the decade, however, its membership was deeply divided on candidate selection. Dick Chichester and James Phelan questioned the board's nomination process and its use of membership fees "as a slush fund to try and run Rehoboth." This, coupled with the association's unpopular support for a beach fee and the lack of "big issues," resulted in its membership dwindling to 150. Two years later, with only eight members attending its annual meeting, serious discussion about "deactivating" the group ensued. The group, however, refocused, as it recruited former cofounder Francis Fabrizio to serve as president. By the end of 1984, membership had increased to nine hundred.

4. For example, in one board meeting, Mary Campbell (an influential and long-standing board member) expressed frustration at the mayor's "apparent lack of foresight" in contacting her to select three association members for a sign ordinance revision.

5. Materials used to develop this section, including interviews, are Coalition for the Prevention of Gay Bashing. (1988, July 22). Letter to the editor. *Whale*, p. 6; Dancehall opposition is widespread. (1988, August 6). Voice. *Whale*, p. 4; Davis, V. (1988, April 30). Petition underway to stop Rehoboth dance hall project. *Whale*, pp. 1, 3; Fried, M. (1988, July 23). Uncle Miltie supports Shields and Nelson [letter to the editor]. *Whale*, p. 4; Gene Lawson. (1988, August 10). *Whale*, p. 7; Lawson, E., Jr. (1988, August 17). Polling place actions disturb candidate [letter to the editor]. *Whale*, p. 5; Lewis, K. (1988, July 23). Gays have the same rights as non-gays [letter to the editor]. *Whale*, pp. 5–6; Murray, M. (1988, June 21). Rehoboth building owners will have to pay to convert. *News Journal*, p. B3; Plowman, T. (1988, May 4). Rehoboth petition was discriminatory [letter to the editor]. *Whale*, p. 4; Pummer, C. (1988, August 16). Owners, residents clash over Rehoboth club. *Morning News*, p. B2; Pusey, R., & Pusey, B. (1988, August 17). Important hearing Friday [letter to the editor]. *News Journal*, p. 11; RBHA board minutes. (1985, September 11); RBHA board minutes. (1986, August 16); RBHA board minutes. (1988, June 20); *Rehoboth Beach Homeowners Association newsletter*. (1988, June). Interviews: Felton III; Lawson II; Pisapia IV; Slavin I; Thompson IV.

6. Materials used in this section, including interviews, are Davis, V. (1988, August 24). ABCC hands down Surfside liquor decision tomorrow. *Whale*, pp. 1, 2; Davis, V. (1988, August 27). ABCC denied Strand-Surfside liquor license. *Whale*, pp. 1, 2; Lewis, C. (1988, August 20). Rehoboth liquor license stirs spirited debate. *Morning News*, pp. 1, 4; RBHA board minutes. (1988, September 19); Rife, D. (1988,

August 26). Shore nightspot denied liquor license. *Evening Journal*, pp. 1, 6; Susice, W. (1988, August 24). Liquor license denied: Owners plan to appeal. *Coast*, p. 1. Interviews: Courville and Jerome II; Lawson II.

7. The association directly paid $3,000 in legal fees. Another $950 from residents of the Pines neighborhood for the Puseys' attorney were deposited into the association's account, which added another $50 to round off Fuqua's payment.

CHAPTER 10

1. Materials used for the depiction of SunDance, including interviews, are Archibald, A. (1995, June 30). Sundancing. *Letters*, p. 16; Archibald, M. (2003, August 22). Sundance 2003 heartbeat of the silver rainbow. *Letters*, pp. 8–9; Archibald, M. (2005, August 12). Sundance 2005 eighteen years of sundancing. *Letters*, pp. 6–7; Archibald, M. (2007, August 10). Remembering my first—Sundance that is. . . . *Letters*, pp. 6–7; Elkins, S. (1994, August 25). SunDance in Rehoboth: Seven years of celebrating. *Letters*, p. 18; Elkins, S. (1996, September 13). The way I see it. *Letters*, p. 3; SunDance '91 slated Labor Day weekend. (1991, August 24). *Whale*, pp. 16–17; Sundance '96. (1996, September 6). *Cape*, p. 23. Interview: Archibald I.

2. Materials used for the description of AIDS in this section, including interviews, are AIDS awareness program set for Thursday at YMCA. (1988, January 20). *Whale*, p. 2; Barron, J. (1988, March 30). Gay and minority groups compete for AIDS money. *New York Times*; Blair, J. (2001, August 4). Ideas and trends; Healthy skepticism and the marketing of AIDS. *New York Times*, Sec. 4, p. 14; Boost, D. (n.d.). At the club: Locating early Black gay AIDS activism in Washington, DC. *Arcade*. https://arcade.stanford.edu; Bykowicz, J. (2008, November 24). Doors reluctantly close for once-thriving HERO. *Baltimore Sun*. https://www.baltimore -sun.com/news/bs-xpm-2008-11-24-0811230207-story.html; Centers for Disease Control and Prevention. (1989, August 18). Current trends first 100,000 cases of Acquired Immunodeficiency Syndrome—United States. *Morbidity and Mortality Weekly Report*, 38(32), 561–563; Centers for Disease Control and Prevention. (1991, July 26). *Morbidity and Mortality Weekly Report*, 40(29), 493–495, 501–502; Dalton, H. (1989, Summer). AIDS in blackface. *Daedalus*, *118*(3), 205–227; Davis, V. (1987, September 26). AIDS support under new auspices. *Whale*, p. 1; Delaware Division of Public Health HIV/AIDS Epidemiology. (2010). *2010 Delaware HIV/AIDS surveillance report*. Delaware Health and Human Services. Dover; Elflein, J. (2021). *Deaths by HIV disease in the U.S. from 1990 to 2018*. Statista. https://www.statista .com/statistics/184594/deaths-by-hiv-disease-in-the-us-since-1990/; Harriman, J. (1988, April 20). Pending probe, $15,000 in minority AIDS money. *Morning News*, p. 1; Henderson, R. (1987, May 31). HERO in the fight against AIDS. *Sun Magazine, Baltimore Sun*, pp. 12–14, 16–20; Lawrence, J. (1987, October 14). Senate says federal AIDS education material can't promote homosexuality. *AP News*. https:// apnews.com/article/65c596e0514c81b20536d9cbf33c066f; Levenson, J. (2004). *The secret epidemic: The story of AIDS and Black America*. Pantheon; McCarthy, J. (2019, June 28). Fear and anxiety during the 1980s AIDS crisis. Gallup Vault. https:// news.gallup.com/vault/259643/gallup-vault-fear-anxiety-during-1980s-aids-cri

sis.aspx; Murphy, M. (1988, October 15). Sussex County AIDS Committee provides support for resort victims. *Whale*, pp. 7, 19; Murphy, T. (2019, December 16). In Baltimore's fight against HIV, making sure Black gay and bisexual men don't get left behind. *TheBody*. https://www.thebody.com/article/baltimores-fight-against-hiv-black-gay-bisexual-men; Oloizia, R. (n.d.). Medical Arts Building and the Health Education Resource Organization (HERO). *Explore Baltimore Heritage*. Retrieved March 14, 2022, from https://explore.baltimoreheritage.org/items/show/555; Padamsee, T. (2020). Fighting an epidemic in political context: Thirty-five years of HIV/AIDS policy making in the United States. *Social History of Medicine*, *33*(3), 1001–1028; Roane, J. T. (2019). Black harm reduction politics in the early Philadelphia epidemic. *Souls*, *21*(2–3), 144–152. https://doi.org/10.1080/10999949.2019.1697131; Royles, D. (n.d.). AIDS and AIDS activism. *The encyclopedia of Greater Philadelphia*. https://philadelphiaencyclopedia.org/essays/aids-and-aids-activism/; Royles, D. (2017, July 6). Race, homosexuality, and the AIDS epidemic. *Black Perspectives*. https://www.aaihs.org/race-homosexuality-and-the-aids-epidemic/; Royles, D. (2020). *To make the wounded whole: African American responses to HIV/AIDS*. University of North Carolina Press; Salvo, J. (2020, August). In the club: Finding early ebony gay AIDS activism in Washington, D.C. [blog]. https://joyeriasalvo.cl/during-the-club-finding-early-black-gay-aids/; Schoettler, C. (1996, January 20). Garey Lambert, AIDS activist projectionist, writer lauded as "the voice of the affected population." *Baltimore Sun*, p. 3B; Short, M. (1988, January 30). Lewes AIDS buddy training draws small crowd interested in support. *Whale*, p. 3; Short, M. (1988, April 23). Call for action to stem rising tide. *Whale*, p. 1; Short, M. (1989, August 19). Beach targeted for AIDS education gay group says it's not enough. *Whale*, p. 2; Short, M. (1990, July 14). Delaware AIDS activists for ACT UP chapter. *Whale*, p. 1; Short, M. (1990, July 18). ACT UP does. *Whale*, p. 1; Specter, M. (2021, June 14). How ACT UP changed America. *New Yorker*; Strubb, S. (2014). *Body counts, a memoir of politics, sex, AIDS, and survival*. Scribner. Interview: Hodge I.

3. Materials used for the depiction of Keith Lewis, including interviews, are Gays seek dialogue with Rehoboth mayor. (1985, August 18). *Morning News*, p. C3; Lewis, K. A. (1985, March 6). Contradictory [letter to the editor]. *Whale*, p. 4; Lewis, K. A. (1985, July 31). Advisory board on gay concerns needed [letter to the editor]. *Whale*, p. 4; Lewis, K. A. (1987, March 25). AIDS is a tragedy [letter to the editor]. *Whale*, p. 4; Powell, D. (1990, July 15). AIDS activists picket Roth's home. *Sunday News Journal*, p. B4; A protest against the Moral Majority [flyer]. (ca. 1983, March). Sears Papers. Interview: Dominguez IV.

4. Dominguez, I. (ca. 1987). AIDS and minorities concerns [first draft preface]. *AIDS Advisory Task Force Report on AIDS in Delaware*. Sears Papers. His title was later changed and pruned from its more radical comments to a final version, *AIDS and Human Relations Concerns*.

5. Materials used in this section, including interviews, are Archibald, M. (1995, June 30). Sundancing. *Letters*, p. 16; Bahr, J. (1991, September 12). Suddenly, last summer. *Letters*, p. 1; Barnett, R. (2005, July 15). Before it was Poodle Beach. *Letters*, p. 40; Barnett, R. (2008, September 12). Wigs and wind. *Letters*, p. 42; Drag

volleyball. (1992, September 17). *Letters*, p. 5; Forney, D. (1981, October 28). Group rentals: Meat axe or scalpel? [editorial]. *Whale*, p. 4; Glen(da). (2007, September 18). Local beat. *RBG*, p. 6; Hogenmiller, T. (1981, November 4). Rehoboth commissioners discuss three point group rental plan. *Whale*, p. 1; Hogenmiller, T. (1981, December 16). Rehoboth shoots down most stringent group rental proposals. *Whale*, p. 1; Hogenmiller, T. (1984, June 6). Resort Realtor, arrested, questions group. *Whale*, p. 1; Jacobs, F. (2003, August 22). The tradition continues! Drag volleyball on Poodle Beach. *Letters*, p. 16; Jacobs, F., & Stiff, L. (2000, June 2). Sunny days and party nights at Carpenter Beach. *Letters*, p. 16; Keller, J. (2020, July 29). Annual drag volleyball event cancelled. *Blade*. https://www.washingtonblade.com/2020/07/29/annual-drag-volleyballevent-cancelled; Murray, M. (1981, November 4). Resort to crack down on group rentals. *Morning News*, p. C1; Soulsman, G. (1989, August 13). Delawareans see progress. *Sunday News Journal*, pp. G1–2; Soulsman, G. (1989, August 13). A failed revolution. *Sunday News Journal*, p. G1; Van Dyne, L. (1978, July). Greetings from Rehoboth. *Washingtonian*, p. 86. Interview: Park et al. I.

6. Materials used in this section, including interviews, are Expanded statement of purpose [press release]. (ca. 1989). ARG. Sears Papers; Four candidates vie for two seats on Rehoboth Board. (1989, August 9). *Whale*, p. 7; Hughes, P. (1988, October 15). Rehoboth's proposed bar ban draws boos. *Whale*, pp. 1–2; Hughes, P. (1988, October 26). Taproom room ban topic of Rehoboth hearing Friday. *Whale*, p. 1; Hughes, P. (1988, October 29). Merchants speak out against proposed Rehoboth bar ban. *Whale*, p. 3; Hughes, P. (1988, November 2). Rehoboth bar ban takes effect amid howls of protest. *Whale*, p. 1; Hughes, P. (1988, November 5). Rehoboth merchants organize to combat city. *Whale*, pp. 1–2; Hughes, P. (1988, December 3). Rehoboth group mounts petition drive on bar ban. *Whale*, p. 1; Hughes, P. (1989, January 21). ARG to appeal Rehoboth petition refusal. *Whale*, pp. 1–2; Hughes, P. (1989, February 8). Surfside returns to ABCC for liquor license. *Whale*, p. 1; Hughes, P. (1989, March 25). ABCC hears plea for Surfside liquors license. *Whale*, p. 2; Hughes, P. (1989, April 22). Sugrue says no to another term as commissioner. *Whale*, pp. 1–2; Hughes, P. (1989, April 29). Surfside Diner liquor license granted but Strand remains dry. *Whale*, p. 1; Hughes, P. (1989, May 20). McTighe says ARG has homeowners backed in corner. *Whale*, pp. 1–2; Hughes, P. (1989, July 5). McTighe retiring from Rehoboth; cites poor health. *Whale*, pp. 1, 8; Hughes, P. (1989, July 22). ARG to drop lawsuit after Rehoboth election. *Whale*, p. 2; Hughes, P. (1989, July 29). ARG fails to back candidates for Rehoboth election. *Whale*, p. 1; Jackson, A. (1988, November 23). Business ban is a greed issue [letter to the editor]. *Whale*, p. 5; Kastor, E. (1989, August 6). The battle for Rehoboth. *Washington Post Magazine*, p. 34; Lawson, E., Jr. (1988, October 26). If it is not broke, don't fix it [letter to the editor]. *Whale*, pp. 4–5; RBHA board minutes. (1989, January 9); RBHA board minutes. (1989, September 18); Short, M. (1988, October 5). Rehoboth hearing on dance hall and tavern ban Oct. 28. *Whale*, p. 1; Theis, J. (1988, November 23). No one benefits from business ban [letter to the editor]. *Whale*, p. 6; Wolfe, N. (1988, November 2). Repressive law not good for resort [letter to the editor]. *Whale*, p. 5. Interview: Thompson IV.

7. Behind the scenes, Smith met with Wolfe and Hooper at the Country Club and, according to Smith, "wanted him to know that their organization was not made up of gays." RBHA board minutes. (1989, February 16).

8. Materials used in this section, including interviews, are Blugerman, B. (1989, June 17). Blugerman explains position as candidate [letter to the editor]. *Whale*, p. 4; Blugerman, B. (1989, July 29). Blugerman comments on candidates debate [letter to the editor]. *Whale*, p. 4; Blugerman, B. (1989, August 5). Blugerman states campaign platform [letter to the editor]. *Whale*, p. 4; Christian first, homeowner second. (1989, August 5). Voice. *Whale*, p. 5; Comments on recent Blugerman statements. (1989, July 22). Voice. *Whale*, p. 4; Darley, R. (1989, August 9). Darley states campaign platform [letter to the editor]. *Whale*, pp. 5–6; Darley, R. (1989, August 12). Rehoboth candidate shares ideas [letter to the editor]. *Whale*, p. 4; Derrickson, D. (1989, August 9). Derrickson responds to Bruce Blugerman [letter to the editor]. *Whale*, pp. 4–5; Four candidates vie for two seats on Rehoboth board. (1989, August 9). *Whale*, pp. 7, 29; Hubbell, F. (1989, August 2). Darley deserves voter support [letter to the editor]. *Whale*, p. 4; Hughes, P. (1989, June 14). Blugerman to file for Rehoboth commissioner seat. *Whale*, p. 1; Hughes, P. (1989, July 1). Rehoboth candidate says "gay" label a campaign tactic. *Whale*, pp. 1, 3, 27; Hughes, P. (1989, July 26). Candidate forum brings Rehoboth issues to forefront. *Whale*, pp. 1, 8, 31; Murray, M. (1989, August 10). In Rehoboth, ugly politics comes as shock. *News Journal*, p. B1; Murray, M. (1989, August 13). Rehoboth rejects bars, nightclubs. *Sunday News Journal*, p. B1; Plowman, T. (1989, August 9). Darley is Rehoboth Homeowners' puppet [letter to the editor]. *Whale*, p. 4; Rehoboth Beach voters support ban on new bars. (1989, August 14). *Evening Star* (Hanover, PA), p. 10; Rubin, R. (1989, August 6). In Rehoboth, a proposed ordinance threatens an uneasy peace. *Philadelphia Inquirer*, p. 1; Salin, J. (1989, August 9). Salin endorses Darley and Derrickson [letter to the editor]. *Whale*, p. 4; Shachoy, P. (1989, July 15). Voter endorses candidate Blugerman [letter to the editor]. *Whale*, p. 5; Shields, B. (1989, July 26). Shields endorses Darley, Derrickson [letter to the editor]. *Whale*, p. 4, 6. Interview: Ackerman III.

CHAPTER 11

1. Materials for this section are drawn from Alliance for Responsible Government. (1989, August 26). ARG comments on the bar ban defeat [letter to the editor]. *Whale*, p. 4; Blugerman, B. (1989, August 23). Lawson responds to recent allegations [letter to the editor]. *Whale*, p. 4; Elkins, S. (1999, August 13). The way I see it. *Letters*, p. 3; Gay may have brought it on himself. (1989, September 11). Speak out. *Whale*, p. 4; Guzda, M. K. (1989, August 18). No room for change. *Baltimore Sun*, pp. 1E, 4E; Hughes, P. (1989, August 16). Court test pledged of business ban. *Whale*, p. 1; Rossillio, M., Jr. (1989, September 6). Rehoboth is a homophobic resort [letter to the editor]. *Whale*, p. 4; Smith, J., & Fabrizio, F. (1989, August 17). Letter to Homeowners. RBHA. Sears Papers; Thoughts on homosexuality. (1989, August 4). Speak out. *Whale*, p. 4; Williams, J. (1989, September 10). An open letter to the gay community [letter to the editor]. *Whale*, p. 5.

2. Materials used for this section, including quotations, are Barrish, C. (1989, August 28). 6 arrested in drug raid on Rehoboth Beach club. *News Journal*, pp. A1, A7; Hughes, P. (1989, August 30). Strand drug bust leaves liquor license in question. *Whale*, pp. 1–2; Keen, L. (1989, September 1). Police raid Rehoboth Strand. *Blade*, p. 4; Lawson, G. (1989, September 13). Lawson responds to recent allegations [letter to the editor]. *Whale*, p. 4; Murray, M. (1989, September 3). Drug bust batters gay Rehoboth club. *Sunday News Journal*, pp. C1–2; Murray, M. (1989, September 3). Undercover investigation posed special problems, state police say. *Sunday News Journal*, p. C2; Speak out. (1989, September 6). *Whale*, p. 4. Interviews: Archibald III; Felton III; Lawson III; Pisapia IV; Slavin I.

3. Materials used for this section, including interviews, are Hughes, P. (1989, September 2). ABCC revokes Strand gathering permit in wake of drug bust. *Whale*, pp. 1–2; Hughes, P. (1989, September 2). Strand AIDS fundraiser nets $10,000 despite lack of liquor. *Whale*, p. 6; Hughes, P. (1989, October 18). Felton, Pisapia say bias has them down but won't leave soon. *Whale*, p. 6; Smith, J. (1990, August 1). Letter to Delaware Alcohol Beverage Control Commission. Sears Papers. Interviews: Felton III; Lawson III; Pisapia IV.

4. Materials used for this section, including interviews, are CARB wants annex of West Rehoboth. (1990, May 9). *Whale*, p. 1; Hughes, P. (1989, June 27). Hamilton seeks Rehoboth mayor's post. *Whale*, pp. 1, 6; Hughes, P. (1989, September 2). Dick Hamilton: Preacher, manager, activist. *Whale*, pp. 7, 24; Hughes, P. (1990, July 4). Vought won't seek second term as mayor. *Whale*, pp. 1, 31; Hughes, P. (1990, July 7). Cooper joins race for mayor's seat in Rehoboth. *Whale*, pp. 1–2; Hughes, P. (1990, July 14). Rehoboth political foes square off as election nears. *Whale*, pp. 1, 6; Pringle, B. (1989, December 21). Parking law opponents seek vote. *News Journal*, p. B4; RBHA board minutes. (1989, September 18); RBHA board minutes. (1990, April 7); RBHA board minutes. (1990, June 9); RBHA board minutes. (1990, July 13); RBHA board minutes. (1990, September 21); RBHA board minutes. (1990, October 29); RBHA board minutes. (1990, November 19); Rehoboth Beach candidates: Sam Cooper. (1990, August 8). *Whale*, p. 7. Interview: Lawson III.

5. Materials used for this section, including quotations, are St. George, D. (1999, August 29). How the tide was turned. *Washington Post Sunday Magazine*, pp. 7–11, 18–22. Interviews: Archibald I, II, III; Felton I, IV; Lawson III; Pisapia IV.

6. Materials used for this section, including interviews, are Albuquerque, F. (1985, February 4). Temple loses army recruitment lawsuit. *Daily Pennsylvanian*, pp. 1, 7; Archibald, M. (1999, May 21). Summer love 1999. *Letters*, p. 6; Archibald, M. (2000, February 4). Gay uncles and Auntie Mama. *Letters*, p. 6; Archibald, M. (2007, March 9). Weevils wobble (but they don't fall down). *Letters*, p. 6; Archibald, M. (2007, May 6). No parking problem. *Letters*, p. 6; Archibald, M. (2008, August 8). Change of heart. *Letters*, p. 6; Bahr, J. (1991, May 23). How does your garden grow? *Letters*, p. 2; Jim Bahr: Fighting the establishment for rights. (1985, March 15). *Daily Pennsylvanian*, p. 3; Lambda also rises. (1991, May 23). *Letters*, p. 3; Lasko, D. (1986, November 24). Sexual dysfunction in gays researched. *Daily Pennsylvanian*, p. 8; Lipman, J. (1981, August 2). Homosexuals seek new image. *CNJ*, pp. A1, C1; Lipman, J. (1981, August 2). Little agreement on "cause" of homosexuality. *CNJ*,

p. C1; Lipman, J. (1981, August 3). Homosexual teens face rough path. *CNJ*, p. 7. Interviews: Archibald III; Bahr II, III; Felton III; Pisapia and Bahr I.

CHAPTER 12

1. Materials used for this section, including interviews, are Another thumbs up for Mr. Belle. (1991, September 4). Speak out. *Whale*, p. 2; Bahr, J. (1991, July 18). The best and worst of Rehoboth Beach. *Letters*, p. 1; Bahr, J. (1991, July 24). Rehoboth incident points out need for consciousness raising [invited editorial]. *Whale*, p. 5; Belle, J. V. (1991, August 10). Rehoboth should discourage homosexual activity. *Whale*, p. 2; Bullough, V. (Ed.). (2002). *Before Stonewall*. Harrington Park; Chibbaro, L., Jr. (1987, June 19). Rehoboth lifeguard disciplined over gloves. *Blade*, p. 3; Chibbaro, L., Jr. (1991, July 26). Four protesters arrested at Rehoboth's gay beach. *Blade*, pp. 1, 17; Deparle, J. (1989, December 11). 111 held in St. Patrick's AIDS protest. *New York Times*. https://www.nytimes.com/1989/12/11/nyregion/111-held -in-st-patrick-s-aids-protest.html; Gays still considered outcasts. (1991, August 28). Speak out. *Whale*, p. 2; Harper, W. (1991, July 31). Rehoboth events bogged the mind [letter to the editor]. *Whale*, p. 4; Hughes, P. (1991, May 25). Differing "family" views lead to two versions of Rehoboth stickers. *Whale*, p. 6; Hughes, P. (1991, July 24). Rehoboth nude bather arrest sparks massive protest. *Whale*, pp. 1–2; Lawson, E., Jr. (1991, August 14). Survival of community dependent upon welcoming all. *Whale*, p. 4; Marcus, E. (2002). *Making gay history*. Harper; Silverman, V., & Stryker, S. (2005). *Screaming queens: The riot at Compton's Cafeteria*. Documentary film; Stein, M. (2005, May 9). The first gay sit-in. History News Network. http:// hnn.us/articles/11652.html; Tired of reading about homosexuals. (1991, September 4). Speak out. *Whale*, p. 2; Why should we adjust our way of life? (1991, August 10). *Whale*, p. 5; Interview: Bahr and Pisapia I.

2. Materials used for this section, including interviews, are Bad News/Good News Department. (1991, August 15). *Letters*, p. 1; Bahr, J. (1991, July 5). CAMP craft. *Letters*, p. 1; Bahr, J. (1991, July 18). Best and worst of Rehoboth Beach. *Letters*, p. 1; Hughes, P. (1990, October 24). Resort homeowners gear up to block Strand liquor sales. *Whale*, pp. 1–2; Hughes, P. (1990, December 26). Noisy nightspot neighbor call patio plan restrictive. *Whale*, pp. 1, 6; Hughes, P. (1991, June 26). Hyde panel to define Rehoboth restaurants. *Whale*, pp. 1, 8; Hughes, P. (1991, July 13). Bar or restaurant? *Whale*, pp. 7, 24; Hughes, P. (1991, July 17). Rehoboth showdown appears imminent over noise. *Whale*, p. 1; Hughes, P. (1991, July 24). RBHA will support Konesey, Pool as noise issue builds. *Whale*, pp. 1–2; Hughes, P. (1991, July 27). Noise, restaurant definition confabs sure to draw crowds. *Whale*, pp. 1–2; Hughes, P. (1991, August 14). Rehoboth police get new underage drinking weapon. *Whale*, p. 2; I agree with Mr. Vandergraft. (1991, June 5). Speak out. *Whale*, p. 4; It was meant to be. (1991, August 29). *Letters*, p. 6; Kesler, N. (1991, June 5). Bill ok'd giving locals more liquor license say. *News Journal*, p. B3; MacKay, D. (1991, June 6). Overheard Memorial weekend. *Letters*, p. 3; MacKay, D. (1991, July 18). Tell me more. *Letters*, p. 2; MacKay, D. (1991, August 15). Tell me more. *Letters*, p. 2; MacKay, D. (1991, August 29). Tell me more. *Letters*, p. 2; Marshall, D. (1991, May 18). Revised Pusey

bill heads for House. *Whale*, pp. 1–2; Marshall, D. (1991, June 8). It's a go: Pusey liquor bill awaits signature of governor. *Whale*, pp. 1, 6; Morris, T. (1991, July 18). Rehoboth politics. *Letters*, pp. 2, 5; Murray, M. (1991, January 12). Rehoboth sets deck, patio hours. *News Journal*, p. A3; Pisapia, V. (1991, July 18). Rehoboth food; Rehoboth politics. *Letters*, p. 6; Pringle, B. (1991, July 19). Plan to restrict early-hours music draws criticism. *News Journal*, p. E1; Pringle, B. (1991, August 5). In Rehoboth, a quieter, gentler campaign. *News Journal*, p. A3; Pusey, B. (1990, December 19). Proposed Patio/Deck ordinance is fair [letter to the editor]. *Whale*, pp. 4–5; Rehoboth is a product of slow evolution. (1991, August 10). *Whale*, p. 4; Short, M. (1990, December 26). Tighter ABCC control? *Whale*, pp. 1, 6; Sievert, B. (1991, August 29). Letter to the editor. *Letters*, p. 4; Vandergraft, J. (1991, May 11). Patio controversy outrages reader. *Whale*, p. 4. Interviews: Bahr IV; Hodge I; Thompson IV; Yochim II.

3. Materials used for this section, including interviews, are Archibald, M. (2008, October 10). Leading us home. *Letters*, p. 6; Bahr, J. (1991, June 6). CAMPgrounds. *Letters*, p. 1; Bahr, J. (1991, June 20). CAMP it up. *Letters*, p. 1; Bahr, J. (1991, September 12). Suddenly, last summer. *Letters*, p. 1; Bahr, J. (1991, October 10). CAMPNotes *Letters*, p. 1; Bahr, J. (1992, August 6). Letters from CAMP Rehoboth: A (re)introduction. *Letters*, p. 2; CAMP Rehoboth financial summary. (1992, May 14). *Letters*, p. 2; Courville, B. (2022, July 7). Personal communication. Sears Papers; Elkins, S. (1997, July 25). The way I see it. *Letters*, p. 3; MacKay, D. (2000, July 14). Being scene. *Letters*, p. 46; McCoy, T. (1992, April). Tales of the beach. *Letters*, p. 4; Ognibene, F., & Ercole, J., Jr. (1992, July 9). Letter to the editor. *Letters*, p. 2; RBHA board minutes. (1991, September 16); Walz, K., & Ward, B. (1992, July 9). Letter to the editor. *Letters*, p. 3. Interviews: Archibald III; Bahr II, III, IV; Dominguez and Welch V; Hodge I, II; Janssen; Thompson IV.

4. Although *Letters* began publishing covers in its second year, consisting of either photographs or original artwork, it was not until 1997 that a cover photo of an interracial group of men appeared.

5. Materials used for this section, including interviews, are Bahr, J. (1991, September 12). Suddenly last summer. *Letters*, p. 1; Bahr, J. (1991, September 12). Women's bonfire set. *Letters*, p. 3; Bahr, J. (1992, July 9). CAMP director. *Letters*, p. 2; Bahr, J. (1992, August 20). Little shop of horrors. *Letters*, p. 2; Hughes, P. (1991, August 10). Supreme Court overturns Surfside Diner decision. *Whale*, p. 1; Hughes, P. (1991, November 6). Rehoboth delays eatery defining vote. *Whale*, pp. 1, 6; Hughes, P. (1991, November 27). Rehoboth sets Dec. 13 hearing on restaurant terms. *Whale*, pp. 1–2; Hughes, P. (1992, May 27). Rehoboth should run city, not restaurants, merchant says. *Whale*, p. 3; Hughes, P. (1992, June 3). Darley, MacDonald get RBHA nod in bids for council seats. *Whale*, p. 1; Hughes, P. (1992, June 10). Third candidate assures election in Rehoboth Beach. *Whale*, pp. 1, 8; Hughes, P. (1992, June 24). Rehoboth election campaign moving into high gear. *Whale*, pp. 1–2; Hughes, P. (1992, July 22). City denies 11 right to register in August election. *Whale*, pp. 1, 6; Hughes, P. (1992, July 22). Rehoboth candidates see need for new money. *Whale*, pp. 1–2; Janssen, B. (1992, April 30). Hit list. *Letters*, p. 15; Marshall, D. (1992, August 12). Rehoboth police link vandalism. *Whale*, pp. 1, 6; Murray, M. (1992, August 5). Candidate finds lesbianism a non-issue. *News Journal*, pp.

B1, B6; Murray, M. (1992, August 11). Home pelted with paint bombs. *News Journal*, p. 6; Osborne, P. (1992, September 25). Liquor board conditionally oks licenses. *News Journal*, p. B12; Osborne, P. (1992, September 25). Taxes cost restaurant its license. *News Journal*, p. B10; Price, B. (1992, August 20). Janssen defeat a triumph. *Letters*, p. 6; RBHA board minutes. (1992, May 18); RBHA board minutes. (1992, June 15); Rehoboth is the product of slow evolution. (1991, August 10). *Whale*, p. 4; Short, M. (1991, August 3). In the balance. *Whale*, p. 23; Short, M. (1992, August 8). Rehoboth goes to the polls today. *Whale*, pp. 1–2; Stewart, A. (1991, September 4). 11 arrested on alcohol-sale charges. *News Journal*, p. B1; Svetvillas, K. (1992, August 9). *Sunday News Journal*, p. B1; What's wrong with dining patios? (1991, October 5). Speak out. *Whale*, p. 4. Interviews: Bahr II; Moss; Thompson IV.

CHAPTER 13

1. Materials used for this section, including interviews, are Bahr, J. (1992, October 1). CAMP director. *Letters*, p. 2; Bauman, A. (1993, May 18). Surge in hate crimes baffles gays. *News Journal*, p. A1; Bauman, A. (1993, July 24). Gays: Victims shunned by legal system. *News Journal*, pp. A1, A5; Boykin, K. (1996). *One more river to cross*. Doubleday Dell; Chibbaro, L., Jr. (1994, July 15). Gays raise a racket over noise ordinance. *Blade*, pp. 1, 5; Hughes, P. (1992, April 25). Rehoboth police implement crackdown in wake of three assaults. *Whale*, pp. 1–2; MacKay, D. (1992, November 27). Being scene. *Letters*, p. 8; van Hertum, A. (1992, August 21). *Blade*, p. 8; Interview: Bahr III.

2. Materials used in this section are Bauman, A. (1993, July 9). Teen accused in gay-bashing goes to trial. *News Journal*, p. A1; Bauman, A. (1993, July 22). Teen gay-basher sent to Ferris School. *News Journal*, p. B3; Bauman, A. (1993, July 24). Gays: Victims shunned by legal system. *News Journal*, pp. A1, A5; Bauman, A. (1993, August 25). Gay-bashing defendant says he'll testify against alleged ringleader. *News Journal*, p. B1; Bauman, A. (1993, September 28). Beating victim speaks out on beach attack. *News Journal*, p. B1; Bauman, A. (1993, September 29). Assault on gays nets 4 years. *News Journal*, p. B1; Chibbaro, L., Jr. (1993, July 16). Rehoboth magistrate drops anti-gay harassment charge. *Blade*, p. 8; Doyle, C. (1993, May 26). *Letter to Steve Elkins*. Reprinted in *Letters*, June 3, 1993, p. 24; Elkins, S. (1993, June 3). Equal protection, zero tolerance. *Letters*, p. 2; Elkins, S. (1993, June 17). Communication is a two-way street. *Letters*, p. 2; Elkins, S. (1993, July 15). Justice and forgiveness. *Letters*, pp. 2, 4; Hager, M. (1993, May 18). 3 hurt in Rehoboth gay-bashing. *News Journal*, p. A1; Humphrey, T. (1993, May 25). Gays can find spot on beach. *News Journal*, p. B1; Lincoln youth gets probation. (1993, October 8). *Cape*, p. 2; Maccubbin, D. (1993, July 29). Letter to the Magistrate Charles. *Letters*, pp. 3, 11; MacIntire, C. (1993, October 1). Judge cites intolerance of lifestyles, rights. *Cape*, pp. 1, 4; Murdza, T. (1993, May 20). Champions of vision. *Letters*, p. 4; Turner, V. (1993, June 3). Fireside. *Letters*, p. 10; Youth gets probation in gay-bashing incident. (1993, October 15). *Cape*, p. 2.

3. Materials used for this section, including interviews, are Archibald, M. (1993, March 18). CAMPScene 93, act 1, scene 1. *Letters*, p. 2; Bahr, J. (1992, October 1).

CAMP director. *Letters*, p. 2; CAMP board minutes. (1993, January 18); CAMP board minutes. (1993, March 11); CAMP board minutes. (1993, June 14); CAMP Rehoboth Board installs new officers. (1992, November 27). *Letters*, p. 2; Price, B. (1993, January 22). Letter to Victor Pisapia and Jim Bahr. Sears Papers; Interviews: Archibald III; Bahr III; Dominguez V; Fezuk I; Hodge V.

4. Materials used for this section, including interviews, are Bauman, A. (1993, August 17). Man charged with crime not yet in the books. *News Journal*, p. B1; Bauman, A. (1993, August 17). Noise law stirs a loud squabble. *News Journal*, p. B1; Hunt, B. (1993, August 26). Editorial. *Letters*, p. 4; MacIntire, C. (1993, August 20). Rehoboth noise ordinance leaves business people feeling betrayed. *Cape*, p. 3; MacIntire, C. (1993, August 20). Strand's Elkins getting flak over noise and ownership allegations. *Cape*, p. 3; Rehoboth to consider noise law revisions. (1993, August 6). *Cape*, p. 2; Strand, Westside Cafe close doors, file bankruptcy. (1993, November 19). *Cape*, p. 2; Vernon, T. (1993, August 20). Batten down the hatches, folks [editorial]. *Cape*, p. 6; Interviews: Lawson III; Slavin I.

5. Materials used for this section, including interviews, are Archibald, M. (2008, May 16). Changing tides. *Letters*, p. 6; Archibald, M. (2008, June 27). The people of CAMP and the dance of love. *Letters*, pp. 6–7; Elkins, S. (1994, May 19). The way I see it. *Letters*, p. 3; Elkins, S. (1997, July 25). The way I see it. *Letters*, p. 4; Moore, W. (1994). Moore threatens non-resident voting [letter to the editor]. *Cape*, pp. 6, 8; Price, B. (1994, August 31). Underground goes down under. *UnderGround*, pp. 4, 6, 14; Vernon, T. (1994, June 17). Rehoboth UnderGround: A new resort "rag" begins publication. *Cape*, p. 47; Interviews: Dominguez V; Fezuk I.

6. Materials used for this section, including interviews, are Bauman, A. (1994, March 12). Rehoboth passes noise ordinance. *News Journal*, p. A3; Cat. (1994, June 22). Hard-core dance floor at XLR-8. *UnderGround*, p. 6; Chibbaro, L., Jr. (1994, July 15). Gays raise a racket over noise ordinance. *Blade*, pp. 1, 5; Elkins, S. (1994, June 16). The way I see it. *Letters*, p. 3; Elkins, S. (1994, September 8). SunDance 94 clears $62,500. *Letters*, p. 22; Gay bashing in West Rehoboth. (1994, July 14). *Letters*, p. 6; Hanumaiah, S. (1994, August 11). Letter to the editor. *Letters*, p. 8; Hayes, S. (1994, June 18). Whisper ordinance? [letter to the editor]. *Letters*, p. 8; Murdza, T. (1993, August 26). Tales of the beach. *Letters*, pp. 6–7; Nym, S. (1994, July 20). Que sarong sarong soiree. *UnderGround*, pp. 14, 21; Nym, S. (1994, August 31). Making waves. *UnderGround*, pp. 14, 18; Parham, D. (1994, June 30). Being scene. *Letters*, p. 26; Parham, D. (1994, July 14). Being scene. *Letters*, p. 18; Parham, D. (1994, August 11). Being scene. *Letters*, pp. 18, 22; Price, B. (1994, June 22). CommonbonD performs at Nomad. *UnderGround*, p. 8; Printz, M. (1994, August 25). Louder than words. *Letters*, p. 14; Rehoboth to consider revised noise ordinance. (1994, August 12). *Cape*, p. 2; Sarong soiree equals success. (1994, August 3). *UnderGround*, p. 9; *State of Delaware v. Eugene Lawson.* Court of Common Pleas of the State of Delaware in and for Sussex County. (1994, September 14). C.A. No: 94-06-0799. Motion to Dismiss. Sears Papers; Vernon, T. (1994, January 28). Sparks fly in latest Rehoboth noise proposal. *Cape*, pp. 1, 4; Vernon, T. (1994, February 18). Resorts cracking down on late night noise. *Whale*, p. 4; Vernon, T. (1994, June 10). Police issuing no warnings on Baltimore Avenue. *Cape*, pp. 1, 9; Vernon, T. (1994, July 1).

Rehoboth police halt regular visits to nightclub following complaints of harassment. *Cape*, pp. 1, 9, 11; Vernon, T. (1994, July 15). Both sides search for compromise on Funland noise complaint. *Cape*, pp. 9–10; Williams, B. (1994, October 6). Letter to the editor. *Letters*, p. 4; Interviews: Felton I; Hodge I; Mosiej I; Yochim II.

CHAPTER 14

1. Materials used for this section, including interviews, are Chibbaro, L., Jr. (1998, August 28). Activists protest toy raid. *Blade*, p. 8; Chibbaro, L., Jr. (1998, September 11). Avengers protest in Rehoboth. *Blade*, p. 6; Effxx Menswear. (1997, July 25). Letter to the editor. *Letters*, p. 4; Elkins, S. (1997, July 25). The way I see it. *Letters*, p. 3; Elkins, S. (1998, September 18). The way I see it. *Letters*, p. 3; Elkins, S. (2000, July 28). The way I see it. *Letters*, p. 3; Feeney, T. (1998, September 6). Gays divided over Rehoboth's image. *Sunday News Journal*, pp. A1, A8; Letter to mayor and commissioners from Mary F. C. Campbell, president. (1998, September). Sears Papers; Mayyasi, A., & Priceonomics. (2016, June 26). How Subarus came to be seen as cars for lesbians. *Atlantic*; Nardi, P. (n.d.). Gays and lesbians in the media. *Encyclopedia of communication and information.* Retrieved August 19, 2022, from https://www.encyclopedia.com/media/encyclopedias-alma nacs-transcripts-and-maps/gays-and-lesbians-media; Rehoboth gift shop owner arrested for violating adult entertainment law. (1998, July 10). *Cape*, p. 16; Russell, D. (1997, August 8). Letter to the editor. *Letters*, p. 4; Shop cited for sex toys. (1998, July 5). *News Journal*, p. B3. Interview: Slavin I.

2. Materials used to develop this section are Elkins, S. (1999, September 18). The way I see it. *Letters*, p. 4; Evans, A. (1995, February 13). Rave sullies Rehoboth's image. *Cape*, p. 6; Vernon, T. (1995, January 27). All night "rave" in Rehoboth leads to LSD arrest. *Cape*, p. 4; Vernon, T. (1995, April 28). Teens dispute club's drug image. *Cape*, p. 15; Vernon, T. (1995, May 19). Rehoboth oks swan song for all night entertainment. *Cape*, p. 12; Vernon, T. (1995, June 2). Residents, Chief Doyle square off over Channel Z. *Cape*, pp. 1, 10–11; Vernon, T. (1995, October 6). Fates smile on future of historic but empty Rehoboth building. *Cape*, pp. 64–65; Vernon, T. (1995, October 6). Hope may be on horizon for abandoned Rehoboth building. *Cape*, pp. 12, 16; Vernon, T. (1997, May 23). Set sail for Rehoboth's newest shops. *Cape*, pp. 42, 44.

3. Materials used to develop this section are Adamson, A., & Frisby, M. (1998, October 1). Truck flips on Xway. *Philadelphia Daily News*, pp. 3, 73; Heimer, S. (1998, November 9). City, state police increase truck inspections, patrols, ticketing. *Philadelphia Daily News*, pp. 4, 32; Pisapia, V. (2020, November 23). Personal communication. Sears Papers; Truck crushed Dover woman in Philadelphia. (1998, October 2). *News Journal*, p. B3; Vernon, T. (1998, October 9). Community activist Pusey dies in crash. *Cape*, p. 14.

4. Materials used for this section are Glenda. (1999, July 29). Your roving reporter. *RBG*, p. 33; L. S. (1999, October 15). Speak out [letters to the editor]. *Letters*, p. 4; Minnuto, T. (1996, August 23). Beginnings. *Letters*, pp. 30, 34; Minnuto,

T. (2000, May 19). Being scene. *Letters*, p. 82; Parham, D. (1995, August 11). Being scene. *Letters*, p. 28; Peterson, E. (1999, September 18). CAMP columnist receives national writing award. *Letters*, pp. 46–47; Riss, C. (2002, June 21). Everything's coming up *Follies*! *RBG*, pp. 7–8; Roberts, R. (1999, February 24). The great sand rush. *Washington Post*; Russellina, M. (1999, July 29). Your roving reporter. *RBG*, p. 34; Santomartino, T. (1999, May 7). Bears invade the beach. *Letters*, p. 42; Santomartino, T. (1999, June 4). Leather beach. *Letters*, p. 30; Santomartino, T. (1999, September 17). Bears at the beach. *Letters*, p. 66; Shilling, B. (1998, July 17). Speak out [letters to the editor]. *Letters*, p. 4; Tipton, R. (2015, June 5). Whitman doesn't speak for every gay man [letter to the editor]. *Cape*, p. 4.

5. Materials used for this section, including interviews, are Becker, B. (1999, July 2). CAMPtown. *Letters*, p. 16; Elkins, S. (1999, September 17). The way I see it. *Letters*, p. 3; Foery, K. (1999, May 21). School daze. *Letters*, p. 40; Jacobs, F. (2000, August 25). Women's group casts wide net[;] catches challenging conversation. *Letters*, p. 12; Minor, K. (2000, July 14). First night. *Letters*, p. 30; Soulsman, G. (1994, June 16). The coming out of Anyda Marchant. *News Journal*, p. D1; Vernon, T. (1994, December 23). Cloud 9. *Cape*, p. 48. Interviews: Janssen; Stiff II.

6. Materials used for this section, including interviews, are Antolini, P. (1997, July 11). An open letter to CAMP Rehoboth readers. *Letters*, p. 4; Caddell, T. (1997, June 11). Rehoboth woman, 33, is found dead. *News Journal*, p. B2; Chibbaro, L., Jr. (1997, July 4). Woman's death an "accident." *Blade*, p. 6; Cloud 9 has hip food that's always a groove. (1998, February 13). *Cape*, p. 68; Elkins, S. (1997, June 13). The way I see it. *Letters*, p. 3; McCoy, T. (1997, July 11). Letters to the editor. *Letters*, p. 4; Murray, M. (1997, July 4). Arrests cause stir at beach. *News Journal*, p. 1; Murray, M. (1997, August 9). Rehoboth pair enter rehab. *News Journal*, p. B2; No new report issued on Berdini death. (1997, June 20). *Cape*, p. 1; Paige Phillips Berdini, restaurant owner [obituary]. (1997, June 19). *Cape*, p. 32; Rehoboth restaurateur's June 8 death termed "suspicious." (1997, June 13). *Cape*, p. 13; Sanginiti, T. (1997, July 3). Pair face drug charges in death. *News Journal*, p. B1; Vernon, T. (1997, July 4). Berdini death tied to overdose; Felton, Beel arrested. *Cape*, pp. 1, 15. Interview: Thompson IV.

7. Materials used for this section, including interviews, are Aguirre, M. (2002, July 12). CAMP profile. *Letters*, p. 78; Archibald, M. (1999, May 21). Summer love 1999. *Letters*, p. 16; Brown, K. P. (1997, May 16). Jamé Foks. *Letters*; Elkins, S. (2000, March 10). The way I see it. *Letters*, p. 3; How loco? Plumb Loco! (1997, May 30). *Letters*, pp. 16–17; Jacobs, F. (2002, April 5). Women's conference sets future standard. *Letters*, p. 8; Ladies teas scheduled for Labor Day weekend. (1998, September 1). *RBG*, p. 6; Shaw, M. (2000, August 25). The Women's Project of CAMP Rehoboth defines its mission. *Letters*, p. 12; Steele, K. (2001, April 6). Heaven's to Betsy! *Letters*, pp. 6, 16; Stiff, L. (2015, October 23). I hear the music. *Letters*; Taormino, T. (2000, September 12). Trouble in utopia. *Village Voice*. Interviews: Archibald IV; Fezuk II; Stiff II.

8. Materials used for this section, including interviews, are Cormier, R. (2006, August 22). What a drag! *News Journal*, pp. E1, E6; Kester, K. (1998, June 12).

Renegade rocks with many faces of a star. *Cape*, pp. 69–70; Letter to the editor. (1999, April 9). *Letters*, p. 4; *RBG* interview. (1998, July 1). *RBG*, pp. 10–13; *RBG* interview: Howard Hicks. (1997, August 8). *RBG*, pp. 22–24. Interviews: Carpenter I, II; Thompson V.

CHAPTER 15

1. Materials used to develop this section, including interviews, are Archibald, M. (2016, July 15). Black and White. *Letters*, p. 6; CAMP Rehoboth board minutes. (1999, July 26); Canady, D. (2000, June 16). Letter to the editor. *Letters*, p. 4; Kastor, E. (1989, August 6). The battle for Rehoboth. *Washington Post Magazine*, p. 17; Sudler, H. (2014). *Summerville*, p. 86. Archer; We're back. (1999, March 23). *RBG*, p. 3. Interviews: Fezuk I; Sudler I; Williams, F., I.

2. Materials used to develop this section, including interviews, are Pate, A. (2001). *West of Rehoboth*. Morrow; Sudler, H. (2014). *Summerville*. Archer. Interviews: Fezuk I; Harmon and Paskins; Slavin I; Sudler I.

3. Materials used to develop this section, including interviews, are Aguirre responds to RBHA letter. (2001, September 14). Letter to the editor. *Cape*, p. 7; Answers to questions submitted by "concerned members of RBHA." (ca. 2001, October). Sears Papers; Campbell, M. (2001, April). Letter to members of the Rehoboth Beach Homeowners Association. Sears Papers; Campbell, M. (2001, August 31). RBHA responds to concerned members [letter to the editor]. *Cape*, pp. 6–7; Decker, H. (2001, August 5). Press release. Sears Papers; Maldives, M., & Mills, S. (2001, September 21). RBHA could have powerful presence [letter to the editor]. *Cape*, p. 7; Mary Campbell: Progressive woman [obituary]. (2015, April 24). *Cape*, p. 26; Mavity, R. (2010, December 21). Hoyte Decker: Rehoboth's everywhere man. *Cape*, pp. 14–15; Oliver, G. (2001, May 18). Letter to the editor. *Letters*, pp. 4–5; RBHA board minutes. (2000, October 16); RBHA board minutes. (2000, November 20); RBHA board minutes. (2001, January 15); RBHA board minutes. (2001, March 26); RBHA board minutes. (2001, May 21); Voth, D., et al. (2001, May 15). An open letter to the board of the Rehoboth Beach Homeowners Association and the general membership. Sears Papers. Interview: Aguirre I.

4. Materials used to develop this section, including interviews, are Aguirre, M. (2001, August 24). Letter to the editor. *Letters*, p. 4; CAMP Rehoboth board minutes. (2000, April 24); LOVE 2000 benefit cuts $40k+ check for charity. (2000, August 31). *RBG*, pp. 48–49; McGuiness, Derrickson win Rehoboth election. (2000, August 18). Rehoboth to vote on Saturday. *Cape*, p. 4; Meet the candidates. (1999, July 15). *RBG*; Pack, R. (1999, August 20). Incumbents win in Rehoboth. *Cape*, p. 18; RBHA board minutes. (2001, July 16); Rehoboth Beach Homeowners Association endorses incumbents. (1999, July 1). *RBG*; Rehoboth commissioners' race heats up with the addition of 3rd candidate. (1999, May 20). *RBG*; Rehoboth committee appointment causes stir. (2001, September 21). *Cape*, p. 4; Reynolds-Hughes, B. (2001, April 20). Rehoboth to vote on Saturday. *Cape*, p. 11; Vernon, T. (1999, August 13). Rehoboth voters to elect two commissioners, mayor. *Cape*, pp. 1, 13; Vernon, T. (2000, August 11). Aguirre filing fuels election in Rehoboth.

Cape, pp. 1, 15; Vernon, T. (2000, August 11). Rehoboth Beach voters go to the polls Saturday. *Cape*, pp. 1, 15, 20; Vernon, T. (2000, August 11). Rehoboth to vote on Saturday. *Cape*, pp. 1, 14; Vernon, T. (2001, August 7). Incumbents retain seats in Rehoboth election. *Cape*, p. 11; Voth, D. (2004, August 27). An interview of the interviewer. *Letters*, pp. 48–49. Interview: Aguirre I.

5. Materials used to develop this section are Aguirre, M. (2001, October 26). Aguirre explains RBHA concerned members [letter to the editor]. *Cape*, pp. 1, 12–13; RBHA general meeting minutes. (2001, October 20); Taylor, B., Jr. (2001, October 24). Rehoboth Homeowners insiders are voted down. *Coast*, pp. 1–2; Taylor, B., Jr. (2001, November 14). Homeowners group seeks to mend fences. *Coast*, pp. 10–11; Vernon, T. (2001, October 19). RBHA concerned members forge new directions, initiatives. *Cape*, pp. 15–16; Vernon, T. (2001, October 26). RBHA members turn the tide at the annual meeting. *Cape*, pp. 1, 12–13; Vernon, T. (2001, October 28). RBHA members turn the tide at the annual meeting. *Cape*, p. 7.

CHAPTER 16

1. Material used to develop this section is Elkins, S. (2001, June 1). The way I see it. *Letters*, p. 3.

2. Materials used to develop this section, including interviews, are Aguirre, M. (2001, June 13). Rehoboth Beach commissioners go on record against discrimination. *Letters*, p. 6; Aguirre, M. (2002, August 16). Aguirre cites a number of firsts [letter to the editor]. *RBG*, p. 7; Archibald, M. (2016, June 7). Reflections on a rainbow theory. *Letters*; Commissioners vote to prohibit discrimination. (2003, May 30). *Letters*, p. 4; Deiner, P. (2004, March 3). Heated argument mars commission meeting. *News Journal*, p. B3; Keegan, A. (2002, August 23). Rehoboth: Gay friendly and now gay representation. *Letters*, p. 26; Poll: 8 in 10 Delawareans believe state should vote on equal rights. (2002, June 21). *RBG*, p. 9; Reardon, A. (2004, March 5). Tempers flare. *Cape*, p. 15; Vernon, T. (2002, June 21). Rehoboth streetscape project dominates candidates' forum. *Cape*, pp. 5, 22; Vernon, T. (2002, July 19). Voter procedure registration flap in Rehoboth. *Cape*, p. 20; Vernon, T. (2002, July 26). Rehoboth homeowners hear candidate views during annual forum. *Cape*, pp. 17–18; Voth, D. (2004, August 27). *Letters*, pp. 48–49. Interviews: Aguirre I; Spain III.

3. Materials used to develop this section, including interviews, are Bonville, D. (2010, February 1). West Rehoboth and West Side New Beginnings backgrounder. https://www.facebook.com/notes/quest-fitness-kayak-inc/west-rehoboth-and-west-side-new-beginnings-backgrounder/291138183016/; Community land trust gears up for art auction. (2005, October 14). *Letters*, pp. 4–5; Deoul, S. (2008, July 25). Four "G's" and a God shot. *Letters*, pp. 40–41; Jacobs, F. (2003, February 7). The Renegade after 25 years. *Letters*, pp. 8–9; Keegan, A. (2004, August 20). Religion history key elements of Lewes renovation. *Cape*, pp. 60–61; Martinac, P. (2002, October 10). Antiracist diversity. *RBG*, p. 20; Milbourne, L., & Bonville, D. (2008, July 23). Letter to the editor. *Letters*, p. 4; Murray, M. (2003, April 23). So long, Renegade. *News Journal*, p. B3; Murray, M. (2005, July 5). West Rehoboth

fights to keep sense of community. *News Journal*, pp. 1–2; Reed, J. (2003, August 23). West Rehoboth walled off by developer [Letter to the editor]. *News Journal*, p. 8; Riss, C. (2003, February 7). Renegade to be torn down, what's next? *Letters*, p. 60; Sievert, B. (2003, March 7). Memories are made of this. *Letters*, p. 12; Spitz, M., Fitzgerald, K., & Medisch, L. (2005, August 26). Letter to the editor. *Letters*, p. 4; Sudler, H. (2002, August 16). *Summerville*, Pt. VII. *RBG*, p. 23. Interviews: Hodge I, II; Thompson VI.

4. Materials used to develop this section, including interviews, are Archibald, M. (2007, July 27). Building a house. *Letters*, pp. 6–7; Archibald, M. (2007, August 16). Remembering my first—Sundance that is. . . . *Letters*, pp. 6–7; Archibald, M. (2007, September 14). A leap of faith: Building the future. *Letters*, pp. 6–7; Archibald, M. (2008, May 30). Fundraising fatigue? *Letters*, pp. 6–7; Archibald, M. (2008, June 27). Final thoughts. *Letters*, p. 30; Archibald, M. (2009, August 8). Change of heart. *Letters*, p. 6; Campbell, M. (2004, August 6). Give Gossett and Sargent consideration [letter to the editor]. *Cape*, p. 8; CAMP forum. (2004, July 30). *Letters*, pp. 6–8; CAMP forum. (2008, July 25). *Letters*, pp. 28–31; Cresson, J. (2004, August 17). Gossett, Sargent win seats in Rehoboth Beach. *Cape*, p. 1; Dear neighbors [political advertisement]. (2004, August 6). *Cape*, p. 2; Elkins, S. (2008, June 13). The way I see it. *Letters*, p. 3; Elkins, S. (2009, June 5). The way I see it. *Letters*, p. 3; Flood, C. (2018, August 2). Patrick Gossett: Fixing problems from the inside out. *Cape*, p. 12; Greto, V. (2008, September 6). The divas. *News Journal*, pp. 4–5; In Donna St. George's words. (2008, June 27). *Letters*, p. 29; Konesey, J. (2004, August 6). Sargent and Gossett are best candidates [letter to the editor]. *Cape*, p. 8; Mavity, R. (2012, January 20). Mayor taps Gossett for Rehoboth seat. *Cape*, p. 1; Oliver, G. (2001, May 18). Letter to the editor. *Letters*, pp. 4–5; Pruitt, G. (2009, May 27). Sussex County AIDS board votes to dissolve agency. *Letters*, p. 22; Rehoboth homeowners to talk wastewater. (2009, January 16). *Cape*, p. 3; Rubenstein, J. (2008, May 16). A new moon rising. *Letters*, p. 98; Slavin, J. (2004, August 6). Give emphatic vote to Gossett [letter to the editor]. *Cape*, p. 8; Soulsman, G. (2007, August 25). Do you feel the magic? *News Journal*, pp. E1, E3; Spence, K. (2005, May 20). Rehoboth passes FAR reduction. *Cape*, pp. 1, 20; Yesbek, B. (2011, October 11). 30 years comes around once in a blue moon. *Cape*; Yesbek, B. (2016, May 20). Blue Moon: More than just great food and fun times. *Cape*, pp. 37, 40. Interviews: Aguirre I; Decker I; Domingue and Welch V; Lawson III; Moss I; Slavin I; Stiff II.

EPILOGUE

1. Materials used to develop this section, including interviews, are Archibald, M. (2000, February 4). Dreaming the world: CAMP Project Action Committee. *Letters*, p. 6; Bahr, J. (1991, May 23). CAMP Rehoboth: An introduction. *Letters*, p. 1; Black History Month exhibition and presentation. (2019, February 8). *Letters*; Boykin, S. (2011, September 6). Rehoboth 4th on gay-couples list. *News Journal*, p. 11; Carpenter, K. (2015, November 16). Thank you, CAMP Rehoboth for workshop. *Cape*, p. 7; Carpenter, K. (2021). Personal correspondence. Sears Papers; Chibbaro, L., Jr. (2011, August 20). DC same sex couples up 40%. *Blade*; Chibbaro, L., Jr.

(2023, May 11). CAMP Rehoboth names new executive director. *Blade*; Danksy, S. (2013, March–April). The perseverance of camp. *Gay and Lesbian Review*; Elkins, S. (1997, July 25). The way I see it. *Letters*, p. 3; Flood, C. (2020, July 27). Rehoboth's handling of complaint raises concerns. *Cape*, pp. 2, 16; Knausgaard, K. (2015, May 25). The inexplicable. *New Yorker*, p. 32; Parks, L. (2001, August 24). Artwork colors his world. *Delaware Beachcomber*, pp. 6, 10; Rosenstein, P. (2003, August 22). The Rehoboth Beach GLBT community is maturing. *Letters*, p. 22; Sontag, S. (1964). On camp. In *A Susan Sontag reader* (1983), pp. 105–120. Vintage; St. George, D. (1999, August 29). Days of reckoning. *Washington Post Magazine*, p. 8; Tavernise, S. (2011, August 25). New numbers and geography for same-sex couples. *New York Times*, p. A1; U.S. Census Bureau. (2022). Characteristics of same-sex couple households: 2005 to present. Census.gov. Interviews: Archibald and Elkins; Carpenter I, II; Mariner.

2. Materials used to develop this section, including interviews, are Archibald, M. (2000, May 5). The beat goes on (after the march). *Letters*, p. 8; Archibald, M. (2008, June 13). Remembering why. *Letters*, p. 6; Dollard, J. (1937). *Caste and class in a southern town*. Yale University Press; Durkheim, E. (1893/1992). *Division of labor in society*. W. D. Halls (Trans.). Free Press; Durkheim, E. (1897/1952). *Suicide*. Routledge and Kegan Paul; Elkins, S. (2000, March 10). Speak out. *Letters*, p. 4; Foucault, M. (1998). *The history of sexuality: Vol. 1: The will to knowledge*. Penguin; Gamson, J. (1995). Must identity movements self-destruct? A queer dilemma. *Social Problems*, 42, 390–407; Kotlowitz, A. (1999) *The other side of the river*. Anchor; Lynd, R., & Lynd, H. (1929). *Middletown: A study in contemporary American culture*. Harcourt, Brace; Lynd, R., & Lynd, H. (1937). *Middletown in transition: A study in cultural conflicts*. Harcourt, Brace; Murray, M. (1984). "Homeowners" group urges vote in Rehoboth. *Morning News*, p. 4; Phelan, S. (1989). *Identity politics: Lesbian feminism and the limits of community*. Temple University Press; Vidich, A., & Bensman, J. (1968). *Small town in mass society: Class, power, and religion in a rural community* (2nd ed.). Princeton University Press. Interviews: Dominguez and Welch V; Hodge I.

James T. Sears is an independent scholar focusing on queer history. He is the author or editor of numerous books, including *Growing up Gay in the South*; *Lonely Hunters: An Oral History of Lesbian and Gay Southern Life, 1948–1968*; *Behind the Mask of the Mattachine: The Hal Call Chronicles and the Early Movement for Homosexual Emancipation*; and *Rebels, Rubyfruit, and Rhinestones: Queering Space in the Stonewall South*. A former Fulbright Scholar, he has taught at Trinity University, Indiana University, Harvard University, Penn State University, and the University of South Carolina, and was a research fellow at the University of Queensland and the University of Southern California. He continues to lecture throughout the world.